Sing Me a Story! Tell Me a Song!

Join us on the web at

EarlyChildEd.delmar.com

Sing Me a Story! Tell Me a Song!

Creative Thematic Activities for Teachers of Young Children

Hilda L. Jackman

THOMSON

DELMAR LEARNING

Australia Canada Mexico Singapore Spain United Kingdom United States

THOMSON

DELMAR LEARNING

Sing Me a Story! Tell Me a Song! Creative Thematic Activities for Teachers of Young Children
Hilda L. Jackman

Vice President, Career Education SBU:
Dawn Gerrain

Director of Editorial:
Sherry Gomoll

Acquisitions Editor:
Erin O'Connor

Editorial Assistant:
Ivy Ip

Director of Production:
Wendy A. Troeger

Production Editor:
Joy Kocsis

Director of Marketing:
Wendy E. Mapstone

Channel Manager:
Donna J. Lewis

Cover Illustration:
Laurent Linn

Interior Illustrations:
Laurent Linn

Composition:
Stratford Publishing Services, Inc.

For permission to use material from this text or product, submit a request online at http://www.thomsonrights.com

Any additional questions about permissions can be submitted by email to thomsonrights@thomson.com

Library of Congress Cataloging-in-Publication Data

Jackman, Hilda L.
 Sing me a story! Tell me a song! : creative thematic activities for teachers of young children / Hilda L. Jackman.
  p. cm.
 Includes biliographical references.
 ISBN 1-4018-3729-8
 1. Early childhood education--Activity programs--United States--Handbooks, manuals, etc. 2. Curriculum planning--United States--Handbooks, manuals, etc. 3. Project method in teaching--United States--Handbooks, manuals, etc. I. Title.

LB1139.35.A37J33 2004
372.13--dc22

2004044024

NOTICE TO THE READER

Contents

Contents By Curriculum Areas

LANGUAGE EXPERIENCES

DRAMATIC PLAY

POEM

PUPPET PLAY

ACTIVITIES

MUSIC

ACTIVITIES

MOVEMENT

SENSORY ART

ACTIVITIES

COOKING AND CREATIVE FOOD EXPERIENCES

ACTIVITIES

MATH

ACTIVITIES

SCIENCE

ACTIVITIES

SOCIAL STUDIES

ACTIVITIES

Preface

*W*hen teachers of young children get together at conferences, workshops, and staff development meetings, they like to exchange ideas and activities. This book is intended to be like a newly found "teaching friend" that will offer creative curriculum activities to help new teachers, teachers already practicing in early childhood education, administrators, supervisors, college educators, students, and those homeschooling.

The easy-to-follow format uses themes to integrate the curriculum for young children from **infancy through eight years of age**. Theme teaching involves creating many activities around a central idea. These activities are blended into every part of the curriculum within a flexible time frame, ranging from several days to a few weeks. The activities are designed for the classroom teacher to select and combine as needed in order to meet the needs and interests of the children.

The basic concepts of this teaching resource emphasize the following:

1. Themes and activities reflect the philosophy suggested by the National Association for the Education of Young Children (NAEYC) for Developmentally Appropriate Practice in Early Childhood Programs (DAP), such as:

   ▶ the critical role of teachers in understanding and supporting children's development and learning

   ▶ the concept of classrooms or groups of children as communities of learners

   ▶ the importance of each child in the group

   ▶ the significant role of families in early childhood education, including support for their cultures and communities

2. Themes and activities take into consideration the age, stage of development, prior learning, and experiences of young children.

3. Themes and activities emphasize and integrate different aspects of development and learning, such as:

   ▶ visual

   ▶ auditory

   ▶ tactile

   ▶ olfactory

   ▶ taste

   ▶ creativity

   ▶ language

   ▶ critical thinking

   ▶ problem solving

   ▶ social and emotional development

   ▶ cultural development

   ▶ coordination

   ▶ motor development

4. Themes and activities are developmentally appropriate, and they underscore the importance of individual differences and cultural diversity among young children. This allows children to learn at their own pace and style.

5. Themes and activities encourage the development of positive self-esteem and a sense of "I can do it" in young children.

6. Activities have been "child tested." They are easily adaptable to large group, small group, or individual instruction.

The Text

As teachers of the youngest children, we have a significant responsibility to the children in our care. Decades of research by neuroscientists and others have found that a child's foundation for behavior and learning for the rest of his or her life is laid in the early years.

Therefore, an early childhood program should be based on fulfilling the developmental needs of young children. It also should adapt to the individual and cultural differences of children. Understanding the interrelationship among development, learning, and experiences is essential to provide the highest-quality care and education for young children.

Multicultural and antibias considerations are essential each time you set up an appropriate, warm, supportive environment for young children. Establishing this environment enables children to make connections to their reality as well as the larger world, to develop positive self-esteem, and to receive approval, recognition, and success. The themes and activities in this book provide opportunities for children to develop an awareness of cultural similarities and differences that will build understanding and respect for others.

Establishing guidance guidelines in an early childhood environment includes setting clear, consistent, and fair limits for classroom and playground behavior. This directs younger children toward appropriate ways to relate to others and function in a group environment, and it helps older children set their own limits. Setting limits means security for children.

SECTIONS AND THEMES

This book is divided into six broad **sections**, with individual **themes** comprising each section. The thematic approach introduces children to activities that require active exploration, problem solving, and the acquisition of specific concepts or skills. Each theme is designed to merge play with child-initiated and teacher-created experiences. Thirty themes are identified in this text.

THEMATIC WEBS

The curriculum **web** diagram for each theme assists in categorizing thoughts and determining what needs to be emphasized in each theme. The process of webbing is a form of brainstorming that explores and organizes connections between ideas. The web at the beginning of each theme is a starting place, to which you can add your own ideas, topics, and activities to meet the needs of your children. Creating webs helps you remain flexible.

THEME GOALS

Goals for each theme are written in a *developmentally sequenced* listing to aid in your planning for the ongoing development of children as they grow and learn.

Additionally, teachers should be aware that the goals and concepts children achieve in association with a particular theme do not end when the unit is over. Children continue to explore and apply their knowledge within succeeding themes.

VOCABULARY

Vocabulary development is not done in isolation. It is a part of language development and progresses from the repetition of words to the understanding and acquisition of words. The **vocabulary** words included in each theme are only suggestions. Vocabulary should be an outgrowth of teacher and children sharing experiences relating to the theme. Review what children *know,* continue with what children *want to find out,* and conclude with what children *have learned.*

BULLETIN BOARDS

The children-created **bulletin board** featured in each theme should come from ideas suggested by the children, as should the process of creating the final product. The bulletin board ideas in this book are only recommendations. The bulletin board should be a visual extension of what is happening in your classroom. Remember to place bulletin boards at a child's eye level.

THEMATIC ACTIVITIES

Selecting developmentally appropriate **activities** begins with what the teacher knows about each child in the classroom. Understanding the developmental changes that may occur in the years from infancy through middle childhood is critical in making curriculum decisions. The **developmentally appropriate materials and supplies charts for curriculum areas (Appendix B)** can assist you in making such determinations.

The activities presented in each of the themes provide for all areas of a child's development: physical, cognitive, social, emotional, cultural, language, aesthetic, and creative. At the same time, these learning activities enable children to achieve curriculum goals, skills, and concepts through the following:

- fingerplays, poems, and flannelboard stories
- dramatic and puppet play
- music and movement
- creative food experiences
- sensory art
- math
- science
- social studies
- children's books

Each activity is introduced by an illustrated **icon** that suggests its appropriateness for specific ages:

Note: In no case was any activity, chant, fingerplay, song, or poem of known authorship used without credits. The vast majority of these have been shared with me by young children, teachers, and students I have taught in my college courses. Other material is either from old folk songs, traditional games, or is completely original content.

BOOKS

A selected bibliography of **children's books** is included with each theme. Books are an essential part of curriculum development. Children's interests should motivate the selection of children's literature, a vital part of early childhood learning. Learning is basically the process of associating that which is new with what is already known, and stories can be a powerful tool to accomplish this for young children. Interactions with children through books help us enfold literature into language and literacy development.

FAMILY LETTERS

Special letters sent home on a periodic basis help promote trust and a partnership between teachers, families, and young children. These letters also can help develop open communication between home and school by sharing opportunities for learning experiences that families need to help their children develop and grow.

This book contains 30 letters, one for each theme, plus a special one for families of infants. These can be personalized to fit the group of children and families in your classroom. Messages are more effective if they are personal and specific to your program.

The letters

- encourage families to share with you what they know about their children and what is important to them as families.
- encourage families to keep in touch with you so that you can answer any questions or concerns mentioned in the letter.
- contain general early childhood information.
- discuss the theme the children are exploring and offer activities families can do with children at home to extend or emphasize classroom experiences.
- encourage family involvement in events and activities, thereby strengthening teamwork between families and teachers.

Appendices

Appendix A of this book contains full-page enlargements of music presented in various themes. These may be photocopied for ease of use and for sharing. Appendix B offers developmentally appropriate materials and supplies for curriculum areas. Appendix C includes blank lesson plans and a suggested infant letter.

CD-ROM

The CD-ROM (Windows and Mac compatible) that accompanies this book contains the following teaching tools: a detailed table of contents, thematic outlines, lesson plans, family letters, and the collection of rebus charts and patterns from the text. Including the rebus charts and patterns on the CD-ROM allows for reproducing in 8½-by-11-inch format. The family letters, which also appear in the text, are included here to make producing and personalizing them easier for teachers. The letters are in four categories for families of toddlers, preschool children, primary-grade children, and a special letter for families of infants, which is also included in the text. Letters are written for each theme. They are suggestions and intended to be personalized with what is happening in *your* classroom. The lesson plans and thematic outlines are additional tools included on the CD-ROM.

THEMATIC OUTLINES

The outlines on the CD-ROM are a complete list of each theme and activity contained in the text. The outlines are intended as an additional guide for your theme and activity selection.

LESSON PLANS

After theme selection, webbing, and activity choices, the process of **lesson planning** is the next step in curriculum development. Lesson plans should be based on the developmental stages, learning styles, abilities, and interests of the children.

The three examples of lesson plans offer ways to

- apply the theme across the curriculum.
- support theme-related and nonrelated activities.
- integrate thematic instruction with other required program elements.

The activities included in the lesson plans for infants, toddlers, preschool, and kindergarten through third-grade children are selected from several of the themes suggested in this resource book. Both completed and blank lesson plan forms are included on the CD-ROM.

Get Ready to Play, Explore, Learn, and Sing

Young children entering early childhood programs are eager to sing, play, explore, and learn about themselves and their world. A developmentally appropriate classroom should give the children a multitude of opportunities to select activities from a variety of curriculum areas. This thematic curriculum resource book is designed to help you offer appropriate experiences and activities for each child in your care.

I hope you and the children experience much enjoyment, exploration, and discovery from these creative learning experiences.

Acknowledgments

A book is always a collaboration of many ideas and experiences. A sincere and heartfelt *thank you* goes out to the numerous children, teachers, families, college students, and colleagues with whom developmentally appropriate themes and activities were shared over many years.

Special recognition and many thanks must go to

Laurent Linn, my son, whose amazing illustrations demonstrate the exuberance of early childhood. He expresses with his pen to paper what I try to say with words.

Philip Jackman, my husband, who was *always* there with a rhyming word, an original fingerplay or poem, and continuous patience, encouragement, and love.

Jo Eklof, my friend and colleague, whose charming songs reflect the affection and respect she feels for the children and the world in which we live.

Janet Galantay, **Roberta Robinson**, **Nita Mae Tannebaum**, and **Bea Wolf**, my friends and exceptional teachers of young children, who contributed their activities and expertise that added so much to this book.

Stephen Linn, my son, whose additional support and encouragement always came at the right moment during this project.

Jared Cohen, my nephew, who continues to tell me what kids like to do, even though he has grown beyond the early childhood years.

To the Thomson Delmar Learning staff, especially Erin O'Connor and Ivy Ip, thank you!

To Linda DeMasi, thanks!

And to my reviewers, a special thanks for all your comments.

Julie Bakerlis, M.S.
Quinsigamond Community College
Worcester, MA

Jennifer E. Berke, Ph.D.
Mercyhurst College, North East Campus
North East, PA

Wendy Bertoli, M.Ed.
Lancaster County Career and Technology Center
Lancaster, PA

Heather Fay
Childtime Children's Center
Akron, OH

Jennifer Johnson, M.Ed.
Vancy-Granville Community College
Henderson, NC

Judith Lindman, M.Ed.
Rochester Community and Technical College
Rochester, MN

About the Author

*H*ilda Jackman, Professor Emerita with the Dallas County Community College District, describes her life's work simply. "It has always been," she says, "about children and families." From her early years in children's theatre, through the years when she was establishing herself as a writer, producer, and puppeteer in children's television, through her undergraduate years, to her earning a master's degree in early childhood education, to raising two sons—the emphasis has always been the same. This devotion to her goal—children and families—led to years of experience as a teacher of young children and eventually to the position of center director. Her ability, dedication, and reputation resulted in her selection as the person to establish the Child Development/Early Childhood Program and Parent-Child Study Center at the newly opened Brookhaven College, a position she held for 18 years until retiring. Since then she has found another career—but one still tied to children and families—as a writer, first with her textbook, *Early Education Curriculum: A Child's Connection to the World*, and most recently with *Sing Me a Story! Tell Me a Song!* Many of the activities that you will read about in this book are ones that the author has enjoyed sharing with all of the children and teachers she has known over her long career. The author also works as an early childhood consultant and a presenter of workshops and staff development, and she is active in several early childhood professional organizations. But no matter what she does, as the author herself puts it, "My life has always been about children and families."

All About Me!

*T*he *children* are at the center of all we do in early childhood education. Developmentally appropriate curriculum is based on knowledge about how children develop and learn. Their age and experience also should be taken into consideration.

With this in mind, select thematic activities from this section, realizing that not all of the children in your class have to do the specific activity at the same time. Let *their* individual differences, abilities, and interests guide you. The activities are designed to meet the diversity of your children.

The following themes are included in Section I — All About Me!:

Theme 1 — My Body

Theme 2 — My Friends

Theme 3 — My Family

Theme 4 — My Self

Theme 5 — My Home

Theme 6 — My Community

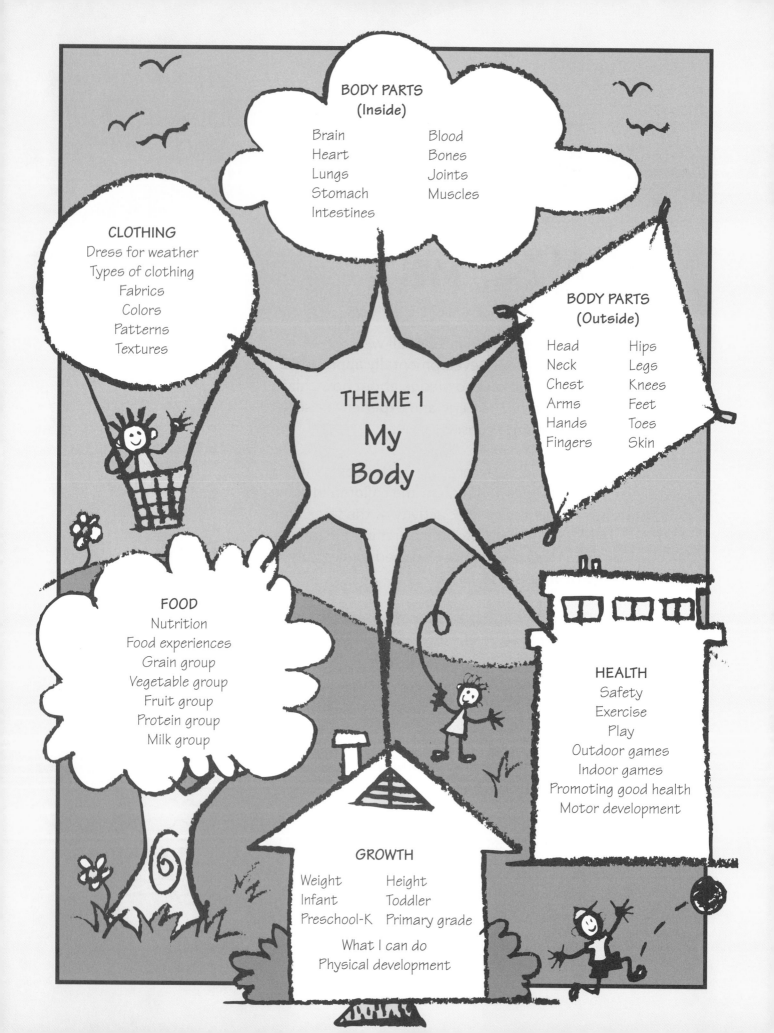

BODY PARTS
(Inside)

Brain	Blood
Heart	Bones
Lungs	Joints
Stomach	Muscles
Intestines	

CLOTHING

Dress for weather
Types of clothing
Fabrics
Colors
Patterns
Textures

BODY PARTS
(Outside)

Head	Hips
Neck	Legs
Chest	Knees
Arms	Feet
Hands	Toes
Fingers	Skin

THEME 1

My Body

FOOD

Nutrition
Food experiences
Grain group
Vegetable group
Fruit group
Protein group
Milk group

HEALTH

Safety
Exercise
Play
Outdoor games
Indoor games
Promoting good health
Motor development

GROWTH

Weight	Height
Infant	Toddler
Preschool-K	Primary grade

What I can do
Physical development

THEME GOALS

To provide opportunities for children to learn the following:

▶ Every person is special.

▶ Everyone has a body with many parts.

▶ The body can move in many ways and do many things.

▶ Food, exercise, and sleep help our bodies grow.

▶ Eating fruits and vegetables and drinking milk keep our bodies healthy.

Children-Created Bulletin Board

This bulletin board allows each child to draw her face on a paper plate. There is no right or wrong way to do this. A new "face" can be drawn to replace the one being displayed. Each child's "face" may change several times during the theme. This bulletin board helps children develop an awareness of diversity.

▶ Use large-size paper plates for older infants and toddlers to scribble and draw on with crayons.

▶ For older children, add materials to the paper plates, such as markers, paints, construction paper, buttons, yarn, and pipe cleaners.

▶ To get children started, have them look into a mirror and describe what they see, such as the color of their eyes, hair, and skin. This helps them draw self-portraits.

VOCABULARY STARTERS

Let the children add words. Include pictures where appropriate.

brain — a place inside of our head that helps us think, remember, and learn new things.

heart — a muscle in the chest that pumps blood to all parts of the body.

height — the distance between the top of the head to the bottom of the feet when standing.

lungs — two balloonlike sacs inside of the chest that fill up with air when we breathe in and empty when we breathe out.

stethoscope — an instrument that doctors use to hear your heart beat in your chest.

stomach — a special sac inside of our body that catches the food we chew and swallow.

weight — how heavy the body is.

LANGUAGE EXPERIENCES

FINGERPLAY:
Two Little Fingers

Two little fingers crawling up your arm,
　(crawl two fingers up child's arm)
Now they're on your shoulder trying to stay warm.
　(crawl fingers up to shoulder and "snuggle" them
　between shoulder and neck)
Two little fingers crawl into your hair,
　(crawl fingers into child's hair)
Cover your ears because they're almost there.
　(crawl fingers down to ears)
Two little fingers jump on your knee,
　(jump two fingers to child's knee)
See how they get there as fast as can be.
　Now they jump up to your eye,
　(two fingers jump up to eye)
And it's time to wave bye-bye.
　(wave bye-bye with two fingers)

POEM:

"Looking in the Mirror"

When I look in my mirror
I'm happy to see
Someone I like
And that someone is me.

When you look in your mirror
It really is true
There's someone to like
And that someone is you.

Philip Jackman

Introduce a full-length, nonbreakable mirror or small hand mirror to explore individual characteristics, such as eyes, skin, hair, mouth, nose, and clothing.

ALL ABOUT ME BOOK

This is a book the child starts at the beginning of the school year and adds to throughout the year. Simplify this project for younger children by including only those items toddlers can do developmentally. The book could contain the following:

▶ hand-, foot-, finger-, or thumbprints

▶ chart of weight and height

▶ pasted pictures from magazines, or drawn pictures of favorite foods, colors, and shapes

▶ any dictated story

▶ a picture of the child, family members, and friends

▶ address, phone number, birth date

▶ what the child likes to do

STORY STARTER:

"When I Was a Baby"

With younger children, you can do the following:

▶ Let them tell you a story about themselves as babies.

▶ Later, put the stories into each child's *All About Me* book.

With older children, you can do the following:

▶ Let them dictate or write story sentences about when they were babies. Put these on sentence strip paper.

▶ Mix the sentences up, and have the children read each line and put them in the correct sequence.

▶ This activity can be extended by the children. They can make a book of the story and illustrate each line.

TIME FOR A RHYME

With the children, list words that rhyme with body parts. For example:

- heart (smart, chart)
- head (bed, red)
- hand (band, stand)
- feet (seat, treat)

- knee (see, me)
- leg (peg, beg)
- eye (pie, good-bye)
- ear (near, tear)

DRAMATIC PLAY

DOLL CORNER

- Select sock or soft dolls that depict different cultures and are easy to wash.
- The clothing on the dolls also should be washable.
- The clothes should be easy to take off and put on.

BATHE THE BABY

- Provide dolls and a plastic tub with one or two inches of water.
- Children can add tear-free baby shampoo and bathe the baby dolls.
- Older toddlers can squeeze a few drops of liquid soap into the tub. Encourage them to beat the soap into suds with an eggbeater.
- Preschoolers like using washcloths and small bars of soap.
- Have several towels ready for drying the baby.

CLOTHING STORE

- Set up the dramatic play center with boxes of clothing and related items, such as coats, shirts, skirts, gloves, hats, purses, and sunglasses.
- Divide the space into two "dressing rooms," one for girls and one for boys.
- Have a nonbreakable mirror available for the children to see how the clothes look on them.

SUPERMARKET/GROCERY STORE/MERCADO/ FARMER'S MARKET

- With the children's help, set up and extend the dramatic play area.
- Provide the following:

cash register
calculator
play money or money the children make
price tags
markers, pens, and colored pencils
sales slip pad
empty food containers, some with print in different languages to represent foods from diverse cultures

artificial fruits and vegetables
grocery sacks
coupon pages and scissors
shopping lists with words and pictures of items
telephone
signs in several languages with pictures to explain what is for sale

PUPPET PLAY

THUMB FACE PUPPET

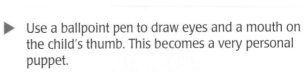

- Use a ballpoint pen to draw eyes and a mouth on the child's thumb. This becomes a very personal puppet.
- Play can be extended if a child wants to make all fingers into puppets.
- Finger face puppets also can personalize fingerplays.

CHILD STICK PUPPET

▶ This puppet can be made out of cardboard, tagboard, or construction paper.

▶ Attach puppet to a craft stick or dowel rod.

▶ Younger children can make a smaller child and attach a straw instead of a stick.

▶ Encourage children to add eyes, a nose, a mouth, ears, hair, clothes, and shoes.

▶ Provide crayons, markers, paints, and construction paper. Be sure to include a variety of colors that can be used to depict different skin tones.

▶ Include many colors of yarn for hair and clothing decoration.

▶ This activity promotes self-awareness and positive self-esteem.

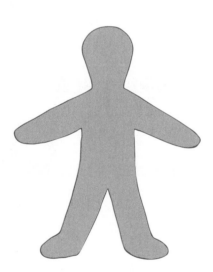

MUSIC

MUSICAL BEAT ACTIVITY: "Everybody Do This"

The teacher does the motions first, then asks for suggestions from children.

Everybody do this, do this, do this
Everybody do this, just like me.
Everybody clap hands, clap hands, clap hands
Everybody clap hands, just like me.
Everybody wiggle fingers, wiggle fingers, wiggle fingers
Everybody wiggle fingers, just like me.
Everybody bend knees, bend knees, bend knees
Everybody bend knees, just like me.
   (Stamp feet, shake shoulders, nod head, etc.)

SONG: "Body Rap"

C'mon, girls and boys, do the body rap.
If you think you can do it just clap-clap-clap.
Now, first you bend over and touch your toes,
And then you stand up and pat your nose.
Put your two hands down and lean on your knees.
Then turn around, turn around as nice as you please.
Now stand up straight, put your arms out wide,
And swing your hips from side to side.
Put your hands on your waist, stick your elbows out
   straight,
And twist back and forth like you open a gate.
Now point to your eyes and blink-blink-blink.
Make your mouth big and wide like you're taking a drink.
Put your hands on your head, put them right on top.
Now bend both your legs and go hop-hop-hop.
Stop where you are, stand up straight again.
Put your hands on your ears, and stick out your chin.
The last thing you do is to clap-clap-clap,
And that's the way you do the body rap.

Philip Jackman

MOVEMENT

OBSTACLE COURSE

▶ Set up a simple mini-obstacle course indoors for infants and toddlers to crawl through (cloth tunnels), climb over (large pillows), crawl under (sheets draped over small tables), and walk over (small, sturdy stairs).

- For older children, set up an obstacle course outdoors with cardboard boxes, hollow blocks, balance beams, hoops, and cloth tunnels.

- Encourage children to crawl or walk through the course slowly, walk sideways or backward around the course, or any other way they can think of. Verbalize their position in space by saying, "You are under the table," or, "You are on top of the pillows."

- Encourage older children to change the course or create a new one after the first one is mastered.

- Set up several short courses, or have another activity going on at the same time so children do not have to wait a long time between turns.

BASIC MOVEMENTS

Children need to become aware of the many ways they can move, as well as understand the flexibility of their bodies.

- Make your body as tall as you can by stretching high.
- Make your body as small as you can by curling into a ball.
- Move across the room as if you are ice skating.
- Move across the room fast. Move slowly.
- Walk across the room on your heels. Walk on your toes.
- Walk across the room taking big steps. Take small steps.
- Swim across the room.
- Swing your arms back and forth, over and around, and side to side.
- Twist and turn like a washing machine.
- Pull an imaginary wagon across the room.
- Shake like jello.
- For younger children, simplify the movements, and demonstrate what you want them to do. Continue to do the movements with them.

WALK THE LINE

- Place an 8-to-10-foot strip of masking tape on the floor.
- Children can crawl, walk forward, backward, sideways, or heel to toe, or jump along the line.
- This is a great way for children to learn balance and coordination safely.

SENSORY ART

DRAW A CHILD

- A favorite activity of toddlers is for the teacher to draw around them while they are lying on a large piece of brown wrapping paper or butcher paper.

- An older child can choose a partner, and the two can draw around each other.

- Each child then adds eyes, nose, mouth, ears, hair, and clothing with materials from the art scrap box.

- Place the drawings around the room.

FINGERPRINTS AND FOOTPRINTS

Fingerprints

- Spread pieces of construction paper or butcher paper on the table in the art center.

- Set out ink pads and magnifying glasses.

- Children make thumb- and fingerprints by placing individual fingers first on ink pads and then on the paper.

- Place a plastic tub with soapy water and paper towels nearby for children to wash their hands when they are finished using ink pads.

- Children can then examine their fingerprints with a magnifying glass.

- Children can look at each other's prints and discuss the similarities and differences.

- To extend this activity, encourage children to use the magnifying glass to look at the skin on their hands and arms. Compare the skin with their fingerprints. Examine several strands of hair with the magnifying glass.

- This activity encourages children to investigate and experiment with a magnifying glass while providing a sensory experience. The children also discover more about their bodies.

Footprints

- Next, encourage the children to make footprints. Begin by covering the floor or outdoor sidewalk with newspaper, and then place long pieces of brown wrapping paper or butcher paper over the newspaper. Tape the corners so that the paper will stay in place.

▶ The children remove their shoes and socks and then stand at one end of the paper.

▶ Help children step into tubs or containers to which you have added enough tempera paint to coat their feet without dripping. Paint is slippery, so you may need to assist some children as they walk on the paper.

▶ At the other end of the paper, place a tub of warm, soapy water and some towels. The children will end the activity by stepping into the tub of water.

▶ This special "feet painting mural" can be placed anywhere in the room or school to show what is happening in your classroom.

WEAVING

▶ Collect enough plastic strawberry baskets for each child to have one to work with. Ask families to help you collect these.

▶ Children select lengths of brightly colored yarn.

▶ Dip one end of the yarn in glue, which will work as a weaving needle when it hardens.

▶ Encourage children to weave the yarn in and out of the holes in the basket until the basket is covered.

▶ This activity helps children develop small muscle skills.

CREATIVE FOOD EXPERIENCES

LET'S MAKE CRACKER FACES

Toddlers need some guidance in spreading the peanut butter or cream cheese. The main purpose of this activity is to give the children an opportunity to try.

You will need the following:

   round crackers (such as Ritz)

   peanut butter (or cream cheese or margarine for children who are allergic to peanut butter)

   raisins

   miniature marshmallows

1. Wash hands.
2. Spread the peanut butter or cream cheese on crackers.
3. Add raisins and marshmallows to make a face.
4. Eat!

LET'S MAKE CRACKER FACES!

Wash hands.

Spread some peanut butter on round crackers.

Then add raisins and marshmallows

to make a face!

EAT!

HEALTHY SNACKS

▶ celery sticks spread with peanut butter or pimiento cheese

▶ apple wedges or slices, which can be dipped into honey

▶ strawberries or pineapple chunks

▶ dried fruits: apples, raisins, apricots

▶ juice popsicles

▶ gelatin, made by the children in the morning and eaten in the afternoon

MATH

MATCH THE SOCKS

Younger children enjoy this activity. They can play this with you, with another child, or by themselves. Toddlers sometimes need more assistance.

▶ Ask families to send you pairs of old socks of all sizes.

▶ Place the socks in a colorful basket.

▶ Ask the children to match the socks according to color, size, pairs, and texture.

LOOK HOW I'VE GROWN

▶ Have children bring baby pictures from home.

▶ Take individual pictures of the children when they first come into your class.

▶ Take a current picture of each child.

▶ Put all of the pictures up to create a special wall in the classroom. Children can show each other how they have grown.

▶ During circle or individual time, have each child tell how she has grown. For example: "I can help serve and clean up at snack, I am taller, my feet are bigger, I can take turns and share."

▶ Demonstrate to the toddlers how they have grown. Show them their baby pictures. Have them look in a mirror to see how they have changed. Talk to them about all of the things they can do now.

▶ Measure and weigh the children at different times during the year to show how they have grown.

▶ Children enjoy knowing how tall they are and how much they weigh. Even though they may not understand what the numbers mean, they seem to gain a sense of self-identification from them.

LET'S MEASURE

Older children enjoy doing this activity.

▶ Make different-size footprints, right and left.

▶ Cut them out and laminate.

▶ Discuss the dimensions of the footprints with the children. Which is the smallest? Which is the largest? Which ones are right feet? Which ones are left feet? How can you tell?

▶ Line them up from smallest to largest or any other way the children decide. They can even create a pattern.

▶ The children can measure their own feet and shoes.

SCIENCE

EXPLORING SHADOWS

▶ Read Asch's *Bear Shadow*, Dodd's *Footprints and Shadows*, or Hoban's *Shadows and Reflections*. All are listed in the Children's Books section of this theme.

▶ What is a shadow? Let the children discover the answer.

▶ By experimenting with different objects in the room, children can discover which ones cast shadows and which ones do not.

▶ Children will discover that shade is a dark place that light cannot reach. A shadow is the shape cast by whatever is in front of the light.

▶ It is fun for the children to outline their shadows on the sidewalk with chalk. They can help each other do this. They also can measure how long or how short their shadows are. Try this at different times during the day. Do the shadows change?

▶ Show toddlers exactly where their shadows are. Move their arms to help them find their shadows. Say, "Wave your arms. See the shadow's arms wave?"

▶ What happens when the children dance or wiggle?

FOOD, HEALTHY FOOD

Together, you and the children cut food pictures from old magazines that you and their families have collected.

Ask for the magazines several months before you do this activity so you will have plenty available.

▶ From the cut-out pictures, create a food group chart. This opens up an opportunity for the class to discuss healthy foods.

▶ If the children cannot find their favorite foods among the pictures, they can draw them and put them on the chart in the appropriate place.

▶ You can download the Food Guide Pyramid for Young Children by going online to: www.usda.gov/cnpp/kidspyra.

CLOTHING FABRICS ARE ALL WET

This activity develops problem-solving and observation skills.

▶ Collect all kinds of fabric scraps: corduroy, wool, flannel, satin, nylon, vinyl, plastic, and cotton.

▶ In small groups, the children take turns using an eyedropper to drop water on each piece of fabric. Then they sort the fabric into two categories: those that absorb water and those that repel water. Ask the children which fabrics they would wear as outer clothing during a rainstorm.

▶ What do children wear when it is raining? Can they describe the fabric content of their umbrellas?

SOCIAL STUDIES

WE ARE ALIKE, WE ARE DIFFERENT

▶ Select several books relating to similarities and differences, and read them to the children. Choose from the list of suggested books at the end of this theme.

▶ While reading the book to younger children, it is helpful to point to the different parts of the face and body on each child.

▶ Next, ask the child to point to her own nose, eyes, mouth, and so on.

▶ After reading the books to older children, provide supplies and materials they can use to create their own "alike" and "different" pictures.

▶ Place the books in the book center, and put the pictures around the room or on the bulletin board.

PUZZLING FACES

▶ Collect many large pictures of children's faces from catalogs, magazines, newspapers, and posters. If you prefer, collect pictures of the entire child, not just the face.

▶ Glue each picture to a piece of cardboard or foam sheet, and let dry.

▶ With light pencil marks, mark the photo into puzzle pieces.

▶ Cut into puzzle pieces.

▶ Put each puzzle into an 8-by-10 envelope or a resealable plastic bag.

▶ Introduce these to the children with the emphasis on the placement of the eyes, nose, mouth, ears, and hair. With older children, discuss position, such as top and bottom, left and right.

▶ Discuss similarities and differences. If the puzzles are of the entire child, talk about the different body parts.

▶ Place the puzzles in the manipulative center.

CHILDREN'S BOOKS

Aliki. (2003). *All By Myself*. New York: HarperTrophy.

Aliki. (2003). *I'm Growing*. New York: HarperCollins.

Asch, Frank. (1988). *Bear Shadow*. New York: Aladdin.

Brown, Tricia. (1984). *Someone Special Just Like Me*. Photographs by Fran Ortiz. New York: Henry Holt.

Bryant, Jill, and Catherine Heard. (2002). *Making Shadow Puppets*. Illustrated by Laura Watson. Buffalo: Kids Can.

Cisneros, Sandra. (1994). *Hairs—Pelitos: A Story in English and Spanish*. Illustrated by Terry Ybanez. New York: Alfred A. Knopf.

Danziger, Paula. (1994). *Amber Brown Is Not a Crayon*. New York: Putnam.

Dillon, Leo, and Diane Dillon. (2002). *Rap a TapTap: Here's Bojangles—Think of That*. New York: Blue Sky Press.

Dodd, Anne W. (1994). *Footprints and Shadows*. New York: Aladdin.

Dupasquier, Philippe. (2002). *123, Follow Me!* Cambridge, MA: Candlewick Press.

Heide, Florence P., and Judith Gilliland. (1990). *The Day of Ahmed's Secret*. Illustrated by Ted Lewin. New York: Lothrop, Lee & Shepard.

Hoban, Tana. (1990). *Shadows and Reflections*. New York: Greenwillow.

Hoffman, Mary. (1991). *Amazing Grace*. New York: Dial.

Kates, Bobbi Jane. (1992). *Sesame Street's We're Different, We're the Same.* Illustrated by Joe Mathieu. New York: Random House.

Kissenger, Katie. (1994). *All the Colors We Are: Todos Los Colores de Nuestra Piel.* Photographs by Wernher Krutein. St. Paul, MN: Redleaf Press.

Morris, Ann. (1993). *Bread, Bread, Bread.* Photographs by Ken Heyman. New York: Mulberry.

O'Brien, Claire. (1997). *Sam's Sneaker Search.* Illustrated by Charles Fuge. New York: Simon & Schuster.

Rogers, Fred. (1986). *Going to the Potty.* Photographs by Jim Judkis. New York: Putnam.

Simon, Seymour. (2002). *Eyes and Ears.* New York: HarperCollins.

Van Cleave, Janice. (1998). *Play and Find Out about the Human Body.* New York: Wiley.

Winter, Susan. (1994). *A Baby Just Like Me.* New York: DK Publishing.

Family Letter (Preschool)

Dear Family,

Our theme is "My Body." We will provide opportunities for the children to learn the following:

- *Every person is special.*
- *Everyone has a body with many parts.*
- *Our bodies can move in many ways and do many things.*
- *Food, exercise, and sleep help our bodies grow.*
- *Fruits, vegetables, and milk keep our bodies healthy.*

We will be talking about the following:

- *inside body parts*
- *health and safety*
- *outside body parts*
- *food*
- *growth*
- *clothing*

To reinforce the concepts we are working on at school, here are some things to do at home with your child:

- *Talk with your child about when he or she was a baby and how he or she has grown.*
- *Take "time for a rhyme." Rhyme words with names of body parts. This is a good activity for you and your child to do on the ride home.*
- *Let your child help you match socks on laundry day.*
- *Take a walk, or exercise together.*
- *Start a growth chart. If you already have one, talk about it together.*
- *Talk with your children about healthy foods and food groups.*

Join us for family participation opportunities at school:

- *Help measure and weigh children.*   Date _____   Time _____
- *Help when we make "paint footprints."* Date _____   Time _____
- *Come take snapshots.*   Date _____   Time _____

The wish list for this theme includes:

empty food boxes for our dramatic play grocery store
grocery sacks
plastic berry baskets
old magazines
fabric scraps
yarn scraps
pairs of old, clean socks

Thanks!

THEME GOALS

To provide opportunities for children to learn the following:

▶ Everyone can be a friend and have a friend at the same time.

▶ Friends can be people or animals.

▶ Friends can be family or other people outside of the family.

▶ Friends are like you in some ways and different from you in some ways.

▶ Friends show they are friendly in many ways, such as sharing, helping, listening, talking, and playing together.

Children-Created Bulletin Board

This bulletin board offers an opportunity for children to work together cooperatively, to develop respect for each other's creativity, and to care about what they are accomplishing together.

▶ Discuss what a quilt is. Invite a quilt maker or family member to visit the class and show the children examples of quilts.

▶ Read Flournoy's *The Patchwork Quilt*, Johnston and dePaola's *The Quilt Story*, Bourgeois's *Oma's Quilt,* or Polacco's *The Keeping Quilt*. All are listed in the Children's Books section of this theme.

▶ Provide precut, assorted colored or white squares of paper.

▶ Older children can cut other papers into desired shapes and glue them onto the squares of paper.

▶ The children select <u>fabric</u> crayons or markers and create designs on the paper squares.

▶ Each individual fabric crayon drawing on paper can then be ironed onto an individual small fabric square by an adult.

▶ Sew these together to make the friendship quilt.

VOCABULARY STARTERS

Let the children add words.

friend — a person you like and who likes you.

helpful — to do friendly things that make someone else's play or work easier.

listen — to pay attention and hear what someone else is saying.

neighbor — someone who lives near you.

share — letting someone use what you have.

thoughtful — to pay attention to what someone else feels or wants.

LANGUAGE EXPERIENCES

POEM:
"I Have A Friend"

I have a friend and
My friend has me.
We're great friends,
As you can see.
We play together
In the rain and sun,
Come join us and have some fun.

FINGERPLAY:

Friends

Two houses, clean and neat
  (hold up two fists facing each other)
Open doors wide, so friends can meet.
  (open fists and hold up all the fingers)
"Hello" to you, and "hi" to you,
  (all fingers wave "hello" to each other)
Let's decide what we will do.
  (fingers face each other)
It's sunny so let's run and play.
  (fingers run and play)
Friends have fun every day.
  (hands clasp together)

POEM:
"One Little Friend"

Based on the traditional folk song, "Five Little Ducks," this can be used as a transition activity to move the children from inside to outside play.

One little friend went out to play
On the playground one fine day.
He (she) was having so much fun
He (she) called another friend to come.
Two little friends went out to play
On the playground one fine day.
They were having so much fun
They called another friend to come.

Repeat until all the children in the classroom have been counted.

TODDLER TELEPHONE TALK

This activity promotes language development for young toddlers.

▶ Encourage two children on individual telephones (toy or discarded real ones) to talk to each other.

▶ Guide them by saying, for example:
   "I like to call my friend on the telephone."
   "You can call your friend on the telephone."
   "Hello, friend."
   "How are you today?"
   "Good-bye, friend."

▶ Then, step back and let the children talk to each other.

▶ You may have to repeat this on several days before the children begin to pick up the phones and "talk" to their friend.

DRAMATIC PLAY

ANIMAL FRIENDS

The following activity is designed to integrate several curriculum areas. The activity can be extended over the entire time that the "My Friends" theme is emphasized.

▶ Ask the children to bring a favorite stuffed animal "friend" to class.

▶ At group time, invite each child to introduce his friend to the other children.

▶ Encourage several children at a time to go to the dramatic play or housekeeping center and plan a pretend birthday party for their stuffed animals or for each other.

▶ With older children, talk about friendship, acceptance, and belonging.

▶ Begin to read the book by Margery Williams, *The Velveteen Rabbit*, or another book from the list at the end of this theme. Continue reading the book over several days.

PUPPET PLAY

BANANA PUPPET

Older infants and toddlers enjoy this activity. It is best to do this right before snack time.

▶ On an unpeeled banana, draw two eyes and a mouth.

▶ Make several banana puppets.

▶ Have one banana "talk" to the children. Add a second banana.

▶ After a few minutes, peel the bananas, cut them into small pieces, and serve as a snack with milk.

▶ Older toddlers can peel the banana and cut it in two with a plastic knife. They can share with their friends.

SOCK PUPPET

▶ Have children bring some of their old socks from home in the colors tan, beige, cream, brown, peach, or white. Child-size socks fit their hands better than adult-size socks.

▶ Guide children to make a sock puppet similiar to their own skin colors.

▶ Suggest making a puppet with a partner.

▶ Have felt scraps, yarn, fabric scraps, markers, and glue set up at the art table.

▶ Older children could sew on buttons using dull-pointed needles and thick thread.

▶ This activity promotes hand-eye coordination, small muscle development, creativity, and language development.

MUSIC

SONG: "Name Song" by Bea Wolf

Reproduced by permission of B. Wolf - 1995
Copyright B. Wolf - 1993

(See page 301 for enlargement.)

SONG: "It's So Good to Be with Friends" by Jo Eklof

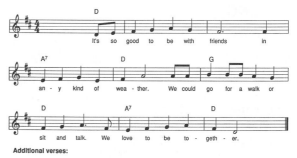

Additional verses:

It's fun in the snow with friends in cold and snowy weather.
We could shiver and play all through the day. We love to be together.

It's fun to swim with friends in warm and sunny weather.
We could splash and play all through the day. We love to be together.

© 1998 by Jo Eklof. All rights reserved. Used with permission.

(See page 301 for enlargement.)

SONG STICKS

This activity is designed for older children.

▶ Each time the children learn a new song, print the title of the song on a craft stick or tongue depressor.

- Add a sticker or small picture to help the children read the song stick.
- Place the sticks in a decorated can or box.
- Have the children close their eyes and take turns drawing a song stick.
- Next, the class sings the song picked.
- Let the children tell you when it is time to stop this activity. Some will want to drop out earlier than others.
- Continue with children who want to proceed, and let the others choose another activity center.

MOVEMENT

TODDLERS TOGETHER

- To encourage parallel play outdoors, have a wagon available. This invites two children to share.
- One child rides, and the other child pulls.
- They can then take turns riding and pulling.
- You may need to help the children get started. Give them a lot of praise when they take turns.

THE FRIENDS GO MARCHING

This is a variation of a traditional activity, "The Ants Go Marching." It can be both a movement/music and a transition activity.

The friends go marching two by two,
Hurrah, hurrah.
The friends go marching two by two,
Hurrah, hurrah.
The friends go marching two by two,
It's the greatest thing to do.
As we all go marching around the room,
Boom, boom — boom, boom.

- Expand this activity by adding extra verses, such as: friends go jumping, stomping, skipping, tiptoeing, and walking.
- Add musical instruments to emphasize the beat.

I'M A RAG DOLL

This activity can be done inside or outside, with or without music. Simplify it for younger children.

- Have a rag doll to show the children. This will help them understand the concept.
- Ask the children to stand up straight and tall, with feet together and head erect.
- Place arms stiff at children's sides, tummy in and chest out.
- Inhale, exhale, and relax body.
- Now become a rag doll. Bend at the waist. Hang head down and sway it from side to side.
- Bend the knees and swing from side to side.
- Drop to the floor, still relaxed.
- Then, reverse the process until all children are standing up straight and tall.
- Become a rag doll again.
- See if any of the children want to give the rag doll any directions of what to do.

FOLLOW A FRIEND

This activity is similar to "Follow the Leader," but with this exercise each child has a partner.

- Have the children form two circles, one inside the other. The inner circle faces the outer circle. This gives each child a partner.
- Start by having the outer circle of children do an action, such as patting the head. The inner circle repeats the action.

- Each child selects an action that his partner follows. The children can speed up and slow down various rhythmic exercises.
- After a few minutes, the inner circle changes places with the outer circle and decides on the action to be followed.
- Older children can expand this activity. One child becomes a mirror that reflects all he sees his partner do. For example, the children could pretend to put on clown makeup, do exercises, or become distorted mirrors like those found in amusement parks.

SENSORY ART

PARTNER PAINTING

This activity promotes taking turns and sharing for young children.

- Set up the easel with two brushes and two colors of paint.
- Have the children paint their picture standing side by side.
- At first you may want to closely supervise the children.
- Encourage children to "use their words" if there is a disagreement. Model appropriate behavior, if necessary.

THREE-DIMENSIONAL FRIENDS

This activity is designed to help children listen, follow directions, and create a three-dimensional picture.

- Place skin-toned construction paper (black, brown, tan, peach, and cream), scissors, rulers, and glue in the art center.
- Guide the children, two or three at a time, into the activity.
- Use one sheet of paper for the background.
- Cut other paper into strips about one inch wide.
- Fold, curl, or pleat the paper strips for hair, nose, and other features. You may need to help some children with curling and pleating. Younger children can use yarn to make hair.
- Glue the pieces onto the background sheet.
- Allow glue to dry.
- The children can play with and display their three-dimensional pictures of their friends and themselves.

RAINBOW OF FRIENDS

This activity encourages group participation and problem solving.

- Provide a prism (a triangular piece of glass that breaks up a ray of light into a color spectrum) for the children to experiment with.
- Talk about the colors of the rainbow.
- Cut a large sheet of butcher paper into the shape of a rainbow arc. Older children can work together to cut the rainbow.
- Have the children create the rainbow. They decide which colors to use and their placement.
- Children decide if they want to use crayons, markers, watercolors, or tempera paint.
- Let the mural dry.
- Later, the children can create "self-portraits" of themselves to add to the rainbow.

FRIENDSHIP HEART

This is an activity for two or three children to do together to encourage cooperation and sharing with friends.

- Cut a medium-size heart out of cardboard or poster board for each group of children.

- ▶ Place the hearts, strips of colored tissue paper, two or three small plastic dishes of diluted white glue, cotton swabs, and scissors on the art center table.
- ▶ Encourage the children to tear off small pieces of tissue paper.
- ▶ Glue them onto the heart, using swabs to help spread the glue.
- ▶ Older children can draw a heart design and cut the heart out themselves.
- ▶ Children also may like to make small tissue paper balls to glue onto the heart.
- ▶ When each heart is complete, ask the children to tell you what they learned about friendship while making the heart.

CREATIVE FOOD EXPERIENCES

CINNAMON TOAST

You will need:

    1 teaspoon cinnamon
    3 tablespoons sugar
    4 tablespoons butter or margarine
    4 slices of bread

Heat oven to 375 degrees.

1. Wash hands.
2. Mix cinnamon and sugar.
3. Add softened butter or margarine, and mix well. Spread on pieces of bread. Bake 5 minutes or until light brown.
4. Eat!

- ▶ For toddlers, give each child a plate with a piece of toast on it.
- ▶ Guide children in spreading some soft butter or margarine on the toast using a plastic knife. Model the appropriate way to use knives.
- ▶ Mix cinnamon with sugar in several salt shakers, and let the children sprinkle the cinnamon-sugar on their buttered toast.

FROSTED GRAHAM CRACKERS

You will need:

    1 cup powdered sugar
    1/4 cup margarine
    food coloring
    1 teaspoon vanilla extract
    1 box graham crackers
    nuts or shredded coconut
    1 tablespoon milk

FROSTED GRAHAM CRACKERS

Wash hands.

Mix sugar, margarine, and 2 to 3 drops of

food coloring. Mix vanilla and milk. Slowly add

vanilla-milk flavoring, a drop or 2 at a time.

Spread over graham crackers. Decorate with

chopped nuts and/or shredded coconut.

YUM! Eat and enjoy!

---

1. Wash hands.
2. Make this recipe several times with different small groups of children.
3. Mix sugar, margarine, and two to three drops of food coloring.
4. Mix vanilla and milk.
5. Slowly add vanilla-milk flavoring, a drop or two at a time, until you have a spreadable consistency. Spread over graham crackers. Decorate with chopped nuts or shredded coconut. Enjoy!

MATH

FAVORITE FOODS

▶ During circle time, ask about children's favorite foods. Emphasize what they and their friends *like*. It will not be necessary to ask about foods they dislike; they will tell you during the discussion.

▶ Take the information, and with the children, make a favorite food graph. See theme 10 for an example of a simple graph.

▶ To extend this activity, review the food groups with the children and make a graph of favorite foods within each food group. Older children can make a food pyramid.

FIND A FRIEND FOLDER GAME

▶ Take an ordinary file folder, open it, and draw a maze on the right page.

▶ Place "Start" and "Stop" on the maze.

▶ At the stop point, have an illustration, a picture, or a sticker of a child.

▶ On the cover of the file folder, write "Find a Friend."

▶ Laminate the folder.

▶ Provide a rub-off crayon or washable marker.

▶ The child playing the game begins at "Start" and marks a path to the friend at "Stop."

▶ To simplify the activity, place numerals 1 through 10 at places in the maze to guide the child.

▶ Older children can make more difficult mazes.

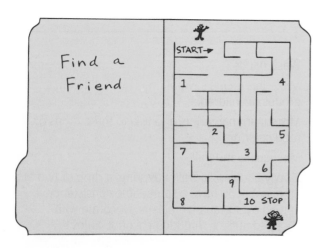

WHAT'S MISSING?

▶ Fill a picnic basket full of picnic items.

▶ Place all of the items on a cloth napkin for the children to see and name.

▶ To simplify for younger children, use only a few items.

▶ Have children close their eyes while you take an object away.

▶ Have children guess which item is missing.

▶ Continue this with several items.

▶ To extend, let the children, two at a time, take the picnic basket to the manipulative center and play the "What's Missing" game.

▶ To further extend, play a "What's Missing" game by grouping together several related items.

SCIENCE

THE FRIENDLY GARDEN

▶ Before planting a garden, explain the process of a seed growing into a plant, using a flannelboard to illustrate. The pieces can be handled easily by the children.

▶ Let the children select which flower seeds they want to plant. This emphasizes that a class of friends can plant and grow a garden together.

▶ Talk about how plants need water, warmth, and sunlight to grow and live. Ask older children open-ended questions so they can tell you what the plants will need in order to grow.

▶ With the children's help, prepare an area in one corner of the playground for a garden. Or, take the sand and water table outside, and fill it with potting soil.

▶ Have the children drop the flower seeds into the soil and cover them with more soil.

▶ Use a stick and the seed package picture to make a sign for identification of the plant.

▶ Watch the garden each day, and water as needed. With your help, the older children can pull weeds as necessary.

▶ This activity can be varied by planting vegetables. The process is the same.

A FRIENDLY RAINBOW

This activity extends and integrates the sensory art activities. This is a great activity to do outside in the bright sunshine.

▶ Place several shallow bowls of water in the sun.

▶ Place a drop or two of oil on the surface of each bowl of water. Use eyedroppers if you want the children to drop the oil onto the water.

▶ Ask the children open-ended questions, such as, "How many colors do you see?" "Do the colors you see match the colors in the rainbow?" "When did you see a rainbow?" "If you stir the water with a stick, do the colors change? Try it and see."

SOCIAL STUDIES

FRIENDS ARE SPECIAL PARTY

This activity integrates all of the curriculum areas. Begin by suggesting to the children, "We are a class of friends, so let's have a Friends Are Special Party!"

▶ The children choose a day and time for the party.

▶ Children write invitations to the party and post them on a special bulletin board for the families and the students in the class to see.

▶ Children make a list of what they will need for the party and how much it will cost.

▶ Give children suggestions for what they can make or bake for the party, such as the frosted graham crackers recipe in the cooking portion of this theme.

▶ The list is given to the teacher or to a family member who has volunteered to purchase the party supplies.

▶ Place additional construction paper in the art center for the children to use in making party hats.

▶ Have children select the music they want to play and the songs they want to sing.

▶ Then it is party time!

▶ To expand this party idea, the children can visit a class of younger students and bring the party to them. This extends the concept of friendship.

PUZZLE PIECES

▶ Select puzzles depicting children from other countries. The younger the child, the fewer pieces there should be in the puzzle.

▶ Introduce the puzzles during group time. Talk about the country where the children in the puzzle live. With the children's help, find the places on a globe or map.

▶ Invite two or three children to work as friends to put the puzzle together.

▶ Encourage the children to talk about what the children in the puzzle are doing. Ask open-ended questions.

CHILDREN'S BOOKS

Ajmera, Maya, and John D. Ivanko. (2002). *Animal Friends.* Watertown, MA: Charlesbridge.

Aliki. (1995). *Best Friends Together Again.* New York: Greenwillow.

Appelt, Kathi. (2002). *Bubba and Beau, Best Friends.* Illustrated by Arthur Howard. San Diego: Harcourt.

Bauer, Marion D. (2002). *Frog's Best Friend.* Illustrated by Diane Hearn. New York: Holiday House.

Bourgeois, Paulette. (2002). *Oma's Quilt.* Illustrated by Stephanie Jorisch. Buffalo: Kids Can Press.

Bunnett, Rochelle. (1992). *Friends in the Park.* Photographs by Carl Sahlhoff. New York: Checkerboard Press.

Carle, Eric, and Kazuo Iwamura. (2003). *Where Are You Going? To See My Friend: A Story Friendship in Two Languages.* New York: Orchard Books.

Cheltenham Elementary School Kindergartners. (1991). *We Are All Alike . . . We Are All Different.* New York: Scholastic.

Cosby, Bill. (2003). *Friends of a Feather: One of Life's Little Fables.* Illustrated by Erika Cosby. New York: Harper-Entertainment.

Ehlert, Lois. (2002). *In My World.* San Diego: Harcourt.

Flournoy, Valerie. (1985). *The Patchwork Quilt.* Illustrated by Jerry Pinkney. New York: Dial.

Isadora, Rachel. (1990). *Friends.* New York: Greenwillow.

Johnston, Tony, and Tomie dePaola. (1985). *The Quilt Story.* New York: Putnam.

Kellogg, Steven. (1992). *Best Friends.* New York: Dial.

Minarik, Else H. (2002). *Maurice Sendak's Little Bear: Little Bear's New Friend.* Illustrated by Heather Green. New York: HarperFestival.

Polacco, Patricia. (1992). *Mrs. Katz and Tush.* New York: Bantam Books.

Polacco, Patricia. (1988). *The Keeping Quilt.* New York: Simon & Schuster.

Rogers, Fred. (2000). *Let's Talk About It: Extraordinary Friends.* New York: Putnam.

Rogers, Fred. (1987). *Making Friends.* New York: Putnam.

Rylant, Cynthia. (1998). *Poppleton and Friends.* Illustrated by Mark Teague. New York: Scholastic.

Williams, Margery. (1991). *The Velveteen Rabbit.* New York: Doubleday.

Ziefert, Harriet. (2001). *39 Uses for a Friend.* Illustrated by Rebecca Doughty. New York: Putnam.

Family Letter (Toddler)

Dear Family,

We will be talking about friendship as we begin our theme, "My Friends." We will provide opportunities for the children to learn the following:

- Everyone can be a friend and have a friend at the same time.
- Friends can be people or animals.
- Friends can be family or other people outside of the family.
- Friends are alike in some ways and different in some ways.
- Friends show they are friendly in many ways, such as by sharing, helping, listening, talking, and playing together.

We will be talking about the following:

- qualities of friendship
- who can be a friend
- things friends do together
- where I visit my friends

Things to do at home with your young child include:

- You are your child's first friend. Spend time talking and playing together.
- Invite another child over to play.
- Help your child have "gentle hands" with a tame family pet or stuffed animal.
- Read stories about friends and friendship.
- Make friends with a friendly puppet. For example, use a sock, or draw a face on a banana.

Family participation opportunities at the center:

- Come anytime for some quality rocking chair time.
- Come for a toddler and friend picnic.
  Date _____   Time _____
- Send snapshots (covered in clear contact paper) of baby's friends and family to put low on the wall.

Our wish list for this theme includes:

pictures of friends together
stuffed toy friends
picture books about friends
nonworking, real telephones

Thanks!

THEME GOALS

To provide opportunities for children to learn the following:

▶ A family is two or more people who are connected by love or kinship.

▶ Families may have relatives other than those who live together, such as grandmothers, grandfathers, aunts, uncles, and cousins. Some people are part of more than one family.

▶ Each member of a family is important and special.

▶ Families live all over the world.

▶ Family members are alike in some ways and different in others.

▶ Members of a family work, play, and learn together. They also help each other.

▶ Some families have special foods that they eat and certain days that they celebrate together.

▶ Some families have and care for pets.

Children-Created Bulletin Board

This bulletin board encourages children to think about all of the members of their families and to understand and be accepting of the family units of their friends. The tree concept shows how families change and grow.

▶ You and the children make a family tree out of brown paper bags or brown wrapping paper.

▶ The paper can be crumpled and crushed to add texture.

▶ Staple to a bulletin board to form a tree shape.

▶ Take a walk outside to look at the leaves on the trees. The leaves the children will make should reflect the colors currently on the trees outside,

depending on the season in which you use this theme.

▶ Children cut out leaf shapes for the tree.

▶ Children write their names on some leaves and family member's names on others.

▶ If the children bring family photos to display, let them place these all around the tree.

VOCABULARY STARTERS

Let the children add words.

blended family – people from different family units living together.

daughter – a child of a father and mother who can be a girl or a woman.

extended family – includes aunts, uncles, and so on.

occupation – what people do to earn money for themselves and their families.

one-parent family – a child or children living with one parent, a father or a mother.

relatives – people who belong to your family or to the families of your grandmothers, grandfathers, aunts, and uncles.

son – a child of a father and mother who can be a boy or a man.

tradition – something that has been done or said over and over again in a family, such as special holidays, foods, songs, and stories.

vacation – a special time when people do things or go places to have fun.

LANGUAGE EXPERIENCES

FINGERPLAY: Grandpa's Glasses

These are grandpa's glasses,
   (make two circles with the thumbs and index fingers, and put them in front of your eyes like glasses)
This is grandpa's hat,
   (put both hands over your head in a point to make a hat)
This is how he folds his arms,
   (place one arm over the other arm)
Just like that.
These are grandma's glasses,
   (repeat gesture and make glasses)
This is grandma's hat,
   (repeat hat gesture with both hands)
This is how she folds her hands,
   (clasp hands together)
And puts them in her lap.

FAMILY MEMBER BINGO

This activity is designed for older children, especially those who are just starting to read. It can be played with the entire class or with two or three children at a time.

▶ Make enough bingo cards for each child to have one card.

▶ Write the names of family member relationships on each card (see the pattern sample).

▶ Each card should have the relationship names in a different order. On a few of the cards, write the same names twice, while leaving one or two names off so that each card will be different.

▶ Laminate each card.

▶ Write the family relationship names on individual sentence strip paper or on large cards. Laminate. The printing should be large enough for the children to see and match on their cards.

▶ Give the children enough large buttons or large plastic circles to cover all of the family names on their cards.

▶ Then play the game just like bingo. Call out the name you hold up, and have the children match it on their cards. Call the name several times. The first child to cover all of the names on her card wins the game.

▶ To extend this activity, make and laminate matching name pieces to be placed on an individual board. Place the card and the pieces in the language or manipulative center for one child to play.

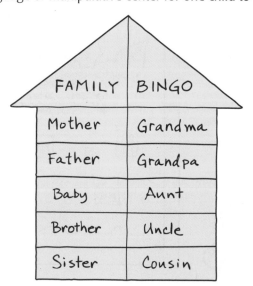

ASK QUESTIONS

Read the book *A Chair for My Mother*, by Vera Williams. Ask the children open-ended questions, such as:

- Have you ever been furniture shopping?
- With whom did you go?
- Do you save money?
- Where do you put the money you save?
- What are you going to do with your money?
- Should we save pennies to buy something for the classroom?

▶ Vote on what to buy. This relates to the math activity in this theme.

▶ Place *A Chair for My Mother* in the book center for the children.

DRAMATIC PLAY

TODDLER PRETEND PLAY

It is easy and fun to play "let's put the baby to bed" with a toddler and a doll. This can be an activity for the teacher to do with one child.

▶ Start by saying, "You be the mommy, and I'll be the daddy. This box can be the baby's bed, and here is the baby's blanket."

▶ Continue to talk through the activity, guiding the child through the step-by-step process of putting the baby to bed, covering the baby, and kissing it good night.

▶ Other children may want to do the same thing, so have enough dolls, boxes, and blankets for two or three children. Use washcloths or hand towels as doll blankets.

▶ This activity helps toddlers role-play what happens at home. It also emphasizes caring relationships that develop within a family.

HOME LIVING CENTER

From time to time, take an inventory of the home living center. You will probably want to replace or add new items.

▶ What about aprons, bibs, tablecloths, artificial flowers, newspapers, magazines, cookbooks, dustpans, brooms, mops, and dusters?

▶ In addition, ask the children to bring one item from home that they would like to add to the center.

FAMILY VACATION

▶ Expand the home living/dramatic play center to be about three times its usual size. You can close another center to have room for this.

▶ Take one part of the expanded area and make it the "getting ready to go on vacation" space.

▶ In this area, place suitcases, clothes to pack, shoes, toy or discarded cameras, sunglasses, sunhats, scarves, backpacks, maps or road atlases, envelopes, picture postcards, travel brochures, and travel posters.

▶ For younger children's "luggage," use small suitcases, camera cases, briefcases, or backpacks.

▶ In another area, arrange chairs in rows with two or three chairs side by side to form seats in a car, bus, train, or plane.

▶ The children can start in the home living center for the planning stage of the vacation. They can even make lists of what to take and what to do on the vacation.

▶ They then move to the suitcase area to pack for the trip.

▶ Finally, they move to the transportation area where their "vehicle" is ready to go.

▶ This activity encourages planning together as a family, sequencing, placing things in order, problem solving, sharing, taking turns, and creativity.

PUPPET PLAY

PAPER CUP FAMILY POP-UPS

▶ You will need Styrofoam or paper cups, craft sticks, yarn, construction paper, fabric scraps, markers, glue, and tagboard, cardboard, or poster board.

▶ Cut poster board or tagboard circles sized to fit vertically inside of the cup. Let older children cut the circles themselves. This develops problem-solving skills.

▶ The children create faces on the circles. They can add hair and hats. Suggest that they make faces look like family members.

▶ Glue a circle to a craft stick, and let dry.

▶ Push the end of the stick gently through the bottom of the cup, where a slit has been cut.

▶ Pull the stick down to hide the family member's face.

▶ Push the stick up to make the person pop up.

MUSIC

SONG: "I Am a Member of My Family" by Jo Eklof

Additional verses:
We love each other..........
We're kind to each other..........
We laugh with each other..........
We take care of each other..........
We play with each other..........
We smile at each other..........
We hug each other..........
We cheer up each other..........

(See page 302 for enlargement.)

"MAMA'S COOKIES" CHANT

▶ Use a simple clapping pattern or a patting-the-knee pattern.

▶ Infants enjoy having you hold their hands and clap them together.

▶ Older children can vary the clapping patterns from simple to complex. Add clap — pat — clap — pat or clap — pat — snap/clap — pat — snap, for example.

▶ Add musical instruments to emphasize the beat.

▶ After repeating the chant several times, let the older children try to do the chant by themselves. Then one child takes a line, then another. Try to go from one child to the next without any inter-ruption. Children can add to the chant by supply-ing other family names.

Here is the chant, adapted from an American traditional game:

Mama baked some cookies for the cookie jar.
   (Children repeat the line.)
I ate a cookie from the cookie jar.
   (Children repeat the line.)
Brother ate a cookie from the cookie jar.
   (Children repeat the line.)

Sister ate a cookie from the cookie jar.
   (Children repeat the line.)
Daddy ate a cookie from the cookie jar.
   (Children repeat the line.)
We all love the cookies from the cookie jar.
   (Children repeat the line.)

"HUSH LITTLE BABY"

This traditional song, which has been passed down through several generations, can be sung or chanted, or told like a story. Vary the song by using papa, grandma, or grandpa instead of mama some of the time. Add flannelboard characters or stick puppets to help illustrate it for younger children.

Hush, little baby, don't say a word,
Mama's going to buy you a mockingbird.
If that mockingbird won't sing,
Mama's going to buy you a diamond ring.
If that diamond ring turns to brass,
Mama's going to buy you a looking glass.
If that looking glass gets broke,
Mama's going to buy you a billy goat.
If that billy goat won't pull,
Mama's going to buy you a cart and bull.
If that cart and bull turn over,
Mama's going to buy you a dog named Rover.
If that dog named Rover won't bark,
Mama's going to buy you a horse and cart.
If that horse and cart break down,
You'll be the sweetest little baby in town.

MOVEMENT

MUSICAL SHEET

Share this movement idea with families. It is fun to do at school and at home. Ask family members to send old bedsheets or small blankets from home to use as "parachutes." Younger children may use a lightweight blanket instead of a sheet.

This is a great outdoor activity, one the children can do at school with their friends or at home.

▶ Form a circle with the children, holding the outer edges of the sheet.

▶ Put on a record, tape, or CD. Use music of different cultures, styles, and tempos.

▶ Have the children breathe deeply as they raise and lower their arms, making the sheet seem to move with the music.

▶ After the children can raise and lower their arms comfortably, have them run up and back, still holding onto the edges of the sheet.

▶ To vary this activity, place assorted sizes of soft, lightweight balls on top of the sheet.

BEANBAG TOSS

This activity promotes large muscle development.

▶ Place a large plastic laundry basket outside or a large box with a hole cut out of the side. Children enjoy decorating the basket or box.

▶ Older children can paint a smiling face on the box with the hole becoming a big red mouth.

▶ Have beanbags of all shapes, sizes, and colors available. Every beanbag should be different, so each child can identify her own.

▶ You and the children can make up different games to play with the beanbags. For example, start with the throw line close to the basket or box so the children can more easily hit the opening. Slowly move the line further away from the opening. Continue this until the children tell you to stop!

▶ Some children like to try throwing the beanbags with both hands, first with the right, then with the left.

FOLLOW THE HULA HOOPS

Place several hula hoops or tires around the playground. Arrange them in a pattern that will make it easy for the children to progress from one hoop to the next. This exercise promotes cooperative play, group problem solving, and physical development.

▶ Each child selects a beanbag.

▶ Set up a starting line. Each child tries to throw the beanbag into the first hoop. If she misses, she takes a second throw from the spot where her beanbag landed, continuing until the beanbag lands in the hoop.

▶ The child then stands inside the first hoop and throws the beanbag into the second hoop.

▶ The children continue through the hoops, going from one hoop to the next, until they reach the finish line.

▶ After the children have played this, they can make up their own rules and move the hoops into different configurations.

SENSORY ART

FAMILY LACING MATS

This activity is fun for older toddlers and young preschoolers. It promotes hand-eye coordination and small muscle development.

▶ Using a pencil, draw several different sizes of heads and faces on foam sheets or the back of placemats.

▶ Cut out the faces.

▶ Punch large holes just inside the edges of the faces.

▶ Draw eyes, nose, and smiling mouth on each face.

▶ You will need 10-to-15-inch cotton shoelaces.

▶ Tie one end of the lace to the face shape, and show the child how to push the string through the holes.

FAMILY BOOK

▶ Have children draw pictures of each family member, pets included.

▶ If a child does not want to draw, have her cut family pictures from magazines.

▶ Suggest that children draw family members together on the last page of the book.

▶ Children can dictate or write something for each page. This will encourage them to read their books.

▶ Older children can draw a picture of the family doing something or going somewhere, then tell the story in writing.

▶ Provide wrapping paper, wallpaper scraps, and fabric pieces to make the front and back book covers.

FAMILY CULTURAL YARN ARTISTRY

Place a world globe or map in your classroom.

Throughout the year, you can guide the children to discover the countries their family members come from or where they now live. If you use a map, mark each country with a pushpin for visual effect.

Invite the families to share their cultures with the children. This will reinforce the concept that the class is a family.

Mexican Yarn Pictures

▶ Invite the children to select pieces of brightly colored yarn and a piece of cardboard for each picture they plan to make.

▶ Place glue at different places on the cardboard to make a design.

▶ Then press the yarn into the glue, coiling it or making rows to create the designs. Sometimes it is helpful to use a craft stick to move the yarn into place.

▶ Let dry.

▶ Display these creative art pieces around the classroom.

Huichol Indians of Mexico: "Ojo de Dios" (God's Eye)

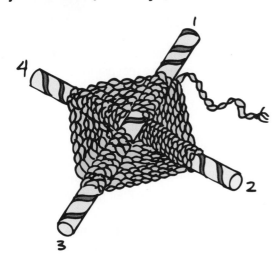

This weaving activity is designed for older children.

▶ Provide pieces of brightly colored yarn, glue, pencils, and two craft sticks, tongue depressors, or straws for each child.

▶ Suggest that the children cross the two sticks in the middle and glue them together. Allow sticks to dry.

▶ Lightly mark in pencil the ends of the sticks with the numbers 1, 2, 3, and 4.

▶ Tie the yarn around the stick near the center. Then wind the yarn once around stick 2. Continue winding around sticks 3 and 4.

▶ Proceed in this manner until you reach the ends of the sticks.

▶ Tie the end of the yarn, and tuck it into the woven design.

CREATIVE FOOD EXPERIENCES

CHINESE EGG DROP SOUP

You will need:

  1 egg
  3 cups clear chicken broth
  1 tablespoon cornstarch
  2 tablespoons cold water

1. Wash hands.
2. Pour broth into a saucepan. Bring to a boil.
3. Measure water and cornstarch into a container with a lid, and shake energetically.

CHINESE EGG DROP SOUP

Wash hands.

Pour 3 cups clear chicken broth into a saucepan and bring to a boil. Measure 2 tablespoons cold water and 1 tablespoon cornstarch into a container with a lid and shake. Pour cornstarch mixture into the broth. Stir with a fork until smooth. Break an egg into a small bowl and beat with a fork. Slowly pour the beaten egg into the broth. Stir until all the egg has been added and cooked. Remove from heat and serve!

4. Pour cornstarch mixture from the container into the broth. Stir with a fork until smooth.
5. Break an egg into a small bowl, and beat with a fork.
6. Slowly pour the beaten egg into the broth.
7. Stir until all of the egg has been added and cooked.
8. Remove from heat, and serve.
9. This recipe serves four. Make it several times with small groups of children.

Let the children see what happens when the egg cooks in shreds as it is dropped into the broth.

FAMILY SNACK

You will need:

  peanuts or small pecan pieces
  sunflower seeds
  pumpkin seeds
  raisins
  dried apricot, pineapple, apple, or peach pieces
  shredded coconut

chocolate or butterscotch chips
dry cereal pieces

1. Wash hands.
2. Mix ingredients.
3. Eat!
4. Place remaining snack mix in a closed plastic container.

Note: Omit the nuts for any child allergic to them.

FAMILY RECIPE BOOK

▶ Have families send in simple recipes that children enjoy at home.

▶ Plan to try each recipe on a different day. This could extend over several weeks or months.

▶ From these recipes, create a class cookbook, and add to it throughout the year.

▶ Each child's recipe becomes a page in her Family Book. (See sensory art Family Book in this theme.)

MATH

PENNIES IN A JAR

This activity ties in with the book *A Chair for My Mother*, as discussed in the language experiences part of this theme.

▶ Collect pennies in a large, unbreakable jar. The jar should be small enough to be filled in a reasonably short time.

▶ The pennies can be collected by you, other teachers, families, and the children.

▶ Have the children guess how many pennies will be in the jar when it is ¼ full, ½ full, and full.

▶ Measure and mark the jar.

▶ Some children may want to use the pennies to see how high they can count. This is fine, as long as they put the pennies back into the jar.

WHO IS MISSING?

▶ Provide pictures of different family members cut from magazines, or use real photos sent from home.

▶ Include a variety of ages, cultures, and clothing.

▶ Place three or more pictures on a table or on the floor where all of the children can see them. The number of pictures you use will vary according to the developmental abilities of the children.

▶ Ask the children to close their eyes while you remove one of the pictures.

▶ Let the children tell you which picture is missing.

▶ Then allow the children to take turns removing one picture, so that the other children can guess which one is missing.

▶ To make it more difficult for older children, keep adding pictures.

MATCH THE STICKS

▶ Using 10 craft sticks or tongue depressors, number each stick from 1 to 10.

▶ Make a duplicate set of sticks.

▶ Using stickers of faces, birds, butterflies, and so on, or dots of colored glue, add the corresponding number of stickers or dots on each numbered stick.

▶ The children then match the two sets of sticks.

▶ To expand the activity, select one set of numbered sticks, and invite the children to arrange the sticks in order from 1 to 10, or backward from 10 to 1.

▶ Older children can put two or more sticks together and add the number of sticker objects on the combined sticks.

SCIENCE

LET'S SEE WHAT WE CAN SEE

▶ On a partly cloudy day, spread out several blankets on the grassy area of your playground.

▶ Have the children lie on their stomachs and explore what they can see from that position.

▶ Next, have them turn over on their backs and explore what they see above. This is a great time to talk about cloud formations.

▶ Introduce Shaw's book *It Looked Like Spilt Milk*, listed in the Children's Books section of this theme.

▶ You can learn a lot about how the children see and think about their world.

▶ Families can do this activity at home, giving them special time with their children.

ARE ROCKS ALIKE, OR ARE THEY DIFFERENT?

▶ Collect all kinds of rocks. Have the children and their families help you.

▶ Save egg cartons, old muffin tins, paper plates, and margarine tubs for sorting and grouping the rocks.

▶ Encourage small groups of children to sort rocks that are alike in some way, and put them in various containers.

▶ This usually stimulates a lot of discussion about the color, size, shape, texture, and pattern of rocks.

▶ The children continue with their discovery of rocks and bring in new ones from home once this activity is introduced in class.

▶ Older children can experiment with ways to tell which rocks are hard and which are soft. For example, try a simple scratch test with a penny. Which rocks can be scratched by a penny? Which ones cannot?

▶ Make books available to assist with rock identification.

▶ Place the rocks in the science center, and let the children keep going back to find new ways to classify them.

▶ Before placing the rocks in the science center, discuss the appropriate use of rocks and safety factors.

SOCIAL STUDIES

The following curriculum suggestions are built on activities presented in this theme.

POTLUCK FAMILY FEAST

This can be a culminating class project for the family theme.

▶ Ask each family to bring a favorite dish, or one that represents the family's culture.

▶ Have families also bring recipes to be included in the class cookbook.

▶ The feast can be at lunch or dinner.

▶ A variation can be a breakfast feast.

POSTCARDS

▶ Have families ask relatives who travel or live in other cities or countries to send postcards to the children.

▶ You and the children can then place the cards on the map of the world in the classroom.

▶ You may get so many that you will have to rotate the cards. When they are not on the map, put them in boxes labeled with the city's or country's name.

FAMILY TREE

▶ Have the children and their families make a family tree showing their family members.

▶ Encourage the families to share their family trees with the class.

FIND THE COUNTRY

▶ Books included in the last part of this theme offer insights into families from many countries.

▶ On a map or globe, find Africa, China, England, Israel, Japan, Mexico, Puerto Rico, Russia, Taiwan, and the United States.

CHILDREN'S BOOKS

Altman, Linda J. (2002). *Singing with Momma Lou.* Illustrated by Larry Johnson. New York: Lee & Low.

Bailey, Debbie. (1999). *Families.* Illustrated by Susan Huszar. Toronto: Annick Press.

Bourgeois, Paulette. (2002). *Oma's Quilt.* Illustrated by Stephanie Jorish. Buffalo: Kids Can Press.

Chania, Michael. (1994). *Grandfather Four Winds and Rising Moon.* Illustrated by Sally J. Smith. Tiburon, CA: H. J. Kramer.

Cole, J. (1997a). *I'm a Big Brother.* New York: Morrow.

Cole, J. (1997b). *I'm a Big Sister.* New York: Morrow.

Cooney, Barbara. (1985). *Miss Rumphius.* New York: Puffin.

Dorris, Arthur. (1991). *Abuela.* Illustrated by Elisa Kleven. New York: Dutton.

Downey, Roma. (2001). *Love Is a Family.* Illustrated by Justine Gasquet. New York: Scholastic.

Edwards, Michelle, and Phyllis Root. (2002). *What's That Noise?* Illustrated by Paul Meisel. Cambridge, MA: Candlewick Press.

Fisher, Valorie. (2002). *My Big Brother.* New York: Atheneum.

Flournoy, Valerie. (1985). *The Patchwork Quilt.* Illustrated by Jerry Pinkney. New York: Dial.

French, Vivian. (2002). *A Present for Mom.* Illustrated by Dana Kubick. Cambridge, MA: Candlewick Press.

Greene, Stephanie. (2002). *Falling into Place.* New York: Clarion.

Greenfield, Eloise. (1991). *Daddy and I.* Illustrated by Jan A. Gilchrist. New York: Black Butterfly Board Books.

Hudson, Wade. (1993). *I Love My Family.* New York: Scholastic.

Johnston, Tony, and Tomie dePaola. (1985). *The Quilt Story.* New York: Putnam.

Keats, Ezra Jack. (1998). *Peter's Chair.* (Rev. ed.). New York: Harper.

Kulka, Susan. (1992). *How My Family Lives in America.* New York: Bradbury Press.

McCaughrean, Geraldine. (2002). *My Grandmother's Clock.* Illustrated by Stephen Lambert. New York: Clarion.

McGill, Alice. (2002). *Here We Go Round.* Illustrated by Shane Evans. Boston: Houghton Mifflin.

Morris, Ann. (1990). *Loving.* Photographs by Ken Heyman. New York: Lothrop, Lee & Shepard.

Ostarch, Judy, and Anthony Nex. (1993). *My Family.* (Board Book). New York: Price/Stern/Sloan.

Palacco, Patricia. (1988). *The Keeping Quilt.* New York: Simon & Schuster.

Scott, Ann Herbert. (1992). *On Mother's Shoes.* Illustrated by Glo Coalson. New York: Clarion.

Shaw, Charles G. (1988). *It Looked Like Spilt Milk.* New York: HarperTrophy.

Smith, Cynthia L. (2002). *Indian Shoes.* New York: Harper-Collins.

Swanson, Susan M. (2002). *The First Thing My Mama Told Me.* San Diego: Harcourt.

Williams, Vera B. (1982). *A Chair for My Mother.* New York: Mulberry Press.

Family Letter (Primary grade)

Dear Family,

We are very excited to begin our new theme, "My Family." The children will have opportunities to learn the following:

- *A family is two or more people who are connected by love or kinship.*
- *Families may have members other than those living together.*
- *Each family member is important and special.*
- *Family members can be alike or different.*
- *Family members work, play, learn together, and help each other.*
- *Some families eat special foods and have celebrations.*
- *Some families include pets.*

We will be talking about the following:

- *relationships of family members*
- *where our family members live*
- *family activities*
- *family favorite songs, books, and so on*

Try some of the following things to do at home with your child:

- *Look through family photo albums together.*
- *Talk about things you did when you were a child, such as games, songs, and activities.*
- *Find special ways to include your child in preparing for family celebrations.*
- *Plan a family night of stories, songs, and games with no TV.*
- *Rent a video or DVD of one of your favorite childhood movies, and watch it with your child.*

Family participation opportunities at school include:

- *Send in family snapshots to share.*
- *Ask out-of-town relatives to send postcards to the class.*
- *Take part in the family feast.*

    Date _____   Time _____

- *Help create a cookbook from recipes turned in by other children's families in the class.*
- *Share the family tree that you and your family made.*

Wish list for this theme includes:

road maps	*paper sacks*
postcards	*paper plates*
rocks of all kinds	*postage stamps*
old luggage (small and medium)	*envelopes*
nonworking cameras	*stationery*

Thanks!

THEME GOALS

To provide opportunities for children to learn the following:

▶ I am special because I am **me**. There is no one else just like me.

▶ I am still discovering how to do new things.

▶ I can use my mind and my senses to accomplish many things.

▶ I can play and do things by myself or with friends and family.

▶ I can show my emotions and say how I feel without hurting others.

▶ I can say "no" to things that will hurt me or others.

Children-Created Bulletin Board

This bulletin board gives children an opportunity to express how they feel about themselves. Throughout the theme, the bulletin board changes as the children learn more about feelings, self-esteem, self-motivation, and self-control.

▶ Cut poster board cards in various shapes, such as circles, squares, rectangles, and triangles.

▶ Have each child select one card in his favorite shape.

▶ Write or have the child write anything about himself on the card, including the suggestions that follow in the "Special Recipe."

"Special Recipe for (Child's Name)"

Two big (color) eyes,
One great smile,
(Long, short — color) hair,
Smooth (color) skin,
One cup of niceness,
Two cups of laughter.

▶ Children add anything they want about themselves. Give a few examples to get them started: "Add one cup of books. Stir in puzzles. Mix together and discover (child's name)."

▶ You may find it easier to do this with each child individually.

▶ Put the finished recipes on the bulletin board.

▶ Have the children add photos of themselves or pictures they draw of themselves.

▶ As they learn to do more things during this theme, children can add to the original recipe.

▶ Drawings that express feelings also can be added.

▶ Adding new items will make this an interactive bulletin board.

VOCABULARY STARTERS

Let the children add words.

creative — discovering new ways of doing things.

feelings — what you mean when you talk about or show being happy, sad, afraid, angry, or surprised.

learn — to know and understand something you did not know or understand before.

self — whatever is just about you and nobody else.

thoughts — what happens when you get ideas and decide to do things.

LANGUAGE EXPERIENCES

BALL NAME GAME

All you need for this activity are the children and a large ball. This is a good transition activity. When a child's name is called, he can choose a learning center and go to it.

▶ Everyone sits on the floor in a circle.

▶ Talk about how special everyone's name is.

▶ Roll the ball to a child. Everyone says the child's first name.

▶ Ask the toddler to roll or bring the ball back to you. Continue rolling the ball and saying each child's name.

▶ The preschooler can roll the ball to someone else. Everyone says that child's name. The ball passes from one child to another until each child's name is called and repeated.

▶ Extend this activity by rolling the ball to a child and saying the child's last name.

▶ Continue until each child's last name has been called.

WHOSE VOICE IS THIS?

Use a tape recorder to tape each child's conversational voice, giggling, laughing, or singing.

▶ Record each child privately, away from the other children. If children do not know what to say, help them say something with you. This way you are recording your voice too.

▶ Next, play back what each child recorded and have the other children guess whose voice they hear.

▶ Talk about how each person's voice is unique.

▶ Place the tape recorder in the music center. The children can listen to the voices whenever they wish.

LET'S SHARE

▶ Read Hutchins's *The Doorbell Rang*, listed in the Children's Books section of this theme.

▶ Discuss the concept of sharing as a way of showing someone you care about him.

▶ Ask open-ended questions such as: "What have you shared?" "With whom did you share it?" "Why do you need to share?" "How do you feel when someone shares with you?" "What are some things we could share in the classroom?"

▶ *The Doorbell Rang* is about sharing cookies. Buy or bake a giant cookie, and let the children find ways to share.

DRAMATIC PLAY

I AM HAPPY

This activity can be done indoors or outdoors.

▶ Give the children opportunities to show emotions (happy, sad, angry, afraid, and surprised) by the way they run, walk, hop, throw a ball, or move their bodies.

▶ Role-play appropriate ways to handle situations.

▶ Ask children to share what makes them feel happy, sad, and so on.

▶ This could be repeated throughout the year to help children deal with their feelings.

▶ Puppets can also help children talk about how they feel.

PANTOMIME TIME

▶ Read Carle's *The Mixed-Up Chameleon*. See the Children's Books section of this theme.

▶ Ask open-ended questions, such as: "Why do you think the chameleon was feeling unhappy?" "What feelings do you have about the chameleon?"

▶ Help the children decide which "chameleon character" they want to pantomime. Act without using words. One child can even be the sun and another the fly.

▶ Read the story again.

▶ The children pantomime their roles as the story unfolds.

▶ To extend this activity, have the children create paper costumes of the different "chameleon characters."

▶ The children also can draw their own chameleons.

PUPPET PLAY

TENNIS BALL PUPPET FRIEND

Let the children name this puppet. For the purpose of describing this activity, we will call the tennis ball puppet "Happy." This activity promotes positive self-esteem, self-motivation, and self-control.

▶ To make Happy, an adult should cut a slit in the middle of the ball across from one seam to the next. (See the illustration for clarification.) **Caution:** Be careful when cutting. A tennis ball is difficult to cut. It is hard to hold without slipping.

▶ Use markers or "puff paint" to make eyes, eyebrows, nose, and mouth.

▶ To make Happy "talk," press the sides of the ball.

▶ Use a box to make a special home for the puppet.

▶ Let a different child take Happy home each day after school and bring him back the next day.

▶ Happy reports on his overnight (or weekend) adventure at the child's home.

▶ This gives the child an opportunity to develop a voice for the puppet and tell what happened.

▶ You and the children can write in a special book what happens to Happy. Where did he go? What did he eat? Whom did he see? Where did he sleep?

▶ The children also can illustrate their books.

▶ Children vote on who gets to take Happy home.

▶ Next, you and the children can make a calendar and count the days until Happy goes home with the next child.

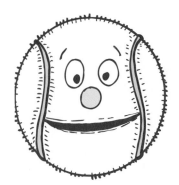

FEELINGS PUPPET

Children of all ages enjoy this activity.

▶ Put tongue depressors, crayons, and markers out for the children to use.

▶ Encourage the children to make a set of "feelings" puppets.

▶ Children can draw faces on the tongue depressors that show happy, sad, fearful, angry, and surprised expressions.

▶ Give the children envelopes in which to put their "feelings." They place the envelopes in their individual cubbies. When the children want to express how they feel, they can pull out their "feelings" puppet.

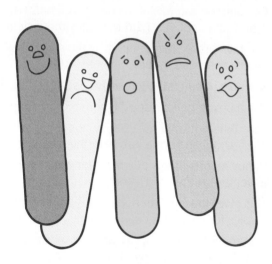

MUSIC

SONG: "Hello, Hello"

PRESCHOOL-K   PRIMARY-GRADE

The following song is a *musical beat* activity. It also can be chanted.

Hello, hello,
We sing in many ways.
Hello, hello,
Let's sing them now today.

In the following verses of this "Hello" chant, a simple method of indicating the beat is used. Though the chant is original, the system of indicating the beat is adapted from Sally Moomaw's *More Than Singing* (1997), published by Redleaf Press, St. Paul, MN.

Use a drum or other musical instrument to reinforce the beat. A vertical line (|) above a syllable means that it is accented. An asterisk (*) indicates a pause (or "rest," as in music) in the phrasing. In addition, phonetic pronunciations are provided under the foreign words.

English

*Hel-lo * hel-lo **
*We sing in ma-ny ways **
*Hel-lo * hel-lo **
*Let's sing them now to-day **

Spanish

*Ho-la * ho-la **
(oh-la oh-la)
*We sing in ma-ny ways **
*Ho-la * ho-la **
*Let's sing them now to-day **

French

*Bon-jour * bon-jour **
(bone-zhoor bone-zhoor)
*We sing in ma-ny ways **
*Bon-jour * bon-jour **
*Let's sing them now to-day **

German

Gu-ten tag gu-ten tag
(goo-ten tog goo-ten tog)

Italian

*Ci-a-o * Ci-a-o **
(chee-ah-oh chee-ah-oh)

Japanese

Kon-ni-chi- wa Kon-ni-chi- wa
(koh-nee-chee-wah koh-nee-chee-wah)

Chinese

*Ni-hao * ni-hao **
(nee-how nee-how)

Korean

*An nung * an nung **
(ahn nyong ahn nyong)

Vietnamese

*Chao * Chao **
(Chow Chow)

Hebrew

*Sha-lom * sha-lom **
(sha-lome sha-lome)

Arabic

*Mar-h-ba * mar-h-ba**
(mar-hah-bah mar-hah-bah)

MOVEMENT

EXERCISES FOR OLDER INFANTS AND TODDLERS

▶ **Push the chair,** to practice walking.
Have the infant on his feet holding onto the back of a low, sturdy child's chair. Help him push the chair while practicing walking.

▶ **In and out of the box,** for coordination.
Use a heavy cardboard box or tub, and place the baby inside. Encourage him to climb in and out.

▶ **The rocking chair,** for fun and to strengthen muscles.
Have the infant sit on the floor next to you. Bring your knees up, and rock back and forth. Encourage the child to do the same.

▶ **Pop-up,** for upper body and stomach strength.
Do this exercise together. Have the baby sit on the floor and bend over. Quickly have him straighten his legs while sitting upright and stretching his arms up high. Hold for two seconds, then quickly return to bent-over position. Repeat.

LET'S WAVE, WOBBLE, AND WIGGLE

Do this activity with or without recorded music, or try it using the traditional tune "The Bear Went over the Mountain."

My thumbs, my thumbs want to pop up.
My thumbs, my thumbs want to pop up.
My thumbs, my thumbs want to pop up.
That's what they like to do.

Continue the pattern with the following changes:

My hands, my hands want to shake . . .
My arms, my arms want to wave . . .
My head, my head wants to wobble . . .
(That's what *it* likes to do.)
My legs, my legs want to wiggle . . .
My feet, my feet want to dance . . .
Now all of me wants to jump . . .
(That's what *I* like to do.)

End with:

Oh, I am starting to giggle,
I am starting to giggle,
I am starting to giggle,
I think I'll just sit down!

I'M THE LEADER

▶ Everyone forms a big circle. Select one of the children to be the leader.

▶ Suggest that he hop, jump, or crawl, and say, "Do it just like me."

▶ The other children then try to do what he does.

▶ Continue with the children taking turns.

▶ This is one of those quick activities that can be used anytime.

RIGHT, LEFT, RIGHT, STOP!

This movement activity helps with recognition of left and right.

▶ Let the children help you come up with other ideas.

▶ Older children like to combine several body movements at one time.

▶ Children like to do this at home with family members too.

March with feet	Sway with upper body
Left, right,	Right, left,
Left, right,	Right, left
Left, right,	Right, left,
Stop!	Stop!

Raise arms	Move head
Left, right,	Right, left,
Left, right,	Right, left,
Left, right,	Right, left,
Stop!	Stop!

SENSORY ART

EXPRESSING FEELINGS

To ease the times a child may feel frustrated, angry, or full of energy (and "using his words" won't help), bring out the clay or play dough. Many types and textures are available. Recipes for play dough are provided in themes 6 and 10.

▶ Set up a special space for the child to have some alone time with the clay or play dough.

▶ For a toddler, a special place to pound on the plastic pounding bench can help defuse feelings.

MAKE AN "I'M SPECIAL" VEST

Do this project with each child individually, if possible.

▶ Take a large paper grocery sack and invert it.

▶ Cut straight up the center of one of the wide sides to where the bottom creases.

▶ Here, cut a large round circle out of the bottom of the sack.

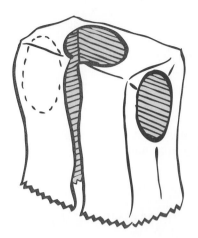

▶ On each narrow side of the sack, cut a vertical oval that starts at the bottom crease and descends about eight inches.

▶ The child puts the vest on by placing his head through the large round opening, with the long vertical slit to the front and arms through the two side ovals.

▶ Have each child decorate the "I'm Special" vest with crayons, markers, felt and fabric scraps, construction paper, feathers, cotton balls, and all kinds of shapes, stickers, and buttons.

▶ Put magazines and catalogs out as well, and suggest that children cut out pictures of what they like and glue these to the vest.

TWO-DIMENSIONAL ART GALLERY

In a school hallway, walkway, or entrance area, display some of the children's art along with posters or pictures of famous paintings.

▶ Mat and attractively exhibit all of the art, so that the children's creativity is treated the same as that of well-known artists.

▶ Let the children help you mount the exhibition.

▶ This is a good way to introduce the children to great works of art and the painters who created the works.

▶ Many children's books on art are available to share with the children, for example, *Getting to Know the World's Greatest Artists Series*, published by Children's Press, and *New York's Metropolitan Museum of Art Series*, published by Viking.

CREATIVE FOOD EXPERIENCES

HAPPY FACES

You will need the following:

a loaf of bread
cream cheese
peanut butter
apple jelly
raisins
nuts

HAPPY FACES!

Wash hands.

Cut circles from bread with a round cookie cutter.

Spread bread with cream cheese, peanut butter,

or apple jelly. Use raisins and nuts to make

eyes, nose, and mouth.

ENJOY!

---

1. Let the children cut circles from bread with a round cookie cutter.
2. Spread bread with cream cheese, peanut butter, or apple jelly. Children sometimes use all three.
3. Use raisins and nuts to make eyes, nose, and mouth. Enjoy!

Note: Omit peanut butter and nuts for those children who are allergic.

LET'S MAKE A CAKE

This recipe is easy for the children to do and can give them a sense of accomplishment. It also is a fun one to pass on to families.

1. Wash hands.
2. Put one can of fruit, with the juice, into a buttered 9-by-13-inch metal or glass pan.
3. Dump one box of white or yellow cake mix over the fruit.
4. Cut one stick of butter or margarine into small pieces.
5. Dump shortening pieces on top of the cake mix.
6. Bake at 350 degrees for 30 to 40 minutes.
7. Eat!

MATH

THE LANGUAGES OF MATH

This activity encourages learning to count from one to five in many languages. It also helps build self-esteem for children of other cultures.

English	Spanish	French	German	Italian
one	uno (ōō-no)	un (ŏon)	eins (īnes)	uno (ōō-no)
two	dos (dose)	deux (dŏŏ)	zwei ([ts]vye)	due (dōō-eh)
three	tres (trais)	trois (t(r)wah)	drei (dry)	tre (treh)
four	cuatro (kwáh-tro)	quatre (ká-tra)	vier (fear)	quattro (kwáh-tro)
five	cinco (seén-ko)	cinq (sank)	funf (fŏonf)	cinque (cheén-kay)

English	Chinese	Japanese	Hebrew	Arabic
one	yi (yee)	ichi (ée-chee)	achat (a-(h)áht)	wahid (wáh-hid)
two	er (uhr)	ni (nee)	shta'yim (shtah-yéem)	ithinin (ith-nín)
three	san (sahn)	san (sahn)	shalosh (shah-lṍśh)	thalatha (ta-lá-ta)
four	si (suh)	shi (shee)	arba (ar-báh)	arba'a (ar-báh)
five	wu (woo)	go (go)	hamesh ([h]ah-meśh)	kamisa (k(h)aʹhm-sa)

MATH COOKIES

Relate this activity to Hutchins's book *The Doorbell Rang*. See the language experience activity in this theme. This activity promotes problem solving, one-to-one correspondence, and cooperation.

▶ You and the children make three dozen "cardboard cookies." These can be made easily out of heavy cardboard or poster board cut into circles.

▶ Decorate the cookies with markers and crayons.

▶ Some of the cookies should be alike.

▶ Make up math games that can be played with the cardboard cookies.

▶ Younger children can sort the cookie circles by color or by the number of "chocolate chip dots" on the cookies. They also can practice making a straight line with the cookies.

▶ Older children can practice counting and sorting the cookies into pairs, as well as figuring out how many children are in the class, whether they can share the cookies equally, and what they have to do to share the cookies equally.

SCIENCE

FIXING THINGS

▶ Collect broken toys, torn books, or anything that can be fixed with masking tape, clear tape, or glue.

▶ You and the children decide how to repair the broken or torn items.

▶ Children may work in pairs to figure out how the broken pieces might fit together again.

MY BODY IS MADE OF HINGES

This project has many levels. The beginning levels are appropriate and interesting for preschoolers. The entire procedure is fascinating for older children. To introduce this activity, have a variety of hinges in a box.

▶ Demonstrate how the hinges work, and allow the children to experiment with them for several days.

▶ Next, talk about hinges in the room, and then show how children's bodies have "hinges."

▶ Let children bend their fingers, wrists, knees, and so on, to music.

▶ Introduce silhouette pieces, such as: head, neck, trunk, arms, hands, legs, and feet. These can be made from black construction paper or shiny, lightweight black art paper.

▶ Have a prepared figure put together with brads to show how the body moves.

▶ Prepare the silhouette body parts for each child, and place the pieces in individual envelopes.

▶ Go through magazines and catalogs for action poses.

▶ Encourage each child to select one picture. Using glue sticks, glue it on half of an 8½-by-11-inch piece of white paper.

▶ On the side of the page opposite the picture, have the child position the silhouette body parts in the same position. Children may need your watchful eye to do this.

▶ When each child is satisfied with the pose, he glues the parts, one at a time, onto the paper.

▶ Place all of the finished silhouette pictures on the bulletin board.

SOCIAL STUDIES

CELEBRATING BIRTHDAYS AND SPECIAL MONTHS

Birthdays are special days for children. Help them celebrate by setting up a big classroom calendar that you and the children design.

▶ Have each child write his name and birth date on the calendar.

▶ Since some cultures and religions do not emphasize birthdays, also include on the calendar special events that happen each month in your community or nationally.

▶ You can celebrate birthdays and other special days at the same time.

▶ Play special recorded music, eat a new snack, or read a new book to celebrate the child's birthday.

Here are some suggestions for special events to celebrate. You and the children can decide how you will observe the day.

September	Monarch Butterfly Migration Month Good Neighbor Day (fourth week)
October	Popcorn Month Apple Month Teddy Bear Day (Oct. 27)
November	National Children's Book Week (third week) Homemade Bread Day (Nov. 17)
December	Birds in the Snow Week (fourth week) Poinsettia Day (Dec. 12)
January	National Soup Month New Year's Day in 123 nations (Jan. 1)
February	Black History Month Presidents' Day (second week)
March	National Nutrition Month Children's Poetry Day (March 21)
April	Week of the Young Child (Consult the National Association for the Education of Young Children for specific dates: 1-800/424-2460.) Earth Day (April 22)
May	Be Kind to Animals Month National Safe Kids Week (second week)
June	Children's Day (second week) Flag Day (June 14)
July	Blueberry Month National Ice Cream Day (third week)
August	National Clown Week (first week) Family Day (second week)

CHILDREN'S BOOKS

Aliki. (1986). *Feelings.* (Rev. ed.). New York: HarperTrophy.

Anderson, Peggy P. (2002). *Let's Clean Up!* Boston: Houghton Mifflin.

Carle, Eric. (1996). *The Grouchy Ladybug.* New York: HarperCollins.

Carle, Eric. (1984). *The Mixed-Up Chameleon.* New York: HarperTrophy.

Carlson, Nancy L. (1997). *ABC I Like Me.* New York: Viking Press.

Catalanotto, Peter. (2002). *Matthew ABC . . .* New York: Atheneum.

Christopher, Matt. (1993). *The Lucky Baseball Bat.* Illustrated by Dee Derosa. New York: Little, Brown.

Cowell, Cressida. (2003). *Super Sue.* Illustrated by Russell Ayto. Cambridge, MA: Candlewick Press.

French, Simon. (2002). *Guess the Baby.* Illustrated by Donna Rawlins. New York: Clarion.

Getting to Know the World's Greatest Artist Series. (1990). Chicago: Children's Press

Got, Yves. (2003). *Sam's Busy Day.* (Boxed Board Books). San Francisco: Chronicle.

Hayward, Linda, and Norman Gorbaty. (1997). *Mine: A Sesame Street Book about Sharing.* (Board Edition). New York: Random House.

Hill, Elizabeth S. (2002). *Chang and the Bamboo Flute.* Illustrated by Lesley Liu. New York: Farrar, Straus & Giroux.

Hoffman, Mary. (2002). *The Color of Home.* Illustrated by Karin Littlewood. New York: Putnam.

Hutchins, Pat. (1989). *The Doorbell Rang.* New York: Mulberry Books.

Isadora, Rachel. (2003). *On Your Toes: A Ballet ABC.* New York: Greenwillow.

Lebrun, Claude. (1997). *Little Brown Bear Is Growing Up.* New York: Children's Press.

MacCarone, Grace. (1995). *The Lunch Box Surprise.* New York: Cartwheel Books.

Mayer, Mercer. (1995). *I Am Sharing.* New York: Random House.

McGee, Marni. (2002). *Wake Up, Me!* Illustrated by Sam Williams. New York: Simon & Schuster.

Merriam, Eve. (1994). *Poems: Higgle Wiggle, Happy Rhymes.* Illustrated by Hans Wilhelm. New York: Mulberry Press.

New York's Metropolitan Museum of Art's Series. (1993). *What Makes . . . a . . . ?* New York: Author and Viking.

Raposo, Joe. (2001). *Imagination Song.* Illustrated by Laurent Linn. New York: Random House.

Reiser, Lynn, Rebecca Hart, and Corazones Valientes Organization. (1998). *Tortillas and Lullabies/Tortillas y cancioncitas.* New York: Greenwillow.

Singer, Marilyn. (2003). *Boo Hoo Boo-Boo.* Illustrated by Elivia Savadier. New York: HarperCollins.

Stuve-Bodeen, Stephanie. (2002). *Elizabeti's School.* Illustrated by Christy Hale. New York: Lee & Low.

Waber, Bernard. (2002). *Courage.* Boston: Houghton Mifflin.

Wells, Rosemary. (1997). *Noisy Nora.* New York: Dial.

Weninger, Brigette. (1998). *What's the Matter, Davy?* Illustrated by Eve Tharlet. New York: North South Books.

Wollman, Jessica. (2002). *Andrew's Bright Blue T-Shirt.* Illustrated by Anna L. Escriva. New York: Doubleday.

Zemach, Kaethe. (2003). *Just Enough and Not Too Much.* New York: Arthur A. Levine/Scholastic.

Zolotow, Charlotte. (1985). *William's Doll.* Illustrated by William Pene DeBois. New York: HarperTrophy.

Family Letter (Preschool)

Dear Family,

We are starting another theme this week, "My Self." We will provide opportunities for the children to learn the following:

- *I am special because I am **me**. There is no one else like me.*
- *I am still discovering how to do new things.*
- *I can use my mind and my senses to accomplish many things.*
- *I can play and do things by myself or with friends and family.*
- *I can show emotions and say how I feel without hurting others.*
- *I can say "no" to things that will hurt me or others.*

We will be talking about the following:

- *feelings*
- *verbal expression*
- *nonverbal expression*
- *self-esteem*
- *self-motivation*
- *self-control*

Things you can do at home with your preschool child include:

- *Welcome "Happy" (the tennis ball puppet) when it comes home with your child. It will be in the box it "lives in," but "Happy" enjoys getting out sometimes. "Happy" should be included in family activities, such as going where your child goes and sleeping in the room with your child.*
- *Sing songs with your child, and record them on a tape recorder. This gives the family a special musical cassette.*
- *Make cookies or a cake with your child.*
- *Let your child help you repair things around the house.*

Family participation opportunities at school will include:

- *Help us make "I'm Special" vests.*
  Date _____ Time _____
- *Come visit the children's art gallery.*
- *Help us make silhouettes.*
  Date _____ Time _____

Our wish list for this theme includes:

magazines and catalogs
posters of famous paintings
tennis balls
large paper sacks
heavy cardboard

Thanks!

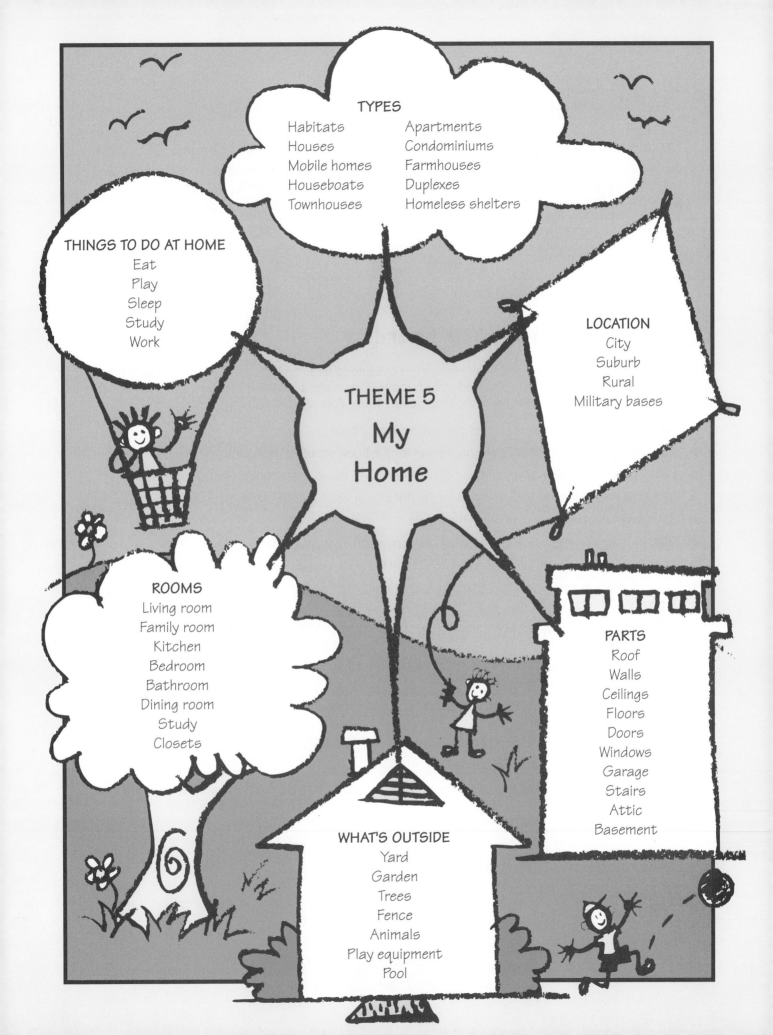

TYPES

Habitats
Houses
Mobile homes
Houseboats
Townhouses

Apartments
Condominiums
Farmhouses
Duplexes
Homeless shelters

THINGS TO DO AT HOME

Eat
Play
Sleep
Study
Work

LOCATION

City
Suburb
Rural
Military bases

THEME 5
My Home

ROOMS

Living room
Family room
Kitchen
Bedroom
Bathroom
Dining room
Study
Closets

PARTS

Roof
Walls
Ceilings
Floors
Doors
Windows
Garage
Stairs
Attic
Basement

WHAT'S OUTSIDE

Yard
Garden
Trees
Fence
Animals
Play equipment
Pool

THEME GOALS

To provide opportunities for children to learn the following:

▶ A home is a place where you live, sleep, eat, work, and play.

▶ A home can be built from brick, stone, wood, metal, cement, mud, and straw.

▶ Homes come in many types, sizes, and shapes.

▶ Homes can be found in many locations, such as cities, rural areas, and suburbs.

▶ Homes are different in different parts of the world.

Children-Created Bulletin Board

This bulletin board of a house-shaped book encourages children to recall and classify the rooms in their homes and the furnishings, objects, and activities located in each room. If the majority of the children in your class live in apartments, mobile homes, or on a farm, make the shape of the home correspond to this.

▶ Cover the bulletin board with butcher paper or wrapping paper.

▶ Cut a large, house-shaped front and back cover for the book out of poster board.

▶ Leave the covers blank so the children can draw windows, doors, and doorknobs on them.

▶ Using the cover for a pattern, cut pages for the book from white butcher paper.

▶ Cut a page to represent each room in the home.

▶ With the help of the children, title and label each page with a room name.

▶ Punch three holes on the left side of each page and the book covers.

▶ After assembling the book pages, attach loose-leaf rings, ribbons, yarn, or pipe cleaners twisted together to form rings through the holes.

▶ Ask the children to select a title for their Big Book. While the children are watching, print it on the front cover, and say the words as you write.

▶ Let the children help you number the pages. Many times, they will think of this without you suggesting it.

▶ Throughout the duration of the "My Home" theme, have the children cut and paste pictures of objects and furnishings that belong in each room. These can be cut from magazines and catalogs or drawn by the children.

▶ Continue to personalize the book whenever the children have a suggestion.

▶ "Read" the book often with the children.

▶ Expanding this activity can integrate many areas of curriculum. The children may want to make their own *little* house book.

COVER

VOCABULARY STARTERS

Let the children add words. Include pictures where appropriate.

apartment — a building that has many homes inside.

duplex — a house that is divided into two homes.

farmhouse or **ranch house** — a house in the country where a farmer or rancher and her family live.

home — a place where you live.

houseboat — a home made to float on the water like a boat.

mobile home — a home that can be moved from one place to another.

shelter or **habitat** — a structure that protects you from the weather and keeps you safe.

LANGUAGE EXPERIENCES

FINGERPLAY:
Houses

Here's a nest for Robin Redbreast.
  (cup hands with palms up)
Here's a hive for Busy Bee.
  (hands cupped together with fingers up)
Here's a hole for Bunny Rabbit.
  (make a circle with thumbs and index fingers)
And here's a house for me.
  (tips of fingers touching, palms apart)

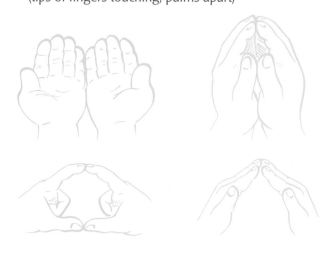

POEM:
"My House"

My house, my house is very tall.
It has a ceiling and a wall.
It has a window and a door.
It has a carpet on the floor.
My house, my house is clean and bright.
It has a lamp that I can light.
It has a table and a chair.
It has a closet with clothes to wear.
My house, my house, it is the best.
It has a bedroom where I rest.
It has a kitchen with food to eat.
It has a stove and oven to heat.
My house, my house, it has a hall.
It has some pictures on the wall.
It has a bookcase filled with books.
It has a coatrack with some hooks.
My house, my house is very fine.
It's warm and snug and it is MINE!

Philip Jackman

WHAT'S THAT SOUND?

This activity helps children develop listening skills and creative and abstract thinking. For younger children, do the following:

▶ Record on a tape recorder simple sounds around the house, such as a faucet running, a telephone ringing, a timer going off, and music playing.

▶ Play the tape, and ask the children to identify what is making the sound. Use pictures to help younger preschoolers with the identification.

▶ Record additional sounds with the children's help.

▶ Go outside, and listen for new sounds to record.

For older children, do the following:

▶ Record more complex sounds, such as a washing machine, a dishwasher, a toilet flushing, a toaster popping up, a clock ticking and its alarm ringing, a doorbell sounding, someone knocking on a door, a garage door opening, and a closet door opening and closing.

▶ Go through the same process: play the sounds, have the children guess what is making the sound, and record additional indoor and outdoor sounds.

▶ Have the children identify from which room in the house the sound came.

▶ Extend this activity by having the children pretend to be the object and act out what it does while making the sound.

DRAMATIC PLAY

THE NAPPING HOUSE

This activity promotes paying attention to what the author and the illustrator were saying, the sequencing of events, and using dramatic play to express what was happening.

▶ After reading Wood's *The Napping House* (see the Children's Books section in this theme), have the children first make the sounds of each character asleep, then the sounds each character makes when awakening.

▶ Ask open-ended questions about the book, such as: "What did you see happening to the colors of the illustrations of the book?" "Were the colors at the beginning different from those at the end of the book?" "Why were those colors used?" "What was happening outside of the house?" "What was happening inside of the house?"

▶ To broaden this activity, make materials available for the children to paint their own illustrations of *The Napping House*.

LET'S GO CAMPING

▶ Change and expand the home living/dramatic play area into a campground.

▶ Pitch a tent, either indoors or outdoors, and put cots or mats inside.

▶ Add camping equipment, such as blankets, paper cups, plates, plastic knives, forks, spoons, and flashlights.

▶ Ask families to send one item they might use when camping.

▶ This activity extends the concept that even when a family goes on a camping vacation, the tent becomes a home.

▶ Talk about other times and places when people lived in tents.

LET'S BUILD A HOUSE WITH BOXES AND BLOCKS

▶ Put pictures of all types of houses in the block center.

▶ Place unit and hollow blocks, sanded pieces of wood, various sizes and shapes of boxes, and milk carton blocks in the area.

▶ Add multiethnic family figures, small animals, and small cars and trucks.

▶ Encourage the children to build homes.

▶ Have the children label the rooms in each home.

▶ Arrange the houses into neighborhoods, and add streets for the cars and trucks.

▶ Extend this for older children by placing boxes of various sizes in the block center. The children can color or paint the boxes, draw windows, and glue several together to make an apartment building.

▶ Using masking tape, make a street down the center of the building site.

▶ Children may decide to add buildings, such as a school, child care center, grocery store, or hospital.

▶ Keep the center like this for several days or weeks. The children will help you decide.

▶ Another way to keep the children involved is to take the house building outdoors.

▶ Fill the sand and water table or a plastic tub with water and dirt.

▶ Let the children build mud houses.

PUPPET PLAY

KITCHEN GADGET PUPPETS

This is an activity for older children to promote cooperation, problem solving, creativity, literacy, and language development.

▶ Collect wooden spoons, new dishwashing sponges with handles, splatter shields (shields that fit onto pans to prevent splattering while cooking), and large sieves. Ask families to send in one kitchen gadget with their child.

▶ Talk about how puppets can be made from many things. Show children the selection of gadgets. What would they do to make these into puppets?

▶ Guide children to the table where you have already set up glue, markers, felt, yarn, craft moveable eyes, and construction paper.

▶ Place yourself nearby with the hot glue gun to help with fast gluing.

▶ Step back and let the children create puppets.

▶ To extend this activity, suggest to the children that they could write a short puppet play and use their newly made characters to bring the play "to life."

MUSIC

KITCHEN BAND

▶ Collect pots, pans, spoons, empty plastic bottles, empty oatmeal containers, and rhythm sticks.

▶ The children select their "instruments" and make a circle or a line.

▶ Play an audiotape, or a CD of marching music, such as "76 Trombones" from *The Music Man* or a John Philip Sousa march.

▶ That is all you need to have a children's marching band.

PLAY THE PIANO

This activity is designed for older toddlers and young preschoolers to promote listening skills and small muscle development.

▶ Gather the children around the tables in the classroom.

▶ Ask children to pretend that the table in front of them is a *piano*. "Hold your fingers on your table as if you are playing the piano."

▶ Say, "First, we'll play some very soft music." Demonstrate moving your fingers lightly, touching fingertips gently to the table.

▶ Say, "Now let's play some very loud music." Demonstrate moving your fingers, touching fingertips to the table with a very heavy, firm touch.

▶ Next, play slow, then fast, music.

▶ Guide the children into moving all fingers up and down independently from each other. This exercises individual finger muscles.

▶ Once the children have a general idea of what to do, play some recorded piano music.

▶ Ask the children to follow along with the music and play softly, loudly, slowly, and fast when the music does so.

SONG: "Here's the Way We . . ."

Sing these verses to the tune of "Here We Go 'Round the Mulberry Bush."

Here's the way we get out of bed,
Get out of bed, get out of bed,
Here's the way we get out of bed,
So early in the morning.
Here's the way we wash our face,
Wash our face, wash our face,
Here's the way we wash our face,
So early in the morning.

Continue with:

Here's the way we brush our teeth.
Here's the way we drink our milk.
Here's the way we eat with a spoon.
Here's the way we open the door.
Here's the way we play outside.

Sing about the rooms in a house:

Here's the way we walk to the kitchen.
Here's the way we sleep in the bedroom.
Here's the way we play in the family room.

The children will help you add more verses.

MOVEMENT

JACK-AND-JILL-IN-THE-BOX

Jack-in-the-box, (child stands)
Push Jack in. (child crouches down)
Turn the handle,
See Jack again. (child jumps up)
  Jill-in-the-box, (child sits down)
  Sits so still.
  Won't you come out?
  Yes I will. (child jumps up)
Jack-in-the-box,
Close the top. (child squats down)
Turn the handle,
And up Jack pops. (child jumps up)
  Jill-in-the-box,
  Where is she? (child sits down)
  Open the lid,
  And there she'll be. (child jumps up)

MUSICAL BEAT: Johnny Builds with One Hammer

"Hammer" a musical beat with a pretend hammer in the right hand as you begin to sing or chant:

Johnny builds with one hammer, one hammer, one hammer,
Johnny builds with one hammer all day long.
(hammer with pretend hammers in the right and left hands)
Johnny builds with two hammers, two hammers, two hammers,
Johnny builds with two hammers all day long.
(hammer with pretend hammers in the right and left hands and with the right foot "hammering" on the floor)
Johnny builds with three hammers, three hammers, three hammers,
Johnny builds with three hammers all day long.
(hammer with pretend hammers in the right and left hands and with the right foot and left foot hammering on the floor)
Johnny builds with four hammers, four hammers, four hammers,
Johnny builds with four hammers all day long.
(hammer the same as above, and add the head going up and down like a hammer)
Johnny builds with five hammers, five hammers, five hammers,
Johnny builds with five hammers all day long.
(reverse the process, and end up with no hammers)
Johnny builds with no hammers, no hammers, no hammers,
Johnny builds with no hammers all day long.

SENSORY ART

MAKE MILK CARTON BLOCKS

▶ With the children's help, cut off the tops of two milk cartons, and push the open end of one carton into another carton to make a sturdy block.

▶ Ask the children to cover the blocks with wallpaper scraps, construction paper, or contact paper.

▶ Older children can color or draw brick designs on the blocks.

▶ For toddlers, make the blocks and let them decorate, or give some of the blocks made by the older children to the younger ones.

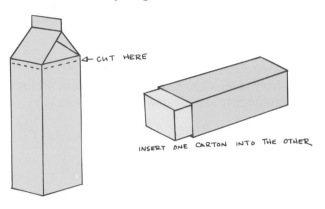

CONSTRUCT A HOUSE

▶ Place construction paper, craft sticks, and glue at a table.

▶ Suggest to children that they build the shape of a house, an apartment house, or any other type of house with the craft sticks and glue.

▶ After the glue dries, children can add windows and doors.

▶ Children may build several structures or create original designs of craft sticks placed on the paper. It is the process that is important!

A DIAGRAM OF MY HOUSE

Older children enjoy this activity. It stimulates abstract thinking, recall, and language development.

▶ Before you begin this project, show children examples of several room diagrams or maps.

▶ Then, place different sizes of paper, rulers, pencils, markers, and crayons on a table.

▶ Ask each child to draw a diagram or map of the inside of her house.

▶ To further develop this concept, have families help measure the child's room. Note the doors and windows as well as the furniture in the room. Have the child draw the room on graph paper.

▶ Prepare a place in the classroom to display the finished drawings.

DESIGN A ROOM

Children enjoy doing this with a partner.

▶ Collect small- to medium-size boxes with lids.

▶ Supply glue, scissors, fabric and wallpaper scraps, construction paper, markers, crayons, and tagboard.

▶ Guide children into designing a room inside of a box. The lid becomes the ceiling.

▶ Let the children decide which room it will be.

▶ Children can wallpaper the sides of the box (walls of the room), cut out windows and doors, make curtains for the windows, and construct simple furniture.

CREATIVE FOOD EXPERIENCES

A SANDWICH TREAT

You will need the following:

1/4 cup undiluted frozen orange juice
1/2 cup peanut butter*
8 slices of bread

1. Wash hands.
2. Mix concentrated orange juice and peanut butter.*
3. Spread on bread that is plain or toasted.
4. Cut into small pieces.
5. Enjoy!

*Note: Plan another food experience if some children are allergic to peanut butter.

BANANA MILK SHAKE

You will need the following:

1 cup of ripe banana, sliced
1/2 teaspoon vanilla
1 cup liquid nonfat milk

1. Wash hands.
2. Beat banana until creamy.

3. Add vanilla.
4. Mix.
5. Stir in milk.
6. Chill and serve. Makes one pint.

SKILL DEVELOPMENT IN THE KITCHEN

These ideas can be done at the center, school, or home. Pass them on to the families.

▶ Try a tasty way to develop finger-thumb ability by putting a pinch of grated cheese on a cracker.

▶ Motivate a child to place a raisin in the middle of a round cookie or cracker, and watch her eye-hand coordination.

Skill Development in the Kitchen

stir   pour   peel
squeeze   scrub
beat
roll   spread   snap
shake   tear   compare

More ways to help a child begin to master skills through learning experiences in the kitchen include:

stir (spoon)
pour (measuring cup)
peel (a hard-boiled egg)
squeeze (orange)
beat (milk or egg)
scrub (potato)

roll (rolling pin)
spread (plastic knife)
snap (green beans)
shake (salt)
tear (lettuce)
compare (apples)

MATH

MATH SETS OF THREE

▶ Select several books or poems to read to children that include the number *three,* such as *The Three Little Pigs, The Three Kittens,* and *Three Billy Goats Gruff.*

▶ Talk about the concept of "three," and use flannel-board pieces of the characters in the stories to demonstrate this.

▶ Then place the flannelboard activities in the manipulative center for children to tell the stories again.

▶ An extension of this is for children to build the house from the *Three Little Pigs* or the bridge from *Three Billy Goats Gruff.*

▶ Ask children to look for sets of three around the room, such as three crayons, three chairs, three windows, three people, and three blocks.

SORT KEYS

▶ Collect keys of all sizes.

▶ Place keys in the math center for children to sort, or place in order from smallest to largest or from largest to smallest.

▶ Draw large outlines of the keys on paper or tagboard. Then make patterns for children to use in a matching game.

BUILD WITH GRAHAM CRACKERS

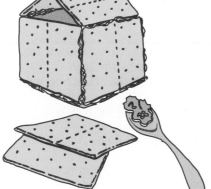

▶ To introduce this activity, talk or read about how a house is built. See the Children's Books section in this theme for some suggestions.

▶ Show pictures of houses being built.

▶ Guide the children to where you have set up graham crackers, peanut butter, and frosting.

▶ Wash hands.

▶ Everyone starts with a square graham cracker placed on a piece of waxed paper.

▶ The children spread a thin layer of peanut butter or frosting (for children allergic to peanut butter) along all of the edges of the graham cracker.

▶ Next, place another graham cracker standing up on one edge of the flat cracker. Younger children can "build" onto a one-pint milk or juice carton with graham crackers. This provides a framework for their small hands.

▶ Continue this process to build a structure that looks like a room of a house.

▶ Place another flat graham cracker to make a ceiling, forming a cube, or place two crackers "cemented" with peanut butter or frosting at the top to form a peaked roof.

▶ To complete this activity, children can eat their graham cracker room. Some may choose to eat before they are finished.

SCIENCE

PLEASE TOUCH

▶ Set up a science table in your room filled with safe objects that stimulate children to explore, experiment, and discover.

What Floats and What Sinks

▶ Place a small plastic tub with water on the table.

▶ Nearby, have objects for children to test to see which ones sink and which ones float.

▶ Talk about why some things sink and some float.

▶ Suggestions for items are objects found around the house: a plastic measuring spoon, a wooden spoon, keys, straws, nails, several pennies, a crumpled foil ball, a rock, a shell, corks, and a sponge.

Magnets

▶ Put all sizes of magnets on the science table.

▶ For younger children, nonaluminum baking sheets work well for putting on and taking off the magnets.

▶ Metal popcorn or cookie tins work well and provide storage space.

▶ Give each older child a single magnet to experiment with. Let each discover which objects are attracted to the magnet and which are not. Have assorted items available.

Discovery with Plastic Bottles

▶ Fill one-half of a clean plastic bottle with water, and replace the top.

▶ In a second clean plastic bottle, place some sand.

▶ Place each bottle in the water-filled tub.

▶ Which sinks? Which floats?

▶ How much water is needed for the bottle to float? How much sand is needed for the bottle to sink or float?

SOCIAL STUDIES

SHELTERS AND HABITATS

PRESCHOOL-K   PRIMARY-GRADE

This plan of instruction familiarizes children with pictures of homes, shelters, and habitats around the world. It promotes observation, problem solving, creative thinking, and small-muscle skills. Ann Morris's *Houses and Homes* and *National Geographic* magazine are good resources. The Children's Books section of this theme offers additional resources.

▶ Temporary habitats include tents, recreational vehicles, igloos, teepees, and caves.

▶ Permanent habitats are homes, apartments, condominiums, mobile homes, adobes, duplexes, townhouses, and farmhouses.

▶ Ask open-ended questions, such as: "How are the houses alike?" "How do they differ?" "Who usually lives in these habitats?" "Are any of these homes the same as where you live?" "Are they different?" "Why can't we live outside all of the time like some animals do?" "Why do people live in homes?"

▶ Next, have large sheets of paper, crayons, markers, craft sticks, fabric and paper scraps, glue, tape, and Styrofoam pieces accessible.

▶ Encourage children to create the type of temporary habitat they would live in if they lived in a very hot climate, or the type of habitat they would want if the weather were extremely cold.

▶ Give children plenty of time to finish this project. It could take several days.

▶ Take pictures of children's structures to put on the bulletin board.

CHILDREN'S BOOKS

Ackerman, Karen. (1992). *This Old House.* New York: Macmillan Children's Book Group.

Angelou, Maya. (1994). *My Painted House, My Friendly Chicken.* Photographs by Margaret C. Clarke. New York: Clarkson N. Potter.

Banks, Kate. (2003). *Mama's Coming Home.* Illustrated by Tomek Bogacki. New York: Farrar, Straus & Giroux.

Barton, Byron. (1990). *Building a House.* New York: Greenwillow.

Bowers, Tim. (2002). *A New Home.* San Diego: Harcourt.

Brown, Margaret Wise. (1995). *Goodnight Moon/Buenas noches, Luna.* Illustrated by Clement Hurd. New York: Rayo.

Brown, Margaret Wise. (1989). *Big Red Barn.* New York: Harper & Row.

Bunting, Eva. (1996). *Going Home.* Illustrated by David Diaz. New York: HarperCollins.

Dorros, Arthur. (1992). *This Is MY House.* New York: Scholastic.

Gibbons, Gail. (1990). *How a House Is Built.* New York: Scholastic.

Hayward, Linda. (2001). *Jobs People Do: A Day in the Life of a Builder. New York:* DK Publishing.

Jackson, Thomas C. (1994). *Hammers, Nails, Planks, and Paint: How a House Is Built.* New York: Scholastic.

Marzollo, Jean, and Ashley Wolff. (1998). *Home Sweet Home.* New York: HarperTrophy.

Morris, Ann. (1994). *Houses and Homes.* Photographs by Ken Heyman. New York: A Mulberry Paperback Book.

Pinkney, Gloria Jean. (1992). *Back Home.* Illustrated by Jerry Pinkney. New York: Dial Books for Young Readers.

Pinkwater, D. Manus. (1993). *The Big Orange Splot.* New York: Scholastic.

Reasoner, Charles. (1995). *Whose House Is This?* (Board Book). New York: Price Stern Sloan.

Rockwell, Anne. (1991). *In Our House.* New York: HarperCollins Children's Books.

Rowe, Julian, and Molly Perham. (1994). *Build It Strong.* Chicago: Children's Press.

Stevens, Janet. (1985). *The House that Jack Built.* New York: Holiday House.

Wood, Audrey. (1984). *The Napping House.* Illustrated by Don Wood. San Diego: Harcourt.

Family Letter (Preschool)

Dear Family,

Our theme is "My Home." We will provide opportunities for children to learn the following:

- A home is a place where you live, sleep, eat, work, and play.
- A home can be built from many different materials.
- Homes come in various types, sizes, and shapes.
- Homes can be found in numerous locations.
- Homes are different in different parts of the world.

We will be talking about the following:

- types of homes
- location of homes
- what is outside
- parts of a house
- rooms in a house
- things to do at home

Things to do at home with your preschool child include:

- Identify sounds around the house, such as a clock ticking, a doorbell ringing, the washing machine, and the dryer.
- Put up a tent in the backyard or the family room, and camp out with your child.
- Using pots, pans, spoons, empty oatmeal containers, and plastic bottles, make a "kitchen band" and play music.
- Help your child make a diagram of the house or her or his room.
- Take a walk around the neighborhood. Talk about the kinds of homes you see. Are there any houses being built in the neighborhood? Talk about how a house is built.

Family participation opportunities at school will include:

- Read books to the children.
  Date_____ Time_____
- Help when we make our Big Book bulletin board.
  Date_____ Time_____
- Help when we build graham cracker houses.
  Date_____ Time _____

Our wish list for this theme includes:

all sizes and types of boxes and milk cartons

empty, clean plastic bottles with caps

empty oatmeal containers

all sizes of keys

camping items, such as flashlights and camping dishes

kitchen gadgets, such as wooden spoons, new dishwashing sponges with handles, and large sieves

Thanks!

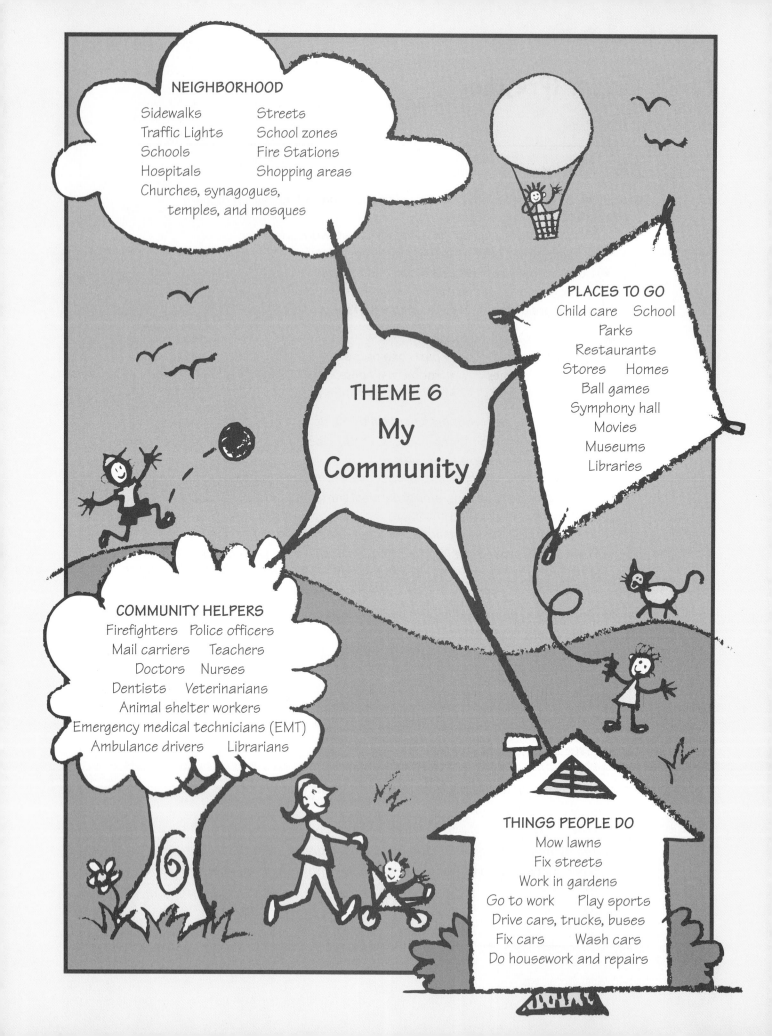

NEIGHBORHOOD

Sidewalks   Streets
Traffic Lights   School zones
Schools   Fire Stations
Hospitals   Shopping areas
Churches, synagogues,
    temples, and mosques

PLACES TO GO

Child care   School
        Parks
     Restaurants
Stores   Homes
     Ball games
    Symphony hall
       Movies
      Museums
      Libraries

THEME 6
My
Community

COMMUNITY HELPERS

Firefighters   Police officers
Mail carriers   Teachers
   Doctors   Nurses
 Dentists   Veterinarians
  Animal shelter workers
Emergency medical technicians (EMT)
Ambulance drivers   Librarians

THINGS PEOPLE DO

Mow lawns
Fix streets
Work in gardens
Go to work   Play sports
Drive cars, trucks, buses
Fix cars   Wash cars
Do housework and repairs

THEME GOALS

To provide opportunities for children to learn the following:

▶ We all live in a community that is made up of many people.

▶ Members of a community work in many different places, such as stores, offices, homes, and schools, and indoors and outdoors.

▶ Some people wear special clothes or uniforms when they work and use special tools or machines.

▶ Family members need to work in the community to buy what the family needs, such as housing, food, clothing, and transportation.

▶ We should respect and get along with community members who may think, dress, and act differently than we do.

Children-Created Bulletin Board

This bulletin board will keep changing during the time the "My Community" theme is emphasized. Creating the bulletin board fulfills several purposes: keeping the children interested in their community; offering a space where children can put their drawings, comments, and thank-you notes; and keeping families aware of the ongoing community involvement of their children.

▶ Divide the bulletin board into two sections.

▶ One area will be for photographs that you and the children take of people from the community who visit the school and for photographs you take of community helpers working at their jobs.

▶ The other section will be for photocopies of the thank-you letters the children send to community helpers and the drawings they create.

▶ Change the bulletin board every time a new community person is introduced to the children.

VOCABULARY STARTERS

Let the children add words.

community — a place where a group of many people lives, works, and plays together.

community helpers — a man or a woman who works at a job that helps the people who live in the community.

job or **occupation** — what a person does to earn a living for himself and his family.

neighbors — people who live or work close to your house.

respect — treating other people with kindness and understanding.

LANGUAGE EXPERIENCES

MAILBOXES

▶ Collect and make mailboxes out of shoe boxes, milk cartons, or tissue boxes.

▶ Have each child make one for himself. Include a box for the teachers.

▶ Have each child write his name on a box, or place on it a photograph for those children who are not yet recognizing their names.

▶ Provide envelopes and "stamps" (stickers, Easter Seal stamps, or magazine coupon stamps, for example) in the writing center.

▶ The children can write letters or draw pictures and "send" them to their classmates by placing them in the appropriate classroom mailboxes.

WRITE THANK-YOU LETTERS

▶ Have the children write thank-you letters or notes to community members who visit the class and to those visited during field trips.

▶ Younger children can draw pictures to accompany the thank-you note you write.

▶ Suggestions for people to visit or invite include: firefighter, police officer, nurse, doctor, veterinarian, animal caretaker from the zoo, storyteller from the library, museum staff member, doll collector, dance teacher, member of an orchestra, square dance group, bell choir.

LETTERS OR GREETING CARDS TO THE FAMILY

▶ It is fun for the children to write letters or make greeting cards to send to family members.

▶ Mail them or take a field trip to the post office to mail them.

▶ Have the children keep track of how long (how many days) it takes mail to get to their houses. Was the family member surprised?

DRAMATIC PLAY

PROP BOXES

▶ In a sturdy box, collect authentic items that represent a certain job or occupation.

▶ Label each box clearly for identification.

painter — several sizes of brushes, roller, bucket, sandpaper, masking tape, paint-stirring sticks, cap, gloves, old clothes, and a smock or an apron. Let younger children paint on boxes with water. Older children can paint with tempera.

baker/chef — hat, apron, spoons, rolling pin, dough, flour, and sifter. See Sensory Art activities in this theme for a play dough recipe.

firefighter — hats, several pieces of garden hose, raincoats, boots, and gloves.

gardener or **florist** — plastic flowers, pots with dirt, watering can, garden gloves, and hand shovel.

post office worker or **letter carrier** — play money (children can make their own with crayons, markers, and scrap construction paper), rubber stamps and stamp pad, postmarked stamps or stickers, envelopes, mail bag (large purse), hat, scrap paper, markers, pencils, and tape.

TELEPHONE DIRECTORY

▶ In the dramatic play/home living area, set up a special place with a small table, a nonworking telephone, a phone message pad and pencil, and a telephone book.

▶ Make a class telephone directory by having each child write his name, address, and telephone number on a blank piece of paper in a small loose-leaf notebook.

▶ Add telephone numbers for community services, such as the library, grocery store, and zoo.

▶ Place directory by the telephone.

▶ Suggest to the children that they begin writing down telephone messages and numbers when they "answer the phone" in the dramatic play area.

▶ An extension of this activity could be to set up a "telephone space" made from a refrigerator box.

▶ Place another copy of the class telephone directory in the booth along with an actual telephone book or yellow pages.

MY TOWN — MY NEIGHBORHOOD

This activity encourages creativity, observation, problem solving, cooperation, and spatial awareness skills.

▶ Take a walk around the neighborhood surrounding your center or school.

▶ Point out buildings, businesses, houses, street names, and roads. In some communities, it may be necessary to walk a wider area to find any buildings or businesses.

▶ For this activity you will need to close some of the centers in the room and expand the dramatic play area.

▶ Using boxes of varying sizes, construct a community.

▶ Talk about which buildings are needed, such as houses, apartments, stores, fire and police stations, hospitals, banks, churches, shopping malls, airports, movie theaters, and schools.

▶ On a large piece of cardboard, place the buildings as they are located in your community.

▶ With the children, name and label the buildings and the streets.

▶ If you have enough room on your playground, use larger boxes, and make a town that includes cars, buses, and trucks.

▶ See Math activities in this theme for a further extension of this project.

PUPPET PLAY

COMMUNITY HELPER PUPPETS

▶ Cut cardboard circles 8 to 10 inches in diameter, or use large paper plates.

▶ For infants and young toddlers, draw large, simple facial features on the cardboard circle.

▶ Attach a stick, such as a paint stirring stick or tongue depressor, to make a puppet.

▶ Play peekaboo by placing the face in front of an adult's or a baby's face.

▶ Let older children make a set of stick puppet faces by themselves.

▶ Children can add construction paper hats that represent community helpers, such as firefighters, police officers, letter carriers, and construction workers.

MUSIC

THE ORCHESTRA

Introduce the children to the concept of a community orchestra. Start with Rubin and Daniel's book, *The Orchestra*, listed in the Children's Books section of this theme.

▶ Play several classical music selections, such as Britten's *A Young Person's Guide to the Orchestra*, Prokofiev's *Peter and the Wolf*, and Saint-Saëns's *Carnival of the Animals*. Choose short excerpts of these to play at any one time.

▶ Visit your local library for these selections and to find children's books to accompany the music.

▶ To further develop this activity, add puppets, flannelboard characters, or musical instruments as the children become familiar with the music.

MAKE MUSICAL INSTRUMENTS

▶ Collect bathroom tissue rolls, paper towel tubes, waxed paper, rubber bands, new combs, aluminum pie plates, paper plates and cups, and cereal and oatmeal boxes.

▶ Guide the children into making and decorating the following:

drums — from oatmeal boxes.

plate shakers — with clothespins or birdseed placed between two aluminum pie plates, or paper plates tied together with yarn.

cup shakers — with dried beans inside of two paper cups taped together with masking tape.

flutes — from paper towel tubes. Punch a line of several holes to about two inches from the end. Cover the end with a square of waxed paper held in place with a rubber band.

rhythm sticks — from dowel sticks cut to specification at the hardware store.

humming combs — with waxed paper loosely wrapped around a comb, place to the lips and hum.

MOVEMENT

LET'S DANCE

Infants enjoy all kinds of music. Toddlers enjoy dancing to lively music, especially when you tie bells to their shoestrings. Tie some on your shoes too.

▶ Place the infant on his back, hold his ankles, and move his feet to the rhythm of the music you are singing or playing.

▶ Take the baby's hands and move his arms up and down, or clap his hands together as the music plays.

ACT OUT A STORY WITH DANCE

▶ Read a story or poem to the children, such as Stecher's *Max, the Music Maker*, listed in the Children's Books section of this theme.

▶ Let the children be the orchestra. They can play rhythm instruments or the ones they made as you read the book.

▶ Have the children dance or act out the story by walking quickly and slowly, running in place, tapping along, or moving with scarves or crepe paper streamers.

▶ Try having half the class be the orchestra while the other half dances.

MORE DANCING

▶ Take a field trip to a dance studio, or have a dancer visit your class.

▶ The children enjoy watching a dancer in ballet or tap shoes.

▶ Have the dance teacher or dancer show the children and you how to do some simple steps.

▶ Give the children opportunities to repeat these steps over and over again. Try it with different kinds of music.

SENSORY ART

MAKE PLAY DOUGH

You will need:

> 1 cup flour
> 1/2 cup salt
> 1 cup water
> 1 tablespoon cooking oil
> 2 teaspoons cream of tartar
> vanilla, peppermint, or almond extract

1. Wash hands.

2. Mix all ingredients.

3. Stir over low heat until the mixture forms a ball.

4. Remove from heat, and wrap in waxed paper to cool.

5. Store in an airtight container.

6. The play dough will last much longer if kept in the refrigerator.

7. You and the children can add food coloring before cooking or wait until after cooking so the children can see the change from white to marbled to the final color.

8. Fragrant extracts, such as vanilla, peppermint, or almond, may be added to the play dough.

Theme 10 contains a recipe for *uncooked* play dough.

COMMUNITY TELEPHONES

▶ To make a set of telephones, you will need two empty tin cans, a long piece of string, two toothpicks or nails, and a hammer.

▶ Punch a hole in the bottom of each can with a hammer and nail.

▶ Thread ends of string through the holes.

▶ Tie the string around the toothpicks to keep them from coming out of the cans.

▶ Two children hold the tin can "telephones" and pull the string tight.

▶ The children then take turns talking and listening.

▶ For variation, add more phones and create a "community party line."

WOODWORKING

This activity encourages positive self-esteem, self-motivation, problem solving, large and small muscle development, hand-eye coordination, and creativity.

▶ Visit a community hardware store with the children before setting up the woodworking area. This gives the children a firsthand experience seeing many different types of nails, screws, washers, bolts, hammers, screwdrivers, and wood.

▶ Introduce the children to the woodworking center with its materials, tools, and pictures of houses and buildings under construction at various construction sites.

▶ Children should be closely supervised, with only two at a time using the tools.

▶ Collect real tools and materials, such as small claw hammers (8 to 12 ounces), assorted nails, safety goggles (children's swimming masks work well), clamps, a hand drill, wood glue, sandpaper, rulers, pencils, and paper.

▶ For older children, add a crosscut saw (approximately 18 inches long), screws, and screwdrivers.

▶ Obtain inexpensive grades of wood from carpentry shops, lumberyards, and do-it-yourself discount stores, or ask families to contribute.

▶ In the beginning, children enjoy sanding and gluing the pieces of wood. Add hammering, sawing, and nailing later.

CREATIVE FOOD EXPERIENCES

EAT RICE WITH CHOPSTICKS

▶ Begin this project by reading Dooley's *Everybody Cooks Rice*, listed in the Children's Books section of this theme.

▶ Introduce the children to how food connects one neighbor to another in the neighborhood. Recipes using rice are included at the end of this book.

▶ To further develop children's understanding of other cultures, introduce the use of chopsticks to eat rice.

▶ Chopsticks are useful tools that are part of Chinese, Japanese, Korean, and Vietnamese cultures.

▶ Cook rice according to the instructions on the package.

▶ Give each child a new pair of chopsticks that he can take home after using. Many Asian restaurants give sets of new chopsticks to teachers for the asking.

▶ Demonstrate to the children how to hold the chopsticks by the thicker end.

▶ Put one chopstick at the base of the thumb, and hold the other between the thumb, index, and middle fingers. Move only the finger-held chopstick to pick up rice or small pieces of food.

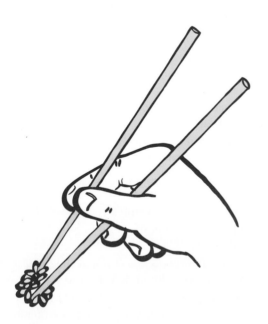

▶ Many young children find the task easier by holding the chopsticks closer to the end where they are picking up food.

▶ Explain to the children that it is rude to point with chopsticks. Avoid licking the chopsticks or spearing food with them.

CHICKEN SOUP WITH RICE

Here is another way to connect language, literacy, and cooking. Read Sendak's *Chicken Soup with Rice*, listed in the Children's Books section of this theme.

You will need the following:

6 cups chicken broth
1 cup chicken, cooked and diced
3/4 cup cooked rice

1. Bring broth to a boil.
2. Add chicken and rice.
3. Reheat and eat.

This recipe serves 8.

MATH

PARTNER TOWER BUILDING

Tower building promotes math skill development, such as problem solving, exploration of spatial relationships, and experimentation with weight and balance. Socialization and cooperation also are emphasized.

▶ In the block center, have one child build a tower or shape and another child duplicate it.

▶ Let the children continue this activity until they tire of it.

▶ To vary the activity, have a small group of children build a tower.

▶ The first child puts a block in place. Each child in the group takes a turn stacking a block on top of what has been built. Continue taking turns until the tower falls.

▶ The children can discuss why they think the tower fell.

▶ Children may want to experiment with stacking blocks another way.

MIXED-UP PEOPLE

Older children like to draw pictures of people, such as firefighters, bakers, nurses, cowboys, ballet dancers, and farmers.

▶ Supply plenty of paper, crayons, markers, and scissors for children to make pictures of people.

▶ Suggest to children that they cut pictures they have made into three pieces, dividing the picture into body, head, and legs.

▶ Put the body of one, the head of another, and the legs of another together to make a mixed-up person.

▶ Leave the materials for the children to come back to draw mixed-up people whenever they choose.

SHAPE CITY

▶ Provide the children with colorful construction paper, scissors, and glue.

▶ Demonstrate how to cut out all sizes of different shapes. Precut the shapes for younger children.

▶ The children glue the shapes onto a piece of paper to make designs of homes, buildings, vehicles, and people. Younger children enjoy just gluing the shapes everywhere on the page, with no specific design in mind.

▶ An extension of this activity is for the children to create a shape city on a long piece of butcher paper.

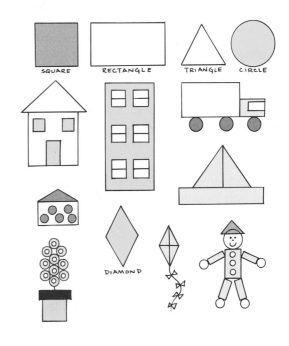

SCIENCE

FIRE PREVENTION

▶ After visiting a fire station or having a firefighter visit the school, reinforce the experience.

▶ Try STOP (don't run — freeze), DROP (fall to the ground), and ROLL (over and over until the fire is out) to put out fire on clothing.

▶ Practice what to do to escape from a smoky room. Crawl to the nearest exit. Stay low, since smoke and hot air rise.

▶ Another vital rule: If the DOOR is HOT, do not open it! Ask the children what it means if the door is hot.

▶ Start a list of fire-safety rules on a large sheet of paper or poster board.

▶ Ask children to contribute rules you have discussed or ones they learned at home.

▶ Continue to add to the list. Post it at the children's eye level.

PULLEYS

▶ Ask open-ended questions relating to children's experiences with tall buildings and apartment houses.

▶ How do the people get from one floor to another?

▶ Introduce the concept of pulleys and elevators.

▶ Next, let the children watch you set up two chairs to support the ends of a wooden dowel or broomstick.

▶ Tie heavy string to the handle of a small basket filled with toy animals and people figures from the block center.

▶ Loop the string over the dowel.

▶ Ask a child to pull the string down on one side of the dowel. This illustrates how a pulley lifts the basket with toys on the other side.

▶ Let the children experiment with the pulley.

▶ Provide materials, and encourage the children to make other pulleys.

▶ Guide the children into adding pulleys into the block area with their buildings.

SOCIAL STUDIES

COMMUNITY BUILDINGS

▶ Show the children pictures of all kinds of buildings in communities around the world.

▶ Obtain the pictures from travel agents, airlines, travel brochures, and magazines such as *National Geographic*. You may want to take some photos as well.

▶ With the children, compare the similarities and differences of the buildings.

▶ Ask open-ended questions, such as: "Who do you think works in this building?" "What is his job?" "Why do you think the building is so tall?" "Why is this building so small?" "What country do you think this building is in?" "What city?"

▶ This discussion can be combined with the Shape City activity in the Math section of this theme.

COMMUNITY MAP

▶ With older children, use a map of your community to show them where their school is. Mark the spot on the map.

▶ Find some of the streets, roads, houses, and buildings in the neighborhood, and mark these.

▶ Let the children make a large floor map of the neighborhood and city.

▶ Provide a large piece of butcher paper, masking tape, construction paper, crayons, and markers. Egg cartons make interesting structures, and paper towel tubes make great tunnels.

CHILDREN'S BOOKS

Bauer, Judith. (1990a). *What's It Like to Be a Doctor?* Mahway, NJ: Troll Associates.

Bauer, Judith. (1990b). *What's It Like to Be a Nurse?* Mahway, NJ: Troll Associates.

Borden, L. (1990). *The Neighborhood Trucker.* New York: Scholastic.

Butterworth, Nick. (1992). *Busy People.* Cambridge, MA: Candlewick Press.

Caseley, Judith. (2002). *On the Town: A Community Adventure.* New York: Greenwillow.

Chen, Chih-Yuan. (2003). *On My Way to Buy Eggs.* New York: Kane/Miller.

Crawford, Andy. (2002). *Touch and Feel Fire Engine.* Photographs by Lynton Gardiner. New York: DK Publishing.

Darling, David. (1992). *Spiderwebs to Skyscrapers.* New York: Dillon Press.

Dooley, Norah. (1991). *Everybody Cooks Rice.* Illustrated by Peter J. Thornton. Minneapolis, MN: Carolrhoda Books.

Flanagan, Alice K., and Christine Osinski. (1998). *Mrs. Murphy Fights Fires.* San Francisco: Children's Press.

Friend, David. (1992). *Baseball, Football, Daddy, and Me.* New York: Puffin Books.

Ganci, Chris. (2003). *Chief: The Life of Peter J. Ganci, a New York Firefighter*. New York: Orchard Books.

Hayward, Linda. (2001). *Jobs People Do: A Day in the Life of a Police Officer*. New York: DK Publishing.

Henderson, Kathy. (1991). *I Can Be a Basketball Player*. Chicago: Children's Press.

MacLean, Christine K. (2002). *Even Firefighters Hug Their Moms*. New York: Dutton.

Merriam, Eve. (2000). *On My Street*. Illustrated by Melanie H. Greenberg. New York: HarperFestival.

Patrick, Denise L. (1993). *The Car Washing Street*. Illustrated by John Ward. New York: Scholastic.

Powers, M. E. (1992). *Our Teacher's in a Wheelchair*. Chicago: Whitman.

Rogers, Fred. (1989). *Going to the Dentist*. New York: Putnam.

Rosa-Mendoza, Gladys. (2002). *Jobs Around My Neighborhood/Oficios en mi Vecindaro*. (Bilingual ed.). Illustrated by Ann Iosa. New York: Me & Mi Publishing.

Rubin, Mark. (1995). *The Orchestra*. Illustrated by Alan Daniel. Buffalo: Firefly Books.

Russel, Joan P. (2001). *Aero & Officer Mike: Police Partners*. Honsdale, PA: Boyds Mills Press.

Sendak, Maurice. (1962). *Chicken Soup with Rice*. New York: Scholastic.

Seymour, Peter. (1990). *Firefighters*. New York: Dutton Children's Books.

Skurzynski, Gloria. (1992). *Here Comes the Mail*. New York: Macmillan Children's Books.

Stecher, Miriam. (1990). *Max, the Music Maker*. Photographs by Alex Meyboom. New York: Lothrop, Lee & Shepard Books.

Tasky, Sue. (1997). *The Busy Building Book*. New York: Putnam.

Van Laan, Nancy. (1992). *People, People, Everywhere*. New York: Knopf.

Ziefert, Harriet. (1991). *City Shapes*. Illustrated by Susan Baum. New York: HarperCollins.

Family Letter (Primary Grade)

Dear Family,

We are beginning our new theme, "My Community." The children will have opportunities to learn the following:

- We live in a community made up of many people.
- Members of a community work in many different places.
- Some people wear special clothes or uniforms when they work and use special tools or machines.
- Family members work in the community to buy what the family needs, such as housing, food, clothing, and transportation.
- We should respect and get along with community members who may think, dress, and act differently than we do.

We will be talking about the following:

- our neighborhood, and who lives and works there
- community helpers
- things that people do
- places to go in the community

Things to do in the community with your child include:

- Take a walk around your neighborhood. Let your child point out things that relate to what he or she is doing in school.
- Look at ongoing construction sites of homes and buildings.
- Ask what he or she is building at school.
- Discuss how specific community helpers have helped your family.
- Eat a dinner using chopsticks, if you have not done so. Let your child show you how.
- Visit a museum, see a play, cheer at a ball game, and enjoy the symphony orchestra in your community.

Come join us for the following family participation opportunities at school:

- Visit the class and share your occupation with the children.
  Date _____ Time _____
- Join us on our neighborhood walk.
  Date _____ Time _____
- Help us in the woodworking center.
  Date _____ Time _____

Our wish list for this theme includes:

nonpostal stamps	milk cartons
envelopes	aluminum pie plates
all sizes of boxes	magazines and catalogs
paper cups and plates	empty oatmeal boxes
tubes from paper towels	

Thanks!

The Senses

*Y*oung children learn through their five senses. Beginning in infancy, children first learn about their world through seeing, hearing, tasting, smelling, and touching. Because of this, it is important to include a curriculum that offers many sensory experiences.

The thematic activities in this section suggest how to interconnect the senses and the total curriculum. They are designed to meet the individual differences, abilities, and interests of the children in your class. Encourage the children to make choices, and be supportive of the activity choices they make.

The following themes are included in Section II, "The Senses":

Theme 7 — Seeing

Theme 8 — Hearing

Theme 9 — Tasting

Theme 10 — Smelling

Theme 11 — Touching

THEME GOALS

To provide opportunities for children to learn the following:

▶ The importance of the five senses, with this theme's emphasis on the sense of sight.

▶ The eyes are the part of the body used to see and help us learn.

▶ We should take good care of our eyes.

▶ Some people cannot see at all or cannot see objects clearly.

▶ Humans cannot see in the dark; we need light to see.

Children-Created Bulletin Board

This bulletin board provides opportunities for interactive discovery. It will change during the time the five senses are being studied. Encourage the children to think of things to put on the bulletin board and to discover what you have added.

▶ Cover the bulletin board with burlap to give the area a new texture as you begin the interconnecting theme of the senses.

▶ In one corner of the bulletin board, place an unbreakable mirror. This allows the children to look closely at the parts of their faces at times throughout the day.

▶ For the theme "Seeing," arrange big cutouts of two eyes at the top of the bulletin board.

▶ Under the eyes, put the words, "Look What I See!"

▶ The children place pictures they have drawn or cut out on the board. They can write or dictate sentences about what they see and put these up.

▶ It is also fun for the children to make faces with eyes the color of their own eyes and add these to the collection.

▶ More objects can be placed on the bulletin board as the children become involved with activities relating to this theme.

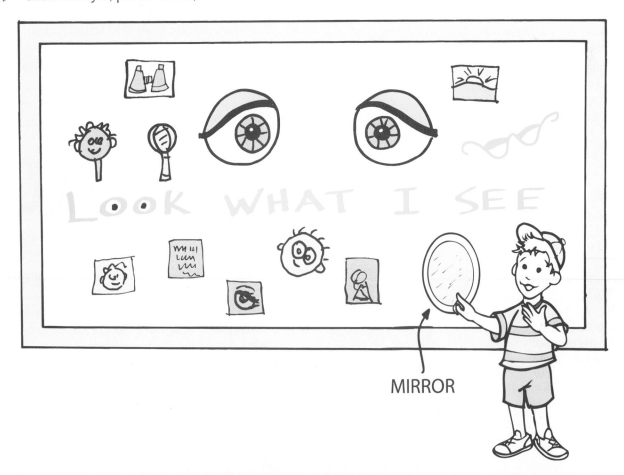

MIRROR

VOCABULARY STARTERS

Let the children add words. Include pictures where appropriate.

eye — the part of the body with which we see.

eyebrows — the hair that grows in an arch pattern above the eyes.

eyelashes — the hairs on the eyelids that help protect the eyes from dust particles.

eyelids — the skin that opens and closes over the eyes.

iris — the colored part of the eye.

pupil — the black spot in the middle of the iris.

vision — being able to see things.

LANGUAGE EXPERIENCES

WHERE ARE YOU?

The very young infant will watch the movements of an adult.

▶ Move to different parts of the room, and call the baby's name.

▶ When the infant turns her head to look for you, give her hugs and verbal praise.

▶ Change positions of the baby, from the back to the stomach or sitting up. This gives the child an opportunity to use different kinds of movement when looking for the adult.

POEM:
"Looking at the World"

When I wake up
What do I do?
I open my eyes
Just like you.
  When I get up
  What do I see?
  I see my bedroom.
  It's all around me.
I go to the window
And look outside.
I see the world

So big and wide.
  It's filled with wonderful
  Things to see.
  Like the sun and flowers,
  Like grass and trees.
Like cars on the street,
Like clouds in the sky.
I love to watch
The world with my eyes.

Philip Jackman

CHILDREN'S POETRY

Most children enjoy making up poems. Using the five senses is a way to get them started.

▶ When it is raining, go outside and sit under a safe, covered area.

▶ Have the children *look* at the rain and describe it in one or more words. Write the dictation exactly as each child says it.

▶ Next, have children close their eyes and *listen* to the rain. Describe this.

▶ Have children stick out their tongues, *taste* the rain, and describe it.

▶ Then, children *feel* the rain on their hands and describe what that feels like.

▶ What does the rain *smell* like? Have children describe the odor.

▶ For older children, thunder and lightning add to the poetry-writing experience.

▶ Follow up by placing children's poems on the bulletin board.

SEEING THE WORLD DIFFERENTLY

▶ When the children are outside, encourage them to look all around them and talk about what they see.

▶ What do children see to their right? To their left? In front? In back?

▶ What do children see when they hang their heads between their legs? Does the world look different upside down?

▶ How does everything look when children crawl through the outdoor play tunnel?

▶ Follow this up by having the children look at the classroom from different points of view.

DRAMATIC PLAY

MIRRORS, MIRRORS EVERYWHERE!

▶ Place mirrors of many shapes and sizes throughout the room. These should be well-secured wall mirrors, unbreakable, and with rounded edges.

▶ Put mirrors in unexpected places, such as the manipulative center and the music center.

▶ Place them at eye, floor, and knee levels.

▶ These mirrors are props that can extend impromptu dramatic play. Observe what the children do when they look in the mirror.

▶ This activity opens up the entire room and offers the children additional ways to see themselves.

▶ As an alternative to mirrors, place foil or other reflecting objects around the room.

LET'S PAINT

▶ Set up a dramatic play area outdoors for the children to role-play being a house painter.

▶ Supply clean quart and gallon paint cans full of water, brushes of various sizes, painter's hats, smocks, and drop cloths.

▶ The children can paint the building, the playground equipment, and other objects.

LET'S LOOK

Turn the dramatic play center into an optometrist's office or eyewear store.

▶ Collect an assortment of old plastic eyeglass frames (regular eyeglasses with lenses removed), and place them into several little baskets.

▶ Near the baskets, place an unbreakable stand-up or wall mirror.

▶ Encourage the children to try on the different glasses to see how they look.

▶ Add eye charts, pictures of people wearing glasses, posters, a cash register, and play money.

PUPPET PLAY

THE "SEEING" PEOPLE PUPPET

To make this puppet, you will need a paper plate about nine inches wide, a tongue depressor or large craft stick, and colored cellophane.

▶ Cut two eyeholes slightly above the middle of the plate. They must be large but can be round, oval, or other shapes.

▶ The rounded side of the plate may be colored by the child with crayons to look like the child or the child's favorite animal.

▶ Then, on the other side of the plate, glue or tape a piece of cellophane a little larger than both eyeholes.

▶ Finally, tape the stick to the back side, allowing enough stick showing below the plate to use as a handle for the child to hold.

▶ Have each child look at classmates, the room, pictures, books, or other colored surfaces.

▶ Ask the children to notice how, for example, the yellow cellophane "eyes" make blue things look black or yellow things look white. A complementary or an opposite color always looks black, while the same color disappears.

▶ Have the children go outside to see how different trees and buildings look through their colored "eyes."

▶ Use different colors of cellophane to extend this activity.

STEP 1   STEP 2   STEP 3

MUSIC

MONKEY SEE, MONKEY DO

This is a traditional song with a beat. Use a simple clapping–patting–stamping pattern to emphasize the beat.

▶ Infants enjoy having you hold their hands and clap them together.

▶ For older children, let them take turns being the leader that others follow. The children enjoy acting like monkeys.

Monkey see, monkey do,
Clap, clap, clap your hands.
Monkey does the same as you,
Clap, clap, clap your hands.
   Monkey see, monkey do,
   Pat, pat, pat your knees.
   Monkey does the same as you,
   Pat, pat, pat your knees.
Monkey see, monkey do,
Stamp, stamp, stamp your feet.
Monkey does the same as you,
Stamp, stamp, stamp your feet.

▶ You and the children can add other actions, such as "shake, shake, shake your head," "wiggle, wiggle, wiggle your body," or "sniff, sniff, sniff your nose."

MOVEMENT

INFANT CRAWL

Babies want to reach and touch everything in sight. When they begin to crawl, give them something to crawl to.

▶ Cover paper towel rolls with brightly colored paper.

▶ Then, place clear contact paper over the roll to strengthen it and make the tube easy to wipe off.

▶ These can be pushed and rolled.

▶ You can make a pull toy from the rolls as well. Just tie several together on a string.

▶ Other ways to encourage infants to crawl include: knock the ends out of large cardboard boxes for a crawl tunnel; pile large cushions on the floor for infants to crawl under, over, and around.

LETTER HOP

This activity promotes the practice of motor skills, sight recognition of letters, and listening skills.

▶ To highlight the letters emphasized during this theme, make big letters and place them on the floor with masking tape.

▶ Have the children outline the letters by walking forward, backward, and sideways, or hopping, skipping, tiptoeing, and marching.

▶ Play music that tells children how fast or slow to move around the letters.

SENSORY ART

IT'S FAR AWAY; NO, IT'S NEAR

▶ Show the children a flower in a vase.

▶ Ask children to look at it closely.

▶ Then move the flower and vase across the room.

▶ Ask the children: "Has the flower changed?" "Does the vase look different or the same?"

▶ Talk about how something looks when it is nearby and how its look changes when it is far away.

▶ Next, place sheets of paper, pencils, and crayons in the art center.

▶ Also include pictures of birds, airplanes, trees, flowers, and people. These should show how an object, such as an airplane, looks when it is far away and when it is nearby.

▶ Ask the children to draw two pictures, such as one showing an object far away and another showing the same object up close.

▶ Talk about the pictures.

LETTERS AND NUMBERS

▶ With the children's assistance, make upper- and lower-case letters and numbers out of different grades of sandpaper, sponges, pipe cleaners, burlap, and velvet.

▶ The children can sort the letters by shape and size, spell their names, differentiate between letters and numbers, and integrate the senses of sight and touch.

ART CAN CATCH THE SUN

▶ Give each child a square sheet of waxed paper.

▶ Let children cover it with glue. For gluing, use small squeeze bottles with long tips to strengthen small muscles.

▶ Completely cover the glue with colorful tissue paper.

▶ Next, children cover the paper with another layer of glue.

▶ Place another sheet of waxed paper on top.

▶ Let dry for several days.

▶ Then peel the waxed paper off.

▶ Have children gently punch one or two holes in the glue/tissue art.

▶ Put a string in the top.

▶ Hang the sun catchers where they receive full sun. Discover the patterns they make, and see what the sun does to the colored tissue.

▶ Encourage children to experiment with other ways to make sun catchers. Promote creativity.

CREATIVE FOOD EXPERIENCES

FORGOTTEN COOKIES

Doing this type of cooking activity with the children will help them understand, in a positive way, that they cannot always have instant gratification. This is a recipe the children will want to do again. It is a good one to share with families, too.

You will need the following:

    2 eggs (only the whites are needed)
    2/3 cup of sugar
    1 teaspoon of vanilla
    6-ounce package of chocolate bits

1. Wash hands.
2. Preheat oven to 350 degrees.
3. Beat two egg whites until stiff peaks are formed. Add the sugar while beating.
4. When the egg whites are stiff, add the chocolate bits and vanilla.
5. Drop by spoonfuls onto a greased cookie sheet.

6. Put into the oven. TURN THE OVEN **OFF**.
7. Forget the cookies for at least two hours.
8. Then, remember what is in the oven and enjoy!
9. Talk about how the egg whites look before and after beating.
10. Discuss how the cookies look before and after baking them.

BREAD PUDDING FOR ALL

This is a great activity to do when you have a large block of time available. The recipe will take about an hour for you and the children to prepare. It makes enough for 20 servings.

You will need the following:

    12 slices of white bread
    8 eggs
    2 cups of sugar
    4 tablespoons margarine
    6 cups of milk
    2 teaspoons of vanilla
    2 teaspoons of cinnamon
    1/2 cup of raisins

BREAD PUDDING FOR ALL

Wash hands.   Preheat oven to 400 degrees.

Break 12 slices of white bread into small pieces and place in 2 long baking dishes.   Beat 8 eggs and 2 cups sugar together in a bowl. Add 2 teaspoons of vanilla and 6 cups milk to the egg mixture and pour over the bread.   Put small pieces of margarine on top.

Add 1/2 cup raisins and sprinkle cinnamon over the top.

Bake in oven for 30 minutes. Cool and eat. YUM!

1. Wash hands.
2. Preheat oven to 400 degrees.
3. Break bread into small pieces, and place in two long baking dishes.
4. Beat the eggs and sugar together in a bowl.
5. Add vanilla and milk to the egg mixture, and pour over the bread.
6. Put small pieces of margarine on top.
7. Add raisins, and sprinkle cinnamon over the top.
8. Bake in the oven for 30 minutes.
9. Cool and eat. Yum!

MATH

MATCH THE FRUITS AND VEGETABLES

- Make a folder matching game of fruits and vegetables.
- Use duplicate pictures from magazines, use stickers, or draw and color them yourself.
- For younger children, use fewer fruit and vegetable pictures.
- Open up a file folder. On one side, paste pictures of fruits. On the other side, paste pictures of vegetables. Double-sided sticky tape can be used to secure the pictures.
- Print in lower case the name of each fruit and vegetable.
- Make a set of matching cards with duplicate fruits and vegetables.
- Laminate the folder and each card.
- Label the front of the folder with two of the pictures and the words "Fruits and Vegetables."
- Glue an envelope or a locking plastic bag on the back of the folder. Put the card pieces into this.
- Put the folder game in the math center for the children.

SORTING IDEAS

- Collect sample cards of paint colors from hardware and paint stores.
- Put the samples in an open box, a basket, or a plastic container in the math center.
- Have the children sort the paint cards by color.
- In another container, place fabric and wallpaper squares. Make these available for the children to sort by patterns.
- This stimulates the children to look around their homes. What colors do they see in their environment? Which surfaces are painted, and which are wallpapered? What patterns are on the fabric of their furniture? Families can be included in this activity.

SCIENCE

WATCH MY EYES

- Give each child a partner.
- Have each pair sit where they can look at each other's eyes.
- Look at the iris, the colored part of the eye.
- Look at the pupil, the black spot in the middle of the iris.
- Turn the lights off in the classroom for a few minutes.
- Then, turn the lights back on. Ask the children to observe their partners' pupils again. Do they look the same? Different?
- Explain that the pupils get larger (open up) in the dark to let more light enter the eye. This helps the eyes to see.
- In bright light, such as sunshine, the pupils get smaller (contract) to let less light enter the eyes.
- The children may want to do this again. Repetition is important to reinforce learning.

LOOK FOR THE DOTS

▶ Put several magnifying glasses out on the science table with a group of black-and-white pictures cut from the newspaper.

▶ The children can do this activity in groups of two or three.

▶ Ask the children to look through a magnifying glass at the newspaper picture. Ask, "What do you see?"

▶ Children will see that each picture is made up of lots of black dots. The dots are largest in the dark areas.

▶ The children will want to share their discovery with their families.

SOCIAL STUDIES

SPECIAL COLLECTIONS

▶ Invite a family or community member to visit the class to share a special collection with the children. Perhaps someone has collected items from all over the world, such as dolls, stamps, or shells.

▶ Each item collected usually has an interesting story connected to it.

▶ The children can ask questions to find out more about how and when the individual started collecting.

▶ Locate all of the countries, states, and cities on maps or globe of the world. This will help the children "see" where the objects came from.

▶ A natural follow-up is for the children to bring their collection of toys, stamps, sports cards, or stuffed animals to share with their classmates.

▶ What about your special collection? You can share too.

CHILDREN'S BOOKS

Aliki. (1989). *My Five Senses.* New York: HarperTrophy.

Carle, Eric. (1973). *I See a Song.* New York: Scholastic.

Cousins, Lucy. (1997). *What Can Pinky See?: A-Lift-the-Flap-Book.* Cambridge, MA: Candlewick Press.

dePaola, Tomie. (1996). *The Bubble Factory.* New York: Grosset & Dunlap.

Dr. Seuss (pseud. for Theodor Geisel). (1997). *And to Think that I Saw It on Mulberry Street.* New York: Random House.

Dr. Seuss (pseud. for Theodor Geisel). (1968). *The Eye Book.* New York: Random House.

Hoban, Tana. (1997). *Look Book.* New York: Greenwillow.

Hoban, Tana. (1988). *Look! Look! Look!* New York: Greenwillow.

Isadora, Rachel. (2002). *Peekaboo Morning.* New York: Putnam.

Johnson, Neil. (1997). *A Field of Sunflowers.* New York: Cartwheel Books.

Martin, Bill Jr. (1983). *Brown Bear, Brown Bear, What Do You See?* Illustrated by Eric Carle. New York: Henry Holt.

Noll, Sally. (1990). *Watch Where You Go.* New York: Greenwillow.

Oppenheim, Joanne. (1986). *Have You Seen the Birds?* Illustrated by Barbara Reid. New York: Scholastic.

Oxenbury, Helen. (1995). *I See.* (Board Book). Cambridge, MA: Candlewick Press.

Raczka, Bob. (2002). *More Than Meets the Eye: Seeing Art with All the Five Senses.* Brookfield, CT: Millbrook Press.

Shaw, Charles G. (1947). *It Looked Like Spilt Milk.* New York: HarperTrophy.

Showers, Paul. (1992). *Look at Your Eyes.* New York: HarperCollins.

Snape, Juliet, and Charles Snape. (1987). *The Boy with Square Eyes, a Tale of Televisionitis.* New York: Simon & Schuster.

Ward, Leila. (1992). *I Am Eyes — Ni Mac Ho.* New York: Scholastic.

Wick, Walter. (2002). *Can You See What I See?* New York: Cartwheel Books.

Winch, John. (1997). *The Old Woman Who Loved to Read.* New York: Holiday House.

Worthy, Judith. (1988). *Eyes.* New York: Doubleday.

Family Letter (Toddler)

Dear Family,

We are beginning to talk about the five senses. Our first theme is "Seeing." The children will learn the following:

- The five senses, starting with the sense of sight.
- The eyes are the part of the body used to see.
- We should take good care of our eyes.
- Some people cannot see at all.
- We cannot see in the dark; we need light to see.

We will be talking about the following:

- our eyes
- the color of our eyes
- what seeing helps us do
- how we can take care of our eyes
- what we see in our world

Some things to do at home with your toddler follow:

- Spend time with your child talking about what each of you see, both indoors and outdoors.
- Look in the mirror with your child, and point out the color of the eye, the eyelashes, eyebrows, and the eyelid that winks and blinks.
- Sort laundry with your child. Look for colors, patterns, and sizes.
- Read books with your child.

Family participation opportunities at school will include:

- Come visit us and share our classroom experiences.
  Date _____   Time _____
- Share your special collection of stamps, dolls, shells, or other objects with the children.
  Date _____   Time _____

Our wish list for this theme includes:

colored cellophane sheets

colored tissue paper sheets

wallpaper or fabric pieces

paper towel rolls

paper plates

paper cups

Thanks!

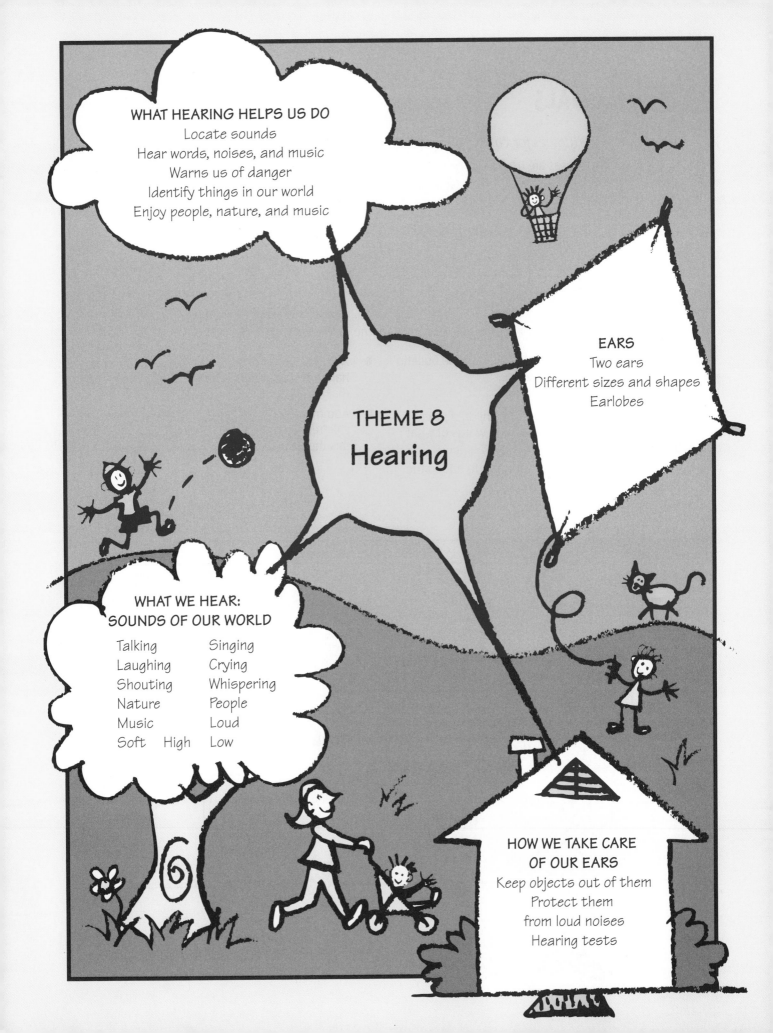

THEME GOALS

To provide opportunities for children to learn the following:

▶ How the five senses are used.

▶ The ears are the part of the body used to hear.

▶ We listen to hear many sounds and find out many things.

▶ We should take good care of our ears.

▶ Some people cannot hear at all, or cannot hear well.

Children-Created Bulletin Board

This bulletin board is a continuation of the one started in Theme 7, "Seeing."

▶ Place two oversize ears on the sides of the bulletin board. Leave the "eyes" in place.

▶ Add the word "Listen!"

▶ During the theme "Hearing," the children place on the bulletin board pictures and words of what they hear.

▶ Children create new faces with ears to add to the bulletin board.

▶ Add small bells on strings or colored ribbon to hang from the bulletin board. The children enjoy making these "jingle."

▶ Add more items to the bulletin board as the children become busy with activities related to this theme.

VOCABULARY STARTERS

Let the children add words.

ear — the part of the body with which we hear.

earlobe — the soft skin at the bottom of the ear.

hearing — the ability to notice sounds with the ears.

listen — to pay attention to what we are hearing.

sound — what we hear with our ears.

LANGUAGE EXPERIENCES

HEAR A SOUND, MAKE A SOUND

Infants enjoy making sounds, hearing sounds around them, and responding to what they hear.

▶ Shake rattles, bells, and tambourines for the babies to see and hear.

▶ Babies will answer the sounds by watching and cooing.

▶ Repeat the sounds many times.

▶ Shake–coo. Shake–coo. A kind of rhythm will occur.

▶ Try many different kinds of sound-making toys and musical instruments.

▶ Let the infant play with the rattle or an appropriate toy, and watch how he plays with it.

FINGERPLAY:
My Little Ears

I have two little ears.
  (point to ears)
They belong to me.
  (point to yourself)
They help me hear.
  (put hand behind ears)
Don't you see?
  (place hands above eyes)
My two little ears
  (point to ears)
Go everywhere I go,
When I'm way up high
  (point up to the ceiling)

Or when I'm way down low.
  (point down to the floor)
My two little ears
  (point to ears)
Love the beat of a drum,
  (pretend to beat a drum)
Or the roar of an airplane
  (make your arms fly like an airplane)
Or a bumble bee's hum-m-m-m.
  (fingers together, fly like a bee)
I have two little ears.
  (point to ears)
They belong to me.
  (point to yourself)
They help me hear.
  (place hands behind ears)
Don't you see?
  (place hands above eyes)

Philip Jackman

DRAMATIC PLAY

FIND WHAT'S NEW

▶ To introduce children to the new items you have added to the dramatic play/home living area, hide a ticking kitchen timer or an alarm clock there. See if the children can find it without any clues.

▶ After they find the timer, ask the children to point out what other new items have been added.

▶ Suggestions of objects to add to the area include: bongo drums, bells, maracas, rain sticks, cymbals, autoharp, kitchen pots and pans, wooden spoons, rhythm sticks, tambourines, and a washboard.

▶ The children can explore the different musical instruments and the sounds they make.

▶ The more they hear, the more children learn about their environment.

▶ For younger children, place a "jack-in-the box" somewhere in the room.

▶ See if the children can find where the music is coming from before it pops open.

▶ Introduce the toy to the children before you hide it in the room so that they will expect the "pop-up."

SCARVES, STREAMERS, AND TAMBOURINES

This activity can be done indoors or outdoors. You will need a large space so the children can move around.

▶ Have the children select scarves, crepe paper streamers, or tambourines that you have made available for them.

▶ Play a variety of music for the children to "act out" what the music is "telling" them to do.

▶ Suggestions for musical selections available in libraries or stores under many different labels and performing artists include:

Composer	Selection
Copeland	*Rodeo*
Dukas	*The Sorcerer's Apprentice*
Grofé	*Grand Canyon Suite*
Rimski-Korsakov	*Flight of the Bumble Bee*
Rossini	*William Tell Overture*
Saint-Saëns	*Carnival of the Animals*
Tchaikovsky	*The Nutcracker Suite*

PUPPET PLAY

RABBIT EARS

For this activity, the children will need small, six-inch, white paper plates, small craft sticks, yarn, pipe cleaners, crayons, and markers.

▶ Help the children cut two ear holes about an inch from one edge of a paper plate.

▶ The children will put their index and middle fingers through these holes to be the rabbit's ears.

▶ Ask the children to draw a rabbit face on one side of the plate. Yarn or pipe cleaners can be used for whiskers.

▶ At the bottom of the face on the opposite side of the plate, tape or glue the craft stick so that it projects down far enough to serve as a handle.

▶ The children may want to make more than one rabbit puppet, so have plenty of plates and sticks available.

▶ By holding the handle with one hand and using the two fingers of the other hand as wiggly ears, the puppets are ready for lots of imaginative play.

MUSIC

SONG: "I Have Two Ears" by Jo Eklof

I have two ears to hear, hear, hear. I have a brain to think. I have two eyes to look, look, look. I have two lids to blink. I have a nose to sniff, sniff, sniff. I have some hands to touch. I have a mouth to give a smile and say, "I love you so much!

(See page 302 for enlargement.)

TEACHER'S TURN

- Put a box of musical instruments in the center of the circle.

- Explain to the children that you are going to close your eyes while each child selects an instrument from the box.

- The children put their instruments behind their backs.

- Your eyes stay closed while one child plays an instrument and you try to guess which instrument it is.

- After the instrument is played and you guess, then open your eyes. Were you right or wrong? It is important for you to guess wrong some of the time.

- Continue playing until all of the children have had a turn.

LISTEN!

After reading Martin and Archambault's book *Listen to the Rain,* listed in the Children's Books section of this theme, give each child a musical instrument to play.

- Some of the instruments can be ones the children made (see Theme 6, Music section). Others can be pots, pans, wooden spoons, maracas, rain sticks, cymbals, triangles, tambourines, and drums.

- Ask the children to listen to the book again and add the musical sounds to match the sound of the rain. An example of the delightful language of the book follows:

> Listen to the rain,
> the whisper of the rain,
> the slow soft sprinkle,
> the drip-drop tinkle.
> . . . the lightning-flashing,
> thunder-crashing,
> sounding pounding roaring rain.

- For follow-up activities, older children can write their own poems about rain or take the poems they created in Theme 7 and add musical sounds.

- Endicott's imaginative illustrations in *Listen to the Rain* may stimulate the children to create their own drawings for their poems.

MOVEMENT

FREEZE

This game is easy for children to understand. It helps them develop bodily control and balance and can be done either indoors or outdoors.

- Have the children evenly scattered in a large play area with their personal space clearly defined.

- Tell the children that when you say "go," they are to move around easily and flowingly, as though they are floating through the air or water.

- Encourage the children to let their head, arms, hands, and legs move loosely "every which way."

- Then, tell the children that when you say "freeze," they are to follow directions and "freeze" in whatever position they are in at that moment.

- Children are to stay motionless until you say "unfreeze." Then, they are to resume moving around.

- Do this "freeze" and "unfreeze" three or four times. Let the children take turns being the one to say "freeze" and "unfreeze."

- To make this activity successful, the children should be careful not to bump into each other and to avoid moving so fast that they lose their balance and fall.

GO IN AND OUT THE WINDOW

This activity is designed to help children coordinate words with actions, follow oral directions, and develop spatial awareness.

Go in and out the window,
Go in and out the window,
Go in and out the window,
Hi, ho, hi, ho, hi, ho.

March in and out the window,
March in and out the window,
March in and out the window,
Hi, ho, hi, ho, hi, ho.

- Arrange the children's chairs in a circle. Leave enough "window" space between each chair for the children to pass through.

- When children sing the traditional song "Go In and Out the Window," they move through the circle of chairs.

▶ Moving into the circle of chairs, children are moving "in the window." Moving out of the circle, they are moving "out the window." The children weave in and out of the circle all in the same direction. You may want to lead the line the first time the song is sung.

▶ Change the words and the movement by marching or tiptoeing, or in other ways the children think of.

SENSORY ART

INFANT WIND CHIME

▶ Collect lightweight items, such as foil pie tins, metal lids from jars, chimes, and anything else that will make fascinating sounds when the wind blows.

▶ Make sure items are safe and will not scratch or cut children's fingers when touched.

▶ Tie items with strings or yarn to a tree limb or clothing hangers so that the wind can move them.

▶ Carry the infants to the wind chime to listen to the sounds it makes.

▶ Talk about the sounds.

▶ Let the babies touch the safe chime pieces if they want to do so.

POPPING BUBBLE PRINTS

▶ Prepare a solution of equal parts water and dish detergent. Put the liquid in several small containers.

▶ Add food coloring or tempera to create desired colors.

▶ Put the containers in a pan.

▶ Have the children blow with a straw into the container until bubbles reach the top. To prevent the children from "drinking" the solution, cut a little hole near the top of each straw.

▶ Make a print by lightly touching plain or manila construction paper to the bubbles. The bubbles will stick to the paper, then pop! This will leave a colorful imprint on the paper.

▶ Let the paper dry.

▶ This is a special way to create class stationery, gift wrap, or unusual art prints.

CREATIVE FOOD EXPERIENCES

CRUNCHY SALAD

You will need the following:

2 carrots	1 teaspoon lemon juice
1 stalk of celery	1/4 teaspoon salt (optional)
2 apples	1/2 cup yogurt or sour cream
1/2 cup raisins	lettuce

1. Wash hands.
2. Wash carrots, celery, and apples.
3. Cut off ends of carrots, peel, then grate. Put in large mixing bowl.
4. Cut out core of apples, and cut the apples into small, bite-size pieces. Add to the mixing bowl.
5. Cut celery into small pieces and put in bowl.
6. Add raisins.
7. Sprinkle with lemon juice and salt.
8. Stir in yogurt or sour cream.
9. Precut all of the ingredients for younger children. They can help you mix the salad.

CRUNCHY SALAD

Wash hands.

Wash 2 carrots, 1 stalk celery, and 2 apples.

Cut off ends of carrots, peel, then grate.

Put in large mixing bowl. Cut out apple cores.

Cut the apples and celery into small bite-size pieces

and add to the mixing bowl. Add 1/2 cup raisins.

Sprinkle with lemon juice and salt.

Stir in 1/2 cup yogurt or sour cream. Mix and eat!

CRUNCHY GRANOLA

You will need the following:

> 1/2 cup chopped unsalted peanuts (the more nuts you add, the crunchier the granola gets)
>
> 1/4 cup hulled sunflower seeds
>
> 1/2 cup coconut
>
> 1/2 cup chopped dried fruit (the more fruit you add, the chewier the granola gets)
>
> 1 teaspoon cinnamon
>
> 1/4 teaspoon nutmeg
>
> 1/2 cup honey (the more honey you add, the sweeter the granola gets)

1. Wash hands.
2. Mix all of the dry ingredients with the honey.
3. Store in an airtight container.

This recipe serves enough for a group of eight children to have one-half cup per child. Omit peanuts for children who are allergic to them.

MATH

ONE-BEAT, TWO-BEAT, THREE-BEAT RHYTHM

This activity helps develop an awareness of sound patterns in mathematical terms.

▶ Give each child a rhythm stick. To make a sound, have the child strike a solid object, such as a box, the table, or the floor.

▶ You also should have a rhythm stick to lead children. Ask them to follow what you do.

▶ First, start a one-beat rhythm, counting "one" on each beat: one–pause/one–pause/one–pause/one, and so on. Stop.

▶ Second, do a two-beat rhythm: one–two–long pause/one–two–long pause/one–two–long pause, and so on. Stop.

▶ Third, do a three-beat rhythm: one–two–three–pause/one–two–three–pause/one–two–three–pause, and so on. Stop.

▶ Fourth, do a four-beat rhythm with no pauses: one–two–three–four/one–two–three–four/one–two–three–four, and so on. Stop.

▶ Then, ask one child to volunteer to lead the group doing the one-beat rhythm, after first reviewing it.

▶ Next, have another child lead the two-beat rhythm, a third child lead the three-beat rhythm, and a fourth lead the four-beat rhythm.

SCIENCE

MATCH THE SOUNDS

▶ Collect small, plastic, 35 mm. film containers.

▶ Divide the film containers into pairs. Partly fill one pair with birdseed. Replace the cap.

▶ Continue this process using dried beans, salt, rice, coffee grounds, medium-size screws, metal washers, paper clips, and macaroni.

▶ Be sure that each set of containers sounds the same when shaken.

▶ Put all of the containers together.

▶ Have the children, one at a time, pick up and shake the containers until they have found a pair that makes a sound match.

▶ This activity sometimes works better in small groups.

▶ For younger children, start with fewer pairs of containers.

▶ The children will want to see what is making the sounds inside of the containers. Closely supervise the younger children while they explore.

BOTTLE SOUNDS

▶ Save five glass bottles that are all the same. Wash them thoroughly. Drinking glasses may be used instead of bottles. They will make different sounds.

▶ Put a few drops of food coloring into a pitcher of water.

▶ Pour different amounts of the water into the bottles.

▶ To get a good range of notes, vary the amount of water in each bottle.

▶ Put the bottles on a table in a row.

▶ Let the children, one at a time, tap each bottle gently above the water line with a spoon or wooden stick. This will create different musical sounds.

▶ Guide the children into sequencing the sounds from lowest to highest.

Note: When the children strike the bottles or glasses, the glass and the air will vibrate. It is the vibration that the children will hear. The different amounts of water combined with the vibration produce the musical sounds of different pitches.

SOCIAL STUDIES

FIELD TRIP

Children enjoy taking field trips. Visit a neighborhood ear, nose, and throat doctor (otolaryngologist) or an audiologist. If a field trip is not possible, ask a doctor, an audiologist, or a nurse to visit the class.

▶ Ask the professional to show the children a plastic ear and explain the parts of the ear.

▶ Using the ear model, have the doctor demonstrate what is done during an ear examination, and talk to the children about hearing safety.

▶ Follow up in the classroom by having the children write a thank-you note to the doctor or audiologist. They can draw pictures too.

▶ Put a copy of the note and the drawings on the bulletin board.

WHISPER GAME

This game is designed to show older children that what they think they hear is not necessarily what someone has said.

▶ Have the children sit in a circle. This works better if there are at least six to eight children playing.

▶ To get children started, whisper a statement into one child's ear, such as, "I have a brown dog that has a white spot on his back, but my kitty is black and has white fur on her paws."

▶ Tell the child to whisper the same words into the ear of the child to the left, and for this child to pass on the message exactly as he heard it to the next child on his left.

▶ This continues until all of the children have done so. The exception will be the last child, who will tell aloud to the whole group what he heard.

▶ Next, say exactly what you said to begin the game.

▶ Usually the message gets jumbled in the telling and hardly resembles the original statement.

▶ Explain to the children that this is how false things are said about people. What is said can even be hurtful and dangerous.

▶ Remind children that it is important to listen carefully and to be sure that they understand what someone says before repeating her or his words to others.

THE ABCs OF SIGN LANGUAGE

▶ Introduce the children to sign language. Explain that it is a special language for people who cannot hear the spoken word.

▶ Sesame Street's book, *Sign Language ABC with Linda Bove,* listed in the Children's Books section of this theme, is one way to acquaint the children with sign language for the deaf.

▶ Ask someone from the local Association for the Deaf or the American Speech-Language-Hearing Association to visit your classroom and share American Sign Language (ASL) with the children. Perhaps a relative of a child in the class knows ASL and will come to visit.

CHILDREN'S BOOKS

Berger, Melvin. (1994). *All About Sounds.* New York: Scholastic.

Brown, Craig. (1992). *City Sounds.* New York: Greenwillow.

Carle, Eric. (1997). *The Very Quiet Cricket.* (Board Book). New York: Putnam.

Cousins, Lucy. (1997). *What Can Pinky Hear?: A Lift-the-Flap-Book.* Cambridge, MA: Candlewick Press.

De Zutter, Hank. (1993). *Who Says a Dog Goes Bow-Wow?* Illustrated by Suse MacDonald. New York: Bantam Doubleday Dell Books for Young Readers.

Dr. Seuss. (1995). *Learn about the Sound of B and Other Stuff.* New York: Random House.

Dr. Seuss. (1987). *Horton Hears a Who.* New York: Random House.

Dr. Seuss (pseud. for Theodor Geisel). (1968). *The Ear Book.* New York: Random House.

Lawrence, John. (2002). *This Little Chick.* Cambridge, MA: Candlewick Press.

Martin, Bill Jr. (1997). *Polar Bear, Polar Bear, What Do You Hear?* (Board Book). Illustrated by Eric Carle. New York: Henry Holt.

Martin, Bill Jr., and John Archambault. (1987). *Listen to the Rain.* Illustrated by James Endicott. New York: Henry Holt.

Miller, Margaret. (1994). *My Five Senses.* New York: Simon & Schuster.

Moncure, Jane B. (1982). *Sounds All Around.* San Francisco: Children's Press.

Oxenbury, Helen. (1995). *I Hear.* Cambridge, MA: Candlewick Press.

Palmer, Hap. (1991). *Homemade Band.* New York: Crown.

Pettigrew, Mark. (1987). *Music and Sound.* New York: Gloucester.

Sesame Street. (1985). *Sign Language ABC with Linda Bove.* New York: Random House/Children's Television Workshop.

Showers, Paul. (1991). *The Listening Walk.* New York: HarperCollins.

Showers, Paul. (1990). *Ears Are for Hearing.* New York: HarperCollins.

Van Kampen, Vlasta. (1990). *Orchestranimals.* New York: Scholastic.

Wells, Rosemary. (1994). *The Night Sounds, Morning Colors.* New York: Dial Books.

Family Letter (Preschool)

Dear Family,

We are continuing to study the five senses. Our theme is "Hearing." We will provide opportunities for the children to learn the following:

- How the five senses are used.
- The ears are the part of the body used to hear.
- We listen to hear many sounds and find out many things.
- We should take good care of our ears.
- Some people cannot hear at all or cannot hear well.

We will be talking about the following:

- our ears
- what hearing helps us do
- how we take care of our ears
- the sounds we hear in our world

Some things to do at home with your preschool child include:

- Play music at home. Share all types of music with your child.
- Read books with your child. Use different voices for the characters.
- Talk about and listen to the sounds you hear every day.

Family participation opportunities for you at school will include:

- Help us make a crunchy salad.
  Date _____   Time _____
- Go with us on our field trip to the ear, nose, and throat doctor or audiologist.
  Date _____   Time _____
- If you know of anyone who could introduce the children to American Sign Language (ASL), please tell us about him or her.

Our wish list for this theme includes:

drinking straws
35 mm. film containers
foil pie tins
metal lids from jars

Thanks!

THEME GOALS

To provide opportunities for children to learn the following:

▶ How the five senses work together.

▶ The tongue is the part of the body used to taste.

▶ The parts of the tongue called "taste buds" are used for tasting sweet, sour, salty, and bitter.

▶ The sense of taste and the sense of smell work together.

▶ We should take care of our mouth, teeth, and tongue.

Children-Created Bulletin Board

This bulletin board is a continuation of the interactive ones in Theme 7, "Seeing," and Theme 8, "Hearing."

▶ Add an open mouth with tongue and teeth to the bottom center of the bulletin board. Leave the eyes and ears already in place.

▶ Add the words "Let's Taste."

▶ Divide the bulletin board into four areas with the words "sweet," "salty," "sour," and "bitter" above the four spaces.

▶ The children add pictures and words of what they taste in the appropriate parts of the bulletin board.

▶ More items can be added as the children become involved with activities relating to this theme.

VOCABULARY STARTERS

Let the children add words.

dental — anything having to do with the teeth.

flavor — the special taste that something has.

taste — the ability to tell the flavors of what we eat.

taste buds — the places on the tongue that help us taste things.

tongue — the movable muscle inside of the mouth that helps us taste and swallow.

LANGUAGE EXPERIENCES

EXPLORE FAVORITE FOODS

Older infants and toddlers have limited experience with foods. Select one fruit or vegetable each week, and explore it thoroughly.

▶ Let families know what foods you will be tasting.

▶ For example, let the children look at a tomato, hold it, smell it, and taste it.

▶ Some of the tomatoes may get "squashed" during this process, so have plenty available to share.

▶ Repeat the name of the fruit or vegetable often so children see the food and hear the correct name at the same time.

▶ Follow up with picture books about fruits and vegetables and pictures placed at children's eye level.

POEM: "I Eat My Peas"

I eat my peas with honey
Every day at noon.
It makes the peas taste funny,
But it keeps them on the spoon.

THE VERY HUNGRY CATERPILLAR

▶ Read Carle's *The Very Hungry Caterpillar* to the children. See the Children's Books section of this theme.

▶ Ask the children to name what they would have eaten if they were very hungry caterpillars.

▶ Write the foods selected on a chart and put it in the art center for the children to refer to later.

▶ Encourage the children to draw the foods they selected, and write the food names on their illustrations.

▶ These pictures can be added to the bulletin board. Some of the children may be creative and cut holes in their pictures, just as Carle did.

▶ As an extension of this activity, select four or five of the children's favorite foods, and have them available for a snack. If possible, select only fruits and vegetables, such as the ones the hungry caterpillar ate.

▶ Ask the children to describe in words which flavors the foods have.

▶ Refer to Theme 23, "Insects and Spiders," for other activities relating to the caterpillar and its metamorphosis into a butterfly.

DRAMATIC PLAY

THE GINGERBREAD MAN

▶ Read *The Gingerbread Man* to the children. Three separate books with different styles of illustration are listed in the Children's Books section of this theme.

▶ Next, ask the children to act out the story. They can take turns being the different characters.

▶ As an extension, ask the children to think of other endings for this folktale.

▶ Doing this type of activity helps children with sequencing, recall, and socialization, and it stimulates imagination and creativity.

▶ Later, make gingerbread children. The recipe is in the Creative Food Experiences section of this theme.

PANCAKES

▶ Read Carle's *Pancakes, Pancakes* or dePaola's *Pancakes for Breakfast* to the children (see the Children's Books section of this theme).

- With older children, ask them to retell the story without using the book.

- Have available some of the items mentioned in the story as props to help with the dramatization.

- Some children may want to act out the story with or without words, while others may want to orally retell the story.

- Make the book available if children cannot remember all of the story.

PUPPET PLAY

GINGERBREAD CHILDREN STICK PUPPETS

This activity relates to the cooking one in this theme.

- The children can further develop Egielski's *The Gingerbread Boy* story by making stick puppets. Theme 1 contains suggestions for patterns.

- Use construction paper reinforced with cardboard or tagboard to make the puppet.

- Have available many colors of construction paper for the children. Some may want to have colorful puppet children.

- Fasten the puppet to a craft stick or dowel rod.

- For younger children, cut smaller child shapes, and attach a straw or small craft stick.

- -

I LIKE SPAGHETTI!

This activity encourages children to think creatively.

PULL

- Put paper plates, markers, crayons, scissors, hole punchers, yarn, glue, and construction paper scraps on a table.

- Talk about making paper plate puppets.

- Ask the children to make a puppet that likes to eat.

- Accept whatever the children make.

- If some children have difficulty getting started, ask open-ended questions to guide them, such as: "What could you do with this paper plate to make it into a face?" "What could you do to show that this puppet likes to eat?" "What about spaghetti?" "What could you do to this paper plate puppet to make it eat spaghetti?"

- Perhaps one or more children will get the idea to make a hole in the puppet's mouth and use yarn for spaghetti. Knot the yarn on the ends so the "spaghetti" will not pull out of the mouth.

- The children also will come up with many other imaginative ways to show how their puppets can "eat."

- For younger children, make a puppet and have them make the puppet "eat spaghetti."

MUSIC

WHAT'S IN THE BOWL?

- Guide the children to sit in a circle.

- Sing the following song to the tune of "Farmer in the Dell."

Jello in the bowl, jello in the bowl,
Jiggle, joggle, wiggle, woggle,
Jello in the bowl.
  Popcorn in the bowl, popcorn in the bowl,
  Pop, pop, pop-pop-pop,
  Popcorn in the bowl.
Mix pancakes in the bowl, mix pancakes in the bowl,
Stir, stir, fast and slow,
Mix pancakes in the bowl.
  Soup in the bowl, soup in the bowl,
  Splish, splash, swish, swash,
  Soup in the bowl.

- It is fun for the children to "jiggle like jello," "pop like popcorn," "stir fast and slow," and "splish like soup."

- Let the children help you make up more verses.

"COOKIES IN THE OVEN"

This song can be sung and acted out by the children. Older children can be divided into groups, with each group singing a different verse or line in each verse. Sing the song to the tune of "Skip to My Lou."

What do I smell? Sniff–sniff–sniff.
What do I smell? Sniff–sniff–sniff.
What do I smell? Sniff–sniff–sniff.
What do I smell with my nose-y.
　It is cookies in the oven. Yum–yum–yum.
　It is cookies in the oven. Yum–yum–yum.
　It is cookies in the oven. Yum–yum–yum.
　That's what I smell with my nose-y.
Open the oven – put them out to cool.
Open the oven – put them out to cool.
Open the oven – put them out to cool.
Then I can eat my cookies.
　Eat my cookies. Chew–chew–chew.
　Eat my cookies. Chew–chew–chew.
　Eat my cookies. Chew–chew–chew.
　I love to eat my cookies!

Philip Jackman

MOVEMENT

TOOTH TOSS

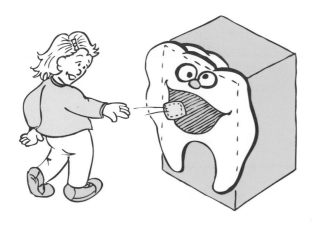

▶ Draw a happy tooth on the side of a sturdy box.

▶ Cut a hole in the smiley mouth large enough for a beanbag to go through.

▶ Have available beanbags of all shapes, sizes, textures, and colors. Every beanbag should be different so each child can recognize her own.

▶ Toddlers can get close to the box to throw their beanbags into the smiley mouth.

▶ Older children enjoy helping you make up rules for the Tooth Toss game. For example, the children who brush their teeth each morning get to toss the beanbag three times for each turn.

DENTAL FLOSS

▶ Have the children divide into two equal groups.

▶ Ask each group to choose a leader and to form a line behind the leader.

▶ Give children a jump rope, a piece of clothesline, or a length of garden hose long enough for one group of children to hold one end, while the other group holds the other end.

▶ This is a cooperative game. Have the rope represent dental floss. The children work together to wipe out germs and tartar by pulling the rope back and forth, like flossing.

SENSORY ART

EGG CARTON FLOSS

This is a fun way to teach young children about dental hygiene.

▶ Cut the bottom of an empty egg carton into three pieces. Discard the top of the carton.

▶ Put the three pieces with white yarn and scissors on a table.

▶ Guide two or three children at a time into cutting a long piece of white yarn to be used as "floss."

▶ Turn the carton pieces over so that the bottom will be face up. These will become pretend teeth.

▶ Help the children wrap the yarn around their fingers as they start to "floss."

▶ Leave the egg cartons and yarn in the manipulative center so that the children can "floss" when they choose to do so.

PEANUT SHELL COLLAGE

This project can connect to several activity areas.

▶ Buy some peanuts in the shell from a grocery or farmers' market.

▶ For a snack, have the children take the peanuts out of the shells, save the shells, and eat the peanuts. This is an interesting small muscle activity too. (Have another snack available for children who are allergic to peanuts.)

▶ Put the peanut shells in a basket or bucket, and make them available in the art center with construction paper, glue, and scissors.

▶ The children can draw and cut out peanut shapes or make any design they wish.

▶ Children then glue the peanut shells onto their drawings.

▶ Add children's finished peanut creations to the bulletin board.

CREATIVE FOOD EXPERIENCES

PEANUT BUTTER BALLS*

You will need the following:

    1/2 cup peanut butter
    1/2 cup nonfat dry milk
    1/2 cup honey

1. Wash hands.
2. With the children's help, measure and put all ingredients in a big bowl. Stir ingredients together.
3. Give each child a portion.
4. Squeeze and pull until the mixture is shiny and soft. (The children love to do this.)
5. Roll into small balls.
6. Identify each child's peanut butter ball with a name label attached to a toothpick inserted in the ball.
7. Place on waxed paper, and refrigerate one hour or longer, until firm.
8. Eat and enjoy!

PEANUT BUTTER BALLS

Wash hands.

Measure 1/2 cup peanut butter.

1/2 cup nonfat dry milk,

and 1/2 cup honey.

Put all ingredients in a big bowl and stir together.

Squeeze and pull until it is shiny and soft.

Roll into small balls and place on wax paper.

Put in the refrigerator.

Wait 1 hour or more until they are firm.

Then, EAT AND ENJOY!

*Substitute another recipe for children who are allergic to peanut butter.

PANCAKES

▶ Read dePaola's *Pancakes for Breakfast,* Numeroff's *If You Give a Pig a Pancake,* or Carle's *Pancakes, Pancakes,* all listed in the Children's Books section of this theme.

▶ Make pancakes with the children for a morning snack. This is easier to do if you use an electric skillet. Follow the directions on a box of prepared pancake mix.

GINGERBREAD CHILDREN

You will need the following:

    5 cups flour
    1 1/2 teaspoons baking soda
    1/2 teaspoon salt
    2 teaspoons ginger
    1 teaspoon cinnamon
    1 teaspoon ground cloves
    1 cup shortening
    1 cup sugar
    1 egg
    1 cup molasses
    2 teaspoons vinegar

1. Wash hands.
2. With the children's help, sift dry ingredients together.
3. Cream shortening and sugar.
4. Stir in egg, molasses, and vinegar. Beat well.
5. Stir in sifted dry ingredients, mixing well.
6. Chill.
7. Roll in pecan-size balls.
8. On an individual piece of waxed paper, have each child put three balls of dough to use for making the gingerbread child. Each child can make an original design.
9. For younger children, use a cookie cutter or help them flatten one ball with a thumb to make the head, roll one into a rope for arms, and roll and curve the other to form legs.
10. Use raisins or red candies for eyes and buttons.
11. Bake in a 350-degree oven for 10 to 12 minutes.
12. For an extra touch, when cookies are cooled, paint a smile on each face. Use a mixture of powdered sugar and milk for icing, and apply with a tooth-pick.
13. Mark each child's name on a chart to match the placement on the cookie sheet(s). This way each child will be sure to get her own.
14. If you are limited in time, use a box of gingerbread mix. The children can still make gingerbread children or shapes with the prepared mix.

MATH

SHARE A PIZZA

This activity can help children learn the concept of how a whole can be divided into halves, fourths, and eighths.

▶ Prior to the activity, create two or more sets of nine-inch plates and plate segments. Each set consists of four *paper* plates: one is left whole, one is cut into two halves, one is cut into four quarters, and one is cut into eight eighths.

▶ Put each set into a plastic, zip-lock bag.

▶ Encourage two children to assemble each set of parts to make three whole plates. The uncut plate is used as a model, making the activity self-correcting.

▶ Have children count the number of parts in each assembled plate.

▶ Younger children like working the puzzle. Older children can comprehend the concept of halves, quarters, and eighths.

▶ Soon after they finish the activity, provide children with one or more nine-inch pizzas, enough to divide up to feed to the entire group.

▶ Ask children's help to problem solve: how should the pizzas be divided to provide enough equal-size pieces to feed the whole class? Then enjoy the pizza!

SCIENCE

TASTING TRAYS

▶ Prepare several trays with various foods for the children to taste.

▶ Be sure *not* to include any foods to which children in your class are allergic.

▶ For younger children, include a few of the foods they have had before, and add one or two new ones.

▶ Introduce preschoolers to foods that are divided into the four taste groups: sweet, salty, bitter, and sour. They may need help in naming the tastes, but they can tell you when the food tastes "yucky!"

▶ School-age children can verbalize how something tastes. Ask them to predict the basic taste of each food item. Have them tell you where on the tongue they detect the different flavors.

▶ Include fresh fruits and vegetables (include radishes, turnips, and potatoes), pretzels, popcorn, potato chips, salted nuts, gumdrops, cookies, pickles, parsley, and unsweetened chocolate on the trays.

▶ Cut these tasting foods into cubes for the children to pick up with toothpicks.

▶ Have the children drink water between each taste to reduce the mixing of flavors.

▶ Prepare another tray with items that look alike, such as sugar, baking soda, baking powder, and cornstarch.

▶ Talk about how these substances look the same but are very different. Explain to children that they should never eat anything if they do not know what it is.

▶ Add a label to each one, and ask the children to taste the differences. It is fine if they do not want to taste.

▶ Extend the tasting activity to another day, and introduce the children to spices, such as cloves, cinnamon, nutmeg, ginger, paprika, and pepper. See Theme 10, "Smelling," and "Smell the Spices" for a follow-up activity.

▶ *Note:* Being able to smell what we are eating is an important part of tasting it. Have the children try closing their eyes and holding their noses while they taste an apple, a banana, or an orange. Can they tell the difference in how the food tastes?

TASTE BUDS

▶ Before introducing this concept to older children, draw a large tongue on white poster board.

▶ Draw around the **front** of the tongue with a colored marker to indicate that the taste buds here taste **sweet** tastes, such as sugar and honey.

▶ Draw around the **sides** of the tongue with a different-colored marker to show that the taste buds here taste **sour** tastes, such as lemon and vinegar.

▶ Draw around the **back** of the tongue with another color to point out that the taste buds here taste **bitter** tastes, such as grapefruit and unsweetened baking chocolate.

▶ Select still another colored marker, and make small dots **all over** the tongue to illustrate that the whole surface of the tongue can taste **salty** tastes, such as pretzels and salted nuts.

▶ Have some sweet, sour, bitter, and salty foods for the children to taste.

▶ As a follow-up activity, have the children draw a tongue on a piece of paper. Then, cut out pictures of foods from magazines, and glue them onto the appropriate taste bud areas of the tongue. Make available the drawing of the tongue used in the Taste Buds activity as a reference for the children.

SOCIAL STUDIES

BREAD, BREAD, BREAD

This activity introduces children to the concept that people all over the world eat bread, and that bread comes in all textures, shapes, sizes, and colors. For younger children, have a bread-tasting party.

▶ Morris's book, *Bread, Bread, Bread,* offers photographs from around the world that show a variety of cultures, as well as the types of bread eaten everywhere. This book is listed in the Children's Books section of this theme.

▶ Ask the children open-ended questions about the families shown in the photographs, the children's own families, what kind of bread they eat at home, and which is their favorite.

▶ Next, invite the children to the snack table to have a "tasting party" of different kinds of bread. Have several uncut loaves so the children can cut slices with your supervision.

▶ Also provide blunt table knives, soft margarine, jellies, and jams.

▶ Talk about which breads taste the same and which taste different. Which ones are new to the children?

▶ Follow up with cooking activities, such as baking corn bread or tortillas.

▶ Take a field trip to a bakery or bagel shop.

CHILDREN'S BOOKS

Aylesworth, Jim. (1998). *The Gingerbread Man.* Illustrated by Barbara McClintock. New York: Scholastic.

Carle, Eric. (1994). *The Very Hungry Caterpillar.* (Board Book). New York: Philomel Books.

Carle, Eric. (1992). *Pancakes, Pancakes.* New York: Scholastic.

Collins, Ross. (2000). *Alvie Eats Soup.* New York: Arthur A. Levine.

Cooke, Trish. (2003). *Full, Full, Full of Love.* Illustrated by Paul Howard. Cambridge, MA: Candlewick Press.

dePaola, Tomie. (1990). *Pancakes for Breakfast.* San Diego: Harcourt.

Egielski, Richard. (1997). *The Gingerbread Boy.* New York: HarperCollins Juvenile.

Ehlert, Lois. (1994). *Eating the Alphabet: Fruits and Vegetables from A to Z.* San Diego: Harcourt.

Gershator, David. (1998). *Bread Is for Eating.* New York: Henry Holt.

Hartley, Karen, and Chris Macro. (2000). *Tasting in Living Things.* Illustrated by Alan Fraser. Des Plaines, IL: Heinemann.

Helmer, Diane Star. (2003). *The Cat Who Came for Tacos.* Illustrated by Vivi Escriva. Morton Grove, IL: Albert Whitman.

Lin, Grace. (2001). *Dim Sum for Everyone.* New York: Knopf.

McCloskey, Robert. (1987). *Blueberries for Sal.* New York: Viking Press.

McMillan, Bruce. (1991). *Eating Fractions.* New York: Scholastic.

Morris, Ann. (1993). *Bread, Bread, Bread.* Photographs by Ken Heyman. New York: Mulberry.

Numeroff, Laura J. (1998). *If You Give a Pig a Pancake.* Illustrated by Felicia Bond. New York: HarperCollins.

Numeroff, Laura J. (1997). *If You Give a Mouse a Cookie.* Illustrated by Felicia Bond. New York: HarperTrophy.

Numeroff, Laura J. (1991). *If You Give a Moose a Muffin.* Illustrated by Felicia Bond. New York: HarperCollins.

Pallotta, Jerry. (1995). *The Spice Alphabet Book: Herbs, Spices, and Other Natural Flavors.* Watertown, MA: Charlesbridge Publishing.

Schmidt, Karen. (1986). *The Gingerbread Man.* New York: Scholastic.

Suhr, Mandy. (1994). *Taste.* Illustrated by Mike Gordon. Minneapolis, MN: Carolrhoda Books.

Westcott, Nadine B. (1992). *Peanut Butter and Jelly: A Play Rhyme.* New York: E. P. Dutton.

Family Letter (Primary grade)

Dear Family,

As we continue to focus on the five senses, we are beginning the theme "Tasting." We will provide opportunities for the children to learn the following:

- How the five senses work together.
- The tongue is the part of the body used to taste.
- Parts of the tongue, called "taste buds," are used for tasting sweet, sour, salty, and bitter.
- The sense of taste and the sense of smell work together.
- We should take care of our mouth, teeth, and tongue.

We will be talking about the following:

- our mouth, taste buds, teeth, gums, and lips
- what tasting helps us do
- how we take care of our mouth
- what we taste

Things to do at home with your child include:

- Conduct taste tests with your child using different healthy snacks. Ask your child to tell you where on the tongue each item is tasted.
- Bake gingerbread, and make pancakes with your child.
- Let your child buy the next loaf of bread when you go grocery shopping.

Family participation opportunities at school include:

- Help us make beanbags. Stop by any time, and pick up the materials.
- Come to our tasting party. Bring any favorite family food (enough for all of the children to taste).
  Date _____   Time _____

Our wish list for this theme includes:

peanut shells

pieces of cardboard and tagboard

paper plates

yarn

Thanks!

THEME GOALS

To provide opportunities for children to learn the following:

▶ How the five senses bring us information about our world.

▶ The nose is the part of the body used to smell.

▶ The sense of smell helps us find out about odors and enjoy food and drink, and it warns us of danger.

▶ We should take care of our noses.

▶ Some people do not have a strong sense of smell or sense of taste.

Children-Created Bulletin Board

This bulletin board builds on the interactive discovery board introduced in Theme 7, "Seeing," Theme 8, "Hearing," and Theme 9, "Tasting."

▶ Add a nose to the middle of the bulletin board with the words "What's That Smell?" Leave the eyes, ears, and mouth already in place.

▶ Add pieces of fabric or cotton balls scented with various fragrances and spices. This adds an interesting smell to the classroom.

▶ Add more items as the children become involved with activities related to this theme.

VOCABULARY STARTERS

Let the children add words.

nose — a part of the body we use to breathe and smell.

nostrils — two holes that let air in and out of the nose.

odor — what makes one thing smell different from any other.

smell — to be able to notice odors with the nose.

sniff — to take air up into your nose so that you can smell something.

LANGUAGE EXPERIENCES

FOOD SMELLS GOOD

For younger children, provide words that go with the smells.

▶ Introduce one food a day.

▶ Have the children smell the food before they taste it. This helps them connect smell and taste in a concrete way.

▶ Talk about what the children smell.

▶ Start first with foods that are familiar to the children, such as bananas, peanut butter, and chocolate pudding.

▶ Later in the day, read a book or show the children pictures representing the food they ate earlier.

POEM: "My Favorite Smells"

Chocolate chip cookies baking,
Mommy's perfume,
Pizza!
Daddy's shaving cream,
Fried chicken!
Pine trees,
Fresh popped corn!
If you ask me, then I will tell
The favorite things my nose likes to smell.

▶ Continue with the children relating their favorite things to smell.

POPCORN, WE LOVE POPCORN

This activity furthers the children's awareness of the five senses and how they are related to each other. It also introduces new vocabulary words.

▶ Have the children wash their hands.

▶ Place unpopped corn in a bowl, and pass it around so that the children can select two or three kernels each.

▶ Ask open-ended questions, such as: "How does the unpopped corn look?" "How does the unpopped corn feel?" "Do the kernels have any smell?"

▶ Throw away the unpopped corn that the children have handled.

▶ With a popcorn popper (placed away from the children), begin popping the untouched kernels.

▶ Talk about what sounds the children hear. Ask them to make the sounds. Start with one child, then continue to add the sounds until you have a "popcorn chorus."

▶ Serve each child an individual portion of popped corn.

▶ While they are eating, have the children describe how the popcorn tastes.

▶ Continue asking questions while the children are finishing. "What did you learn about popcorn?" "What part of our body helped us know what it looked like before it was popped?" "What part of our body helped us know how the popcorn smells?" "What part of our body helped us know how the popcorn tastes?" "What part of our body helped us hear the corn popping?"

▶ This type of questioning helps children develop skills, such as sequencing, recall, processing, and language acquisition.

DRAMATIC PLAY

IT'S A BAKERY!

▶ Turn the dramatic play/home living area into a bakery.

▶ Divide the space into two parts.

▶ The front part should be the counter where "baked goods" are displayed and sold.

- The children can make scented play dough or clay cookies, cakes, and breads. See Theme 6 and the Sensory Art section of this theme for play dough recipes.

- Add a cash register, telephone, order pads, pencils, play money, bags, and boxes.

- Have the children make signs showing how much the bakery items cost.

- Next, make the other part of the area into the "kitchen" of the bakery.

- Put bowls, cutting boards, rolling pins, cookie cutters, cookie sheets, candy molds, cookbooks, aprons, hairnets, a broom, and a dustpan in the back part of the bakery.

- Have available several plastic tubs with warm water and paper towels for the children.

- This is usually a favorite dramatic play area.

PUPPET PLAY

PAPER SACK PUPPET FACE

- Put out lunch-size paper sacks, old magazines, catalogs, glue, markers, crayons, yarn, construction paper, and fabric scraps for the children to use.

- Encourage the children to cut out noses, eyes, ears, and mouths from pictures in the magazines.

- Guide the children into gluing the parts of a face onto the sack to make their puppets.

- Once the children see how they can make funny faces on their paper sack puppets, they may want to make more than one.

- As long as the children are interested, give them plenty of time to create.

- Older children may add yarn hair, fabric clothes, and construction paper arms, hands, and legs to complete their puppets.

MUSIC

POP GOES THE POPCORN

- The children form a circle. They are "unpopped corn."

- One child stands in the middle with arms outstretched. He is the "popcorn machine."

- As they start singing the song, the children start walking in one direction, with the center child rotating with them.

- At the word "pop," all of the children jump and pretend to be "popcorn popping."

- Start singing again, but reverse the direction.

- Then change direction again for the third verse of the song.

- Sing to the tune of "Pop Goes the Weasel."

Round and round the popcorn machine
The popcorn tumbles and tumbles,
But when it gets hot in the popcorn machine
POP! Goes the popcorn.
  Turn and turn the popcorn machine.
  We like to hear it popping.
  So let's make more in the popcorn machine,
  Pop! Goes the popcorn.
Circle and circle the popcorn machine,
It is fun to pop the kernels.
Let's try once more with the popcorn machine,
POP! Goes the popcorn!

MOVEMENT

LET'S PLAY!

Take this activity outdoors. Smelling the fresh air while actively playing is important for young children.

- You will need a medium-size, lightweight blanket with a hole cut in the middle and lightweight bouncing balls.
- Be sure to have enough balls for each child.
- Each player places his ball on the blanket and everyone grabs and lifts the blanket with two hands.
- Then everyone starts pumping the blanket up and down to remove the balls through the hole in the middle.
- Once you get the children started, step back and watch the fun.

SENSORY ART

SMELL THE WATER

- Toddlers love water play. For a change, add different-scented extracts to the water table. Try peppermint, lemon, or almond.
- For younger toddlers, use tearless baby shampoo to bubble the water.

UNCOOKED PLAY DOUGH

You will need the following:

    1 cup flour
    1 cup salt
    1 tablespoon cooking oil
    1 cup water
    food coloring (optional)
    scented extracts

1. Wash hands.
2. Mix dry ingredients.
3. Add oil.
4. Slowly add water until the mixture sticks together but does not feel sticky. Knead the play dough well.
5. Add scented extracts, such as vanilla or peppermint.
6. Store in an airtight container.

When the children play with this play dough, it smells so good! Theme 6 contains the recipe for cooked play dough.

Make your favorite play dough recipe, and add one of the following to make it a new kind of sensory experience:

tissue paper	coffee grounds
cornmeal	rose petals
different colors of grated crayons	colored sand
grated lemon or orange rinds (smells great!)	cake decorating food colors (vivid colors)
cinnamon, vanilla, mint oils (smells great!)	

CREATIVE FOOD EXPERIENCES

BANANA CHOCOLATE SHAKE

You will need the following:

    1 cup milk
    1/2 ripe banana
    3 ice cubes
    2 tablespoons sweetened cocoa powder

1. Wash hands.
2. Place all ingredients into a blender.
3. Mix until smooth.
4. Pour into cups, and eat with a spoon.
5. Serves 2. It is easier to make small amounts at one time in the blender.

BANANA CHOCOLATE SHAKE

Wash hands.

Place 1 cup milk, 1/2 ripe banana, 3 ice cubes, and

2 tablespoons sweetened cocoa powder into

a blender and mix until smooth.

Pour into cups and eat with a spoon!

GREEN EGGS AND HAM

▶ Read Dr. Seuss's *Green Eggs and Ham.*

▶ Invite the children to imagine and describe how green eggs would smell and taste.

▶ Then you and the children can make green eggs for morning snack.

▶ In an electric skillet, scramble eggs with green food color added.

▶ Ask the children to talk about how green eggs actually smell and taste. Do they taste any different than regular scrambled eggs?

▶ Encourage the children to tell their families about this special treat. They can cook some at home too.

MATH

GRAPHING FAVORITE SMELLS

This is a good activity to do after the children have been vigorously involved in the discovery of various odors.

▶ Ask each child to tell you his two favorite smells.

▶ Write them down exactly as dictated.

▶ Then, you and the children can make a graph to show which aromas were the most popular. When sharing the graph, use math vocabulary, such as most, more, fewer, and least.

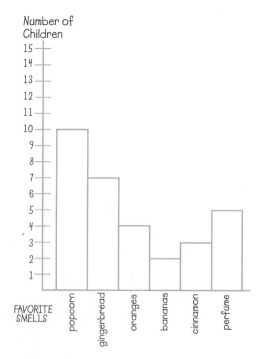

SENSORY BLOCKS

▶ Collect many different types of textures, such as lace, carpet, vinyl, terry cloth, corduroy, sandpaper, and fake fur. Many community businesses will give you odds and ends or remnants of materials.

▶ For samples that do not have a natural odor, spray with pleasant fragrances.

▶ Next, cover small boxes with these different materials. Some of the children may want to help you with this task.

▶ Put the boxes in the block center so the children can explore the smells and textures as they build with boxes and blocks.

SCIENCE

WHAT'S THAT SMELL?

Pleasant experiences are often remembered through the sense of smell. There are several ways to get the children involved in identifying odors. One is to make smell bottles.

▶ Accumulate small, clear jars, such as baby food jars. Remove the labels, and wash thoroughly.

▶ Put a cotton ball scented with a few drops of extract in each jar.

▶ For a young toddler, hold the cotton balls, one fragrance at a time, under the child's nose. Talk about the odors, and show the picture.

▶ Try punching a few holes in the tops of the jars.

▶ You also may leave the lids alone and let the children open and close them, which promotes small muscle development. Remind the children to put the lids back on the jars when they finish their turns.

▶ Suggestions for the smells include: vanilla, lemon, peppermint, almond, and butterscotch extracts; onion juice; pickle juice; vinegar; and colognes.

▶ Fruit peels, such as orange, grapefruit, and lemon, dropped into the jar, also are aromatic.

▶ Have pictures, such as of an orange, a lemon, or an onion, for younger children to match with the scents.

▶ Providing words to go with the smells is very important for toddlers.

SMELL THE SPICES

Another way to involve children in the discovery of new smells is to make spice cards. This activity works best when it is done in small groups.

▶ In the art center, put out index cards, containers of diluted white glue, small paintbrushes, and a variety of spices.

▶ The children brush glue onto the cards.

▶ Then they sprinkle one spice onto each card.

▶ Shake the excess off into a wastebasket or on a newspaper for easy cleanup.

▶ Include spices that are somewhat familiar to the children, such as ginger, cinnamon, and nutmeg.

▶ Even though garlic and salt are not spices, it is interesting for the children to discover that garlic salt has a distinctive odor, while salt has none.

OTHER SMELLS IN THE ROOM

▶ Leave out scratch-and-sniff stickers and index cards in the manipulative center for the children to explore.

▶ Additional aromas in the classroom can be provided by placing potpourri, cinnamon sticks, or cloves in baskets.

▶ Put these baskets around the room, preferably using one odor at a time.

▶ To further develop the concept of smells in the environment, bring in a vase of flowers or a potted, flowering plant. Place these in the science center.

▶ Let the children discover the flowers without you pointing them out.

SOCIAL STUDIES

LET'S GRIND CORN

Introducing children to the process of grinding corn will help connect them to other cultures. Corn is the staple of many cultures, most of which grind the kernels to produce cornmeal. The children can do the same thing in the classroom. This project can be integrated into many curriculum areas.

▶ Collect an assortment of pictures showing corn growing, being ground, and being used in cooking.

▶ Have actual ears of corn in their husks, as well as dried corn, a box of cornmeal, sifters, spoons, funnels, cups, and a *matate*, or Mexican mortar and pestle.

▶ Put the items in the discovery center, along with the pictures.

▶ Cover a table and floor with newspaper. Put the cornmeal with funnels and other utensils on the paper.

▶ Encourage a group of three or four children to practice pouring and measuring.

▶ Put the matate and dried corn on another table. Invite another three or four children to grind the corn. You may have to demonstrate the process for younger children.

▶ Let the children taste the difference between commercial cornmeal and the fresh meal. Use one box of cornmeal just for tasting.

▶ *Note:* A large, hard, flat rock, washed thoroughly, can be used as the mortar, and a smaller hard rock can be the grinding tool.

▶ Read Politi's *Three Stalks of Corn,* listed in the Children's Books section of this theme. Younger children enjoy the pictures, and older children enjoy the story as well.

▶ To further develop this idea, invite family members to cook with the children and share how they use cornmeal in their recipes. Some family members may grind their corn with a matate and offer to bring their own to share with the children.

CHILDREN'S BOOKS

Cole, Joanna. (1994). *You Can't Smell a Flower with Your Ear!: All About Your Five Senses.* Illustrated by Mavis Smith. Los Angeles: Price Stern Sloan.

dePaola, Tomie. (1989). *The Popcorn Book.* New York: Holiday House.

Dr. Seuss (pseud. for Theodor Geisel). (1960). *Green Eggs and Ham.* New York: Random House.

Fowler, Allan. (1991). *Smelling Things.* San Francisco: Children's Press.

Hartley, Karen, and Chris Macro. (2000). *Smelling in Living Things.* Des Plaines, IL: Heinemann.

Low, Alice. (1994). *The Popcorn Shop.* Illustrated by Patti Hammel. New York: Cartwheel Books.

Machotka, Hana. (1992). *Breathtaking Noses.* New York: Morrow Junior Books.

McMullan, Kate. (2000). *I Stink!* Illustrated by Jim McMullan. New York: HarperCollins.

Murphy, Mary. (1997). *You Smell: And Taste and Feel and See and Hear.* New York: DK Publishing.

Pinderhughes, John. (1997). *My Five Senses: A Shape Little Nugget Book.* New York: Golden Press.

Pinkney, Andrea. (1997). *I Smell Honey.* New York: Red Wagon.

Politi, Leo. (1994). *Three Stalks of Corn.* New York: Aladdin.

Royston, Angela. (1993). *The Senses.* (A Lift-the-Flap Body Book.) Illustrated by Edwina Riddell. New York: Barron's Juveniles.

Ruis, Maria, Jose M. Parramon, and J. J. Puig. (1985). *Smell.* New York: Barron's Juveniles.

Shappie, Trisha Lee. (1997). *Where Is Your Nose?: A Peekaboo Book with Flaps and a Mirror!* Illustrated by Judith Moffatt. New York: Cartwheel Books.

Suhr, Mandy. (1994). *Smell.* Illustrated by Mike Gordon. Minneapolis, MN: Carolrhoda Books.

Family Letter (Preschool)

Dear Family,

We are beginning our new theme, "Smelling," as we continue studying the five senses. The children will learn the following:

- How the five senses bring us information about our world.
- The nose is the part of the body used to smell.
- The sense of smell helps us find out about odors and warns us of danger.
- We should take care of our noses.
- Some people do not have a strong sense of smell or sense of taste.

We will be talking about the following:

- the nose and parts of the nose: nostrils, bridge, and tip
- what smelling helps us do
- how we take care of our nose
- what we smell

Things to do at home to reinforce your child's school activities include:

- Make popcorn.
- Let your child smell the cologne, perfume, or shaving lotion used at your house.
- Talk about the different smells while you cook.

Family participation opportunities at school include:

- Come make green eggs with us.
  Date _____   Time _____
- Come grind corn with us.
  Date _____   Time _____

Our wish list for this theme includes:

paper sacks

tissue paper

index cards

newspapers

empty, clean baby food jars

Thanks!

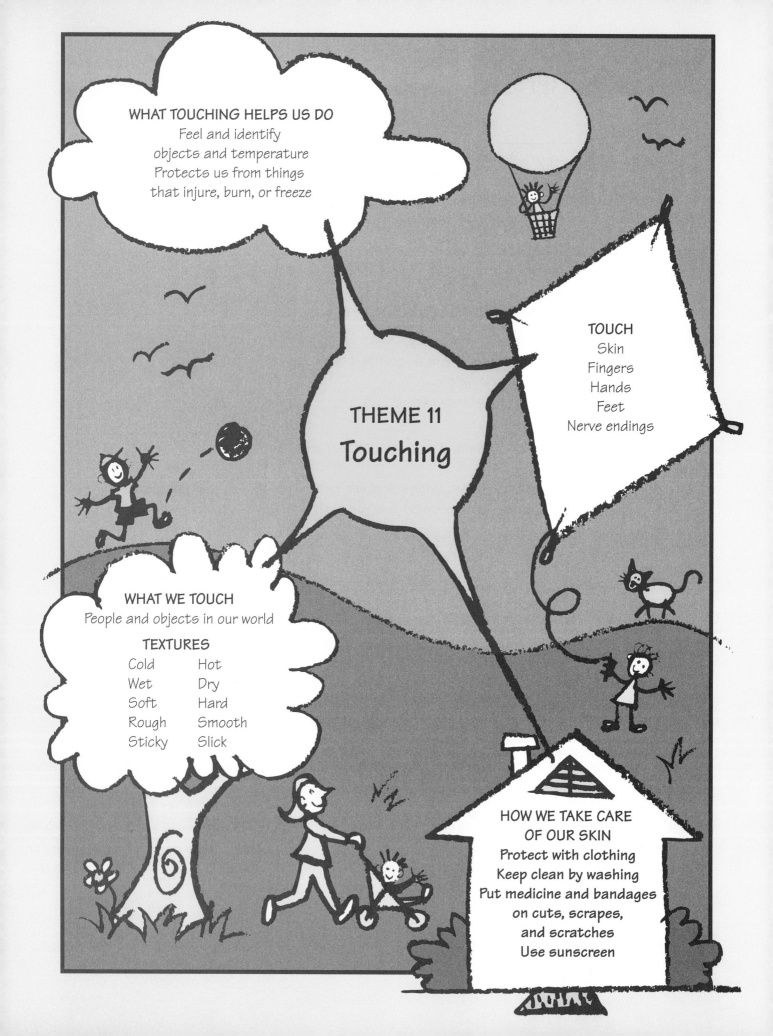

THEME GOALS

To provide opportunities for children to learn the following:

▶ How the five senses help us every day.

▶ The skin is the part of the body that gives us our sense of touch.

▶ We usually use our fingers to touch and identify things.

▶ Our skin protects us and keeps us safe by telling us when things are too hot, if we are too cold, or if we are hurt.

▶ We should take care of our skin.

Children-Created Bulletin Board

This bulletin board builds on the ones developed for the four senses presented in Themes 7, 8, 9, and 10.

▶ Add two large hands to the bulletin board. Place one on the bottom left and the other on the bottom right.

▶ Put the words "Please Touch!" on the board.

▶ Attach various textures to the burlap already in place, such as rough sandpaper, smooth plastic, sticky tape, contact paper, soft fabric and cotton balls, and small pieces of wood.

▶ Add more things as the children become involved with activities related to this theme.

VOCABULARY STARTERS

Let the children add words.

feel — to be able to notice things with our skin.

skin — the outer covering of our body.

temperature — how hot or cold something is.

texture — what the outside of something feels like.

touch — to feel things through your skin.

LANGUAGE EXPERIENCES

WORD DESCRIPTIONS

▶ Start the children thinking about the sense of touch and how to use words to describe how things feel. For example: soft like a pillow, hard like a rock, smooth like a mirror, rough like sandpaper, wet like water, dry like sand, cold like an ice cube, and hot like a bright lightbulb.

▶ Accept whatever words the children use. The objective is to get them associating words with the sense of touch.

▶ Add to this activity. Fill several large plastic tubs with cotton balls, gravel, sand, birdseed, carpet pieces, and rice.

▶ Put these tubs next to each other in a line.

▶ Have the children walk from one tub to another with their *bare feet*.

▶ If some children do not want to take off their shoes, ask if they would like to use their hands to touch instead of their feet.

▶ As they walk, ask the children to describe how each texture feels.

▶ Later, children can create pictures to further express their feelings about the experience.

BIG BOOK

This culminating activity helps the children assimilate what they have learned about their five senses. The project provides opportunities for the children to plan, reflect on, and review their learning experiences.

▶ Create a class Big Book on the senses.

▶ The children should be the decision makers regarding what goes into the book.

▶ With children's input, design a cover and a table of contents. How many pages should there be for each one of the senses? How should the children's drawings and dictated words be incorporated into the book? Should they create new content?

DRAMATIC PLAY

HOT POTATO

This game can be played inside or outdoors, with the children sitting or standing in a circle.

▶ Give children a lightweight beanbag. This can be stuffed with newspaper, small Styrofoam packing pieces, wadded balls of newspaper, or tissue paper instead of beans.

▶ Pretend the beanbag is a "hot potato."

▶ As it is passed to the children, they quickly toss it to someone else.

"PLEASE TOUCH" STORE

▶ With the children's help, make the dramatic play area a special place by putting up a sign that says "Welcome to the Touch Store! Please touch everything!"

▶ Label the areas with signs that say "Soft," "Hard," "Rough," "Smooth," "Sticky," "Prickly," and other texture words.

▶ Let the children explore the classroom. When they find something that belongs in an area of the "store," they bring it there.

▶ Be sure to have unique items placed around the room so that the children have fresh things to examine.

▶ The children may find that they need more space to expand the store. Be prepared to open the classroom even more.

PUPPET PLAY

HUMPTY DUMPTY

This puppet can be made by you and your preschoolers. Primary-grade children can make the puppets to give to the younger children to enjoy.

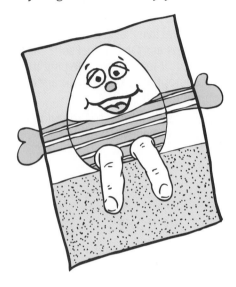

▶ Put cardboard or tagboard sheets, sandpaper, construction paper, yarn, ribbon, markers, and crayons on a table.

▶ Have the children draw an egg-shaped Humpty Dumpty sitting on a sandpaper wall.

▶ Cut two holes for the children to place two fingers in the puppet. The fingers become Humpty's legs.

▶ It is fun for the children to sing or say the nursery rhyme while playing with their puppet.

▶ Children like to place Humpty in other situations besides falling off the wall.

▶ Children may suggest making more nursery rhyme puppets. Have plenty of materials available so that they can continue to create puppets.

MUSIC

A MUSICAL GAME

The object of this activity is to encourage the children to imagine objects of different sizes, shapes, and textures, and to sing a song at the same time.

▶ Each verse of the song presented in this activity suggests picking up a different type of object.

▶ As the song is sung, the children can walk around the play area, indoors or outdoors, while picking up imaginary objects and putting them in imaginary baskets.

▶ Give toddlers actual little baskets and ask them to walk around and put things in their baskets while you sing. Put out small blocks and toys for them to pick up.

▶ The song is sung to the tune of "Paw-Paw Patch." This is a traditional song with some new words added. You may want to explain to the children that paw-paws are a small, brown, podlike fruit named by Native Americans. They do not taste very good, but early settlers in the eastern part of the United States ate them.

Let's take a walk and look around.
Let's take a walk and look around.
Let's take a walk and look around
Way down yonder in the paw-paw patch.
Picking up paw-paws, put 'em in a basket.
Picking up paw-paws, put 'em in a basket.
Picking up paw-paws, put 'em in a basket
Way down yonder in the paw-paw patch.
Find a little feather and put it in my basket.
Find a little feather and put it in my basket.
Find a little feather and put it in my basket.
Way down yonder in the paw-paw patch.
Find a wiggly worm and put it in my basket, etc.
Find a big rock and put it in my basket, etc.
Find a cute bunny and put it in my basket, etc.
Find an ice cube and put it in my basket, etc.
Find a little bug and put it in my basket, etc.

MOVEMENT

WATER PLAY RELAY

▶ Divide the children into two equal groups for this outdoor activity.

▶ Have each group form a line and stand at least six feet from the other group.

▶ Give the first child in each line a small plastic bucket full of water.

▶ At the other side of the play area, draw a line on the ground that each child must run to and cross before returning with the bucket and handing it to the next child in line.

- At a signal to start, the first child in line runs to the line and back, taking care not to spill the water. If the bucket is prematurely emptied, the game is over. Time to start a new one.

- Each returning child hands the bucket off to the next child, until all children have run with the bucket to the line and back.

- The object of the game, in addition to being the first to finish, is to try to complete it without spilling the water.

- After playing this once, the children can make up their own rules.

TEXTURE WALK

This is an extension of the Word Descriptions activity in the Language Experiences section of this theme.

- Collect all kinds of texture squares, such as carpet samples, doormats, packing materials, linoleum and wooden floor tiles, foam rubber cushions or pillows, and artificial grass.

- Take the squares and line them up to make a textured walk.

- Have the children take off their shoes and socks, and put them in their cubbies.

- The children take turns walking along the textured squares and describing what they feel with their bare feet.

- Children can walk forward, sideways, backward, and on tiptoe. Older children can experiment with other ways of getting across the textured walk.

- To vary the activity, put on a cassette or CD, and ask the children to take a texture walk while "moving to the music."

- Put the texture walk in an out-of-the-way space in the room or on the playground, and leave it there for the duration of the theme so that the children can return to it often.

- Primary-grade children can work with a partner and think up additional uses for the texture walk.

SENSORY ART

LET'S TOUCH

Infants and toddlers learn by touching things and exploring them with their mouths as well.

- Give an infant a small paper bag or a piece of brown wrapping paper, and watch all of the sensory exploration that occurs.

- For toddlers, make a touch bag for each child by placing five or six items in a large paper bag, such as a soft stuffed animal, a feather, a washcloth, a piece of wood, and a rubber ball.

- Ask the children to reach inside of their bags and, without looking, guess what the objects are. Ask them to name them. You supply the words if they cannot.

- Continue this activity, also asking the children such questions as: "Does it feel soft?" "Does it feel rough?" "Does it feel round?" Helping the children discover appropriate words encourages language development.

- Leave the bags on a table so the children can return to them whenever they wish.

MAKE TEXTURE BOXES

There are several ways to create a sensory touch box for toddlers.

Individual Texture Boxes

- Make several individual boxes using shoe boxes.

- Let the children help you make these by gluing different things inside of each box. For example, use sandpaper, scraps of fabric, yarn, feathers, pieces of fur, and leather.

- Leave enough room so that other items the children find can be added. Some of these could be leaves, flowers, and sticks.

Group Texture Box

- Using an appliance box, at least three to four feet square, is another way to create a texture box.

- Put several pounds of sand or gravel in the bottom of the box to stabilize it.

- Close the box, and tape down the flaps securely.

- Ask the children to join you in decorating the box.

- Glue or tape (with double-sided tape) various materials onto the box. Use items that have tactile and three-dimensional qualities, for example, egg cartons, cotton balls, thread spools, several small nonbreakable mirrors, bells, foil, string, yarn, and other items suggested by the children.

LET'S TOUCH AND MATCH

▶ Precut two pieces of each of the following articles: sandpaper, foil, corrugated cardboard, sponges, silk, corduroy, leather, lace, wallpaper, washcloths, butcher paper, and construction paper.

▶ Gather two of the following: craft sticks, feathers, plastic tops from food containers, hair curlers, golf balls, and bells.

▶ Separate the textured pairs by putting one mate in a paper bag numbered 1 and the other in a paper bag marked 2, or A and B.

▶ For younger children, use fewer pairs.

▶ Ask one child to reach into bag 1 without looking and pull out an item.

▶ Have the same child reach into bag 2, again without looking, and try to find the matching piece using her sense of touch.

▶ If a child misses the match, reassure her that it is all right. There will be another turn later.

▶ Continue going around the circle until each child has had a turn to guess correctly.

CREATIVE FOOD EXPERIENCES

MARSHMALLOW AND COCONUT TREAT

You will need the following:

large marshmallows
shredded coconut

1. Wash hands.
2. Sprinkle coconut on a long sheet of waxed paper.
3. Place marshmallows in a slotted spoon, and dip them quickly into a pot of hot water that is well out of reach of the children.
4. Place the slightly cooled marshmallows on the long strip of waxed paper covered with coconut.
5. Let the children roll the marshmallows in the coconut, and then place the coated marshmallows on another piece of waxed paper to dry.
6. Enjoy!

NO COOK ORANGE COOKIES

You will need the following:

30 to 40 vanilla wafers
1/4 cup orange juice
2 tablespoons granulated sugar
powdered sugar

1. Wash hands.
2. Divide the children into small groups. Each group has a specific task to complete.
3. Place vanilla wafers in a plastic zip-top bag, and crush with a rolling pin until finely crumbled. The children can take turns with the rolling pin.
4. Put the crumbs in a large bowl, and add the sugar and orange juice.
5. Mix well.
6. Roll into balls with moistened hands.
7. In a separate bowl, roll balls in powdered sugar. Place on waxed paper.
8. If mixture is too sticky, add more vanilla wafers.

NO COOK ORANGE COOKIES

Wash hands.

Place 30 – 40 vanilla wafers in a plastic zip-top bag

and finely crush with a rolling pin.

Put the crumbs in a large bowl.

Add 2 tablespoons sugar and 1/4 cup orange juice.

Mix well and roll into balls.

Roll balls in powdered sugar and place on wax paper.

EAT!

MATH

FINE MOTOR TOUCH

When children play this math game of putting the correct number of objects into numbered compartments, they develop one-to-one correspondence recognition and fine motor skills.

▶ Save egg cartons.

▶ In the bottom of each egg compartment, write a numeral with a permanent marker.

▶ Put several of these numeral recognition egg cartons in the math center with small plastic tongs and dried beans, small buttons, or pennies. The tongs usually are available in the science section of educational products stores.

▶ Encourage the children to use the tongs to place the correct number of beans, buttons, or pennies in the numbered spaces, and to return them to their original containers.

BUTTON, BUTTON, WHO'S GOT THE BUTTON?

Keep a large plastic jar or other container with a lid filled with buttons of many sizes, colors, and shapes. Many family members usually have loose, mismatched buttons around the house. Ask them to contribute.

▶ Place the button jar in the math or manipulative center.

▶ The children can count, sort, classify, make collages, and match the buttons.

▶ For younger children, use only large-size buttons.

▶ Older children enjoy tossing the buttons into plastic containers and paper cups and counting how many they can get into the container.

▶ The buttons can provide the children with a meaningful activity to occupy them when bad weather cancels their outdoor time.

SCIENCE

IMAGINOLOGY

The focus of this concept is that children like to do new things with familiar materials. This helps encourage problem solving, imaginative thinking, and creativity. Many items around the classroom can be used for this activity.

▶ The children may work individually or with partners. Ask the children to think about and then describe all of the things they can do with the following, one item at a time:

a piece of string or a ball of string

a box	egg cartons
paper sacks	wrapping paper
sandpaper	envelopes
straws	craft sticks

▶ The children will think of more items. Support their ideas by giving them unlimited time, materials, supplies, and plenty of space in which to develop unique creations.

SOCIAL STUDIES

THE BRAILLE ALPHABET

▶ Discuss with the class different ways we communicate with others, such as written words, spoken words, nonverbal reactions, body language, and sign language.

▶ Introduce them to Braille, which is a system of letters and numbers communicated through touch.

▶ Explain that instead of words and letters printed on a page or in a book, Braille letters and numbers are "bumps" on a page.

▶ Ask someone from one of the local associations or services for visually impaired children and adults to visit your class. This person usually can bring copies of the Braille alphabet to show the children.

▶ You may obtain a card with the alphabet and numbers in Braille at no cost by sending a postcard to the American Foundation for the Blind, 15 West 16th Street, New York, NY, 10011.

PRESCHOOL-K   PRIMARY-GRADE

GO ON A FIELD TRIP

▶ Visit a fabric or carpet store by yourself first to arrange a special time for the field trip and to be sure the store is appropriate for young children to visit. Ask the store manager if the children may take a collection of carpet samples back to school.

▶ It is important that the people at the store be available to show the children many textures that they can touch.

▶ Suggest that the individuals set up a special area in the store with preselected materials to share with the group.

▶ Allow enough time for the children to ask questions and talk to the salespersons.

▶ Follow up by sending thank-you notes from the class.

▶ Encourage the children to talk about their experience, to draw pictures, and to dictate stories about it.

CHILDREN'S BOOKS

Boyton, Sandra. (2003). *Fuzzy Fuzzy Fuzzy!* (Board Book). New York: Little Simon.

DK Publishing. (Ed.). (2003). *Touch and Feel Animals.* (Boxed Set). New York: Author.

Harlow, Rockwell. (1987). *The Touch Me Book.* New York: Golden Books.

Hartley, Karen, and Chris Macro. (2000). *Touching in Living Things.* Des Plaines, IL: Heinemann.

Hill, Eric. (1997). *Spot's Touch and Feel Day.* New York: Putnam.

Isadora, Rachel. (1991). *I Touch.* New York: Greenwillow.

Kunhardt, Dorothy, and Edith Kunhardt. (2001). *Pat the Puppy.* New York: Golden Press.

Kunhardt, Dorothy, and Edith Kunhardt. (1990). *Pat the Bunny.* (Board Book). New York: Golden Press.

Kunhardt, Edith. (1998). *Pat the Cat.* New York: Golden Books.

Muntean, Michaela. (1996). *Elmo Can . . . Taste! Touch! Smell! See! Hear!* Illustrated by Maggie Swanson. New York: Golden Books and Children's Television Workshop.

Otto, Carolyn B. (1994). *I Can Tell by Touching.* Illustrated by Nadine Bernard Westcott. New York: HarperTrophy.

Oxenbury, Helen. (1995). *I Touch.* (Board Book). Cambridge, MA: Candlewick Press.

Rose, Julian, and Molly Perham. (1993). *Feel and Touch!* San Francisco: Children's Press.

Wood, Nicholas. (1991). *Touch . . . What Do You Feel?* Mahwah, NJ: Troll Associates.

Family Letter (Primary Grade)

Dear Family,

We are studying the last of the five senses. Our theme is "Touching." The children will learn the following:

- *How the five senses help us every day.*
- *The skin is the part of the body that gives us our sense of touch.*
- *We usually use our fingers to touch and identify things.*
- *Our skin protects us and keeps us safe by letting us know when things are too hot or cold or if we are hurt.*
- *We should take care of our skin.*

We will be talking about the following:

- *our skin and nerve endings*
- *what touching helps us do*
- *how we take care of our skin*
- *what we touch*

Things to do at home with your child include:

- *Talk about what is going on in the classroom.*
- *Encourage your child to investigate the textures around the house and yard.*
- *Use word descriptions of how things feel when you and your child touch various surfaces.*
- *Let your child share cooking experiences with you. It is important for your child to make something and contribute to family meals.*

Join us for the following family participation opportunities at school:

- *Visit our classroom any time to see what we have been creating and discovering.*
- *Join us for our field trip to the fabric or carpet store.*
  Date _____ Time _____

Our wish list for this theme includes:

egg cartons

straws

wrapping paper

buttons of all shapes, sizes, and colors

sandpaper

thread spools

rolling pins

Thanks!

Seasons

Young children are active learners. They enter into whatever they do with spontaneity and energy. The seasons of the year and young children are easily connected. Both are filled with the rhythms and energy of life. The thematic activities in this section offer children opportunities to grow and learn while actively enjoying the rhythms of the changing seasons.

The activities are easily adaptable to large group, small group, or individual instruction. This allows the children to learn at their own pace and style.

The following themes are included in Section III, "Seasons":

Theme 12 — Fall

Theme 13 — Winter

Theme 14 — Spring

Theme 15 — Summer

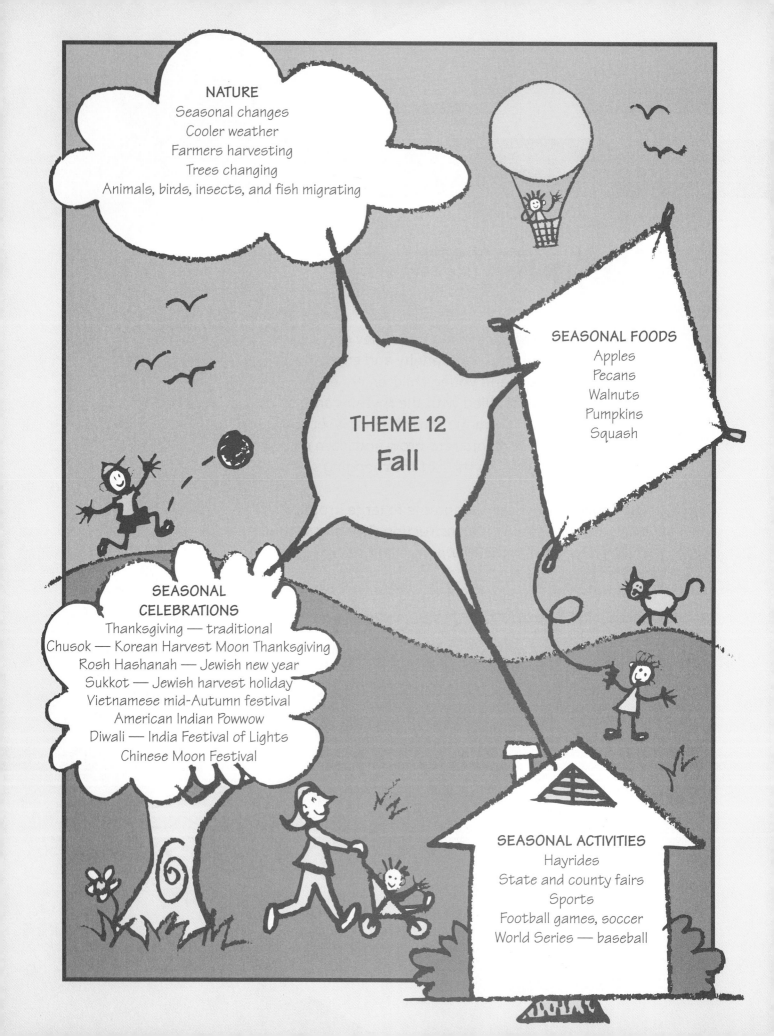

NATURE
Seasonal changes
Cooler weather
Farmers harvesting
Trees changing
Animals, birds, insects, and fish migrating

SEASONAL FOODS
Apples
Pecans
Walnuts
Pumpkins
Squash

THEME 12
Fall

SEASONAL CELEBRATIONS
Thanksgiving — traditional
Chusok — Korean Harvest Moon Thanksgiving
Rosh Hashanah — Jewish new year
Sukkot — Jewish harvest holiday
Vietnamese mid-Autumn festival
American Indian Powwow
Diwali — India Festival of Lights
Chinese Moon Festival

SEASONAL ACTIVITIES
Hayrides
State and county fairs
Sports
Football games, soccer
World Series — baseball

THEME GOALS

To provide opportunities for children to learn the following:

▶ Fall is a season of the year that comes after summer and before winter.

▶ Fall is the time of year that has many changes in nature, such as shorter days and longer nights.

▶ In the fall, many birds and some animals, fish, and insects migrate to warmer climates.

▶ The leaves of trees may change color, and many trees lose all of their leaves.

▶ Fall weather becomes cooler, and we start wearing warmer clothing.

Children-Created Bulletin Board

The children will be active participants in making this bulletin board for the fall theme. The board will change to reflect what happens during each season.

▶ Cover the entire board with pale blue, pink, or green paper. This becomes the background for all four season themes.

▶ With the children's help, cut out a tree trunk from corrugated paper, or crumple paper bags to form a tree trunk.

▶ Staple the trunk to the bulletin board. Add tree branches with black or brown crayons or markers.

▶ Trace each child's hand on medium-green construction paper.

▶ Have each child cut out the hand shape and place it where a leaf would be on the tree.

▶ As the leaves on real trees start changing color, place individual watercolor tablets of yellow, orange, red, or brown on a tray. You can usually push out the tablets from watercolor paint sets available at most stores.

▶ The children, a few at a time, dip their index fingers into a small glass of water. Each child then selects a color and rubs the finger on a paint tablet. The more they rub, the more colorful their prints will be.

▶ Children's paint-loaded fingers are then used to make "fingerprint leaves" all over the tree branches, on the ground, or blowing in the wind.

▶ Collect fallen leaves from a walk around the neighborhood, and glue these onto the bulletin board.

▶ At Thanksgiving time, write what each child is thankful for on colored leaf shapes, and add these to the fall scene.

▶ When the class focuses on planting, growing, and harvesting apples, have the children turn the tree into an apple tree. October is Apple Month.

VOCABULARY STARTERS

Let the children add words.

autumn — another name for fall, the season that comes after summer and before winter.

fall — one of the four parts of the year.

harvest — the gathering of ripe grains, fruits, and vegetables from farms, gardens, and orchards.

migration — the movement of birds, fish, and butterflies from one place to another.

orchard — many fruit trees grown on a large piece of land.

temperature — hotness or coldness of anything.

LANGUAGE EXPERIENCES

SOUNDS ALL AROUND

▶ Create interesting sounds in the environment for infants.

▶ Hum, sing, and talk to infants when you are changing their diapers, feeding them, and holding them.

▶ Respond to infants' "talking" sounds.

▶ Musical toys, musical mobiles, and the voices of adults and other children are important to infants.

▶ Have picture books to share with an individual child.

▶ Each child should be able to interact with the book as well. This means holding, touching, and chewing the book.

- Select board books that encourage this interaction, and present rhythmic language, rhymes, chants, and songs. Some suggestions include:

Ahlberg, Allan, and Janet Ahlberg. (1981). *Peek-a-Boo.* New York: Viking.

Brown, Margaret Wise. (First Board Book ed., 1991). *Goodnight Moon.* Illustrated by Clement Hurd. New York: HarperCollins.

Hathon, Elizabeth. (1993). *Soft as a Kitten.* New York: Grossett & Dunlap.

Kemp, Moira. (1987). *Pat-a-Cake.* Los Angeles: Price Stern Sloan.

Titherington, Jeanne. (1990). *Pumpkin, Pumpkin.* New York: Mulberry.

THE LITTLE RED HEN

Retelling stories using a flannelboard helps the children sequence a story, repeat the language of the story, and dramatize concepts.

- Read the story *The Little Red Hen.* Four versions are listed in the Children's Books section of this theme.
- Ask the children to help you retell the story with the flannelboard characters you have made. Use felt or nonwoven interfacing, found at a fabric store, to make the characters.
- After repeating the story, place the flannelboard and character pieces in any activity center or curriculum area.
- Flannelboard figures can be touched, held, and moved, thus helping the children move between real and abstract.

POEM: "Fall"

Where did the summer go?
First it was hot, but now it's so cool.
We were on vacation, but now we're in school.
Where did the green go?
First plants looked green as green plants could be.
Now they look brown, red, and yellow to me.
Where did the leaves go?
The trees and their branches had leaves all around.
Oh my, now they're falling all over the ground.
What's going on here?
I think that I've figured out what's happening here.
It's what they call "Fall." It's that time of the year.

Philip Jackman

DRAMATIC PLAY

"A" IS FOR APPLE AND "P" IS FOR PUMPKIN

If possible, visit a farmer's market or the produce section of a grocery store with the children. Turn the home living/dramatic play area into a produce stand. This can be accomplished indoors and continued outdoors as a "drive-up" market stand.

- Collect recycled paper grocery bags and fruit baskets.
- Add aprons, a toy cash register, a scale, and real or plastic apples, pumpkins, onions, corn, squash, and nuts.
- Make one side of the produce stand into a "pumpkin patch."
- Add cornstalks, hay bales, straw hats, a scarecrow, and plenty of real pumpkins and gourds. Let the children make the scarecrow.
- Give the children an opportunity to investigate all of these items firsthand.

PUPPET PLAY

IT'S A TURKEY!

Introduce the children to this activity by showing pictures of turkeys and reading books, such as Aronosky's *All About Turkeys,* listed in the Children's Books section of this theme.

- For children who are interested in creating puppets, use the same approach when making some of the leaves for the bulletin board.
- Invite the children to trace around their hands on brown wrapping paper or construction paper.
- If needed, help toddlers and young preschoolers who want to do this activity.
- Have the children cut out the hands. Younger children can paste or glue the leaves on the entire drawing without cutting.
- The thumb becomes the turkey's face, and the four fingers become the turkey's back.
- Add paper, real feathers, or anything else the children decide will personalize their puppets.

▶ Attach a craft stick to make a puppet.

▶ Give the children time to explore the materials and their puppets.

SCARECROW PUPPET

▶ Have materials available so children can make scarecrow hand puppets from two pieces of felt or other fabric cut to fit the child's hand.

▶ Glue or sew the two pieces together.

This illustration is just an example. Creativity should be the emphasis for this activity.

▶ Eyes, nose, mouth, ears, hair, and hat can be attached with Velcro™ or glue.

▶ Use straw for hair and extra decoration. Straw can usually be found at craft stores.

▶ The children can use their puppets in the dramatic play areas as well.

MUSIC

"PICKING APPLES"

This is a rhythm activity appropriate for children of all ages. It encourages them to play with the *rhythm of language.*

Apples, apples, everywhere
Lots of apples for us to share.
Let's go find an apple tree,
Fiddle-dee-dum and fiddle-dee-dee.
There's a nice one. Let me see —
Fiddle-dee-dum and fiddle-dee-dee.
Lots of apples, let's pick some,
Fiddle-dee-dee and fiddle-dee-dum.
I'll pick an apple, and you pick one,
Fiddle-dee-dee and fiddle-dee-dum.
Let's pick more, how about two?
Fiddle-dee-dum and fiddle-dee-doo.
That's not enough. How about three?
Fiddle-dee-doo and fiddle-dee-dee.
Now we've enough for you and me,
Fiddle-dee-dum and fiddle-dee-dee.

Philip Jackman

"OATS, PEAS, BEANS, AND BARLEY GROW"

This traditional song has been passed down from one group of children to the next. Perhaps some of the verses will be new to you and your children. It is fun for the children to act out the words as they are singing.

Chorus:

Oats, peas, beans, and barley grow,
Oats, peas, beans, and barley grow,
Can you or I or anyone know
How oats, peas, beans, and barley grow?

Verse:

First the farmer sows the seed,
Stands erect and rests with ease,
He stamps his foot and claps his hands,
And turns around to view his lands.

Chorus:

Oats, peas, beans, and barley grow,
Oats, peas, beans, and barley grow,
Can you or I or anyone know
How oats, peas, beans, and barley grow?

Verse:

Next the farmer waters the seed,
Stands erect and rests with ease,
He stamps his foot and claps his hands,
And turns around to view his lands.

Repeat chorus.

Verse:

Next the farmer hoes the weeds,

Repeat the rest of the verse.

Repeat chorus.

Verse:

Last the farmer harvests the seed,

Repeat the rest of the verse.

Repeat chorus.

MOVEMENT

LEAF DANCING

Play recorded instrumental music in the background as the children move around, acting out the words to the poem. Ask them to help you make up other verses and actions.

Like a leaf or feather,
in the windy, windy weather,
we'll whirl around and twirl around,
and all fall down together.
Like the birds covered in feathers,
in the windy, windy weather,
we'll fly around and twirl around,
and feel the wind together.

SENSORY ART

LET'S TEAR

This activity helps children with small muscle development and hand-eye coordination. It also gives them a sense of autonomy within appropriate boundaries.

▶ Have children who are interested tear small pieces of tissue and construction paper and glue them onto pumpkin shapes.

▶ Let the children make as many pumpkins as they want.

▶ Leave the materials out, and let children return to the table whenever they want to do so.

COLLECT FALL LEAVES

▶ With the children, collect fall leaves.

▶ Dry leaves. Pressing them in an old telephone book for several days works well.

▶ Toddlers and preschoolers enjoy crumbling up the dried leaves. Place these on a tray.

▶ Put out glue in small containers along with small brushes or cotton swabs for the children to use to spread glue onto construction paper.

▶ The children can create pictures with the dried leaves by experimenting with the materials and with random placement of the leaves.

▶ Let the pictures dry flat.

PARTNER COLLAGE

▶ Guide the children, each with a partner or in a small group, into making a tree, a pumpkin, an apple, or a fall sports collage.

▶ Put out magazines, calendars, colored tissue paper, poster board, construction paper, glue, scissors, yarn, and fabric scraps for the children to use.

▶ Working cooperatively, let the children decide what they want their collage to be and how it should look.

▶ Ask the children to title their collages and write their names at the top.

CREATiVE FOOD EXPERiENCES

IT LOOKS LIKE A PUMPKIN FACE

You will need the following:

English muffins (enough for each child to have one half)

spreadable, orange-colored cheese

vegetables cut into slices and pieces (celery, carrots, black olives, green peppers)

1. Wash hands.
2. Spread the cheese over an English muffin half.
3. Add various vegetables to make silly faces.

LET'S MAKE APPLESAUCE

You will need the following:

6 apples
1/2 cup water
1/8 teaspoon cinnamon
1 teaspoon lemon juice
sugar to taste

1. Wash hands.
2. Peel apples. Remove core from each apple.
3. Cut up the apples, and add water, sugar, and lemon juice.
4. Put apple mixture in a pan, cover, and cook until tender on medium heat, approximately 15 to 20 minutes.
5. Add cinnamon.
6. Mash apples with a fork or potato masher, or press through a colander.
7. Serve and eat!

LET'S MAKE APPLE SAUCE!

Wash hands.

Peel 6 apples. Remove core from each apple.

Cut up the apples and add 1/2 cup water,

 sugar to taste, and 1 teaspoon lemon juice.

Put in a pan, cover, and cook until tender on a

medium heat. Add 1/8 teaspoon cinnamon.

Mash apples with a fork or potato masher or

press through a colander.

Serve and eat!

JOHNNY APPLESEED DAY (SEPTEMBER)

Here is another "apple" idea for the children on a fall day.

▶ Warm some apple cider in a Crock-Pot, and serve for snack.
▶ Talk about how the cider tastes and smells.

MATH

SHOE BOX FOREST

▶ Cover a shoe box with wood-patterned contact paper. Cover the lid *and* the bottom of the box.
▶ Place slits in the box lid. The number of slits depends on the developmental stage of the children.

► For toddlers, use large tongue depressors with leaves drawn or pasted on them.

► Let each child insert the "tree sticks," and take them out. Use words to go with the actions, such as: "You're putting the sticks *in* the box." "Now you're taking the sticks *out* of the box."

► Step back, and let the children play this math game.

► With preschoolers, make slits in the top of the box, and write numerals from 1 to 10 under each slit.

► Make craft sticks into trees by adding green tree-top shapes glued to each stick.

► Put dots on the trees that correspond to each slit in the box.

► The children match the tree with the number of dots on it to the slit on the box with that numeral.

► Put the tree sticks into a resealable plastic bag, and store them in the bottom of the shoe box. When the children are through playing this math game, they put the pieces into the bag, then into the box, and finally put the lid on.

MATCH THE APPLE SEEDS

► Take an ordinary file folder, open it, and draw an apple on the right side.

► The apple can be bright red, yellow, or green. See the Science section of this theme for information about different types of apples. You may decide to make several folder games.

► Divide the apple into puzzle parts, and number them from 1 to 9.

► On the cover of the file folder, write "Apple Seeds."

► Laminate the file folder.

► Draw another apple exactly the same, except place this apple on a piece of tagboard. Divide this apple into puzzle parts, and place apple seeds on each piece, numbering from 1 to 9. Outline each puzzle piece in black (see illustration).

► Laminate the apple.

► Cut the apple into the puzzle slices you have previously marked.

► Put pieces into a resealable plastic bag, and staple or glue to the back of the folder.

► Put the folder game in the math or manipulative center for the children to discover.

SCIENCE

APPLE VARIETIES

Introduce children to the many kinds of apples and how they are grown. Introduce toddlers to the different kinds of apples by preparing a tasting tray. Show them the actual whole apples before cutting them. It is important for the children to see, touch, smell, and taste real apples. Show them pictures of an apple tree.

► An individual apple tree may grow up to forty feet and live more than 100 years.

► Each tree begins with one small seed.

► Read Micucci's *The Life and Times of the Apple,* Gibbons's *The Seasons of Arnolds' Apple Tree,* and Aliki's *The Story of Johnny Appleseed* to the children, all listed in the Children's Books section of this theme.

► Bring several kinds of apples to class for the children to *see, smell, feel,* and *taste.* They can even *hear* an apple when they take a bite.

► Some varieties of apples include:

Red Delicious — sweet and juicy, eat fresh

Gala — sweet and crisp, use in pies, or bake

Golden Delicious — sweet and tender, good in pies, or eat fresh

McIntosh — slightly tart, make applesauce, or eat fresh

Winesap — firm and spicy, good for cider, or eat fresh

Granny Smith — tart taste, use in pies, or eat fresh

Jonathan — sweet and crisp, use in pies, or eat fresh

Rome — slightly tart and crisp, nice size for baking, or eat fresh

Fuji — sweet, spicy, make applesauce, or eat fresh

Braeburn — very firm, good for pies or baked

▶ Have the children help you make a list of the many uses of the apple, including apple cider vinegar, apple bread, and apple butter. Add this list to the bulletin board.

THE SEASONS OF THE APPLE TREE

▶ Introduce the children to the life cycle of the apple tree.

▶ Give each child a large piece of paper and crayons or markers.

▶ Guide children into dividing their paper into fourths, one section for each season of the year.

▶ Write the name of a season in each section.

▶ Have children draw an apple tree as it looks in each season. They can use the books about apples for reference. In winter, the tree has bare branches and tiny buds at the end of each branch; in spring, the tree has small green leaves and apple blossoms; in summer, the tree has leaves and small green apples; and in fall, the tree has big apples on the branches and on the ground.

▶ The children can create other things that are happening, such as honeybees flying around the blossoms in the spring, and people picking the apples in the fall.

SOCIAL STUDIES

CHINESE MOON FESTIVAL

▶ The Chinese hold a festival in September to celebrate the harvest of crops. Since there is a full moon around harvest time, they call the celebration the **Moon Festival.** This is similar to the American tradition of Thanksgiving.

▶ Moon Cakes (round, yellow cakes filled with red bean paste and sesame seeds, or fruits, nuts, and spices) are enjoyed by everyone during this time of year.

▶ The Moon Cake symbolizes the moon and family unity.

▶ Perhaps one of the children in your classroom has a family member who would visit and share how the Chinese Moon Festival is celebrated in his family.

▶ Serve Moon Cakes to the children. These are available at bakeries or grocery stores that sell Asian food.

SUKKOT

▶ **Sukkot** (sŏó-koat) is the Jewish harvest festival celebrated in the fall.

▶ During the holiday a **sukkah** (sŏó-kah), a small hut or booth is built in the courtyard of a Jewish temple or synagogue by the members of the congregation, or in individual family backyards. These structures remind Jewish people of the booths lived in by their ancestors in the desert.

▶ The sukkah is covered with evergreen boughs, palm fronds, or tree branches. The children decorate it with flowers, fruits, and vegetables.

▶ This is a happy festival. Families visit the sukkah and share the fruits of the harvest.

▶ Plan a field trip to visit a Jewish temple or synagogue during Sukkot. This gives the children an opportunity to learn about another festival of Thanksgiving.

POWWOW

▶ A **powwow** is another tradition that takes place in the fall. This is an important experience for many American Indian tribes.

▶ Some powwows and other ceremonies also are held during the year by tribes throughout the United States.

▶ This occasion brings tribes and families together.

▶ Food, singing, drums, and dancing are all part of the powwow.

▶ The dancers wear colorful feathers just as their ancestors did. This is a time when ancient traditions are passed from one generation to another.

▶ Invite a family or community individual to visit the class and share the music, drums, or costumes that are part of the powwow.

▶ Visit your local library or bookstore for further information.

CHILDREN'S BOOKS

Ada, Alma Flor. (2001). *With Love Little Red Hen.* Illustrated by Leslie Tryon. New York: Atheneum.

Ahlberg, Allan, and Janet Ahlberg. (1981). *Peek-a-Boo.* New York: Viking.

Aliki. (1963). *The Story of Johnny Appleseed.* New York: Aladdin.

Aronosky, Jim. (1998). *All About Turkeys.* New York: Scholastic.

Berg, Jean H. (1962). *The Little Red Hen.* Illustrated by Mel Pekarsky. Chicago: Follett.

Birdwell, Norman. (1997). *Clifford's Thanksgiving Visit.* New York: Scholastic.

Brown, Margaret Wise. (1991). *Goodnight Moon.* (First Board Book ed.). Illustrated by Clement Hurd. New York: Harper-Collins.

Bunting, Eve. (1991). *A Turkey for Thanksgiving.* Illustrated by Diane de Groat. New York: Scholastic.

Carle, Eric. (1987). *The Tiny Seed.* Saxonville, MA: Picture Book.

Chanin, Michael, and Sally Smith. (1994). *Grandfather Four Winds and Rising Moon.* New York: Starseed Press.

Ehlert, Lois. (1991). *Red Leaf, Yellow Leaf.* San Diego: Harcourt.

Galdone, Paul. (1973). *The Little Red Hen.* Boston: Houghton Mifflin.

George, Lindsay B. (1995). *In the Woods: Who's Been Here?* New York: Greenwillow.

Gibbons, Gail. (2001). *Apples.* New York: Holiday House.

Gibbons, Gail. (2000). *The Pumpkin Book.* New York: Holiday House.

Gibbons, Gail. (1984). *The Seasons of Arnold's Apple Tree.* San Diego: Harcourt.

Golden, Barbara Diamond. (1995). *Night Lights: A Sukkot Story.* San Diego: Harcourt.

Golden, Barbara Diamond. (1995). *The World's Birthday: A Rosh Hashanah Story.* San Diego: Harcourt.

Hall, Zoe. (2000). *Fall Leaves Fall!* Illustrated by Shari Halpern. New York: Scholastic.

Hall, Zoe. (1994). *It's Pumpkin Time.* Illustrated by Shari Halpern. New York: Scholastic.

Hathon, Elizabeth. (1993). *Soft as a Kitten.* New York: Grossett & Dunlap.

Howe, James, and E. Young. (1994). *I Wish I Were a Butterfly.* San Diego: Harcourt.

Hutchings, Amy. (1994). *Picking Apples and Pumpkins.* Photographed by Richard Hutchings. New York: Cartwheel Books.

Hutchins, Pat. (2000). *Ten Red Apples.* New York: Greenwillow.

Kalman, Bobbie. (1997). *Celebrating the Powwow.* New York: Crabtree.

Kemp, Moira. (1987). *Pat-a-Cake.* Los Angeles: Price Stern Sloan.

Maass, Robert. (1992). *When Autumn Comes.* New York: Henry Holt.

Maestro, Betsy. (1993). *How Do Apples Grow?* Illustrated by Giulio. New York: HarperTrophy.

Marzollo, Jean. (1997). *I Am an Apple.* Illustrated by Judith Moffatt. New York: Scholastic.

Maslowski, Steve. (2003). *Birds in the Fall.* North Mankato, MN: Smart Apple Media.

McQueen, Lucinda. (1995). *The Little Red Hen/La Gallinita Roja.* New York: Scholastic.

Micucci, Charles. (1992). *The Life and Times of the Apple.* New York: Orchard Books.

Muller, Gerda. (1995). *Circle of Seasons.* New York: Dutton.

Rendon, Marcie R. (1996). *Powwow Summer: A Family Celebrates the Circle of Life.* Minneapolis: Carolrhoda Books.

Rius, Maria, U. Wensel, and Jose M. Parramon. (1998). *Fall (The Four Seasons).* New York: Barron's Juveniles.

Rockwell, Anne. (1989). *Apples and Pumpkins.* Illustrated by Lizzy Rockwell. New York: Simon & Schuster.

Schweninger, Ann. (1993). *Autumn Days.* New York: Puffin Books.

Sundgaard, Arnold. (1996). *The Lamb and the Butterfly.* Illustrated by Eric Carle. New York: Scholastic.

Titherington, Jeanne. (1990). *Pumpkin, Pumpkin.* New York: Mullberry.

Wellington, Monica. (2001). *Apple Farmer Annie.* New York: Dutton Books.

Zemach, Margot. (1983). *The Little Red Hen.* New York: Farrar, Straus & Giroux.

Family Letter (Toddler)

Dear Family,

We are starting to learn about the seasons. Our first theme is "Fall."

The children will learn the following:

- *Fall is the season of the year that comes after summer and before winter.*
- *Fall is a time of year that has many changes in nature.*
- *In the fall, many birds and some animals, fish, and insects go where the weather is warm.*
- *The leaves of trees may change color, and many trees lose their leaves.*
- *Fall weather becomes cooler, and we start wearing warmer clothing.*

We will be talking about the following:

- *fall changes in trees and weather*
- *farmers harvesting fruits, vegetables, and grain — especially apples, pumpkins, and nuts*
- *fall holidays and celebrations*
- *fall family activities*

Things to do at home with your child to support our classroom activities include:

- *Go for a walk and look at trees, collect fallen leaves, watch the birds fly south, and notice other changes.*
- *Talk about what you see.*
- *Point out fall colors.*
- *Carve a pumpkin, and eat pumpkin pies.*
- *Take your child to the grocery store to buy apples. Taste the different kinds.*
- *Read books about fall and the other seasons.*

Family participation opportunities at school will include:

- *Come help us make applesauce.*
  Date _____   Time _____
- *Go with us on a field trip.*
  Date _____   Time _____

Our wish list for this theme includes:

  shoe boxes

  paper grocery bags

  magazines and calendars

  feathers

  fall leaves

Thanks!

NATURE
Seasonal changes
Cold weather
Animal hibernation
Plant life dormant
Snow in some areas

THEME 13
Winter

SEASONAL FOODS
Soups
Stews
Dumplings
Hot chocolate
Hot cider
Maple syrup

SEASONAL CELEBRATIONS
Hanukkah — Jewish
Los Posadas (The Inns) Mexican American
Russian Winter Festival
New Year — Chinese, Vietnamese,
Cambodian, and Islamic
Christmas — Christian
Kwanzaa — African American
Martin Luther King's Birthday
President's Day   Valentine's Day

SEASONAL ACTIVITIES
Ice skating
Sledding
Skiing
Hockey
Basketball
Olympics

THEME GOALS

To provide opportunities for children to learn the following:

▶ Winter is a season of the year that comes after fall and before spring.

▶ Winter is the time of year with the shortest days and longest nights.

▶ In the winter, many animals and insects hibernate.

▶ Many plants stop growing, and their seeds, roots, or bulbs live underground waiting for warmer weather.

▶ Winter weather usually becomes very cold, often with snow, sleet, and ice. Heavy clothing helps protect us and keeps us comfortable and warm.

Children-Created Bulletin Board

As the weather changes into winter, so does the interactive bulletin board. Encourage the children to think of what can be added or deleted from the board to show that winter has arrived.

▶ There can be pictures of bears hibernating, children sledding, and sleet or snow falling.

▶ Cotton balls or Styrofoam™ "squiggles" can be glued on to create "snow people" or snow on the tree.

▶ This is an opportunity for children to work cooperatively adding winter scenes to the board.

VOCABULARY STARTERS

Let the children add words. Include pictures, where appropriate.

blizzard — a very big and strong snowstorm.

frost — ice crystals that form on a surface, such as the ground.

hibernation — a time when many animals are resting or sleeping during the winter months.

ice — frozen water.

sleet — frozen raindrops.

snow — frozen water crystals, or flakes, that fall from the sky.

LANGUAGE EXPERIENCES

POEM: "Wintertime"

Woo! Woo! Woo-woo-woo!
When winter comes, hear the cold wind blow.
Look! Look! Look-look-look!
Out of the clouds, here comes the snow!
Hop. Hop. Hop-hop-hop.
The rabbit hurries to his hole so deep.
Shhh. Shhh. Shhh-shhh-shhh.
Don't make a sound — now he's fast asleep.

GETTING DRESSED FOR WINTER

▶ Read Neitzel's *The Jacket I Wear in the Snow* or London's *Froggy Gets Dressed,* listed in the Children's Books section of this theme.

▶ These books are a lot of fun for the children. Neitzel's cumulative rhyme (a takeoff of *The House That Jack Built*) and the lively illustrations describe every stitch of clothing the little girl wears in the snow. London's Froggy keeps forgetting key articles of clothing needed for going out into the snow.

▶ Have the children go through the books' sequence of identifying the appropriate clothes to wear, building on vocabulary.

▶ Have available all of the pieces of clothing mentioned in the books for one or two of the children to dress as the characters in the book. The children love to do this, and it offers a hands-on experience.

DRAMATIC PLAY

THE THREE BEARS

▶ Turn your dramatic play area into the house of "The Three Bears."

▶ Make three sets of ears from fake fur, construction paper, or tagboard, and attach them to headbands.

▶ Get a girl's headband with a bow on it for Goldilocks.

▶ You will need three sets of dishes, eating utensils, and chairs in three different sizes.

▶ Use colored masking tape to make a "path" for the bears to follow when they leave their house for a walk in the woods.

▶ Extend this activity by setting up an adjacent area where the bears will hibernate for the winter.

▶ Ask the children to decide what the bears will need for their long sleep. Add these items gradually.

GIFT WRAPPING CENTER

As the children experiment with wrapping beautiful packages, they are developing small muscles, problem solving, and working cooperatively with other children.

▶ Collect empty boxes of all sizes, wrapping paper of many colors and textures, yarn, ribbon, bows, tape, and scissors.

▶ Set up the dramatic play area as a gift wrapping center, and invite the children to wrap and decorate packages.

PUPPET PLAY

PUSH-UP CANDLE PUPPETS

Festivals of light are held worldwide during the winter months. The candle is an important symbol of these celebrations. The Children's Books section of this theme offers related stories.

▶ To introduce this puppet project, bring different sizes of candles to show the children. Show pictures and read books.

▶ Talk about the candles that are carried door to door during Las Posadas in Mexico.

▶ Have a Hanukkah menorah with candles to demonstrate how candles are lit during this Jewish holiday.

▶ Show how candles are used during the African-American celebration of Kwanzaa.

▶ Talk about how at Christmas candles are used to make homes look warm and cheerful.

▶ The children can go to the art table to make their "candles" and "candle puppets" whenever they choose.

▶ Put paper towel rolls that have been cut in half, colored tissue and construction paper, foil, tape, glue, scissors, crayons, and craft sticks on a table.

▶ Let the older children experiment with ways to make "flames" push up through the "candle."

▶ Let those toddlers who want to explore the materials do so.

▶ Precut candle "flames," and help toddlers glue the "flames" onto craft sticks to push up through the paper towel rolls.

▶ Leave the materials in the art center for several days. Some children like to make more than one puppet.

MUSIC

SONG: "Jingle Bells"

▶ Sing the song "Jingle Bells." Play a record or tape of this as well, and fill the environment with music and bells.

▶ With one or two infants at a time, introduce a variety of bells.

▶ As you play the bells, talk about their shapes and the sounds they make.

▶ Guide each child into holding a bell and making it ring.

▶ Repeat this activity throughout the holiday season.

DANCE WITH TEDDY

▶ Encourage the children to bring their favorite stuffed animal to play with in the classroom. Many of these will be teddy bears. Add any teddy bears already in the room to these.

▶ Invite the children to dance and sing with their teddy bears.

▶ The older children can help you sing and act out the traditional song "Teddy Bear, Teddy Bear."

Teddy bear, teddy bear,
Turn around.
Teddy bear, teddy bear,
Touch the ground.
Teddy bear, teddy bear,
Skidoo.
Teddy bear, teddy bear,
Go upstairs.
Teddy bear, teddy bear,
Say your prayers.
Teddy bear, teddy bear,
Turn out the light.
Teddy bear, teddy bear.
Say good night.

SONG: "Brr, It's Cold Today!" by Jo Eklof

Put on your hat. Put on your gloves Brr, it's cold to-

day. Be sure that you dress up warm-ly when you go out to

play. Put on your coat. Put on your boots. It

looks like win-ter will stay. Oh, it's cold. Yes, it's cold.

Brr, it's cold to-day. Yes! Brr, it's cold to-day!

© 1982 by Jo Eklof. All rights reserved. Used with permission.

(See page 304 for enlargement.)

MOVEMENT

IN AND OUT

This activity promotes gross motor development.

► Wrap several very large boxes with wrapping paper and bows. Leave the ends open.
► Place boxes in the classroom.
► Encourage the children to climb in and out of the decorated boxes.
► After a while, add a pillow at one end of the box. The children will then have to crawl over the pillow to get out.

ICE SKATING

► Give each child two pieces of waxed paper (for use on a carpeted floor) or two pieces of cardboard or tagboard (to use on uncarpeted areas).

► Play "The Skater's Waltz" or other appropriate music.
► Suggest to the children that they "ice skate" using the waxed paper or cardboard as skates.
► Encourage the children to try different arm movements, as well as leg and body movements.
► Ask the children to act out other winter sports, such as skiing or sledding. This is a good activity to relate to the Winter Olympic Games.

JACK FROST

► Play some music in the background that suggests wintertime, such as Tchaikovsky's *The Nutcracker Suite.*
► Have the children sit in a circle. One child is Jack Frost, who sits inside of the circle.
► Jack closes his eyes.
► While the music is playing, have the other children pass an ice cube, enclosed in a plastic bag, from child to child around the circle.
► Then, stop the music! The child with the ice hides it by placing it behind her back.
► Jack Frost opens his eyes and tries to guess who has the ice cube.
► After the guess, the children trade places. The game begins again when the music starts.

LION DANCER

► Read Waters and Slovenz-Low's *Lion Dancer, Ernie Wan's Chinese New Year.*
► Give one or two of the children drums.
► Ask children to play the drums as though they were playing for the Lion Dance.
► Next, give the other children various kinds of percussion instruments to play along with the drums. Some suggestions for creating different sounds follow:
  — cymbals (crashing)
  — wood blocks (clapping)
  — triangle (ting-a-linging)
  — Chinese gong (smashing)

- tambourines (slapping)
- many sizes of drums (pounding)
- chimes (striking)
- bells (jingling)
- castanets (shaking)
- maracas (shaking)

▶ The children can make some of their own instruments. See theme 6 for suggestions.

SENSORY ART

IT'S COLD!

▶ To introduce the concept of cold to very young children, put a small amount of cold water in a plastic tub or the sand and water table.

▶ Talk about how cold the water is.

▶ Start with helping children put just one finger into the water and taking it out quickly.

▶ You can model putting your hand in and letting the water run through you fingers. After that, let the children decide if they want to play in the water.

▶ Once the children are playing in the water, add a few ice cubes.

▶ Continue talking about how cold the ice cubes make the water.

▶ This activity can be easily repeated.

MITTENS

▶ Trace each child's handprint on a colorful piece of felt.

▶ Let interested children decorate their mittens using markers, crayons, and stickers.

▶ Punch a hole at the top of the felt, and string yarn through it.

▶ Hang the mittens around the room for decoration.

▶ Some families like to use these as holiday ornaments.

SNOWFLAKES

▶ Each snowflake is one of a kind. Let the children make their unique snowflakes with marshmallows and toothpicks.

▶ Put out mini-marshmallows, regular-size marshmallows, and toothpicks for the children to make as many snowflakes as they wish.

▶ Children then stick toothpicks into the marshmallows and connect the marshmallows to other toothpicks.

▶ Children will soon have unusual snowflakes to show each other.

▶ Ask the children questions about their creations. "Did you use different-size marshmallows?" "What different patterns did you make?" "How is this snowflake different from this other one?" "Now that you've made this snowflake, what else can you add to it?"

LIGHT-UP PICTURES AND LANTERNS

▶ Provide cotton swabs, tempera paint, manila paper, and salad oil for the children to use.

▶ Put the cotton swabs and tempera paint on separate trays for each child.

▶ Guide the children who are interested to paint designs on the 9-by-12-inch manila paper.

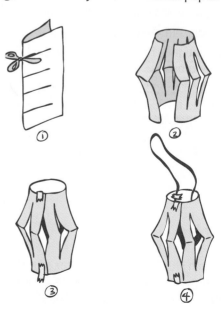

▶ After the paint is dry, have the children use a paintbrush or basting brush to quickly spread a layer of salad oil over the entire picture.

▶ If the children spread too much oil on their picture, this is part of the process. They are learning by doing.

▶ Light should shine through and brighten up the picture when it is hung in a window.

▶ For older children, extend this project by making their light picture into a Chinese festival lantern by doing the following:

— Fold the picture.

— Cut lines across the fold of the paper, almost to the other edge, but not quite (see illustration).

— Unfold the picture. Hold it so the cut lines go up and down.

— Bring the two sides around together.

— Tape the sides together. The lantern will bend on the fold.

— Tape a piece of ribbon or yarn to the top of each lantern, and hang the lanterns around the room as decorations.

CREATIVE FOOD EXPERIENCES

MEXICAN HOT CHOCOLATE — CHOCOLATE CALIENTE

You will need the following:

4 cups milk

5 tablespoons Mexican chocolate or unsweetened chocolate

4 tablespoons brown sugar

2 cinnamon sticks, broken in half

I teaspoon vanilla

1. Wash hands.

2. Combine milk, chocolate, sugar, and cinnamon in a saucepan.

3. Cook over low heat until the chocolate melts and the sugar dissolves.

4. Remove from heat, and add vanilla to milk mixture, beating with an eggbeater.

5. Place a piece of cinnamon stick in a cup for each child, and pour the warm chocolate into the cups.

Safety reminder: Show the children all of the steps in this recipe, but only the teacher should heat this mixture.

STONE SOUP

Read Brown's *Stone Soup,* or Muth's *Stone Soup,* or Forest's *Stone Soup,* listed in the Children's Books section of this theme. Next, you and the children make your own Stone Soup.

You will need the following:

3 small clean rocks, found and washed by you and the children, if possible.

3 stalks of celery

2 large carrots

2 medium onions

2 medium potatoes

3 medium tomatoes

1/2 teaspoon basil

1/2 cup fresh parsley

1 1/2 tablespoons salt

1/2 teaspoon pepper

1/2 cup rice

1. Wash hands.

2. Everyone helps chop or measure an ingredient.

3. Put the ingredients into a big pot and then onto the stove.

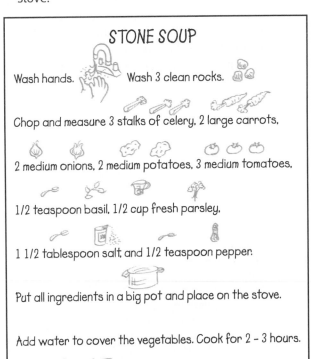

STONE SOUP

Wash hands.   Wash 3 clean rocks.

Chop and measure 3 stalks of celery, 2 large carrots,

2 medium onions, 2 medium potatoes, 3 medium tomatoes,

1/2 teaspoon basil, 1/2 cup fresh parsley,

1 1/2 tablespoon salt, and 1/2 teaspoon pepper.

Put all ingredients in a big pot and place on the stove.

Add water to cover the vegetables. Cook for 2 – 3 hours.

Add 1/2 cup rice to thicken the soup. ENJOY!

4. Add water to cover the vegetables, and cook on low heat for two to three hours. The soup smells so good as it cooks!

5. Add the rice to thicken the soup, and cook until rice is tender.

6. Enjoy!

MATH

HIBERNATION HELPER GAME

This game is for two to four children at a time. Its object is for each child to help her "bear" move from "Start" to safe winter hibernation in the "cave."

▶ On poster board, draw an enlarged version of the sample game board shown in the illustration. Primary-grade children can make the game board and pieces with your assistance, if needed.

▶ Using poster board or tagboard, cut out four bears. Color one black, one brown, one tan, and one red.

▶ Laminate the bear pieces.

▶ From the same material, cut out 30 2-inch by 2-inch squares. In the center of 20 of these, draw a triangle. In the remaining 10, draw a circle.

▶ A triangle shows the number of squares a player can move *forward,* and a circle shows the number a player must move *backward.*

  – Inside *five triangles,* write the numeral 1.

  – Inside *five more triangles,* write the numeral 2.

  – Inside an additional *five triangles,* write the numeral 3.

  – Inside the last *five triangles,* write the numeral 4.

  – Inside *three circles,* write the numeral 1.

  – Inside *three circles,* write the numeral 2.

  – Inside *three circles,* write the numeral 3.

  – Inside *three circles,* write the numeral 4.

▶ Laminate the square pieces.

▶ Before starting, have each player select a bear to move. Also, put the 30 numbered pieces into a bag or box, and shake them up.

▶ Each child, in turn, draws a numbered piece and moves her bear forward or backward the number of spaces indicated. Players cannot move back further than "Start."

▶ Play continues until each bear is safely hibernating in the cave. If all of the numbers are drawn before the bears reach the cave, put the numbers back into the bag, shake them up, and keep drawing.

SCIENCE

WHAT'S THE TEMPERATURE?

▶ Show the children several different kinds of thermometers. Talk about them. Discuss how thermometers are used. Ask: "What do you think this big thermometer does?" Point out the vertical number line.

▶ Measure and record the morning outside temperature for one week. Use the large thermometer.

▶ Draw a large thermometer on poster board, and put it in the classroom. Also create a chart with the days of the week along the top and temperatures up the side.

▶ Use strips of red paper to graph the temperature measured by the mercury on the real thermometer outside.

▶ At the end of the week, children can see which day was coldest or warmest.

HIBERNATION HELPER GAME

SAMPLE GAME PIECES

SOCIAL STUDIES

INTERVIEW THE ANIMALS

To help children understand seasonal changes and how animals adapt to these changes, have them "interview the animals."

▶ Decide which children will be the television news or newspaper reporters and which children will be the animals being interviewed.

▶ Provide microphones (play ones or ones the children have made out of paper towel rolls), bear ears, bunny ears, bird feathers, and other objects the children help think of.

▶ Make up a list of questions to be asked, such as: "Do you sleep all through the winter?" "How do you know when it is time to wake up?" "Do you sleep for part of the winter?" "What do you eat?" "Why do you migrate?" "How do you know where you are going?" "Why don't you go to sleep during the winter?" "Why do you stay active and search for food all winter?"

▶ Discuss how some of these questions can be answered. Provide correct information for the children. For example, deep hibernators that sleep most of the winter are groundhogs, frogs, box turtles, and snakes. Bears, raccoons, and skunks are light hibernators, sleeping for weeks and snacking on food they have stored in their dens. Cardinals, deer, and snowshoe hares stay active during the winter.

▶ Everyone has a lot of fun with this activity. You will also find out what misconceptions the children have.

▶ Older children can do research to find out more about hibernating animals.

CHILDREN'S BOOKS

Adoff, Arnold. (1991). *In for Winter, Out for Spring.* Illustrated by Jerry Pinkney. San Diego: Harcourt.

Berenstain, Stan, and Jan Berenstain. (1996). *The Berenstain Bears' Four Seasons.* New York: Random House.

Borden, Louise. (1992). *Caps, Hats, Socks, and Mittens: A Book about the Four Seasons.* Illustrated by Lillian Hoban. New York: Scholastic.

Brown, Marcia. (1975). *Stone Soup.* New York: Aladdin Books.

Bunting, Eve. (2002). *One Candle.* Illustrated by K. Wendy Popp. New York: Joanne Carter.

Bunting, Eve. (1994). *Night Tree.* Illustrated by Ted Rand. San Diego: Harcourt.

Burden-Patmon, Denise. (1992). *Imani's Gift at Kwanzaa.* Illustrated by Floyd Cooper. New York: Simon & Schuster.

Chiemruom, Sothea. (1994). *Dara's Cambodian New Year.* Illustrated by Dam Nang Pin. New York: Simon & Schuster.

Conway, Diana Cohen. (1994). *Northern Lights.* New York: Kar-Ben Press.

dePaola, Tomie. (1997). *The Legend of the Poinsettia.* New York: Paper Star.

Ehlert, Lois. (1995). *Snowballs.* San Diego: Harcourt.

Ets, Mary Hall, and Aurora Labastida. (1991). *Nine Days to Christmas (Los Posadas).* New York: Puffin.

Forest, Heather. (2000). *Stone Soup.* Illustrated by Susan Gaber. New York: August House.

Fuchs, Diane M. (1995). *A Bear for All Seasons.* New York: Henry Holt.

George, Jean C. (1995). *Dear Rebecca, Winter Is Here.* Illustrated by Loretta Krupinski. New York: HarperCollins.

George, Linda B. (1995). *In the Snow: Who's Been Here?* New York: Greenwillow.

Greene, Carol. (1982). *Read Holidays around the World.* Chicago: Children's Press.

Guiberson, Megan L. (1995). *Winter Wheat.* New York: Henry Holt.

Hirschi, Ron. (1990). *Winter – Invierno.* New York: Dutton.

Keats, Ezra Jack. (1996). *The Snowy Day.* (Board Book). New York: Viking.

Lanton, Sandy. (2003). *Lots of Latkes.* Illustrated by Vicki Jo Redenbaugh. New York: Kar-Ben Press.

Lemelman, Martin. (1998). *Chanukah Is . . .* (Board Book). New York: UAHC Press.

London, Jonathan. (1995). *Froggy Gets Dressed.* Illustrated by Frank Remkiewicz. New York: Puffin.

Lotz, Karen E. (1993). *Snowsong Whistling.* Illustrated by Elisa Kleven. New York: Dutton.

Maslowski, Steve. (2002). *Birds in the Winter.* North Mankato, MN: Smart Apple Media.

Muth, Jon J. (2003). *Stone Soup.* New York: Scholastic.

Neitzel, Shirley. (1994). *The Jacket I Wear in the Snow.* Illustrated by Nancy W. Parker. New York: Mulberry.

Pinkney, Andrea Davis. (1998). *Seven Candles for Kwanzaa.* Illustrated by Brian Pinkney. New York: Puffin.

Preller, James. (1994). *Wake Me in Spring.* New York: Scholastic.

Prelutsky, Jack, and Jeanne Titherington. (1984). *It's Snowing, It's Snowing: Poems.* New York: William Morrow.

Scharfstein, Sol. (1985). *Hanukah Pop-Up Book.* Hoboken, NJ: KTAV Publishing.

Schweninger, Ann. (1993). *Wintertime.* New York: Puffin.

Shostak, Myra. (1997). *Rainbow Candles: A Chanukah Counting Book.* (Board Book). New York: KarBen Press.

Tran, Kin-Lan. (1992). *Tet: The New Year.* Illustrated by Mai Vo-Dinh. New York: Simon & Schuster.

Tresselt, Alvin R., and Roger Duvoisin. (1988). *White Snow, Bright Snow.* New York: William Morrow.

Waters, Kate, and Madeline Slovenz-Low. (1990). *Lion Dancer, Ernie Wan's Chinese New Year.* Photographed by Martha Cooper. New York: Scholastic.

Yerxa, Leo. (1994). *Last Leaf, First Snowflake to Fall.* New York: Orchard Books.

Family Letter (Preschool)

Dear Family,

Our new theme is "Winter." We will provide opportunities for the children to learn the following:

- *Winter is a season of the year that comes after fall and before spring.*
- *Winter is the time of year with the shortest days and longest nights.*
- *In the winter, many animals and insects hibernate.*
- *Many plants stop growing, and their seeds, roots, or bulbs live underground, waiting for warmer weather.*
- *Winter weather usually becomes very cold, often with snow, sleet, and ice. Heavy clothing helps protect us and keeps us comfortable and warm.*

We will be talking about the following:

- *seasonal changes of nature*
- *animal hibernation*
- *seasonal activities*
- *cold weather*
- *seasonal celebrations*
- *seasonal foods*

Try some of the following things to do at home with your child:

- *Talk about the changes in the weather.*
- *Let your child help you bring out winter clothes and put away summer ones.*
- *Let your child help you prepare for your family's holiday celebration.*
- *Enjoy the sights and sounds of the season with your child.*

You are welcome to join us for the following family participation opportunities at school:

- *Help us make "Stone Soup."*
  Date _____ Time _____
- *Come visit us during our "animal interviews."*
  Date _____ Time _____

Our wish list for this theme includes:

  cotton balls and cotton swabs
  Styrofoam™ "squiggles" or packing shapes
  paper towel rolls
  wrapping paper
  small boxes

Thanks!

NATURE

Seasonal changes
Warmer weather
New life
Animals
Plants

Birds
Insects
Trees budding
Migration
Wild flowers

**THEME 14
Spring**

**SEASONAL FOODS
FRUITS AND
VEGETABLES**
Tomatoes
Lettuce
Celery

SEASONAL CELEBRATIONS
Spring festivals — arrival
of spring and planting time
Basanth —Muslim / Holi or Basaat — Hindu
Easter — Christian / Passover — Jewish
Sham Al Naseem — Egyptian
Tu B'Shevat — Jewish tree planting
Cinco de Mayo — Mexican
Urini Nal — Korean Honor the Children
Kodomo-No-Hi — Japan Children's Day
Hina Matsuri — Japan Doll's Day

SEASONAL ACTIVITIES
Picnics   Kite flying
Planting vegetable
and flower gardens
Sports
Track   Tennis   Golf
Baseball   Softball

THEME GOALS

To provide opportunities for children to learn the following:

▶ Spring is a season of the year that comes after winter and before summer.

▶ Spring is the time of year that has many changes in nature, such as longer days and shorter nights.

▶ In the spring, many birds and some other animals, such as fish and insects, migrate to cooler climates.

▶ New life and growth begin: seeds sprout, leaves grow, and flowers bloom.

▶ Spring weather becomes warmer, and we begin wearing less clothing.

Children-Created Bulletin Board

When spring arrives, the bulletin board starts blooming with flowers, fruits, and vegetables.

▶ Here is a suggestion for a flower garden. Provide assorted tissue paper, pipe cleaners, yarn, Styrofoam™ egg cartons, small paper plates, art foam, construction paper, tape, glue, and scissors. Each child can create many flowers for the garden. See the Sensory Art activities in this theme for other additions to the spring bulletin board.

▶ Again, trace around the children's hands on light green construction paper. Cut the shapes to make spring leaves for the bulletin board tree. Let the children do as much as they can or want to do.

VOCABULARY STARTERS

Let the children add words. Include pictures, where appropriate.

blossom — a flower on a plant.

bud — a bump on a plant where a branch, leaf, or flower grows.

garden — a place where vegetables and flowers grow.

rain — water that drops from the clouds.

root — the part of the plant that grows underground.

seed — the tiny pod that has inside of it the beginning of a new plant or tree.

LANGUAGE EXPERIENCES

FINGERPLAY: The Little Acorn

I took a little acorn
And put it in the ground.
  (pick up imaginary acorn with fingers of one hand, and put it into the other cupped hand)
I filled up the hole
And smoothed it all around.
  (pour in "dirt," and rub hand over "hole")
Took my watering can
And made the ground all wet.
  (pick up "can," and pour over "ground")
Then the seed began to sprout
And poked up its head.
  (point index finger up from "ground" hand)
It grew and it grew
And made a lot of leaves.
  (slowly raise arm above head, and open up hand so that fingers become leaves)
It's an oak tree as big
As the tallest trees.
  (extend hand and arm high over head)

Philip Jackman

POEM: Seeds

SEEDS

The little seeds are sleeping under their blanket made of earth.

They dream until the rainclouds cover the sky;

then all the little seeds begin to sigh,

"We are thirsty! We're thirsty!

We need some rain to drink!"

And now there are raindrops falling, raindrops falling,

and all the little seeds are busy drinking up all the

raindrops falling, raindrops falling, and soon ------

the little seeds begin to grow -------

s l o w l y . . . s l o w l y . . .

and some turn into flowers . . .

and others turn into trees,

and many turn into good things to eat!

And all of them are beautiful;

they're very beautiful, reaching up so high

as they try to touch the sky!

Reproduced by permission of B. Wolf
Copyright B. Wolf – 1993

STORY STARTER: "When the Wind Blows"

With younger children, do the following:

▶ Let the children tell you a story about what happens when the wind blows.

▶ You can do this as a group activity or one on one with each child.

▶ Write down what the children say. Later, read it back to them, and let the children draw pictures about the wind blowing.

With older children, do the following:

▶ Let the children dictate or write story sentences about what happens when the wind blows. Put these on sentence strip paper.

▶ Mix up the sentences. Have the children read each line and arrange in the correct sequence.

▶ This activity can be extended by the children. They can make a book of the story and illustrate each line.

DRAMATIC PLAY

FLOWER SHOP

▶ In the spring, flowers bloom in the dramatic play area's flower shop. The children begin by choosing a name for their shop.

▶ If possible, visit a flower shop, and have the florist talk to the children and show them different areas of the shop. Sometimes the florist gives the children flowers to take back to the classroom.

▶ Stock the shop in the dramatic play area with silk flowers, flowerpots, watering cans, gardening gloves, aprons, spray bottles, plastic vases, packets of seeds, and Styrofoam™ balls.

▶ Let the children discover how to stick the flowers into the Styrofoam™ and put these into the flowerpots. This eliminates the need for dirt or potting soil.

▶ If dirt or potting soil is added, place several layers of newspaper on the floor to catch spills for easy cleanup.

▶ The children can pretend to grow seeds, care for the flowers, and make flower arrangements in one part of the shop.

▶ In another area of the shop, put out a cash register, telephone, order pad, pencils, and pictures of flowers, and flower displays. These can be drawn by the children or cut from magazines. The children also may draw their own flower posters and brochures to place around the area.

▶ Allow plenty of time for this creative play. Sometimes the flower shop lasts weeks. Observation of the children's play will tell you when it is time to change.

FROM CATERPILLAR TO BUTTERFLY — FROM SEED TO GROWING PLANT

▶ To help the children assimilate all of the information about what happens in the spring, have them act out the story of Carle's *The Very Hungry Caterpillar* or Ehlert's *Planting a Rainbow.*

▶ This process encourages children to apply new vocabulary, to sequence events, and to use their imagination and creativity.

▶ Repeat this activity. Change it by reading different books to the children, adding props, and taking the dramatic play area outdoors on the playground.

▶ The action and reenactment change with each telling.

PUPPET PLAY

BUTTERFLY PUPPET

▶ To make the butterfly puppet, supply nine-inch paper plates, tagboard cut into strips approximately one inch wide and four to five inches long, pieces of colored tissue paper, crayons, markers, glue, and scissors.

▶ Let the children decide when they are interested in making puppets.

▶ Children can color the entire bottom of a plate with whichever colors and patterns they choose.

▶ Next, children bend the plate in half, with the colored halves showing. These become the wings of the butterfly puppet.

▶ With your assistance, on each side of the plate next to the crease have the children position a tagboard strip, and staple each end to the plate, allowing a little slack where they can insert their fingers.

▶ Finally, have the children glue pieces of colored tissue paper to the inside of the folded plate, allowing the tissue to overhang on the edges so that they "float" when the wings are flapped.

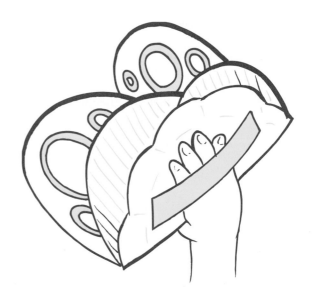

► For older toddlers and young preschoolers, simplify the puppet by having interested children color the plate and glue on the tissue paper. You attach the strips for their fingers.

► Each child inserts his thumb under one strip and his other four fingers under the other strip. When the wings flap, away flies the butterfly!

MUSIC

SPRING RAIN

The following is a *musical beat* activity. It also can be chanted.

Listen to the ràin, pretty ràin.*
Listen to the ràin, pretty ràin.*
Listen to it drìp.
Listen to it dròp.
Listen to the ràin, pretty ràin.*
  Listen to it pàtter on the ròof.*
  Listen to it pàtter on the ròof.*
  Listen to it drìp.
  Listen to it dròp.
  Listen to it pàtter on the ròof.*

Philip Jackman

    This method of indicating beat was introduced in theme 4 and is adapted from Moomaw's *More Than Singing.* Accent syllables with a vertical line (') above them, and pause (rest) where an asterisk (*) is shown. Use a drum or other musical instrument to help reinforce the beat.

MOVEMENT

MOVE WITH THE WIND

This activity works very well outdoors.

► Choose music with varied tempos, some instrumental and some that ask children to sing along.

► Let each child select crepe paper streamers or scarves.

► The children pretend that they are being moved by the wind as they dance and sing with the music.

CATERPILLAR HOPSCOTCH

► With the children's help, make a hopscotch game outdoors using sidewalk chalk. Draw circles until you have the length of the caterpillar you want, varying the sizes of the circles.

► Make a face and an antenna on the first circle, and draw simple legs on the other circles.

► On some of the circles, draw a vertical line down the middle; leave some circles with no lines.

► Encourage the children to find different ways of jumping from circle to circle. Jump on one foot, hop into only the unlined circles, place both feet on the lined ones, and jump with both feet.

► Emphasize the fun of jumping. This skill improves with each child's developmental growth.

► To extend the activity, number the circles. A child calls out a number and tries to throw a bean bag into the circle with the number selected.

► Older children make up their own rules and expand the game as well.

SENSORY ART

FRUIT AND VEGETABLE COLLAGE

This is a one-on-one activity. Help older infants make a collage by doing the following:

► Precut pictures of fruits and vegetables.

► Cut a piece of clear contact paper, about the size of a large piece of construction paper, and place it sticky side up in front of the child.

► While sitting with the child in your lap or next to you, guide him to put a picture on the contact paper.

► Talk to the child as you do this. Say the name of the fruit or vegetable.

► Continue as long as the child wants to.

SPRING COLLAGE

▶ Collect eggshells.

▶ Place the shells, a small amount at a time, in a paper towel, and crush them. The older children can help do this.

▶ Put the crushed shells, different colors of paper, and glue on the art table.

▶ Let the children have fun making a collage with the crushed eggshells and other materials.

FLOWERS EVERYWHERE

▶ Ask your local florist for discarded flowers. Collect as many roses as you can before they turn brown.

▶ Pull the petals off all of the flowers.

▶ Make the petals available for children to glue onto construction paper to make aromatic flower pictures.

▶ You can also create a pleasant sensory experience by adding the flower petals to the sand and water table.

▶ Encourage the children to compare sizes, discuss shapes, identify colors, and smell and feel different textures.

SPRING FLOWERS

▶ To create "spring flowers," gather together coffee filters, pipe cleaners, the bottoms of egg cartons, crayons, and markers.

▶ Cover the table with two or three layers of newspapers. The papers will provide padding and absorb colors that soak through as the children work.

▶ Let the children experiment with the materials. They can decorate a filter, poke a finger in the center, and make a small twist at the bottom.

▶ Fasten a pipe cleaner stem by giving one end of the pipe cleaner a few turns around the twist.

▶ Make a small hole in each of the 12 egg holders in the inverted lower half of an egg carton to create a "garden." The children can "plant" their flowers by inserting the pipe cleaners into the holes.

▶ Children identify their flowers by writing their names on the egg carton at the base of the flowers. They also can place their flowers in the dramatic play flower shop.

CREATIVE FOOD EXPERIENCES

BANANA SNACK

▶ Bananas are a favorite food of infants. Older babies like to squeeze banana slices through their fingers and then taste them.

▶ For a change, let the children try to "cut" the banana into slices themselves by using craft sticks.

▶ Place a section of a banana in front of the child, and demonstrate how this is done with each child. At first, hold the child's hand while placing the craft stick in it and gently "cutting down" on the banana.

▶ Talk about what you are doing.

▶ This activity should be repeated several times while the child is gaining control over his muscles.

BUTTERFLY SALAD

You will need the following ingredients for each serving:

> 2 pineapple rings
> lettuce leaf
> cottage cheese
> celery stick
> green and black olives

1. Wash hands.

2. Place lettuce leaf onto a paper plate.

3. Slice pineapple rings in half to use as an outline of the butterfly's wings.

4. Use the celery stick as the body.

BUTTERFLY SALAD

Wash hands.

Place one lettuce leaf onto a paper plate.

Slice 2 pineapple rings in 1/2 to use as an outline of

the butterfly's wings. Use one celery stick as the body.

Place a small amount of cottage cheese inside of

pineapple rings. Decorate the cottage cheese with

green and black olives.

5. Put a small amount of cottage cheese inside of the pineapple.

6. Decorate the cottage cheese with green and black olives.

MATH

LET'S GO FISHING

- Make several fishing poles using dowel rods that are approximately two to three feet long. Tie a piece of yarn or string to one end, and attach a magnet to the end of the yarn. You might use a hot glue gun to attach the yarn to the magnet.
- Let the children help you make, decorate, and cut out the fish for the fishing pond.
- Attach paper clips to the ends of the fish.
- Place a large piece of blue craft or construction paper on the floor. Cut in the shape of a pond.
- Put the "fish" into the pond.

- Younger children take turns using the fishing rod to try picking up the fish with the magnet.
- To make it more interesting for older children, number the fish from 1 to 10. After the children catch the fish, they add up the numbers to see who caught the most. Help them add up the numbers as needed.

WHERE'S THE BUTTER?

- To create this game, you will need to make and laminate a game folder, "potatoes," and "butter squares."
- The object of the game is for the child to match each "butter square" with a numeral on it to the potato showing the same number of "eyes."
- Laminate a standard file folder. Create 10 potatoes out of brown or tan construction paper, showing "one eye," "two eyes," and up to "ten eyes."
- Write the numeral corresponding to the number of eyes on the back of each potato.
- Cut 10 "butter squares" out of yellow construction paper, and number them from 1 to 10.
- Place the potatoes on the open folder in a random arrangement. Then cut a strip of clear tape and press it down, the lower half on the potato and the upper half on the folder, to form a hinge.
- This makes the game self-correcting. If the child is unable to match the "butter" numeral to the potato "eyes," he can lift up the potato to see if the numbers match.
- Let the children know that you have created a new math folder for them. Explain the game.
- Place this game in the math center for the children to play whenever they wish.

SCIENCE

WHAT HAPPENED TO THE WHITE CARNATION?

▶ After reading books, showing pictures, planting gardens, and visiting a florist shop, continue to talk about the similarities and differences of the plants.

▶ Carefully remove a plant from its container, and place it on newspaper so the roots are visible.

▶ Point to the roots, leaves, stems, and flowers of the plant. Explain that each part of a plant has a certain job. The roots help hold plants in place. Water and food move through the stems. The stems also help the plant stay upright. A tree has a woody, hard stem.

▶ To demonstrate how water moves up through a stem, place a long-stemmed white carnation into a clear container with some water and a few drops of red or blue food coloring. The darker the color, the more dramatic the outcome. For best results, the stem should be freshly cut on a diagonal.

▶ Try this with several flowers. Have the children observe the flower every 10 to 15 minutes and describe any change in the petals. They will notice the petals begin to take on the color of the food coloring.

▶ With toddlers, simplify the activity by showing them the colored water and watching with them as the tinted liquid moves up the stem, changing the color of the carnation. Talk about the color of the flower. What are their favorite colors?

EARTHWORMS

▶ Collect a few earthworms.

▶ Punch holes in the lids of two plastic jars.

▶ Conduct an experiment to help the children understand that earthworms help keep the soil healthy.

▶ Give the children the two jars, and ask them to put a layer of potting soil in the bottom of each.

▶ Next, children add a layer of sand. Continue alternating layers until the jar is almost full.

▶ Spread grated carrots on the top of the soil in each jar.

▶ Sprinkle just enough water in each jar to moisten the soil.

▶ Place a few earthworms in *one* of the jars.

▶ Place the lids on the jars, and cover them with a dark cloth. Ask the children not to disturb the jars until the next day.

▶ Ask the children to predict what changes they might see in the jars the next day. Write down or have children write down what they think will occur.

▶ Do this for several days. Each morning, uncover the jars, and encourage the children to note the changes that have taken place.

▶ If the soil has dried out, add enough water to moisten.

▶ Over time, the children will discover that the earthworms have mixed the layers of potting soil and sand in the jar.

▶ What happened to the carrots?

▶ In the jar without worms, nothing will change.

▶ Explain to the children that the earthworms tunnel through the soil and mix in nutrients that help plants grow.

SOCIAL STUDIES

WHERE DOES FOOD COME FROM?

This is an exploration that you and the children can enjoy together. Though children eat food every day, they probably have little idea how it travels from field or garden to plate, starting as seeds or bulbs, growing, being harvested, and then being processed for eating by canning and freezing.

▶ First talk about the "families" of fruits, grains, and vegetables and how they are determined by the part of the plant we eat. Some examples include:

Fruit — apples, oranges, and pears

Root or bulb — onions, carrots, potatoes, and radishes

Stems — celery and asparagus

Seeds — wheat, rice, peas, corn, and beans

Leaves — cabbage, spinach, and lettuce

Flowers — broccoli and cauliflower

▶ Show pictures of these foods from books, magazines, and seed catalogs. Select some pictures that show the trucks and trains that take the food from the farm to farmer's markets and grocery stores. The Children's Books section of this theme includes some suggestions.

► Older children also enjoy reading about the canning process or visiting a local plant, if possible.

► Talk about the children's favorite kinds of fruits, vegetables, and grains.

► Pick out one or more examples of plant-grown food, and set up a "laboratory" to examine them. A common food, such as peas, is a good sample.

► On a table, arrange several seeds or growing plants, and label them. Next to them, add several fresh pea pods, then a can of peas, and finally a frozen food container of peas.

► Have a taste test by heating some canned peas, cooking some frozen peas, and having some thoroughly washed raw peas for the children to sample.

► Ask the children to describe how they taste. Do they taste the same? Different?

► If possible, ask a farmer, gardener, or fruit grower to visit the classroom and tell the children all about his or her farm, garden, or orchard. Ask if this person can bring some of the produce grown.

CHILDREN'S BOOKS

Bacon, Ron. (1993). *Wind.* New York: Scholastic.

Brown, Craig. (1994). *In the Spring.* New York: Greenwillow.

Carle, Eric. (1998). *Let's Paint a Rainbow.* New York: Cartwheel Books.

Carle, Eric. (1994). *The Very Hungry Caterpillar.* (Board Book). New York: Philomel.

Carr, Jan. (2001). *Splish, Splash, Spring.* New York: Holiday House.

Cassie, Brian, and Jerry Pallotta. (1995). *The Butterfly Alphabet.* Illustrated by Mark Astrella. Watertown, MA: Charlesbridge.

Cooney, Barbara. (1985). *Miss Rumphius.* New York: Puffin.

De Coteau Orie, Sandra. (1996). *Did You Hear Wind Sing Your Name?* Illustrated by Christopher Canyon. New York: Walker and Company.

Demi. (1993). *Little Baby Lamb.* (Soft and Furry Board Book). New York: Grossett and Dunlap.

dePaola, Tomie. (1983). *The Legend of the Bluebonnet.* New York: G. P. Putnam.

Ehlert, Lois. (1988). *Planting a Rainbow.* San Diego: Harcourt.

Ets, Marie Hall. (1978). *Gilberto and the Wind.* New York: Puffin.

George, Lindsay B. (1996). *Around the Pond: Who's Been Here?* New York: Greenwillow.

Gibbons, Gail. (1991). *From Seed to Plant.* New York: Holiday House.

Hill, Eric. (1991). *Spot in the Garden.* (Board Book). New York: Putnam.

Hirschi, Ron. (1996). *Spring/Primavera.* New York: Puffin.

Johnson, Neil. (1997). *A Field of Sunflowers.* New York: Cartwheel Books.

Kalan, Robert. (1991). *Rain.* Illustrated by Donald Crews. New York: Mulberry Books.

Kroll, Virginia. (1993). *A Carp for Kimiko.* Illustrated by Katherine Roundtree. Watertown, MA: Charlesbridge.

Lionni, Leo. (1995). *Inch by Inch.* New York: Mulberry.

Marzollo, Jean. (1997). *I'm a Caterpillar.* Illustrated by Judith Moffatt. New York: Scholastic.

Marzollo, Jean. (1995). *I'm a Seed.* Illustrated by Judith Moffatt. New York: Scholastic.

Maslowski, Steve. (2002). *Birds in the Spring.* North Mankato, MN: Smart Apple Media.

Mudd, Maria M. (1991). *The Butterfly.* Illustrated by Wendy Smith-Griswold. New York: Steward, Tabori, and Chang.

Pfister, Marcus. (1998). *Hopper Hunts for Spring.* New York: North South.

Polacco, Patricia. (1997). *Thunder Cake.* New York: Putnam.

Roberts, Bethany. (2001). *The Wind's Garden.* New York: Henry Holt.

Rockwell, Anne. (2002). *Becoming Butterflies.* Illustrated by Megan Halsey. New York: Walker.

Rockwell, Anne F. (1996). *My Spring Robin.* Illustrated by Harlow and Lizzie Rockwell. New York: Demco Media.

Rucki, Ani. (1998). *When the Earth Wakes.* New York: Scholastic.

Scheer, Julian, and Marvin Bileck. (1985). *Rain Makes Applesauce.* New York: Viking.

Schweninger, Ann. (1995). *Springtime.* New York: Puffin.

Serfozo, Mary. (1990). *Rain Talk.* Illustrated by Keiko Narabashi. Chicago: Children's Press.

Showers, Paul. (1993). *The Listening Walk.* (Rev. ed.). Illustrated by Aliki: New York: HarperTrophy.

Spier, Peter. (1997). *Rain.* New York: Bantam Dell.

Tresselt, Alvin. (1990). *Rain Drop Splash.* Illustrated by Leonard Weisgard. New York: Morrow.

Family Letter (Primary Grade)

Dear Family,

We are studying the four seasons. Our theme is "Spring," and we will provide opportunities for the children to learn the following:

- Spring is a season of the year that comes after winter and before summer.
- Spring is the time of the year that has many changes in nature, such as longer days and shorter nights.
- In the spring, many birds and some other animals, such as fish and insects, migrate to cooler climates.
- New life and growth begin: seeds sprout, leaves grow, and flowers bloom.
- Spring weather becomes warmer, and we begin wearing less clothing.

We will be talking about the following:

- seasonal changes and the new growth of animals, plants, birds, and insects
- seasonal celebrations and the arrival of spring and planting time
- seasonal activities, such as picnics, kite flying, planting vegetable and flower gardens, and sports
- seasonal fruits and vegetables

Strengthen your child's learning by doing some of the following at home:

- Take walks, and look at what is happening to nature in the spring. Talk with your child about what she or he observes.
- Enjoy kite flying and family walks in the rain.
- Plant a garden with your child. Make it a family event.
- As a family, visit the parks and arboretums in your city.

Family participation opportunities at school will include:

- Go with us on our field trip to a local florist.
  Date _____   Time _____
- Spend some time with us in the classroom, and see all of the activities in which we are involved.
  Date _____   Time _____

Our wish list for this theme includes:

flowerpots of all sizes

clean, unused coffee filters

clean baby food jars with lids

plastic vases

earthworms

potting soil

Thanks!

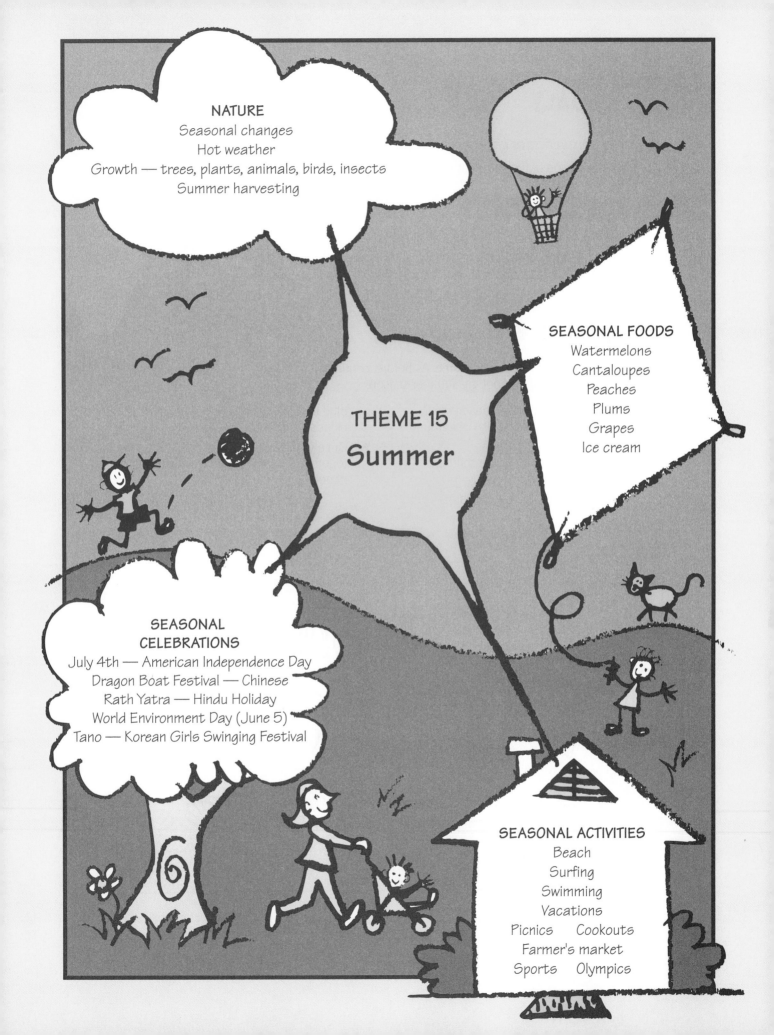

NATURE
Seasonal changes
Hot weather
Growth — trees, plants, animals, birds, insects
Summer harvesting

SEASONAL FOODS
Watermelons
Cantaloupes
Peaches
Plums
Grapes
Ice cream

THEME 15
Summer

SEASONAL CELEBRATIONS
July 4th — American Independence Day
Dragon Boat Festival — Chinese
Rath Yatra — Hindu Holiday
World Environment Day (June 5)
Tano — Korean Girls Swinging Festival

SEASONAL ACTIVITIES
Beach
Surfing
Swimming
Vacations
Picnics   Cookouts
Farmer's market
Sports   Olympics

THEME GOALS

To provide opportunities for children to learn the following:

▶ Summer is a season of the year that comes after spring and before fall.

▶ Summer is the time of year with the longest days and shortest nights.

▶ In the summer, baby birds and other animals grow and learn to take care of themselves.

▶ Most fruits and vegetables grow until they become ripe enough to eat.

▶ Summer weather becomes very hot, and we need to wear lightweight clothing.

Children-Created Bulletin Board

Summer is a continuation of the "Seasons" theme. As before, continue to make the bulletin board interactive. The look of the board will change throughout the summer season.

▶ With the children's help, create a beach scene. Glue sand onto the bulletin board's background paper.

▶ Add seashells, real or drawn by the children.

▶ Have the children tear pieces of construction paper in assorted shades of blue, or paint paper blue to make an ocean or a lake. Add sailboats, clouds, and sun.

▶ Once you get started, the children can work together to make the bulletin board three-dimensional.

VOCABULARY STARTERS

Let the children add words.

beach — a sandy place near a lake or an ocean for playing and sunbathing.

hot — a very high temperature.

ripe — when fruits and vegetables are ready to eat.

shade — a place protected from the heat and light of the sun.

temperature — how hot or cold something is.

LANGUAGE EXPERIENCES

FUN IN THE SUN INDOORS

▶ Use a flannelboard and large flannelboard pieces to tell a story about the summertime.

▶ Make flannelboard pieces that correspond to the experiences of the children, such as the sun, beach balls, sand, small buckets, and shovels. The actual objects should be available in the classroom indoor or outdoor environment.

▶ After you tell a short story, let the older infants and the toddlers put the pieces on the flannelboard, name the articles, and "tell" their story.

LET'S HAVE A READING PARTY OUTDOORS

▶ Take a basket of books, pillows, blankets, and teddy bears outdoors, and have a reading party with the children!

▶ Pitch a tent for a pretend campout, and tell stories.

▶ Have a snack in the tent. Make a "trail mix" with dry cereal pieces, raisins, nuts, and dried fruit.

POEM: "Summertime"

I love to swim in the summertime,
The summertime, the summertime.
I love to swim in the summertime
When the sky is clear and bright.

When we go to the beach in the summertime,
The summertime, the summertime,
When we go to the beach in the summertime,
I like to fly my kite.

I love to sail in the summertime,
The summertime, the summertime.
I love to sail in the summertime,
In a boat that's white and blue.

When we go to the lake in the summertime,
The summertime, the summertime,
When we go to the lake in the summertime,
We'll go fishing. How about you?

Philip Jackman

DRAMATIC PLAY

SURPRISE ENVIRONMENTS

▶ Close off the dramatic play area with a large sheet while "creating" is in progress.

▶ Have a few children set up a special dramatic play area with items they make or bring from home and that are unknown to the other children.

▶ Children will decide what the area will be, which props are needed, and what they will name the dramatic play area. This process is their responsibility.

▶ Add items only if the children ask you to do so.

▶ After you do this, other children will want to set up surprise environments too. That is the whole idea — to get the entire class involved in diverse thinking, problem solving, working together cooperatively, and using their imagination and creativity.

IN THE GOOD OLD SUMMERTIME

▶ Set up a dramatic play ice cream stand outdoors for the children.

▶ Have the children make a sign with the name of the ice cream store, as well as labels for the kinds of ice cream sold and how much the cones cost.

▶ You will need cotton and cotton balls for the ice cream. Color some of the balls with food coloring before setting up. Also gather together containers of sprinkles and toppings, colored pom-poms, scoops, cones, napkins, and pretend money.

MORE OUTDOOR FUN

▶ Create an island! It can be Hawaii, Jamaica, or any place the children choose.

▶ Get a few grass skirts, sunglasses, shells, and non-working cameras.

▶ You and the children can make palm trees, create a beach area by putting sand on a large piece of plastic, and add blue food coloring to a large plastic tub filled with water.

▶ How about some cold lemonade to drink?

▶ The children will tell you what else is needed on their island. They will have a great time, and so will you!

PUPPET PLAY

BEACH PEOPLE PUPPETS

Have fun at the beach! To do that, you will need to create an environment to help children act out what it is like to be at the beach.

▶ Make people puppets! Each one is built around a child's face. For example, one child can be the "sun," a "cloud," or "a wave." (See the illustration.) Help younger children and those who have not been to a beach create their puppets.

▶ Make each puppet with heavy or corrugated cardboard. Out of a large, rectangular piece, cut a face-size hole in the center.

▶ The child who wants to be a sun can decorate the puppet with crayons, markers, or tempera paint in sunny colors.

▶ The children will think of other beach puppets they want to make, such as a beach ball, a round life preserver, or a sand castle.

▶ Encourage the children to create "beach stories" using their puppets. Get them started by sharing books, photographs, and other pictures of beach activities.

MUSIC

LET'S CELEBRATE

▶ Celebrate the Fourth of July with an outdoor "concert."

▶ Make drums (use oatmeal containers), shakers (use paper plates stapled together with birdseed inside), and flutes (use paper towel rolls with waxed paper covering one end and holes punched in one side).

▶ Take these "instruments" outside, along with all of the rhythm instruments and a tape player.

▶ Spread blankets on the grass.

▶ Serve lemonade.

▶ Decorate the playground equipment with red, white, and blue crepe paper.

▶ Let the concert begin. Play festive march music, and have the children play along and march with their musical instruments.

▶ Hold babies in teachers' laps and help them clap to the music. Some infants can crawl around on the blankets, while older ones can be pulled around the playground in decorated wagons.

RAINDROPS PITTER-PATTER AND SUNBEAMS GLOW

This is a *rhythmic* poem. Each verse emphasizes a different mood and season.

▶ Try saying each verse differently. Rain might have a light staccato quality, summer an expansive tone, fall a back-and-forth lilt, and winter a hushed tone.

- The words offer children an opportunity to play with language.
- Each verse suggests an appropriate arm-hand activity, for example: descending hands with wiggling fingers for rain, waving hands with spread fingers for sun, dropping hands sliding back and forth for leaves, and softly swaying falling hands for snow.

In the spring the raindrops go pitter-patter-pit,
Pitter-patter, pitter-patter, pitter-patter-pit.

In the summer the sunbeams glow shiny-shony-shine,
Shiny-shony, shiny-shony, shiny-shony-shine.

In the fall the red leaves dip flitter-flutter-flit,
Flitter-flutter, flitter-flutter, flitter-flutter-flit.

In the winter the snowflakes slip softly-siftly-soft,
Softly-siftly, softly-siftly, softly-siftly-soft.

Philip Jackman

MOVEMENT

SUMMER OLYMPICS

TODDLER · PRESCHOOL-K · PRIMARY-GRADE

- Turn your playground into an Olympic games site.
- Put some napping mats out for the gymnastics event, use the balance beam, set up a track for the runners, and add a sprinkler for the water event.
- Be sure to design the activities for the different developmental stages of the children in your class.
- The children will suggest additional events — be flexible.
- At the end of the day, each child receives a ribbon that says "First Place."

SENSORY ART

WATER EVERYWHERE

INFANT · TODDLER

- Older infants and toddlers enjoy outdoor water play. Sprinkler play, with children walking or running through the water, trying to catch the water in a plastic bucket, or just sitting where the sprinkler "rains" on them, can continue for long periods of time.

- Turn the sprinkler on and off while the children play.
- Tell the children what you are doing. Say: "I'm turning the water off." "See, it is all gone." They will probably look closely at the sprinkler to see where the water goes.
- Say: "Look! Here it comes."
- Let the children help you turn the water on and off.

SUMMER SPRAY

PRESCHOOL-K

- Painting outdoors with spray bottles is fun for preschoolers.
- Take a large piece of butcher paper, and tape or tie it with yarn to the playground fence.
- Cover the grass or ground with a dropcloth.
- Fill three small spray bottles with watered-down paint in primary colors, one each of red, yellow, and blue.
- The more water you add to the paint, the more the children's creations will look like watercolor paintings.
- Ask the children to put on smocks, just as they do when painting indoors.
- Let the children, one at a time or in pairs, with one at each end of the paper, spray paint the paper. They choose which of the three colors to use, or they may even choose all three.
- After the painting dries, create a banner, and hang it from the classroom ceiling, or hang it as a mural on a wall in the classroom for all to see.

WATERCOLOR BUTTERFLIES AND IMAGINATIVE DESIGNS

PRESCHOOL-K · PRIMARY-GRADE

For this project, supply white paper, watercolors, paintbrushes, water, scissors, and a butterfly design, if desired. This activity is designed to introduce the children to a new sensory art technique. Ask the children who are interested to create several designs on the sheets of paper using the techniques that follow.

Wet on Wet

On one of the pictures, the children use the "wet on wet" technique by painting with plain water first. Then they paint over the water design with watercolors. The children will see how the colors run together, creating new colors and interesting patterns.

Wet on Dry

Next, the children paint a picture using the "wet on dry" technique. They paint with watercolors on a dry piece of paper.

▶ Ask open-ended questions, such as: "Do you see a difference in your two paintings?" "Which do you think is your favorite?" "When the pictures dry, would you like to cut the designs out and display them?" "Would you like to put a frame around either of your pictures?" "Would you like to draw some flowers or butterflies and paint them?" "Will you paint your next picture with the *wet on wet* or *wet on dry* technique?"

CREATIVE FOOD EXPERIENCES

SHAKE IT UP

You will need the following:

    2 scoops of ice cream, preferably vanilla
    1 scoop of orange sherbet
    1/3 cup milk
    2 or 3 tablespoons of orange juice

1. Wash hands.
2. Place all ingredients in a blender.
3. Mix until all ingredients are well combined.
4. Enjoy!

(For a change, add peaches instead of orange sherbet.)

EASY SANDWICH SURPRISE

You will need the following:

    a loaf of bread
    fillings such as peanut butter and jelly, or tuna spread

1. Wash hands.
2. Roll out a slice of bread with a rolling pin until it becomes very thin.
3. Spread the filling over the bread.
4. Carefully roll bread lengthwise, and hold together with toothpicks if needed.
5. Slice into bite-size pieces.

The children love making this kind of sandwich, and it is self-correcting — if a piece of bread with filling does not roll, they can eat it anyway!

HAYSTACKS

You will need the following:

    1 small package butterscotch chips
    1 small package chocolate chips
    1 6-ounce package Chinese noodles

1. Wash hands.
2. Melt the butterscotch and chocolate chips over low heat.

HAY STACKS

Wash hands.

Melt 1 small package butterscotch chips and

1 small package chocolate chips over low heat.

Add 1 6-ounce package of Chinese noodles.

Place on wax paper in large spoonfuls.

Shape into balls. Let set.

EAT!

3. Add the package of Chinese noodles.

4. Place on waxed paper in large spoonfuls, and shape into balls.

5. Let set. Eat!

MATH

MATCHING GAME

▶ Children love to find fun things to do in baskets placed around the room.

▶ Fill one basket with a variety of plastic containers and their lids.

▶ The containers should be small enough for the children to handle on their own. Provide plastic ones with tops and some with screw-on lids.

▶ The child can match the containers to her corresponding lids independently or by playing cooperatively with others.

▶ Make this activity available for the children to return to anytime they wish.

BLOCKS AND MATH ARE PARTNERS

▶ Block play is ongoing in every early childhood classroom, no matter what the season.

▶ Stimulate block play by placing some colorful cards nearby with simple pictures of long, short, high, wide, narrow, straight, curvy, and zigzag block designs, along with appropriate word labels.

▶ This is a nonintrusive way to increase mathematical concepts and vocabulary.

▶ Remember to take photographs of the block center creations, or make a simple sketch of the original designs. Be sure to label each picture with the "architect's" name.

SCIENCE

SUN PRINTS

▶ Place objects from the classroom, such as blocks, Styrofoam™ pieces, lids from containers, flannel-board pieces, buttons, shells, and a plastic knife or fork, on dark construction paper, and expose them to sunlight for several hours.

▶ At the end of the day, let the children remove the items and discuss what has happened.

EVAPORATION

▶ Discuss the process of evaporation with the children.

▶ Take two identical small jars, and fill them halfway with colored water. Do not cover the jars.

▶ Put one jar in the sun and the other in the shade.

▶ Have the children predict which will evaporate first.

▶ Discuss and record children's observations each day.

▶ How many days does it take for the water in each to evaporate?

SOCIAL STUDIES

LET'S GO TO THE BEACH!

Summer is the time when people all over the country love to swim, sunbathe, and play at lakes and beaches in our coastal areas.

▶ Read Hayles's *Beach Play* to the children to set the scene; see the Children's Books section in this theme.

▶ Help the children learn more about beaches through pictures, a map, and a miniature beach in your outdoor play area.

▶ Using pictures of beaches that you have collected from travel brochures and magazines, talk with the children about what a beach is (sandy area where the land meets the ocean).

▶ Ask the children if they have ever been to a beach. What do people do there? What do they wear? What do they take with them?

▶ Using a map of the United States that includes an inset map of the Hawaiian Islands, explain that the blue area next to the coastline on our east is the Atlantic Ocean; on the west shore is the Pacific Ocean; and on the south shore is the Gulf of Mexico.

▶ Beaches are located where these blue areas touch the darker-colored land areas.

▶ Have the children show you where beaches are located on your map.

▶ If the children ever want to go to a beach, they should know directions: north, south, east, and west.

▶ Guide the children into showing you where the directions are on the map. Show them the arrow pointing north, usually found in one corner of a map.

▶ It is helpful to write "north," "south," "east," and "west" on the map's four sides.

▶ Invite the children to locate where they live on the map. Ask them in which direction they would have to travel to visit beaches on the west, east, or south. Have them point to the directions on the map.

▶ To extend this activity, have the children make a beach on the playground, and plan a trip to their beach. The existing sandbox or a large piece of plastic on the grass covered with sand becomes the beach. Provide sunscreen, beach balls, a beach umbrella, towels, shells, pails, and shovels.

▶ The children may wear swimsuits and play in the waves (the sprinkler) to complete the environment.

CHILDREN'S BOOKS

Archambault, John, and David Plummer. (1996). *Grandmother's Garden.* Illustrated by Raul Colon. New York: Silver Burdett.

Boelts, Maribeth. (1995). *Summer's End.* Illustrated by Ellen Kandoian. New York: Houghton Mifflin.

Bunting, Eve. (1996). *Sunflower House.* Illustrated by Kathryn Hewitt. San Diego: Harcourt.

Bunting, Eve. (1994). *Flower Garden.* Illustrated by Kathryn Hewitt. San Diego: Harcourt.

Crews, Nina. (1995). *One Hot Summer Day.* New York: Greenwillow.

dePaola, Tomie. (1994). *Four Stories for Four Seasons.* New York: Aladdin.

Ehlert, Lois. (1996). *Eating the Alphabet: Fruits and Vegetables from A to Z.* (Board Book). New York: Red Wagon.

Euvremer, Teryl. (1987). *Sun's Up.* New York: Crown.

Fleming, Denise. (1995). *In the Small, Small Pond.* New York: Henry Holt.

Florian, Douglas. (1998). *A Summer Day.* New York: William Morrow.

Garland, Sherry. (1995). *Summer Sands.* Illustrated by Robert J. Lee. San Diego: Harcourt.

Gershator, Phillis, and David Gershator. (1998). *Greetings, Sun.* New York: DK Publishing.

Haas, Irene. (1997). *A Summertime Song.* New York: Margaret K. McElderry Books.

Hall, Donald. (1995). *Lucy's Summer.* Illustrated by Michael McCurdy. San Diego: Harcourt.

Hayles, Marsha. (1998). *Beach Play.* Illustrated by Hideko Takahashi. New York: Henry Holt.

Hirschi, Ron. (1991). *Summer.* Photographed by Thomas D. Mangelsen. New York: Cobblehill Books.

Kesselman, Windy. (1995). *Sand in My Shoes.* Illustrated by Ronald Himler. New York: Hyperion Books.

Lee, Huy Voien. (1997). *At the Beach.* New York: Henry Holt.

Lerner, Carol. (1996). *Backyard Birds of Summer.* New York: William Morrow.

MacKinnon, Debbie. (1995). *The Seasons: Spring, Summer, Autumn, Winter.* Photographed by Anthea Sieveking. New York: Barron's Juveniles.

Maslowski, Steve. (2002). *Birds in the Summer.* North Mankato, MN: Smart Apple Media.

Peters, Lisa W. (1995a). *The Hayloft.* Illustrated by K. D. Plum. New York: Dial Books.

Peters, Lisa W. (1995b). *The Sun, the Wind, and the Rain.* Illustrated by Ted Rand. New York: Henry Holt.

Rius, Maria, and Jose M. Parramon. (1998). *Summer: The Four Seasons.* New York: Barron's Juveniles.

Rosa-Mendoza, Gladys. (2002). *Fruits and Vegetables/Frutas y Vegetales.* Illustrated by Linda H. Ayriss. New York: Metmi Publishing.

Sanchez, Isidro, and Carmen Peris. (1992). *Summer Sports.* New York: Barron's Juveniles.

Van Leeuwen, Jean. (1997). *Touch the Summer Sky.* Illustrated by Dan Andreasen. New York: Dial Books.

Wallace, Karen. (1999). *Whatever the Weather.* New York: DK Publishing.

Yolen, Jane. (1995). *Before the Storm.* Illustrated by Georgia Pugh. New York: Boyds Mills Press.

Family Letter (Toddler)

Dear Family,

As we continue to study the seasons, we are now starting our theme "Summer." We will offer opportunities for the children to learn the following:

- *Summer is a season of the year that comes after spring and before fall.*
- *Summer is the time of year with the longest days and shortest nights.*
- *In the summer, baby birds and other animals grow and learn to take care of themselves.*
- *Fruits and vegetables grow until they become ripe enough to eat.*
- *Summer weather becomes very hot, and we need to wear lightweight clothing.*

We will be talking about the following:

- *nature and seasonal changes*
- *the growth of trees, plants, animals, birds, and insects*
- *seasonal celebrations, such as the Fourth of July*
- *seasonal activities, such as going to the beach, swimming, picnics, and the Olympic games*
- *seasonal foods, such as watermelon, cantaloupe, and ice cream*

To reinforce what your child is learning in school, try some of the following at home:

- *Go on a family picnic.*
- *Enjoy the Fourth of July with your child.*
- *Decorate your child's tricycle with red, white, and blue crepe paper streamers.*
- *Enjoy water play with your child.*

Family participation opportunities at school will include:

- *Come to our Fourth of July outdoor "concert" on the playground.*
  Date _____   Time _____
- *Come and help us with our summer recipes.*
  Date _____   Time _____

Our wish list for this theme includes:

  small baskets
  clean plastic containers with lids
  plain and corrugated cardboard
  seashells
  plastic buckets with shovels

Thanks!

ENViRONMENT

*C*hildren learn by doing. Young children must explore, discover, and create the environment around them. Encourage children to do what they can for themselves, but provide guidance with some tasks before they become too difficult and frustration begins.

The thematic activities in this section have been developed to assist young children in growing up with a joy of exploration and an appreciation of the environment. A wide variety of experiences, materials, and equipment will accommodate the children's developmental ages and stages.

The following themes are included in Section IV, "Environment":

Theme 16 — Colors in Our World

Theme 17 — Shapes in Our World

Theme 18 — Oceans and Lakes

Theme 19 — Forests

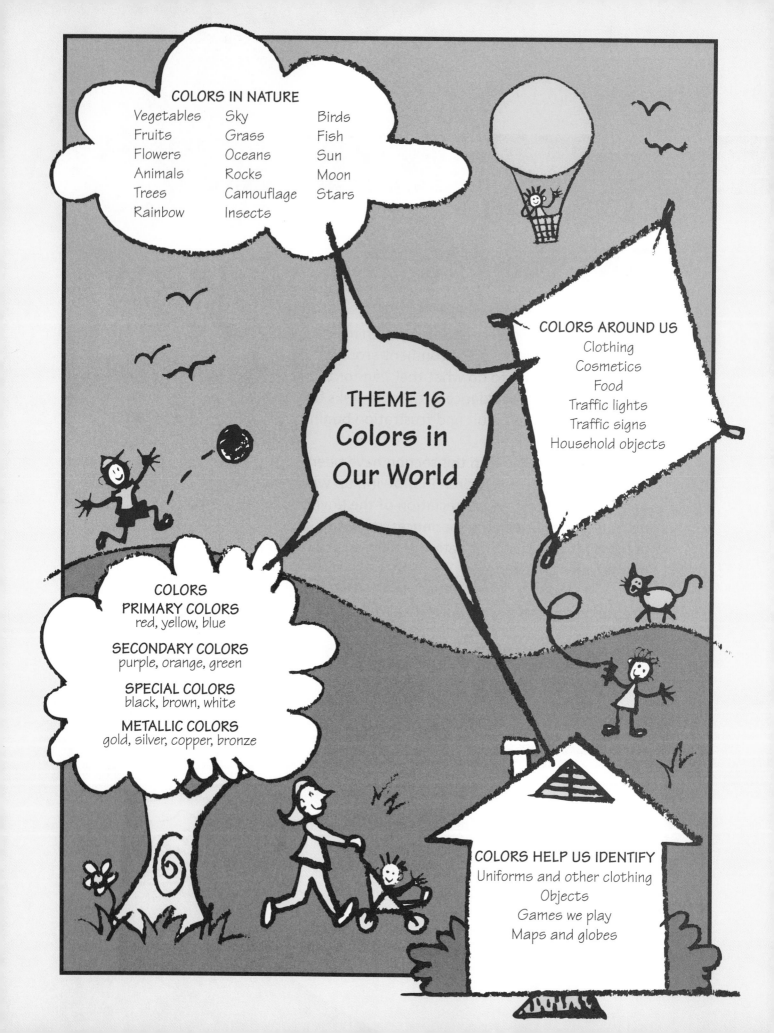

COLORS IN NATURE

Vegetables   Sky   Birds
Fruits   Grass   Fish
Flowers   Oceans   Sun
Animals   Rocks   Moon
Trees   Camouflage   Stars
Rainbow   Insects

THEME 16
Colors in Our World

COLORS AROUND US
Clothing
Cosmetics
Food
Traffic lights
Traffic signs
Household objects

COLORS
PRIMARY COLORS
red, yellow, blue

SECONDARY COLORS
purple, orange, green

SPECIAL COLORS
black, brown, white

METALLIC COLORS
gold, silver, copper, bronze

COLORS HELP US IDENTIFY
Uniforms and other clothing
Objects
Games we play
Maps and globes

THEME GOALS

To provide opportunities for children to learn the following:

▶ Our world is full of color.

▶ Color is important for identifying most things in our world.

▶ Color makes our world more interesting and enjoyable.

▶ Colors have names.

▶ The primary colors are red, yellow, and blue, and when mixed, they produce new colors.

▶ The secondary colors are orange, green, and purple, and they are created by mixing two primary colors.

▶ There are many ways of experimenting with and exploring colors.

Children-Created Bulletin Board

Use this bulletin board to provide the children with concrete examples of how their world is filled with color. As always, include the children in your planning. They will give you a lot of colorful ideas and help you make the board an ongoing project.

▶ Cover the bulletin board with a pastel shade of paper for background.

▶ In the upper left side of the board, place a rainbow made of colored crepe paper or ribbons that the children cut.

▶ Have the children crumple up white tissue paper to make a cloud. Place this in the upper right side.

▶ Have a bright yellow sun peek out from behind the cloud.

▶ In the lower left corner of the bulletin board, have the children create a flower garden. See the

Science activity, "A Garden of Color," in this theme for ways to make the garden.

▶ In the lower right corner of the board, make a blue ocean with waves using cellophane or tissue paper.

▶ Ask the children to draw pictures of themselves or other children, cut these out, and place them anywhere they want on the bulletin board. See the Social Studies part of this theme.

▶ Title the board "Colors in Our World."

▶ Continue to add to the bulletin board throughout this theme.

VOCABULARY STARTERS

Let the children add words.

black — created by mixing all three primary colors.

brown — created by mixing red, yellow, and black.

primary colors — three colors, red, yellow, and blue, from which all of the colors of the rainbow are created.

secondary colors — orange, green, and purple, which are created by mixing any two primary colors.

shade — the darkness or amount of black in a particular color.

tint — the lightness or amount of white in a particular color.

white — the absence of color.

LANGUAGE EXPERIENCES

COLORFUL PEEKABOO

▶ Play peekaboo with the babies.

▶ To make this activity colorful, collect solid-color, see-through scarves.

▶ Hold up a scarf between you and the little one. Play peekaboo.

▶ Talk about the color of the scarf.

▶ Repeat this activity often. It is a fun way to share colors with babies.

A COLOR A DAY

▶ To begin this theme, totally surround the children with a color each day. It is important for children to *experience* color.

▶ For example, children paint with red, wear red, sing about red, eat a red snack, read books about red, and build with red blocks or Legos™.

▶ In small groups, talk about the color of the day. To get the children started, ask open-ended questions, such as: "What do you see that is red?" "How does red taste?"

▶ Write what the children say about each color on a chart. It can be made into a book with their drawings and placed in the book center.

POEM: "Primary Colors"

The primary colors look bright to me.
The first is red, as we all can see,
The second is yellow, plain as can be,
And the third looks blue to me.
  Mix red and yellow — it's orange you'll see,
  Mix red and blue — it's purple you'll see,
  Mix blue and yellow — it's green you'll see,
  And they all look good to me.

Philip Jackman

COLORFUL LANGUAGES

Young children enjoy learning languages. The following names for colors are another way to introduce the colors of the world.

English	Spanish	French	German
red	rojo	rouge	rot
	ró-ho	rōōzh	rote
yellow	amarillo	jaune	gelb
	ah-ma-reé-yo	zhōne	gelb
blue	azul	bleu	blau
	ah-zōōl	blōo	bla-oh
green	verde	vert	grun
	vaiŕ-day	vair	green
purple	morado	violet	purpur
	mo-rah-do	vee-o-lay	pŏoŕ-pŏor
orange	naranja	orange	orangefarben
	na-rahn-ha	o-ranzh	o-rahńj-fár-ben
brown	marron	brun	braun
	mah-rońe	brŏon	brown
black	negro	noir	schwarz
	néh-gro	nwahr	shvarts
white	blanco	blanc	weiss
	blahń-co	blahnc	vice

English	Italian	Japanese
red	rosso	akai
	róh-so	ah-káh-ee
yellow	giallo	kiiro
	jee-ah́-lo	kée-ro
blue	blu	aoi
	blue	ah-oń-ee
green	verde	midori
	vaiŕ-day	mee-dóh-ree
purple	porpora	murasaki-iro
	por-pór-a	mōō-ruh-sáh-kee-eé-ro

English	Italian	Japanese
orange	arancio	mikan
	ah-ráhn-chee-o	mée-kahn
brown	bruno	kasshoku
	brōō-no	kah-shó-kōō
black	nero	kuroi
	náy-ro	koo-róh-ee
white	bianco	shiroi
	bee-áhn-co	she-róh-ee

DRAMATIC PLAY

CRAYON MELT

▶ Ask the children to tell you their favorite crayon color.

▶ Children pretend to be that crayon dancing on a sunny day. This activity works well outdoors.

▶ Children raise their hands above their heads, palms together and fingers pointing up, to make the point of the crayon. Toddlers can just put their hands on their heads.

▶ Play some music for the "dancing crayons."

▶ Remind the children that the sun is shining brightly. What will happen to the colorful crayons?

▶ Comment on the children's actions as they begin to melt. Say: "I think Jared is all melted." "Tamera is melting into a yellow puddle." "Now we have a beautiful lake of many colors."

▶ Continue playing as long as the children want to do so. They can suggest other things that will melt in the sun, such as ice cream cones.

PUPPET PLAY

PURPLE POLKA-DOT PUPPET

▶ Collect clean white socks, child-size, if possible.

▶ Give each child a sock, and ask him to put the sock on his hand.

▶ Ask open-ended questions, such as: "What does the sock look like?" "What kind of puppet can it become?" "What color should it be?"

▶ At the art table, guide the children into making their sock puppets. Provide markers, crayons, and colored plastic tape.

▶ If some children do not want to do anything to the white sock, then that can be the color they choose.

▶ Older children may decide to be more creative with their puppets. Ask them if they know what stripes, polka dots, or plaids look like. Show them with a piece of paper and a marker. The colored plastic tape makes this easy to do.

▶ The main objective is to get the children playing with puppets.

MUSIC

TRADITIONAL SONG: "Mary Wore Her Red Dress"

This activity will encourage young children to look at the colors they and their friends are wearing. It also will make them more aware of the colors in their environment.

▶ After introducing the children to this traditional song, ask them to make up additional words. Examples might be blue jeans, sneakers, shoes, shirt, blouse, hat, ribbon, and headband.

Mary wore her red dress,
Red dress, red dress,
Mary wore her red dress
All day long.

▶ The children can change the focus from clothing to objects in the room or outdoors.

I see a blue ball,
Blue ball, blue ball,
I see a blue ball
On the playground.

I see two red blocks,
Red blocks, red blocks,
I see two red blocks
In the yellow box.

SONG: "When I Wear Red" by Jo Eklof

Additional verses:

Have children make up what to action to do with other colors, for instance, "When I wear green, I always lean."

© 1982 by Jo Eklof. All rights reserved. Used with permission.

(See page 305 for enlargement.)

LET'S PAINT TO MUSIC

▶ Children love to move to music. Select appropriate music from cassettes and CDs of Ella Jenkins, Raffi, Jack Grunsky, Thomas Moore, Steve and Greg, Hap Palmer, Sesame Street, and Red Grammar.

▶ Tape butcher paper to a long table or several round tables.

▶ Set up small containers of different colors of tempera paint, with a brush for each container, at various points around the table.

▶ Each child starts this activity standing at a paint container.

▶ When the music starts, each child begins painting.

▶ The children will play a kind of musical chairs. They stop painting when the music stops. Then,

they move to another point and paint as the music starts again. Everyone stays in and keeps painting. No one gets left out.

▶ The first time you do this, it might be helpful to have the children practice moving around the table, making pretend marks with the brushes as they go.

▶ Hang the "music mural" in the classroom as a wall mural, a banner, or a hanging center divider.

MOVEMENT

COLORS FALL DOWN

This movement activity works best either indoors in a carpeted area or outdoors in a grassy area, where the children can most safely "fall down."

▶ With young toddlers, simply say or chant the song. They can do the actions together.

▶ Have color samples on hand to use as visual clues.

▶ Sing the following song, based on the traditional rhyme:

Ring around a rosey
A pocket full of posies,
Red, yellow, blue,
Red (or yellow or blue) fall down.

▶ For older children, have them divide into three groups. Designate one the "red" group, one the "yellow," and the last "blue."

▶ You name one or more colors to fall down to.

▶ The children join hands in a circle, and all move in one direction as they sing.

▶ After you lead the activity, the children can take turns saying which color(s) they should fall down to.

▶ Vary the activity by announcing which colors the children are to fall down to before they sing, or waiting until the last line to surprise them with which group(s) will fall down.

COLOR RUN

Younger children need help with this activity, but older ones can do it by themselves.

▶ Cut large paper plates in half.

▶ Attach various colors of ribbon or crepe paper streamers along the straight edge by stapling them or tying them through holes punched along the edge.

▶ The children take their rainbow streamers outside and run with them overhead. The faster they run, the more the colors will fly. See illustration.

SENSORY ART

COLORFUL PLACEMATS

With the children's help, make colorful construction paper placemats.

▶ Trace around a plate, spoon, fork, and glass with a black marker.

▶ Laminate each placemat for easy cleaning and durability.

▶ When first introducing colors, use placemats of only one color so all of the children have the same color.

▶ Later the children can choose which colors they want. They can change placemats daily or keep the same color all of the time. Children make the decision.

PASTELS GALORE

▶ Give the children red, yellow, and blue paints.

▶ Encourage the children to create as many colors as they can using these primary colors.

▶ Introduce pastels by adding white to all of the other colors the children created using red, yellow, and blue.

▶ Add watercolors and colored chalk for children to experiment with.

▶ Later, talk about what the children experienced. Write down the names of all of the different colors they discovered. Put this information on the bulletin board.

SHADES OF COLOR

Introduce children to the concept of how a color can have many different shades. Show them a red, yellow, blue, or green ball, the same color of construction paper, and a picture with that color in a book. They are different shades of the same color.

▶ What else do the children see in the classroom that is a different tint or shade of the same color?

▶ Collect magazines, catalogs, and travel brochures. Put these, along with glue, scissors, and various colors of construction paper, on a table.

▶ Ask the children to choose one color and one piece of construction paper.

▶ Explain to the children that they are going to make a "one-color collage" of pictures from the magazines. They then search for all of the shades of the color they chose.

▶ Next, glue the pictures on the construction paper.

▶ Younger children may want to work with a partner.

▶ Older children can extend the activity by designing their collages to range from the darkest to lightest shade of color.

▶ Follow up with a discussion of the many shades of colors the children have discovered. Write down the new words they use to *describe* the colors, such as dark, light, bright, pale, dull, and shiny.

▶ Make the materials available to the children so that they can make additional collages if they wish.

SURPRISE PLAY DOUGH

▶ Put the following items on the art table:
  aprons
  large mixing bowl
  pitcher of water
  measuring cup
  tablespoon
  red, blue, and yellow food coloring
  container of salt
  container of flour
  bottle of vegetable oil
  large spoon
  sandwich-size bags

▶ Have a small group of children wash their hands and put on aprons. You can repeat this activity as many times as needed to give all of the children a chance to participate.

▶ Have several children measure one-half cup of flour each into the bowl until it totals three cups.

▶ Ask another child to measure one cup of salt, and mix it with the flour.

▶ Ask another child to make a well in the dry ingredients and measure a tablespoon of oil into the well.

▶ Add water slowly and mix until the dough is like pie dough.

▶ Divide the dough into sections, and have the children shape the dough into balls.

▶ Place each ball into a plastic sandwich bag labeled with the child's name on masking tape, and close each bag with a rubber band.

▶ Place the balls on a teacher's shelf.

▶ Before the children arrive the next day, make an indentation in each ball, and carefully put in a drop of food coloring, and then reseal the ball.

▶ Reclose each bag.

▶ When the children ask about their balls of dough, hand out the dough and ask them to knead it in the bag.

▶ The children will really be surprised when they see what happens! They can then take the dough out and play with it.

CREATIVE FOOD EXPERIENCES

LET'S DRINK PURPLE

You will need the following:

  1 cup milk
  1/4 cup grape juice
  1 sliced banana

1. Wash hands.
2. Place all ingredients into a blender, and mix.
3. Yum!

Serves approximately three.

LET'S DRINK PURPLE

Wash hands.

Place 1 cup milk,

1/4 cup grape juice, and

1 sliced banana

into a blender and mix together.

YUM!

COLORFUL SALAD

You will need the following:

> strawberries
> blueberries
> bananas
> green or yellow apples
> red or green grapes

1. Wash hands.
2. Wash fruit.
3. Cut up bananas and apples into bite-size pieces.
4. Let children taste each kind of fruit separately before mixing.
5. Put fruit pieces in a big bowl, and mix gently to combine.
6. Eat!

MATH

COLORED STACKING RINGS AND BLOCKS

This exercise is an opportunity to remember that developmentally appropriate basic toys and equipment are the foundation of themes and concepts for young children.

▶ With older infants and younger toddlers, have colored stacking rings and blocks available for them every day.

▶ This individual activity keeps colors and shapes in young children's environment and provides new vocabulary as language skills develop.

COLOR CHALLENGE

▶ Place additional items of one color around the room without the children knowing.

▶ Count and list the number of items of a specific color in the room. For example, count and list all blue items.

▶ Place this information on a chart for the children to refer to *later*.

▶ Ask each child to find blue items in the room, pick up those that can be picked up, and put them in a separate pile next to him.

▶ Children will need to notice items such as the blue on the bulletin board or on someone's shirt.

▶ Each child counts the number of items he found and writes down the number.

▶ With your help, the children add all of the numbers to find the total.

▶ Check the total with your list. Were any items omitted? If so, have the children look again to find the missing items.

▶ Have the children count all of the items again, and compare with your list.

▶ Change this activity on another day. Place items of several colors around the room. This time, tell the children the number of items of each color you have counted.

▶ You will see the children adding up what others find to see if all items have been found.

SCIENCE

WATERCOLORS

▶ A simple way to bring color to the toddler environment is to add a few drops of food coloring to the water table. This can be changed easily and often.

▶ For toddlers and young preschoolers, demonstrate how one color can change into another by having the children add a few drops of yellow food coloring to a glass of water and then watch the color sink and spread.

▶ Add blue drops next. What happens when the colors mix? Continue this activity using different combinations of colored drops to create more colors.

A GARDEN OF COLOR

This activity promotes creativity, problem solving, working together cooperatively, and thinking about how many beautiful colors appear in nature.

▶ Collect books, magazines, and catalogs that have many colorful pictures of all kinds of flowers.

▶ Make these available for the children to look at, not cut up.

▶ Have the children point out and name the different flowers they know. Talk about the different colors of the flowers. For example, a rose can be red, white, pink, or a combination of colors. Can daisies be any other color than white?

▶ Suggest to the children that they can create a garden of colors to put in the flower garden on the bulletin board.

▶ Guide the children to make as many different kinds of flowers as they can out of construction paper. They will tell you which other materials they need to create their garden.

▶ Another decision the children will make is how to group the flowers in the garden. Perhaps they will want to draw them on paper first, plotting out how the flowers will look.

SOCIAL STUDIES

HAROLD AND THE PURPLE CRAYON

TODDLER **PRESCHOOL-K**

Introduce the children to the wonderful world of *Harold and the Purple Crayon* by Crockett Johnson, listed in the Children's Books section of this theme. This book can be the beginning of many fun activities.

▶ After reading *Harold and the Purple Crayon*, give the children paper and purple crayons. Let them tell you where their purple crayons are taking them, and what it is like there.

▶ If some children want a color other than purple, that is fine. Different colors can take them different places in our world of colors.

▶ With preschoolers and kindergartners, you can expand this activity. Attach white butcher paper to the lower part of the walls all around the classroom.

▶ Give each child a portion of the paper and a purple crayon. He can draw pictures and go for a walk, just like Harold.

▶ What a wonderful world the children will create from their imaginations!

THE LAND OF MANY COLORS

PRESCHOOL-K **PRIMARY-GRADE**

The Klamath County YMCA Family Preschool's *The Land of Many Colors,* listed in the Children's Books section of this theme, is another special book you will want to share with the children. It is written by children for children.

▶ Talk about the story with the children. Discuss the messages of peace and respect for differences.

▶ Make purple, blue, and green people, and put them on the bulletin board to add to the "Colors in Our World."

▶ After reading this, the children may want to write and illustrate a story of their own.

▶ Children may want to act out the story with props and simple costumes.

▶ Children can draw and cut out felt characters, then retell the story on the flannelboard.

▶ Together, you and the children can find many ways to expand this activity.

CHILDREN'S BOOKS

Benjamin, Alan. (1992). *What Color? (Que Color).* (Board Book). Illustrated by Hideo Shirotani. New York: Little Simon Books.

Bilgrami, Shaheen. (2003). *Magic Painting Day.* Illustrated by Simone Abel. New York: Sterling.

Burrows, Adjoa J. (2000). *Grandma's Purple Flowers.* New York: Lee & Low Books.

Cabrera, Jane. (1997). *Cat's Colors.* New York: Dial Books.

Carle, Eric. (1998a). *Hello, Red Fox.* New York: Simon & Schuster.

Carle, Eric. (1998b). *Let's Paint a Rainbow: A Play-and-Read Book.* New York: Cartwheel Books.

Crews, Donald. (1995). *Ten Black Dots.* New York: Mulberry.

Demi. (1980). *Liang and the Magic Paint Brush.* New York: Henry Holt.

Dr. Seuss (pseud. for Theodor Geisel). (1996). *My Many Colored Days.* New York: Knopf.

Dundon, Caitlin. (1994). *The Yellow Umbrella.* Illustrated by Sandra Speidel. New York: Simon & Schuster.

Ehlert, Lois. (1997a). *Color Farm.* New York: HarperCollins.

Ehlert, Lois. (1997b). *Color Zoo.* New York: HarperCollins.

Ehlert, Lois. (1991). *Red Leaf, Yellow Leaf.* San Diego: Harcourt.

Fleming, Denise. (1998). *Lunch.* New York: Henry Holt.

Heller, Ruth. (1995). *Color.* New York: Scholastic.

Hill, Eric. (1997). *Spot's Big Book of Colors, Shapes, and Numbers.* New York: Puffin.

Hoban, Tana. (1995). *Colors Everywhere.* New York: Greenwillow.

Hoban, Tana. (1993). *Black on White* and *White on Black.* (Board Book). New York: Greenwillow.

Johnson, Crockett. (1983). *Harold and the Purple Crayon.* New York: HarperTrophy.

Johnson, Stephen T. (2000). *My Little Red Tool Box.* San Diego: Harcourt.

Jonas, Ann. (1989). *Color Dance.* New York: Greenwillow.

Kissinger, Katie. (1994). *All the Colors We Are — Todos los Colores de Nuestra Peil.* Photographed by Wernher Krutein. St. Paul, MN: Redleaf Press.

Klamath County YMCA Family Preschool. (1993). *The Land of Many Colors.* Illustrated by Rita Pocock. New York: Scholastic.

Lianni, Leo. (2000). *A Color of His Own.* New York: Knopf.

Littlefield, Holly. (1997). *Colors of Japan (Colors of the World).* Illustrated by Helen Byers. New York: Lerner Publications.

Liu, Jae Soo. (2000). *Yellow Umbrella.* (with music CD). New York: Kane/Miller.

Martin, Bill Jr. (1983). *Brown Bear, Brown Bear.* Illustrated by Eric Carle. New York: Henry Holt.

Olawsky, Lynn A. (1997). *Colors of Mexico (Colors of the World).* Minneapolis, MN: Carolrhoda Books.

Onyefulu, Ifeoma. (1997). *Chidi Only Likes Blue: An African Book of Colors.* New York: Cobblehill Books.

Van Der Leeden, Ingrid. (1997) *Colors, Colors, Everywhere! (Teething Time Books).* New York: Little Simon Books.

Walsh, Ellen Stoll. (1995). *Mouse Paint.* New York: Voyager.

Winne, Joanne. (2000). *Blue in My World.* New York: Children's Press.

Yenawine, Philip. (1991). *Colors.* New York: Delacorte.

Family Letter (Toddler)

Dear Family,

We are beginning our new theme, "Colors." The children will learn the following:

- Our world is full of color.
- Color is important for identifying most things in our world.
- Color makes our world more interesting and enjoyable.
- Colors have names.
- The primary colors are red, yellow, and blue. When mixed, primary colors produce new colors.
- The secondary colors are orange, green, and purple. Secondary colors are created by mixing two primary colors.
- There are many ways of experimenting with and exploring colors.

We will be talking about the following:

- primary colors
- special colors
- how colors help us
- colors of skin, hair, and eyes
- colors in nature
- colors around us

Try these fun things to do at home with your child:

- Help your child identify objects of different colors in the environment.
- Walk around the house and talk about all of the colors, both inside and outside.
- Talk about the colors of the food you eat.

Family participation opportunities at school will include:

- Come visit our class, and share our colorful experiences with us.
  Date _____   Time _____
- Come help us make flowers for our garden of color.
  Date _____   Time _____

Our wish list for this theme includes:
  children's socks
  pictures of flowers
  colored tissue paper
  colored ribbon
  old magazines
  paper plates

Thanks!

SHAPES

Circle
Square
Triangle
Rectangle
Straight and
curved lines

Diamond
Star
Heart
Octagon

Various sizes
Pentagon
Hexagon
Oval

THEME 17
Shapes in
Our World

SHAPES IN NATURE

Vegetables
Insects
Sun
Shells
Fruits
Birds
Moon

Flowers
Fish
Snowflakes
Mountains
Animals
Rainbow
Trees

SHAPES AROUND US

Cars Trucks Buses
Airplanes
Boats
Traffic signs
Houses and buildings
Baseball diamond
Football field
Skating rink

SHAPES HELP US

Read
Write
Identify objects
Play games

THEME GOALS

To provide opportunities for children to learn the following:

- ▶ Our world is full of shapes.
- ▶ Shape is important for identifying everything in our world.
- ▶ We can see shapes with our eyes and feel them with our hands.

- ▶ Shapes have names.
- ▶ The basic shapes are the circle, square, rectangle, and triangle.
- ▶ A shape comes in many sizes, but it is still the same shape.

Children-Created Bulletin Board

The bulletin board that was created by you and the children for Theme 16, "Colors in Our World," can be used for this theme, "Shapes in Our World," by adding and changing some elements.

- ▶ Change the title of the board to read "Colors and Shapes in Our World."
- ▶ Let the children create a border around the bulletin board. There are several ways to do this.
- ▶ Begin with precut strips of paper in lengths equal to the sides of the bulletin board.
- ▶ The children can do stamp printing with assorted shapes on the strips of paper.

- ▶ Children can cut out shapes from construction paper scraps and make a collage of shapes on the strips.
- ▶ Children can draw their favorite shapes on the border strips.
- ▶ Remove the cloud covering part of the sun to leave a bright sun, a large round circle.
- ▶ Let the children help you add more shapes to the board as the "Shapes" theme continues.

VOCABULARY STARTERS

Let the children add words.

circle — a perfectly round shape.

line — a long mark or the edge of something, either straight or curved.

oval — a shape like an egg.

rectangle — a shape with four sides that are not all equal.

square — a shape with four equal sides.

triangle — a shape with three sides.

LANGUAGE EXPERIENCES

INFANT TALK

▶ Talk about shapes to the babies.

▶ When you roll a ball, talk about circles. Say: "This is a big ball, and it is a round circle." "This is a little ball, and it is a round circle."

▶ When the infants play with empty boxes, such as tissue boxes, small gift boxes, or shoe boxes, talk about the shapes of the boxes.

▶ Cut textured fabric shapes, and glue them to thick pieces of cardboard. Give the shapes to the babies to play with.

▶ Talk about triangles, squares, rectangles, and circles.

▶ Share shapes with the infants as part of their environment.

POEM: "I Am a Shape"

I am a square, a square am I,
I have four sides that you can spy.
I have four corners, all the same,
I am a square, that is my name.
   I am a circle, a circle you see,
   I'm round and round as a ball can be.
   My circling side looks all the same,
   I am a circle, that is my name.
I am a triangle, just look at me,
I have three sides, as you can see.
I have three corners, all the same,

I am a triangle, that's my name.
I am a rectangle, four sides are there,
I have four corners just like a square.
But my sides are different, not all the same,
I am a rectangle, that's my name.

Philip Jackman

A SHAPE STORY

▶ Tell a story to the children.

▶ You can tell the story using the flannelboard and flannelboard characters, or you can draw the story on a flip chart, changing the pages as you progress through the story.

A Shape Story

Once upon a time, there lived a group of circles. They lived and played all by themselves.

(Put the circles, all sizes and colors, on the upper left side of the flannelboard or flip chart.)

In the same town lived a group of squares. They lived and played all by themselves.

(Put the squares, all sizes and colors, on the upper right side of the flannelboard or flip chart.)

There also lived in the town a group of triangles. They lived and played all by themselves.

(Put the triangles, all sizes and colors, on the lower left side of the flannelboard or flip chart.)

And down the street in the same town there lived a group of rectangles. They lived and played by themselves.

(Put the rectangles, all sizes and colors, on the lower right side of the flannelboard or flip chart.)

One day one of the small circles rolled into the center of town and began playing all alone.

(Place a small circle in the center of the flannelboard or flip chart.)

A small square saw the little circle playing all alone and decided to join in the fun.

(Move a small square to the center to join the small circle.)

The circle and the square enjoyed playing together. Just then, the small triangle saw the two shapes playing and wanted to play too. So the triangle joined in the fun.

(Move a small triangle to join the circle and square in the center of the flannelboard or flip chart.)

What do you think happened next?

(The children should answer "a small rectangle joined in the fun." Add a small rectangle to the other shapes in the center of the flannelboard or flip chart.)

What do you think will happen now?

(As the children start telling you what they think will happen, start moving all of the shapes together, and jumble them up all over the flannelboard or flip chart.)

Everyone is having so much fun. Look! Look at what the shapes have done. They have made themselves into a house and a wagon.

(Make a house and a wagon on the flannelboard or flip chart.)

What else can we make?

(Put all of the shape pieces out for the children to pick up. Let a child come up to the flannelboard and make a picture with the shapes. If you are using a flip chart, give the marker to a child and let her make a shape picture. Children can work with a partner to make the picture.)

And now my story is over. The End!

DRAMATIC PLAY

THE SHAPE OF THINGS

Start this activity by clearing a large space in the classroom, or go outdoors on the playground where there is open space.

▶ Help the children define the personal space each will need within the area.

▶ Explain that you are going to ask the children to form shapes with their bodies. There is no right or wrong way to do this.

▶ Ask all of the children to form a straight line with their bodies, either a vertical or horizontal line.

▶ Ask the children to make their bodies into circles, then triangles.

▶ What other shapes can the children make?

▶ Talk about how everything has a shape, and many things combine shapes.

▶ Ask the children to show the shape of a tall candle as it burns down.

▶ Ask the children to demonstrate the shape of a pretzel. Accept any shape they form. (There is a recipe for making pretzels in the Creative Food Experiences section of this theme.)

▶ Ask the children how a growing plant changes its shape.

▶ Make an oval shape of an egg, and show a bird hatching from the egg.

▶ Let the children come up with other shapes to make.

PUPPET PLAY

SACKS AND SHAPES PUPPETS

▶ Put out lunch-size paper sacks, glue, markers, crayons, yarn, construction paper, and fabric scraps for the children to use.

▶ Encourage the children to make a puppet by creating a large shape (circle, triangle, square, rectangle, or oval) for the face, adding facial features to the shape, and then gluing this face onto the paper sack.

▶ Allow enough time for the children to create as many shapes of puppets as they wish.

▶ Older children may add yarn hair, fabric clothes, and construction paper arms, hands, and legs to complete their puppets.

MUSIC

CIRCLE SONG

This can be sung to the melody of the traditional tune "Have You Ever Seen a Lassie?" or recited as a poem.

Have you ever seen a circle, a circle, a circle?
Have you ever seen a circle, which goes 'round and
*   'round?*
It rolls this way and that way, and that way and this way.
Have you ever seen a circle, which goes 'round and
*   'round?*

MUSICAL SHAPES

▶ Ask all of the children to sit on the floor in a circle with you.

▶ Place the following rhythm instruments in the middle of the circle:

triangles

rhythm sticks

sandpaper blocks

drums

bells

castanets

finger cymbals

cymbals

egg-shaped shakers

round maracas

▶ Include enough instruments so that each child will have one.

▶ After each child has selected her instrument, ask her to talk about the shape.

▶ Have each child play the instrument so that everyone can hear the sound each makes.

▶ Next, have everyone play together.

▶ Choose an appropriate cassette or a CD, and let the "shape orchestra" play along with the music.

MOVEMENT

LET'S MOVE!

▶ Continue emphasizing the shape concept by asking the children to move in the way you ask.

– Walk in a line.
– Walk in a circle.
– Walk in a square.
– Walk in a triangle.
– Run in a circle.
– Run in a zigzag pattern.
– Jump in place.
– Jump around a square.
– Hop in place.
– Hop around a triangle.
– Skip in a circle.
– Skip in a rectangle.

Developmentally, some of these instructions may be difficult for younger preschoolers. Accept any way the children move.

CIRCLE GAME

▶ Have the children form a circle, feet apart and touching their neighbor's feet.

▶ One child stands inside of the circle with a volley ball or similar type of ball and tries to throw the ball out of the circle between the players' legs.

▶ The players stop the ball by using their hands.

▶ If the ball goes through, then that child goes in the center and continues the game.

RED LIGHT/GREEN LIGHT

▶ In this game, one child plays the "traffic light," and the rest of the children try to touch "it."

▶ At the start, all of the children form a line about 15 feet away from the "traffic light."

- The light faces away from the line of children, and says "green light!" At this point, everyone moves slowly toward the traffic light.
- At any point, the light may say "red light!" and turn around.
- If the children are caught moving after this has occurred, they are out.
- Play resumes when the traffic light turns back around and says "green light!"
- The traffic light wins if all of the children are out before anyone is able to touch her. Otherwise, the first player to touch the "light" wins the game and becomes the traffic light for the next game.

SENSORY ART

PAPER SHAPES

- Use various shapes of paper for art activities instead of the standard rectangular sheets.
- Place easel paper cut in the shape you are studying on each painting easel in the classroom.

SURPRISE SHAPES

- Without the children knowing, make glue shapes on tagboard, and let them dry.
- Let the children discover and name the shapes by rubbing a crayon over a piece of thin drawing paper on top of the tagboard. Have them use the side of a crayon for best results.

SKYLINES

The main objective of this activity is to have the children identify shapes.

- Collect old magazines with a lot of colorful pictures and advertising.
- Encourage the children to look for rectangles, squares, and triangles in the magazines. After they find the shapes, ask them to cut out the shapes.

- The rectangles, squares, and triangles can be pictures, words, or a combination.
- Glue the shapes onto a half sheet of light blue construction paper to form a skyline. The illustration is one example of using word shapes to form a skyline.
- Both you and the children can have a lot of fun with this project.

CREATIVE FOOD EXPERIENCES

SHAPE SNACK MIX

You will need the following:

    raisins
    dry cereal (round and square)
    sunflower seeds
    butterscotch chips
    sesame seeds
    peanuts
    chocolate chips

1. Wash hands.
2. Mix ingredients.
3. Enjoy!

PRETZELS AND CHEESE SHAPES

You will need the following:

    14-ounce block of cheddar cheese or cubed cheese
    package of stick pretzels

1. Wash hands.
2. Cut cheese into various shapes.
3. Stick the ends of the pretzels into the cheese cubes. The children really have fun with this.
4. Eat and talk about the shapes the children are eating.

- - - - - - - - - - - - - - - - -

LET'S MAKE PRETZEL SHAPES

You will need the following:

> 1 package yeast
> 1 tablespoon sugar
> 1 teaspoon salt (optional)
> 1 1/2 cups warm water
> 4 cups flour
> 1 egg

1. Wash hands.
2. Children help you mix yeast, warm water, and sugar.
3. Stir in flour.
4. Knead until smooth.
5. Give each child a small ball of dough.

LET'S MAKE PRETZEL SHAPES

Wash hands.

Mix 1 package yeast, 1 1/2 cups warm water, and

1 tablespoon sugar. Stir in 4 cups flour and knead until smooth.

Roll a small ball of dough between hands. Make into shape.

Brush 1 egg across top of shape to make shiny.

Sprinkle with salt if desired. Bake at 425 degrees for 15 min.

Let's Eat!

---

6. Roll between hands until approximately ¼ inch across.
7. Form into desired shape.
8. Brush top with egg to make the shape shiny during baking.
9. Sprinkle with salt if desired. Bake at 425 degrees for 15 minutes.
10. Eat!

Make a chart of the placement on the pan of each child's pretzel so she will get the one she has prepared.

MATH

SHOE BOX SORTER

Many commercial shape sorters are available for infants. Here is a suggestion for making an inexpensive one for the infants in your care.

▶ Cut holes in the top of a large shoe box. The holes need to be large enough for shapes to fit through easily and the same shapes as the objects.

▶ Use small square and rectangular blocks and large, peglike objects, such as the bottoms of plastic film containers, to fit into the sorter.

▶ For infants who have mastered this task, line the hole openings with foam rubber. This provides resistance for the baby to push the shapes through.

- - - - - - - - - - - - - - - - -

SHAPES GALORE

▶ Cut fabric scraps into squares, circles, triangles, rectangles, and ovals.

▶ Make sets of the same color, size, shape, and pattern.

▶ Put sets in the manipulative center for children to match fabric pieces.

▶ Children can also sort the shapes according to texture, size, color, or pattern.

▶ To expand this activity, put out a variety of paper and fabric pieces on a table.

▶ Older children can cut the shapes themselves.

▶ Ask the children to name the shapes as they cut. Talk about the sizes and colors too.

SHAPE PATTERNS

This is a small group activity.

▶ Put out a large flannelboard and shapes of many sizes and colors in the math center. You also can have small individual flannelboards, chalkboards, and chalk there as well.

▶ Ask the children to choose partners. The pairs of children will take turns with other pairs at the large flannelboard.

▶ On a large card, set up a simple pattern. Ask the children to arrange the same pattern on the flannelboard. For example, place a circle, square, another circle, and triangle.

▶ Continue holding up patterns for the children to duplicate. Increase the difficulty of each pattern (a square, two circles, a star, two triangles, a rectangle, an oval, and two more rectangles).

▶ For older children, add colors and sizes to the shape patterns. Add new shapes, such as the pentagon, hexagon, and octagon.

▶ Leave the flannelboard(s) and shapes in the math center for the children to create patterns by themselves.

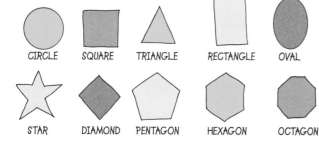

CIRCLE SQUARE TRIANGLE RECTANGLE OVAL

STAR DIAMOND PENTAGON HEXAGON OCTAGON

SCIENCE

NATURAL SHAPES

This activity encourages children to look for the beauty of nature while developing an awareness of color and shape.

▶ Go on a neighborhood walk, and look for shapes in the environment.

▶ Talk about basic shapes. Have the children find examples of these shapes around the classroom, playground, and neighborhood.

▶ Visit an arboretum, flower shop, or grocery store.

▶ Look for all of the different shapes in nature.

▶ Talk about the colors and shapes the children see.

SOCIAL STUDIES

FLAGS OF THE WORLD

This activity is designed to help the children become more aware of the many ways shapes are used in our world. Introduce them to the symbol of a flag by first talking about the flag of the United States. Have an actual flag available, along with pictures of other flags of the world's countries.

▶ Ask the children to look for shapes in the American flag. Then ask them to point out shapes in the other flags.

▶ Have the children make a flag. They can make the United States flag, a flag from another country, or one that they create themselves.

HOUSE SHAPES DRAWING GAME

▶ Before beginning this activity, talk about how many doors and windows are in the children's homes. Have they noticed the shapes around where they live? What shapes can they find in the houses and buildings around their neighborhoods?

▶ Have available construction paper, crayons, markers, and chalk for the children.

▶ Create cards and pictures for the children to use in drawing houses and parts of houses. For example, draw a rectangular door on the cards and windows with squares of glass, and show pictures of a triangular roof, a chimney, steps, and other parts of the house.

▶ You also can number cards to indicate how many doors or windows should be in the house. See illustration.

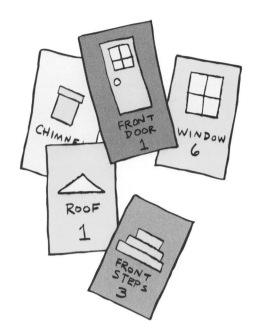

- ▶ Sort the cards by category. Label the piles with a picture indicating each category.
- ▶ Turn each category of cards facedown.
- ▶ The children select a card from each category and draw their houses using the information on the cards.
- ▶ The children decide which color to make their houses.
- ▶ Display the pictures in a special way, or add to the bulletin board.

CHILDREN'S BOOKS

Albee, Sarah. (1996). *Allegra's Shapes.* (Board edition). Illustrated by Peter Panas. New York: Simon & Schuster.

Bolton, Janet. (1994). *My Grandmother's Patchwork Quilt.* New York: Mulberry.

Brown, Anthony. (2003). *The Shape Game.* New York: Farrar, Straus & Giroux.

Callin, Karen. (1992). *Rectangles.* Mankato, MN: Capstone Press.

Dillon, Leo, Diane Dillon, and N. N. Charles. (1994). *What Am I?: Looking through Shapes at Apples and Grapes.* New York: Scholastic.

Fatus, Sophie. (1997). *Holes. (Sally shape series).* New York: Abbeville Press.

Hill, Eric. (1986). *Spot Looks at Shapes.* (Board Book). New York: Putnam.

Hoban, Tana. (1998). *So Many Circles, So Many Squares.* New York: Greenwillow.

Hoban, Tana. (1996). *Shapes, Shapes, Shapes.* New York: Mulberry.

Innovative Kids. (1999). *Soft Shapes.* Illustrated by Bob Fillipowich. Norwalk, CT: Author.

Lamut, Sonja. (1998). *Turn and Learn Shapes.* New York: Grossett & Dunlap.

Mahan, Ben. (1992a). *See a Circle.* New York: McClanahan Books.

Mahan, Ben. (1992b). *See a Square.* New York: McClanahan Books.

Mahan, Ben. (1992c). *See a Triangle.* New York: McClanahan Books.

Morgan, Sally. (1995). *Triangles and Pyramids (The World of Shapes).* New York: Thomson Learning.

Murphy, Stuart J. (1998). *Circus Shapes.* New York: HarperCollins.

Patricelli, Leslie. (2003). *Big Little.* (Board edition). Cambridge, MA: Candlewick Press.

Serfozo, Mary. (1996). *There's a Square: A Book about Shapes (Story Corner).* Illustrated by David A. Carter. New York: Scholastic.

Shannon, David. (1998). *A Bad Case of Stripes.* New York: Scholastic.

Silverhardt, Lauryn. (2002). *Let's Find Shapes.* Illustrated by Vince Giarrano. New York: Simon Spotlight.

Van Fleet, Matthew. (1995). *Fuzzy Yellow Ducklings: Foldout Fun with Textures, Colors, Shapes, Animals.* New York: Dial.

Wood, Amanda. (2003). *Round, Square.* Illustrated by Emma Dodd. New York: Silver Dolphin.

Family Letter (Preschool)

Dear Family,

We will be talking about "Shapes," our new theme. We will provide opportunities for the children to learn the following:

- Our world is full of shapes.
- Shape is important in identifying objects in our world.
- We can see shapes with our eyes and feel them with our hands.
- Shapes have names.
- The basic shapes are the circle, square, rectangle, and triangle.
- A shape comes in many sizes, but it is still the same shape.

We will be talking about the following:

- shapes: the circle, square, triangle, rectangle, oval, diamond, star, heart, pentagon, hexagon, octagon, and straight and curved lines
- shapes in nature
- how shapes help us
- shapes around us

Some things to do at home with your child include:

- Talk about all of the shapes you and your child can find at home, in the yard, and around the neighborhood and community.
- When you are in the car, look for shapes in traffic lights and signs.
- Play board games with your child. These offer different shapes and colors to talk about.
- Let your child help you fold the laundry. Talk about the different shapes you see.

Join us at school for some of the following family participation opportunities:

- Visit our classroom, and join in the activities.
  Date _____   Time _____
- Go with us to the arboretum or grocery store.
  Date _____   Time _____

Our wish list for this theme includes:

paper sacks
old magazines
shoe boxes
fabric scraps
wallpaper scraps
pictures of flags

Thanks!

OCEAN (SEA)

Atlantic Waves Ships
Indian Surf Tugboats
Pacific Beaches Freighters
Arctic Sand Tankers
Salt water Shells Yachts
Source of Swimming Docks
food Harbors

THEME 18
Oceans and Lakes

LAKE RECREATION
Motor boats
Sailboats
Swimming
Water skiing
Fresh water used
for drinking
Dams control flow
of water

OCEAN LIFE

Fish Oysters Seals
Sharks Shrimp Sea lions
Lobsters Octopus Reptiles
Jellyfish Whales Turtles
Crabs Dolphins Snakes

LAKE LIFE

Fish Birds Geese
Ducks Turtles Water plants

KEEP OCEANS, LAKES, AND BEACHES CLEAN

PRACTICE WATER SAFETY

WEAR LIFE JACKET

THEME GOALS

To provide opportunities for children to learn the following:

▶ Water is necessary to all living things.

▶ *Ocean* water is salty.

▶ Most *lakes* have fresh water in them.

▶ Many plants and animals, especially fish, live in oceans and lakes.

▶ The four biggest oceans in the world are the Atlantic, Pacific, Indian, and Arctic.

Children-Created Bulletin Board

Throughout this theme, "Oceans and Lakes," the children can change the bulletin board frequently. The study of water and waves and the fish, mammals, and plant life that inhabit the water offers many opportunities for discovery and exploration.

▶ Title this bulletin board "Oceans and Lakes — Don't Pollute!"

▶ The water background for the board can be done with watercolor paints on butcher paper.

▶ Colored rickrack looks great as the waves.

▶ Form a beach with sand glued onto the paper.

▶ Have the children cut out sandpaper starfish to glue onto the beach, along with seashells.

▶ Place a frog with a long, sticky tongue made from contact paper on the board. Ask the children to put "objects" the frog has caught on his tongue.

▶ You will find activities to add to the bulletin board as you explore this theme with the children.

VOCABULARY STARTERS

Let the children add words. Include pictures where appropriate.

lake — a body of fresh water surrounded by land.

ocean — a great body of salt water.

pond — a small lake.

sea — another name for ocean.

shore — where the land meets the ocean.

surf — waves hitting the shore.

wave — a movement of the surface of the water caused by wind.

LANGUAGE EXPERIENCES

POEM:
"Ocean Friends"

Children enjoy adding hand and body movements to this poem.

When our friends who swim in the ocean blue
Want to say hello, what do they do?
The silvery fish gives its tail a flick,
The lobster's claws go click-click-click,
The great big whale makes a great big splash,
The shark opens wide, then he's gone in a flash,
The octopus waves all his arms at you,
And that's how they say "How do you do?"

Philip Jackman

POEM:
"What a Splash!"

If all the lakes were one lake,
What a great lake that would be!
And if all the oceans were one ocean,
What a great sea that would be!
And if all the people were one person,
What a great person that would be!
And if the great person took a great jump
And jumped as high as could be,
And jumped into the great ocean
What a great splash that would be!

Philip Jackman

A HOUSE FOR HERMIT CRAB

▶ Read Carle's *A House for Hermit Crab,* listed in the Children's Books section of this theme.

▶ This delightful book offers an imaginative look at the underwater neighborhood of Hermit Crab. It also offers many ways to stimulate creativity and language development.

▶ Let the children help you make a list of the things Hermit uses to decorate his houses. Older children can write the list themselves.

▶ Some children may want to draw a picture of the new shell.

▶ Look through other books to find additional sea creatures whose shells could have been used.

▶ Talk about the items the children have outgrown.

▶ Act out the story of *A House for Hermit Crab.*

DRAMATIC PLAY

CAN YOU?

▶ Introduce children to ocean animals they may not have seen before.

▶ Invite someone from a local aquarium or pet store to visit the children and show them a crab, a lobster, an eel, or other creature whose usual home is the ocean.

▶ If possible, plan a field trip to the aquarium or pet store.

▶ Select a video that shows dolphins, an octopus, and other ocean creatures.

▶ After the children have become somewhat familiar with inhabitants of the ocean, ask them if they can do the following:

— Swim like a fish?

— Crawl like a crab?

— Slither like an eel?

— Jump like a frog?

— Dance like a dolphin?

— Hug like an octopus?

▶ Many children will want to show you how they can do all of the movements. Accept whatever they do.

▶ For the younger group, you might need to model the pantomimes for them.

▶ Have available pictures and books about ocean life to show the children.

▶ Play appropriate music in the background.

▶ Let the children add their own ideas to the activity.

UNDERSEA ENVIRONMENT

Let the children change the dramatic play area into an underwater environment. Allow plenty of room and lots of time for this project. This is a cooperative activity. All interested children should be involved.

▶ Have available plenty of books, pictures, maps, and research materials so the children can discover interesting facts about the ocean and the fish, mammal, and plant life that live there.

▶ Have available crayons, colored pencils, markers, crepe paper, construction paper, paper plates, yarn, scissors, and glue.

▶ Children begin to decorate by hanging blue and green crepe paper across the dramatic play area.

▶ Then children can make and hang fish, whales, dolphins, and seaweed from the ceiling or on mobiles attached to a clothesline. You will have to help with this. The clothesline should be above their heads and out of the way of the adults in the room.

▶ Discuss with the children what might be found on the ocean floor. Suggestions could be an octopus cave, a sunken ship, or a coral reef. Any of these can lead to more exploration and research.

▶ This becomes an ongoing project as you and the children add seashells, boats, ships, music, and the sounds of the ocean and lakes. Be prepared to close some centers as the underwater environment continues to grow.

PUPPET PLAY

SPONGE PUPPETS

▶ Collect all sizes of new sponges.

▶ Put these, with scraps of yarn, crepe paper, felt, fabric, toothpicks, craft sticks, and scissors, on a table.

▶ Have the children make ocean creature puppets out of the sponges. Attach yarn or crepe paper "arms" to make an octopus.

▶ Wrap the yarn around toothpicks, and stick them into the sponge, or stick toothpicks through the crepe paper and into the sponge. See illustration.

▶ If the sponge is small enough for the child to hold in his hand, the puppet can be moved around easily.

▶ If the sponge is larger, help the child make some finger holes. Another way to use the puppet is by inserting craft sticks into the sponge to make a stick puppet.

▶ Encourage the children to create voices for their puppets and to act out an underwater adventure in the dramatic play area.

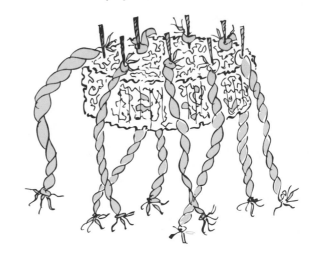

MUSIC

SONG: "The Frog Song" by Jo Eklof

Extend this song by having the children sing additional verses using different animal sounds.

Late last night while you and I were in our beds a-sleep, the frogs came out and sang this song, "rib-bit rib-bit rib-bit rib-bit rib-bit ba-reep!"

(See page 306 for enlargement.)

MOVEMENT

SAIL THE OCEAN BLUE

▶ Have the children imagine that the room or playground is "the ocean blue," and that each child will be one of four types of boat: a rowboat, a motorboat, a sailboat, or a big ship (ocean liner).

▶ Have pictures or books of these boats to give the children something concrete to look at.

▶ Guide the children into trying out each type of boat. Tell them, "Together, let's be a *rowboat*." Using the arms, slowly pull back and push forward on the oars to a "1-2-3-4" count. Move around in a small space of the "lake."

▶ Next, say, "Let's be a *sailboat*." Raise the sail by pulling on a rope, then stretch arms out to either side like a sail, rocking side to side while sailing forward.

▶ Then say, "Let's be a *motorboat*." Turn the key to start it, and then move out from the shore with a "r-r-r-r-r-r" sound. Move around in a large part of the "ocean" or "lake."

▶ Say, "Now here comes the *big ship, the ocean liner*." Put your arms out front, touching the hands together like a ship's prow. "Look out for me! Toot-toot-toot!"

▶ Next the children choose whichever boat they wish to be. Say, "Let's sail the ocean blue!"

▶ Remind the children that it is a big ocean. Some of the boats stay closer to shore, so they must watch out for each other.

▶ Continue to develop this activity by adding various conditions: Say, "Here comes a big wind. What happens to the boats now?" "Watch out, the waves are high!" "Now the ocean is calm again. Whew!"

SENSORY ART

WATER PLAY

Provide opportunities for infants and toddlers to enjoy water play.

▶ Help young infants wash their face and hands with a washcloth. Make this into a game of peekaboo.

▶ Put one-half inch of water into a small plastic tub, and let the children splash water and sail boats.

▶ Add food coloring to the water, and make colored ice cubes. Place these in the water table.

▶ Put large seashells in the water table or sandbox.

▶ Toddlers love to paint *outdoors* with water. Provide several sizes of brushes, and let them paint the sidewalk and the building walls.

MAKE A SAILBOAT

Collect washed, empty plastic soda bottles, sand, colored construction paper, tape, scissors, and markers. This activity is more fun to do outdoors.

▶ You and the children add sand to one plastic soda bottle.

▶ Let the children add a little bit of sand at first to see if the bottle will float in a tub or wading pool with one to two inches of water.

▶ Keep adding sand until the bottle floats without tilting in the water.

▶ Put the top on tightly.

▶ Have the children cut out boat and sail shapes. Tape these onto and around the bottle.

▶ Place the sailboat in the water.

▶ To extend this activity, turn on a small electric fan to create a wind. What happens to the sailboat now?

▶ Some of the younger children may drop in and out of this activity. This is all right. Have other centers open for them to move to.

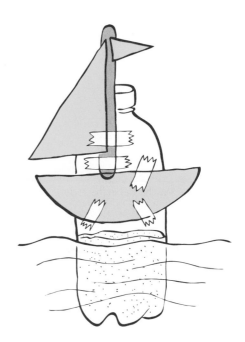

SALTWATER PAINTING

▶ With the children's help, mix warm water, salt, and food coloring into several small containers.

▶ The children, a few at a time, can paint pictures with the mixture on white paper. Try construction paper, newsprint, and computer paper. Will the results be the same or different?

▶ Let the pictures dry. The water evaporates, but the salt remains, creating beautiful pictures.

CREATIVE FOOD EXPERIENCES

FROG FLOAT

You will need the following:

    1 bottle of lemon-lime soda or ginger ale
    lime sherbet
    chocolate chips
    paper cups

1. Wash hands.
2. Have each child fill a paper cup half full with lemon-lime soda.
3. "Float" a scoop of lime sherbet in the soda.

FROG FLOAT

Wash hands.

Fill a cup half full with lemon-lime soda.

"Float" a scoop of lime sherbet in the soda.

Place 2 chocolate chip "eyes" on the sherbet "frog".

Enjoy the treat!

---

4. Pour a handful of chocolate chips out for each child.
5. Place two chocolate chip "eyes" on the sherbet "frog."
6. Enjoy the treat!

FISH SHAPES

You will need the following:

    4 envelopes flavored gelatin
    3 envelopes unflavored gelatin
    4 cups boiling juice or water

1. Wash hands.
2. Combine the seven envelopes of gelatin.
3. Add the boiling juice or water. An adult must do this.
4. Stir until the gelatin is dissolved.
5. Pour into a shallow pan.
6. Chill until firm.
7. Let each child use a fish-shaped cookie cutter to "catch the fish" in the pan of chilled gelatin.
8. You may have to make two "batches."
9. Serve and eat!

STARFISH SANDWICHES

You will need the following:

    wheat or white sandwich bread
    salmon spread or pimento cheese spread
    small jar of pimentos
    black olives

1. Wash hands.
2. You and the children make sandwiches using the salmon or pimento cheese spread.
3. With a star-shaped cookie cutter, press out a star-shaped sandwich.
4. Decorate the individual "starfish" with pimento eyes and olive mouths.
5. YUM!

TUNA CONES

You will need the following:

> 6 1/2-ounce can of tuna (You may need more than one can, depending upon the number of children in your class.)
> 1/3 to 1/2 cup of mayonnaise
> 2 tablespoons sweet pickle relish
> 1/4 teaspoon of salt (optional)
> flat-bottomed ice cream cones, one for each child
> pickle slices

1. Wash hands.
2. Mix tuna, mayonnaise, and sweet pickle relish in a bowl.
3. Scoop mixture into individual ice cream cones.
4. Top with pickle slices.

MATH

COUNT THE SEASHELLS

▶ Collect seashells in a large, unbreakable jar. The jar should be small enough to be filled in a reasonably short time.

▶ The seashells can be collected by you, other teachers, family members, and the children.

▶ Have the children guess how many shells are in the jar when it is one-quarter full, one-half full, and full.

▶ Measure and mark the jar.

▶ Some children may want to use the seashells to see how high they can count. This is fine, as long as they put the shells back into the jar.

WHICH IS SMALLEST? LARGEST?

Make this a small group or an individual activity.

▶ Place two or three dozen seashells of various types in the math center. Use some of the shells from the big jar mentioned in the "Count the Seashells" activity.

▶ Have the children place their seashells in order: smallest to largest, lightest to heaviest, shortest to longest.

▶ Ask the children to think of other ways to sort and classify the shells.

SCIENCE

CREATING ICEBERGS

This is a demonstration that you and the children do together. You may want to conduct it with a small group, then repeat the activity with another small group later in the day.

▶ Freeze a large bowl of water.

▶ Take the ice out of the bowl, and split it into two pieces.

▶ Float one lump of ice in a bowl of tap water.

▶ How much of the ice stays below the waterline?

▶ Now, float the second lump of ice in water with salt added.

▶ Do the children notice any differences? What are they?

▶ Discuss with the children that icebergs occur in oceans. Oceans have salt water.

IS THE SEA SALTY?

▶ Put rock salt, water, containers, strainers, and plastic spoons in the science center.

▶ Ask a few students at a time to pour water over rock salt that has been placed in a strainer.

▶ Put the dissolved salt into a plastic cup.

▶ Give each child a plastic spoon to dip into the water for tasting.

▶ Add the remaining salt water to the cup.

▶ Put the cup aside. Ask the children to check the cup periodically to see when all of the water has evaporated.

▶ How much salt remains?

▶ Repeat the procedure to see if the result is the same. If the outcome is different, what occurred to cause the difference?

SALT WATER AND FRESH WATER

This experiment is easy for the children to do.

▶ Put out two plastic drinking glasses, a plastic pitcher of tap water, table salt, food coloring, and an eyedropper for each color in the science center.

▶ Ask one or several children to fill one glass about halfway with water.

▶ Into the other glass, pour one-half glass of water with two teaspoons of salt added.

▶ Add a few drops of food coloring to the salt water.

▶ Pour the colored salt water into the half glass of fresh water.

▶ The colored salt water moves to the bottom of the glass, *below the fresh water!* Salt water is heavier than fresh water.

SOCIAL STUDIES

DON'T POLLUTE!

It is important for young children to understand the concept of taking care of our world and the community in which we live.

▶ We start by not throwing litter or trash on the floor in our classroom, on the playground, or at home.

▶ For older children, we expand to include keeping trash out of the ocean and lakes and to stop littering our beaches.

▶ Some tips from the Earthworks Group book, *50 Simple Things Kids Can Do to Save the Earth,* listed in the Children's Books section of this theme, follow.

Do not throw litter on the beach, in the ocean, or in lakes. Plastic bags and other plastic garbage thrown into the ocean kill as many as a million sea creatures every year!

When you visit the beach, take along a large garbage bag. Try to fill it with trash, close it tight, then throw it in a garbage can. If there are no receptacles on the beach, take the bag with you, and throw it away at the first garbage can you see.

If you go fishing, never, never, throw a discarded fishing line into the water. Birds and sea creatures can get tangled in it and die.

▶ Primary-grade children can write reports on what they discover from reading books on environmental issues, ecology, and recycling.

MORE WATER THAN LAND

▶ Have available a globe or map of the world.

▶ Talk about how much more water than land there is in the world. Three-quarters of the world is covered by oceans and seas.

▶ Find the Atlantic, Pacific (the largest), Indian, and Arctic oceans on the globe. Which states and cities are near the shorelines? Talk about islands.

▶ Have books and pictures to share with the children depicting different kinds of communities that are built around or near oceans and lakes.

▶ Talk about ocean-related occupations, such as: commercial fishermen; marine geologists, who study rocks and the formation of the ocean floor; marine biologists, who study the animals and plants of the ocean; oceanographers, who explore and study the ocean; and captains and crews of commercial boats and cruise ships.

▶ If you live near an ocean or a lake, ask someone whose occupation deals with the water to visit the class.

▶ Listen to the questions the children ask you about oceans and lakes. Let their interests guide you as you continue to develop curriculum.

CHILDREN'S BOOKS

Arnold, Caroline. (1994). *Sea Lion.* New York: Morrow.

Baldwin, Robert F. (1998). *This Is the Sea that Feeds Us.* Illustrated by Don Dyen. New York: Dawn Publishers.

Carle, Eric. (1988). *A House for Hermit Crab.* New York: Simon & Schuster.

Clements, Andrew. (1997). *Big Al.* (Rev. ed.). New York: Aladdin.

Crews, Donald. (1995). *Sail Away.* New York: Greenwillow.

Crews, Donald. (1988). *Harbor.* New York: William Morrow.

Earthworks Group. (1994). *50 Simple Things Kids Can Do to Save the Earth.* Kansas City, MO: Andrews and McMeel.

Falwell, Cathryn. (2001). *Turtle Splash — Countdown at the Pond.* New York: Greenwillow.

Faulkner, Keith. (1997). *A 3-D Look at Oceans.* Illustrated by Robert Morton. New York: Little Simon.

Fleming, Denise. (1993). *In the Small, Small Pond.* New York: Henry Holt.

Gibbons, Gail. (1998). *Sea Turtles.* New York: Holiday House.

Gibbons, Gail. (1994). *Frogs.* New York: Holiday House.

Gibbons, Gail. (1991). *Whales.* New York: Holiday House.

Hardy, Ann. (1995). *Who Lives in the Oceans, Lakes, and Rivers?: A Baby Animal Sticker Book.* New York: Little Simon.

Heller, Ruth. (1992). *How to Hide an Octopus and Other Sea Creatures.* New York: Grossett/Putnam.

Hulme, Joy N. (1993). *Sea Squares.* (Rev. ed.). New York: Hyperion Press.

Kalan, Robert. (1992). *Blue Sea.* Illustrated by Donald Crews. New York: Mulberry.

Koch, Michelle. (1993). *World Water Watch.* New York: Greenwillow.

Lasky, Kathryn. (1995). *Pond Year.* Illustrated by Mike Bostock. Cambridge, MA: Candlewick Press.

Lionni, Leo. (1995). *On My Beach There Are Many Pebbles.* New York: Mulberry.

Lionni, Leo. (1992). *Swimmy.* New York: Knopf.

MacDonald, Suse. (1994). *Sea Shapes.* New York: Gulliver Books.

McMullan, Kate. (2003). *I'm Mighty!* Illustrated by Tony Oliver. Watertown, MA: Charlesbridge.

O'Mara, Anna. (1998). *Oceans.* Chicago: Children's Press.

Orr, Katherine. (1991). *My Grandpa and the Sea.* New York: First Avenue Editions.

Parker, Steve. (1989). *Seashore.* New York: Knopf.

Pfister, Marcus, and J. Alison James. (1996). *The Rainbow Fish.* (Board ed.). New York: North South Books.

Ranger Rick's Naturescope Guides. (1997). *Diving into Oceans.* New York: Learning Triangle Press.

Winer, Yvonne. (2003). *Frogs Sing Songs.* Illustrated by Tony Oliver. Watertown, MA: Charlesbridge.

Zolotow, Charlotte. (1994). *The Seashore Book.* (Rev. ed.). New York: HarperTrophy.

Family Letter (Primary grade)

Dear Family,

As we continue to study our environment, we are beginning a new theme, "Oceans and Lakes." We will provide opportunities for the children to learn the following:

- Water is necessary to all living things.
- Ocean water is salty.
- Most lakes have fresh water in them.
- Many plants and animals, especially fish, live in oceans and lakes.
- The four biggest oceans in the world are the Atlantic, Pacific, Indian, and Arctic.

We will be talking about the following:

- the oceans
- salt water
- fresh water
- safety on water
- environmental issues
- beaches
- ships and boats
- lake recreation
- fish and mammals

Things to do at home with your child to reinforce our classroom activities include:

- Talk about what you see and read in books, magazines, and newspapers relating to oceans and ocean life.
- If you have taken a vacation at or visited the seashore, look through the pictures and memorabilia from that trip.
- Visit an aquarium or a pet store, and look at fish.
- Help your child start or add to a seashell collection.
- Talk about ways your family is helping to protect the environment.

Participate in these activities at school:

- Come visit us, and see how we have brought the ocean into our classroom.
  Date _____   Time _____
- Help us guess how many seashells are in our big jar.
  Date _____   Time _____
- If you know anyone who fishes for his or her occupation, marine life scientists, or someone who works on a boat or ship, please let us know. We are looking for someone whose work involves the water to visit our class.

Our wish list for this theme includes:
    new sponges
    empty, washed soda bottles
    seashells
    plastic pitcher

Thanks!

PLANT LIFE
Trees
Evergreens
Deciduous — lose leaves
Berry bushes
Moss
Vines
Poison ivy
Poison oak
Wildflowers

THEME 19
Forests

ANIMALS
Deer   Bears
Foxes   Squirrels
Rabbits   Skunks
Raccoons   Opossums
Chipmunks   Turtles
Birds   Snakes

ACTIVITIES
Camping
Hiking
Help forest rangers
Practice safety
Put out campfire
Pick up trash

HOW FORESTS HELP US
Provide lumber for building
Protect environment
Keep soil in place
Prevent flooding

THEME GOALS

To provide opportunities for children to learn the following:

▶ A forest is a home for plants, animals, and insects.

▶ The tallest plants are trees, which provide shelter and food for many animals and insects.

▶ Some trees are called "evergreen," because they do not lose their leaves in the winter.

▶ Broadleaf, or deciduous, trees have leaves in the summer and lose their leaves in the winter.

▶ Bushes, ferns, moss, and toadstools grow low on the forest's floor.

▶ Many animals and birds, such as deer, bears, foxes, rabbits, raccoons, chipmunks, and owls, like to live in the forest.

Children-Created Bulletin Board

Make changes to this bulletin board while the "Forests" theme is emphasized. This bulletin board helps the children stay interested in the environment and how to protect it and teaches them about the plants and animals of the forest.

▶ You and the children can create a three-dimensional bulletin board by taking paper sacks or brown butcher paper and crushing it to create a tree trunk, long limbs, and vines.

▶ Make and glue leaves on the limbs.

▶ Hang the limbs around the bulletin board.

▶ Add a few real twigs and small branches to the bulletin board too.

▶ Then trace children's hands on dark green paper. Have the children cut these out to make an ever-green tree. Place the tree on one side of the board.

▶ Place a banner above the bulletin board that reads: "A Forest Is a Home for Animals and Plants: Take Care of the Forest!"

▶ Ask the children to make animal tracks on strips of paper, and use these as the border around the board. An animal tracks activity is included in the Math section of this theme.

▶ Continue adding to the board throughout this theme.

VOCABULARY STARTERS

Let the children add words. Include pictures where appropriate.

bark — the skin of a tree.

camouflage — the colorings or markings of forest animals that hide them among leaves, bark, and rocks.

forest — a large area of land with many trees, plants, and animals.

tracks — the footprints that animals make.

tree — the tallest plant in the forest.

woods — another name for forest.

LANGUAGE EXPERIENCES

POEM: "I Was Walking in the Forest"

▶ This is a poem with a strong beat. The rhythm can be accented by clapping hands or using rhythm instruments.

▶ Each verse also suggests actions that can be used to illustrate the words. With toddlers, use fewer verses.

▶ Have pictures of the animals to share with the children.

I was walking in the forest
And what did I see
But a wide-eyed owl
Sitting high in a tree.
"Who," he said, "Who, who, who
Who, my friend, are you, you, you?"
   I walked a little farther
   And what did I see
   But a big brown bear
   Getting honey from a tree.
   "Yum," he said, "Yum, yum, yum,
   I love honey in my tum, tum, tum."
I walked a little farther
And what did I see
But a raccoon mama
With her babies three.
"Come here, my babies, 1-2-3
Stay very close, very close to me."
   I walked a little farther
   And what did I see
   But an old woodpecker
   A-peckin' on a tree.
   He pecked, and he pecked, and he peck-peck-pecked

And he said, "All this peckin' is a pain in the neck!"
I was walking in the forest
When what did I see
But a tall forest ranger
Who said to me,
"Be careful in the forest — don't harm trees
And be friends with the birds and animals, please."

Philip Jackman

DRAMATIC PLAY

TEDDY BEAR PICNIC

▶ For infants, place teddy bears and other stuffed animals on the floor around the edges of a blanket.

▶ Hold the younger infants in your lap, and talk about the stuffed animals. Say, "Hello, little bear. Say hello to Anna."

▶ The other babies can crawl to and interact with the animals.

▶ At snack time, plan a "teddy bear picnic" with the toddlers.

▶ Place a large blanket on the playground, and enjoy a picnic with the children and the stuffed animals.

- -

PLAN A TEDDY BEAR PARTY

▶ Ask the children to bring their favorite stuffed animals to class, Beanie Babies™ included.

▶ Have the children plan a party for the teddy bears and all of the stuffed animals.

▶ Encourage several children at a time to go to the dramatic play center to plan the party.

▶ Guide the children in preparing a list of what they will need, writing invitations, and decorating for the party. Ask them to draw or write the invitations any way they wish. Help them if they ask.

▶ Refreshments can be served at snack time.

▶ At the party, read Freeman's *Corduroy*, listed in the Children's Books section of this theme.

PUPPET PLAY

FOREST FINGER PUPPETS

Make this puppet activity open ended. Throughout the "Forests" theme, the children may go to the manipulative or art center and make finger puppets anytime. This offers a visual way to demonstrate what they have learned about forest animals.

▶ Supply markers, crayons, oval-shaped pieces of paper, construction paper, scissors, and double-sided tape.

▶ Guide the children into drawing animal faces on the oval papers or cutting out other face shapes.

▶ Suggest that the children experiment using different kinds of lines, heavy or light.

▶ Children can easily attach the puppets to their fingers with the double-sided tape, or attach the puppets to children's garden gloves.

▶ Encourage the children to make up dialogue between their finger puppets about life in the forest.

▶ With younger children, you might start the conversation with finger puppets of your own.

MUSIC

SONG: "The Bear Lives in the Forest"

This song is based on the traditional "The Bear Went over the Mountain."

The bear lives in the forest.
The bear lives in the forest.
The bear lives in the forest.
He's happy as can be.
   The opossum lives in the forest.
   The raccoon lives in the forest.
   The deer lives in the forest.
   They love to be free.
What else lives in the forest?
What else lives in the forest?
What else lives in the forest?
Oh, please tell me.

SOUNDS OF THE FOREST

Introduce this activity to the children by reading an appropriate book about animals and the sounds they make. Duffy's *Forest Tracks,* listed in the Children's Books section of this theme, is one suggestion.

▶ Play a recorded musical selection that introduces children to the instruments of the orchestra. The following selections suggest animal sounds: Prokofiev's *Peter and the Wolf* and Saint-Saëns's *Carnival of the Animals.*

▶ Place all of the rhythm instruments in the center of the floor during group time.

▶ Ask each child to choose one.

▶ As each child demonstrates the sound her instrument makes, ask: "Does the instrument sound like an animal in the forest?" "Does it sound like the wind in the trees?" "What does it sound like?"

▶ Have all of the instruments play together to combine the sounds into one "forest symphony."

SONG: "Oh, the Forest Is a Lovely Place to Be"

Sing this song to the tune of the traditional "She'll Be Comin 'Round the Mountain." Use rhythm instruments to accompany the song.

Oh, the forest is a lovely place to be,
Oh, the forest is a lovely place to be.
It's got lots and lots of things to see,
And lots of fun for you and me.
The forest is a lovely place to be.
But to keep it lovely you must be its friend,
But to keep it lovely you must be its friend.
So be careful when you camp out,
Douse your fire, be sure it's stamped out.
To keep it lovely you must be its friend.
Oh, the forest is a quiet place to be — sssh,
Oh, the forest is a quiet place to be — sssh.
Since most animals and birds are shy,
If you make noise they'll run or fly.
The forest is a quiet place to be — sssh.
When you leave the forest, you should leave it clean,
When you leave the forest, you should leave it clean.
Pick up your trash when you are through.
Remember: others go there too,
Let's all make sure we leave the forest clean.

Philip Jackman

MOVEMENT

HOP LIKE A BUNNY, SCURRY LIKE A SQUIRREL

In this movement activity, each child picks a forest animal and tries to mimic its posture and movement. It is a good idea to have photos or illustrations of several animals to help the children visualize what they will act out.

▶ Have the children select from among creatures that have clearly contrasting styles of movement, such as bears (big, lumbering), deer (delicate, on tiptoes), rabbits (hopping, sniffing), owls (wide-eyed, head-swiveling), and snakes (watchful, slithering).

▶ For younger toddlers, concentrate on only two or three animals.

SENSORY ART

BARK RUBBINGS

▶ Supply the children with thick drawing paper and crayons.

▶ Go for a walk to look for trees on the playground, around the school, and in the neighborhood.

▶ Have the children rub over the paper with a crayon until the pattern of the bark shows on the drawing paper.

▶ Working with a partner is helpful. One child holds the paper against the tree, while the other partner completes the tree rubbing.

FOREST SPECIAL EFFECTS

Put out glue sticks, white drawing paper, tempera paint in various forest colors, brushes, and new sponges in the art area. Make these available throughout the duration of the "Forests" theme.

▶ Suggest to the children that they use the glue sticks to draw something easy to outline, such as a tree, a flower, the sun, or a bird.

▶ Let the drawing dry.

▶ When the glue is dry, the children color the paper with the paint. For best results, use one color.

▶ Let the paint dry.

▶ After the drawing is completely dry, dip the whole paper in water, then watch what happens to it.

▶ Hang with clothespins on a line placed over several layers of newspapers. Let the picture dry completely, and place the art on the bulletin board for all to see.

CREATIVE FOOD EXPERIENCES

DEER SANDWICHES

You will need the following:

> slices of wheat bread
> peanut butter or plain hummus spread
> raisins
> pretzels
> gumdrops

1. Wash hands.
2. Have the children cut pieces of bread into triangles with plastic knives.
3. Spread with peanut butter or hummus. Be aware of children's allergies.
4. Use raisins for eyes, pretzels for antlers, and gumdrops for noses.
5. Eat and enjoy!

FOREST TREE COOKIES

You will need the following:

> 1 cup of margarine or soft shortening
> 1 1/2 cups of sugar
> 1 egg
> 1 teaspoon of vanilla, almond, or lemon extract
> 2 tablespoons of milk
> 3 cups of flour
> 1 teaspoon of baking powder
> 1/2 teaspoon of salt
> green food coloring

1. Wash hands.
2. Have children complete each of the cooking tasks, two or three children for each task.
3. Cream together the margarine, sugar, egg, vanilla, and milk.
4. Add flour, about a third at a time, baking powder, and salt.
5. Add a few drops of green food color.
6. Mix all ingredients.
7. Chill. Roll out dough with a rolling pin.

FOREST TREE COOKIES

Wash hands.

Cream together 1 cup margarine, 1 1/2 cups sugar, 1 egg.

1 teaspoon vanilla, and 2 tablespoons of milk.

Add 3 cups flour, 1 teaspoon baking powder, and 1/2 teaspoon salt.

Add a few drops of green food color. Mix all ingredients together.

Chill. Roll out dough with a rolling pin and cut cookies with

tree-shaped cookie cutters. Bake at 375 degrees for 10 minutes.

8. Cut cookies with tree-shaped cookie cutters.
9. Bake at 375 degrees for approximately 10 minutes.

As a time saver, substitute ready-to-use cookie dough available at the grocery store.

MATH

MATCH THE ANIMAL TRACKS

▶ Make a folder matching game of animal tracks.
▶ Use fewer, larger animal tracks for younger children.
▶ Open a file folder, and across it spread the animal tracks you have drawn and cut out.
▶ Glue the tracks onto the folder.
▶ Print in lower case, beneath the tracks, the name of the animal that made it.
▶ Make a set of cards with duplicate animal tracks, omitting the name.
▶ Laminate the folder and each card.
▶ Label the front of the folder with two of the tracks and the words "Animal Tracks."

- Glue an envelope or a locking plastic bag on the back of the folder. Place the card pieces in the bag or envelope.
- Place the folder game in the math center for the children.

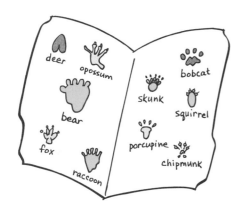

MATH WORD GAMES

- Have available actual objects for the children to count. After they have played the game several times, remove the objects.
- The first time younger children try these activities, let each child choose a partner. It is encouraging to do this in pairs.
- For the first math word game, you need 11 pinecones.

    Two children were gathering pinecones in the forest. The first one gathered four. The second one gathered three more than the first. How many did the second one gather?
- For the second math word game, you need seven acorns.

    A squirrel was gathering acorns for the winter and was hurrying home with seven to store away. However, the squirrel dropped two along the way. How many are left?
- You need four pecans and six walnuts for this one.

    A child was looking in the forest for nuts that had fallen from trees. She found four pecans and six walnuts. How many nuts did the child find?
- You need 11 leaves to start this math word game.

    A deer was nibbling leaves from a branch. When she started there were 11 leaves on it, but when she finished, only three were left. How many did she eat?
- Present the math word games verbally to the younger children. Observe how they solve the problems. Let older children read the games. Observe how they solve the problems.

DO YOU REMEMBER?

- Place objects that relate to this theme, such as acorns, leaves, pinecones, pictures of trees and animals, and pieces of wood, on a tray.
- Start with a few items at a time. Gradually increase the number of objects displayed.
- Ask the child to closely study the objects on the tray.
- Then cover the items with a cloth.
- Ask the child to name them.
- Uncover the tray, and let the child see if she remembered them all.
- Play this like a game. It is self-correcting and non-threatening.
- Add more objects and pictures.
- Repeat the procedure.
- Do this as a one-on-one activity with all of the children over several days.
- Try starting with the items, and then take some away. What is missing?

SCIENCE

LET'S STUDY TREES

For this project, gather pictures, books, magazines, and maps for the children to use.

- Talk about where the trees grow. For example, the tallest trees in the world are redwoods, which grow along the Pacific Coast of North America. Some of the oldest are the pine trees of the Rocky Mountains.

▶ Discuss the following parts of the tree:

crown — the part of the tree above the trunk that is made up of leaves and branches.

trunk — the thick wood stem of the tree.

roots — the tree's anchor, which draws water and food from the soil.

timber — the name given to the wood of the tree.

▶ With the children's help, make a list of things that are made of wood, partly or completely.

▶ Walk around the school, and look for wooden things. Ask the children to walk around the house with their family and identify things made of wood.

▶ Take several days to complete the list. Put it in the science center.

▶ Collect small blocks or pieces of timber. Check with local home improvement or hardware stores and carpenters for scraps.

▶ Label each type of wood with its name for identification.

▶ Put the pieces in the science center, along with magnifying glasses. Ask the children to look for the patterns in the grain of the wood.

▶ Supply a spray bottle filled with water for the children to observe if any changes take place when the wood gets wet.

▶ Provide small tubs of water in which to float the wood pieces. Which pieces sink? Which float?

▶ Leave these in the water, and weigh them several days later. Which pieces have absorbed the water?

▶ Pound nails in some pieces. Which wood is the softest? Which is the hardest?

▶ As a culminating activity, have the children paint the wood pieces and make boats, which they can then take home.

▶ Celebrate Earth Day on April 22. Look at the earth and its surroundings. Clean up the grounds around the school and the neighborhood. If you live near a forest, lake, or wildflower area, take the children on a field trip.

▶ Read Temple's book *Dear World: How Children around the World Feel about Our Environment.* Some excerpts follow:

I love nature. I like being out in the open. The thing I most like is walking in the forest. Then I hear the soft rustling of the treetops which sway gently in the wind. . . . The soft chirping of the birds makes me breathe deeply. Then I always lie down on the soft mat of moss which has grown over the forest floor, and begin to dream.

Mirya Sauerland, age 10
Germany — The Black Forest

I like picking flowers outdoors to make necklaces because then I feel I am playing with the flowers. When it is no longer possible to make such things with wildflowers, the woods and forest will have been destroyed, and I feel uneasy about this. We know that paper is produced from timber and as we don't want the forest to be destroyed, we are recycling milk cartons.

Yukiko Kitamura, age 9
Shikoku, Japan

▶ As a concluding activity for this project, ask the children to write or dictate to you their letters to the world. Display the letters on the bulletin board.

SOCIAL STUDIES

DEAR WORLD

▶ Introduce the children to ways they can protect the environment by reading books about the subject.

▶ Invite visitors from local environmental organizations and a county conservation commission to talk to the children. Perhaps these individuals will take the children on a field trip with their families.

CHILDREN'S BOOKS

Brown, Margaret Wise. (1996). *Four Fur Feet.* Illustrated by Woodleigh Hubbard. New York: Hyperion Press.

Cherry, Lynne. (1990). *The Great Kapok Tree: A Tale of the Amazon Rain Forest.* San Diego: Harcourt.

Dorros, Arthur. (1997). *A Tree Is Growing.* Illustrated by S. D. Schindler. New York: Scholastic.

Duffy, Dee Dee. (1996). *Forest Tracks.* Illustrated by Janet Marshall. New York: Boyds Mills Press.

Freeman, Don. (1976). *Corduroy.* New York: Puffin.

Gise, Joanne. (1990). *A Picture Book of Forest Animals.* Illustrated by Roseanna Pistolesi. Mahwah, NJ: Troll.

Grahame, Kenneth. (2003). *Wind in the Willows.* Abridged and illustrated by Inga Moore. Cambridge, MA: Candlewick Press.

Hines, Gary. (1993). *Flying Firefighters.* Illustrated by Anna G. Hines. New York: Clarion Books.

Hutchins, Pat. (1990). *Good-Night, Owl!* New York: Aladdin.

Jaspersohn, William. (1992). *How the Forests Grew.* Illustrated by Chuck Eckart. New York: Mulberry.

Lauber, Patricia. (1994). *Be a Friend to Trees.* Illustrated by Holly Keller. New York: HarperCollins.

Lockeer, Thomas. (2001). *Sky Tree: Seeing Science through Art.* New York: HarperCollins.

McGee, Marni. (1994). *Forest Child.* Illustrated by A. Scott Banfill. New York: Simon & Schuster.

National Wildlife Foundation. (1998). *Trees Are Terrific (Ranger Rick's Naturescope).* New York: McGraw-Hill.

Pandell, Karen. (1994). *I Love You, Sun. I Love You, Moon.* Illustrated by Tomie dePaola. New York: Putnam.

Pfeffer, Wendy. (1997). *A Log's Life.* Illustrated by Stephanie Lurie. New York: Simon & Schuster.

Ryder, Joanne. (2001). *A Fawn in the Grass.* New York: Henry Holt.

Schimmel, Shim. (1994). *Dear Children of the Earth.* New York: Northwood Press.

Staub, Frank. (1998). *America's Forests.* Minneapolis: Carolrhoda Books.

Stroud, Virginia A. (1996). *The Path of the Quiet Elk.* New York: Dial.

Taylor, Barbara, Kim Taylor, and Jane Burton. (1993). *Forest Life (Look Closer).* New York: DK Publishers.

Temple, Lannis. (1993). *Dear World: How Children around the World Feel about Our Environment.* New York: Random House.

Vyner, Tim. (1995). *The Tree in the Forest.* New York: Barron's.

Waddell, Martin. (1996). *Owl Babies.* Cambridge, MA: Candlewick Press.

Wadsworth, Ginger, and Frank Staub. (1995). *Giant Sequoia Trees (Early Bird Nature Books).* New York: Lerner Publications.

Yolen, Jane, and Laura Regan. (1997). *Welcome to the Green House.* New York: Putnam.

Family Letter (Preschool)

Dear Family,

Our new theme is "Forests." The children will learn the following:

- A forest is a home for plants, animals, and insects.
- The tallest plants are trees, which provide shelter and food for many animals and insects.
- Some trees are called "evergreen," because they do not lose their leaves in the winter.
- Broadleaf, or deciduous, trees have leaves in the summer and lose their leaves in the winter.
- Bushes, ferns, moss, and toadstools grow low on the forest's floor.
- Many animals and birds, such as deer, bears, foxes, rabbits, raccoons, chipmunks, and owls, like to live in the forest.

We will be talking about the following:

- plant life
- berry bushes
- animals
- protecting the forest
- trees
- moss and vines
- how forests help us
- forest rangers

Try some of the following to do at home with your child:

- Talk about ways to protect the environment on a daily basis.
- Go on a walk, and look at the trees. Collect nuts, acorns, and different kinds of leaves that have fallen to the ground. Talk about what you see.
- Go on a picnic with your family, and be sure all members pick up their trash and put it in the garbage can.

Family participation opportunities at school will include:

- Come spend some time with us as we explore the forest. See what is going on in our classroom.

  Date _____   Time _____

- Come join us when we bake "forest tree" cookies.

  Date _____   Time _____

- Please tell us if you know of a local environmentalist who could come to talk to our class.

Our wish list for this theme includes:

recordings of animal sounds	wire coat hangers
music relating to the forest	acorns
pinecones	pictures of trees
pictures of animals	nature magazines

Thanks!

Animals and More

*I*t is important for children to participate actively in their own learning experiences and activities. The curriculum should adapt to their *individual* differences, abilities, and interests.

The thematic activities in this section suggest ways to help you provide appropriate learning experiences for the children in your classroom. Adjust these to individual, small group, or large group involvement. Children enjoy learning about living creatures, and these activities should encourage their enthusiastic participation.

The following themes are included in Section V, "Animals and More":

Theme 20 — Zoo

Theme 21 — Farm

Theme 22 — Pets

Theme 23 — Insects and Spiders

Theme 24 — Fish

Theme 25 — Birds

Theme 26 — Circus

Theme 27 — Dinosaurs

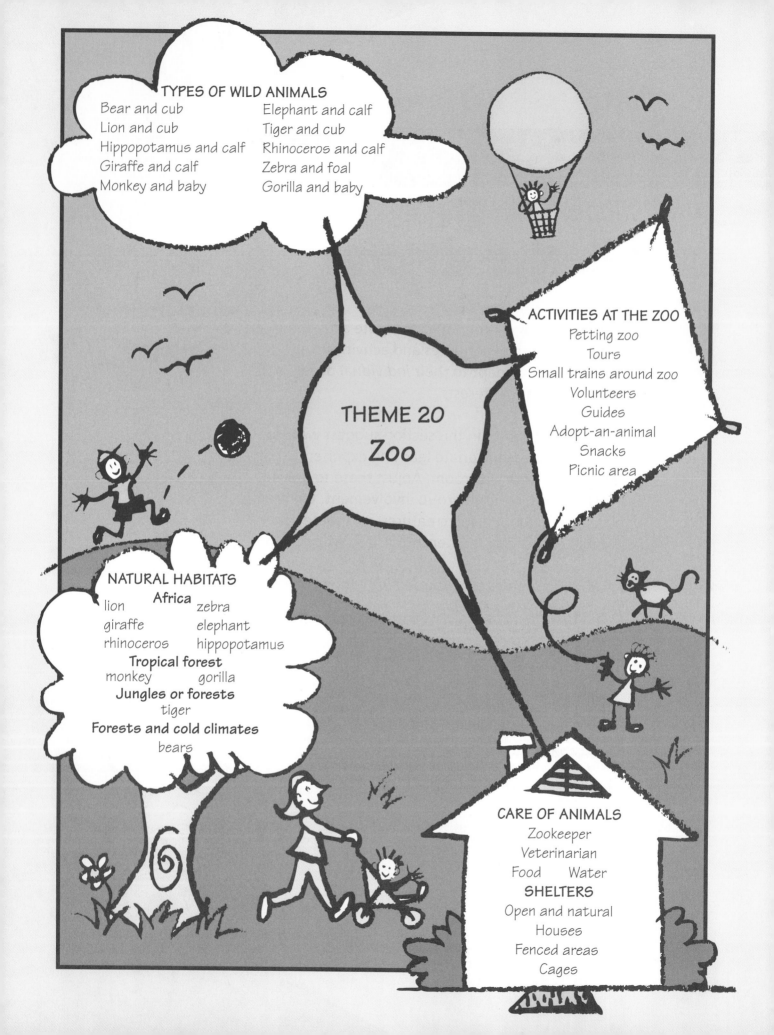

TYPES OF WILD ANIMALS

Bear and cub
Lion and cub
Hippopotamus and calf
Giraffe and calf
Monkey and baby

Elephant and calf
Tiger and cub
Rhinoceros and calf
Zebra and foal
Gorilla and baby

THEME 20
Zoo

ACTIVITIES AT THE ZOO
Petting zoo
Tours
Small trains around zoo
Volunteers
Guides
Adopt-an-animal
Snacks
Picnic area

NATURAL HABITATS
Africa
lion   zebra
giraffe   elephant
rhinoceros   hippopotamus
Tropical forest
monkey   gorilla
Jungles or forests
tiger
Forests and cold climates
bears

CARE OF ANIMALS
Zookeeper
Veterinarian
Food   Water
SHELTERS
Open and natural
Houses
Fenced areas
Cages

THEME GOALS

To provide opportunities for children to learn the following:

▶ A zoo is a place where people can safely see wild animals.

▶ Zoo animals from all over the world are kept in cages, houses, and fenced areas similar to their natural habitats.

▶ Giraffes, bears, elephants, lions, tigers, zebras, monkeys, gorillas, hippopotamuses, and rhinoceroses are some zoo animals.

▶ Baby animals usually are kept with their mothers. Sometimes they are placed in a zoo nursery for extra care.

▶ Zookeepers and veterinarians take care of all of the animals and keep them safe, fed, watered, exercised, and healthy.

Children-Created Bulletin Board

Make the zoo bulletin board interactive by suggesting ways for the children to add to it throughout the theme. The more the class explores the zoo theme, the more the board should reflect the children's exploration.

▶ Cover the surface with tan burlap to give texture to the bulletin board.

▶ String a nylon cord clothesline across the top. With clothespins, attach leaves that the children make, monkeys that are made to hang from the trees, and anything else the children wish to add.

▶ Crush brown paper bags to make the trunks of the trees.

▶ With the children's help, make a craft stick fence across the bottom of the bulletin board.

▶ Title the board "Welcome to Our Zoo."

▶ Place silhouettes of zoo animals on the board. Throughout the theme, the children can put their drawings and pictures on or beside the appropriate animal silhouettes.

▶ You may also put Velcro® pieces on the silhouettes and on the backs of animal pictures. This way the children can match the correct animal picture to the silhouettes.

▶ As with all early childhood bulletin boards, the children frequently should have something new to discover or put on the board.

VOCABULARY STARTERS

Let the children add words.

habitat — a natural place where animals live before they come to the zoo.

veterinarian — a doctor for animals.

zoo — a place where we can see wild animals.

zookeeper — a person who feeds and cares for the animals in the zoo.

zoo nursery — a place for zoo babies needing special care.

LANGUAGE EXPERIENCES

STUFFED ANIMAL PLAY

▶ Hold the baby in your arms or lap.

▶ Introduce the child to a stuffed animal, such as a teddy bear or giraffe.

▶ Say the name, and talk to the infant about the animal.

▶ Hold the animal in front of the baby's eyes.

▶ Slowly move the stuffed animal back and forth, so the child can follow the toy with his eyes.

▶ Stop the activity when the infant tires.

▶ Repeat with the same or a different stuffed animal.

GORILLA FUN

Read Rathman's *Good Night, Gorilla* to the children (see Children's Books section in this theme). This limited-word picture book is delightful — you will probably be asked to read it many times.

▶ Make flannelboard characters of the people and animals in the book. This allows the children to participate in the retelling of the story.

▶ The book, flannelboard, and story pieces can be put in the language center for the children to enjoy whenever they wish.

▶ As a follow-up, the children can act out the story. This helps develop memory and sequencing skills.

DRAMATIC PLAY

ZOO NURSERY

▶ Set up the dramatic play area as a zoo nursery.

▶ Provide doll beds, empty baby bottles, lots of small stuffed animals, baby blankets, aprons, and smocks.

▶ If possible, put several child-size rocking chairs in the area too.

▶ To introduce the children to the zoo nursery, read Smith's *Inside the Zoo Nursery,* listed in the Children's Books section of this theme.

▶ This book explains that baby animals cannot always be kept with their mothers. They go to the zoo nursery for special care by the nursery zookeepers and the veterinarian.

▶ Suggest to the children that they take care of the baby stuffed animals in their own "zoo nursery."

PUPPET PLAY

LET'S MAKE ZOO PUPPETS

▶ For toddlers, put out paper sacks and crayons.

▶ Demonstrate how to make a sack into a puppet by putting your hand inside.

▶ Leave the sacks on the table, and let the children explore playing with the sacks and coloring them.

▶ For preschoolers, put out Styrofoam™ and paper cups, paper plates, paper sacks, construction paper, yarn, crayons, markers, gray paint, paper towel rolls, and craft sticks on a table.

▶ Invite the children to make animal puppets.

▶ A Styrofoam™ cup with a small circle cut in the side is a good beginning for an easy elephant puppet. The child sticks his finger into the cup and out the hole to make the elephant's nose.

▶ Fringe the outer rim of a paper plate all the way around, and it becomes a lion's mane.

▶ Give the children time to experiment with the materials. They will make wonderful zoo puppets.

▶ Follow the puppet making with a parade of animal puppets.

▶ The children who did not want to make a puppet can play rhythm instruments to accompany the zoo parade.

MUSIC

SONG: "Animals Marching in the Zoo"

Before introducing the song to the children, talk about the animals at the zoo. How do children think each animal moves? Ask them: "Which animals do you like the best?" "Which ones do you think you'll be when we sing the song?" Then, have fun! Sing to the traditional tune of "When Johnny Comes Marching Home Again."

The bears are marching in the zoo, hurrah, hurrah.
The elephants are marching too, hurrah, hurrah.
The lions and tigers and tall giraffes,
The rhinos and hippos, and baby calves,
And the monkeys and zebras go marching in the zoo.

▶ For the second verse, sing "playing in the zoo."

▶ For the third verse, sing "eating in the zoo."

▶ For the fourth verse, sing "sleeping in the zoo."

MOVEMENT

ANIMAL ANTICS

This is a large-muscle activity for outdoor play.

▶ Mark a starting point and an ending point on the grass.

▶ The children move from one point to another by following directions, such as:
  — Take two lion leaps.
  — Take four elephant steps.
  — Take three kangaroo hops.
  — Take five monkey jumps.

SENSORY ART

STRIPES, SPOTS, AND PATTERNS

▶ Put out wallpaper and fabric scraps (striped, spotted, and patterned), fake fur and leather scraps, cotton balls, yarn, scissors, glue, crayons, markers, construction paper, and paper plates on a table in the art area.

▶ Leave these materials out throughout the "Zoo" theme.

▶ Encourage the children to create with the materials. It will be interesting to see what things or animals the children make.

SQUIGGLE ART

This activity is designed to encourage creativity, develop flexible thinking, and stimulate brainstorming skills.

▶ Put a "squiggle" on a flip chart. This is just a random line made anywhere on the page.

▶ Have the children look at the line and talk about what they see.

▶ Ask one child to come up and draw his idea to complete the drawing. The drawing should contain the squiggle.

▶ Next, make another line on another sheet of paper on the flip chart.

▶ Ask another child to come up and draw an animal picture that includes the squiggle.

▶ Put out a stack of white paper sheets, each marked with a different squiggle, crayons, markers, and pencils in the art area.

▶ Leave these out so the children can experiment with squiggle art on their own.

CREATIVE FOOD EXPERIENCES

TASTY SNACK

You will need the following:

> 1 banana for each child
> orange juice
> craft or popsicle sticks
> shredded coconut
> chopped peanuts (omit for those children with allergies)

1. Wash hands.
2. Place a small bowl of orange juice in front of each child.
3. Place several servings of shredded coconut and chopped peanuts on waxed paper.
4. Have each child cut his banana into thick slices with a craft stick.
5. Each banana slice is then placed on a craft stick, dipped into the orange juice, and rolled in one or both of the toppings.
6. Enjoy!

ANIMAL MERRY-GO-ROUNDS

You will need the following:

> 1 apple for every two children
> peanut butter
> animal crackers
> pretzel sticks

1. Wash hands.
2. Cut the apple in half ($\frac{1}{2}$ apple per child).
3. Spread peanut butter over the cut side of each apple half (peel is on the bottom).
4. Add animal crackers and pretzel sticks to represent the merry-go-round animals and poles.
5. The children also can separate the zoo animals from the other types in the animal cracker box before they enjoy eating them.

(Use another recipe if some children are allergic to peanut butter.)

ANIMAL MERRY-GO-ROUNDS

Wash hands.

Cut one apple in half.

Spread peanut butter over each apple half.

Add animal crackers and pretzel sticks to make the

merry-go-round animals and poles.

Look at your creation and then eat! Yum!

MATH

LET'S BUILD A ZOO

▶ In the block area, put out stuffed animals, small animal toys, all sizes of blocks and Legos™, berry baskets, boxes, grass, twigs, leaves, and hay.

▶ This will give the children a variety of materials to create a zoo and build areas for the animals.

▶ The bigger blocks, boxes, and stuffed animals usually prove to be the favorites for toddlers.

TALL, TALLER, TALLEST

Introduce this math activity to children by reading books and showing pictures of giraffes in their natural habitats and at the zoo.

▶ Ask the children to look closely at the pictures.

▶ Ask questions such as: "Which legs are the longest on a giraffe, the front ones or the back?" (The front ones are.) "What do you think giraffes eat?" (They eat the leaves and twigs of trees.) "What about the neck and the rest of the giraffe's body?" (The body is one continuous slope from horns to tail.)

▶ Children can draw pictures of the mother, father, and baby giraffes.

▶ Male giraffes are 15 to 20 feet tall. Female giraffes are 10 to 15 feet tall. Newborn giraffes are more than 6 feet tall.

▶ As a class project, have the children use masking tape to mark off 15 feet, 10 feet, and 6 feet on the floor. This should help them visualize the height of giraffes.

▶ Supply tape measures, rulers, yardsticks, paper, and pencils.

▶ As a follow-up to the field trip, talk about what you saw, including the zoo habitats, animals, zoo workers, what was happening, what the animals were doing, and other observations that the children can recall.

▶ With the younger children, read or reread Martin's *Brown Bear, Brown Bear, What Do You See?*

▶ Have the children dictate and illustrate a new book using animals that they saw at the zoo.

▶ Guide the older children to work with a partner to draw a map of the zoo. Ask them to label the areas with the names of the animals that live in each.

▶ Continue this activity for several days. Allow the children plenty of time to complete the project.

SCIENCE

BABY ZOO ANIMALS

A study of the zoo gives children a unique opportunity to observe animals.

▶ Invite a zookeeper, a veterinarian, or an animal rehabilitator to visit the children in your class.

▶ If possible, ask the individual to bring a baby animal that lives in the zoo to visit the class. Some zoos provide this kind of service to schools and child care centers.

▶ Having someone who can answer the specific questions the children ask adds to the interest of this experience and helps the children learn. Someone who works with animals can explain firsthand the habitats, characteristics, and eating and sleeping habits of wild zoo animals.

SOCIAL STUDIES

WHAT DID WE SEE?

▶ In preparation for a field trip to the zoo, read Aliki's *My Visit to the Zoo* and Gibbons's *Zoo,* both of which are listed in the Children's Books section of this theme.

CHILDREN'S BOOKS

Aliki. (1997). *My Visit to the Zoo.* New York: HarperCollins.

Carle, Eric. (1997). *From Head to Toe.* New York: Harper-Collins.

Carle, Eric. (1987). *1,2,3 to the Zoo: A Counting Book.* New York: Putnam.

Deedrick, Tami. (1998). *Community Helpers, Zoo Keeper.* New York: Capstone Press.

Ehlert, Lois. (1997). *Color Zoo.* New York: HarperCollins.

Ford, Miela. (1998). *Watch Us Play.* New York: Greenwillow.

Ford, Miela. (1995). *Bear Play.* New York: Greenwillow.

Friedman, M. (2000). *Animal Crackers.* New York: Golden Books.

Gibbons, Gail. (1991). *Zoo.* New York: HarperTrophy.

Hill, Eric. (1996). *Baby Animals: A Lift-the-Flap-Book.* New York: Puffin.

Hoban, Tana. (1986). *Panda, Panda.* New York: Greenwillow.

Kallen, Stuart A. (1997). *Field Trips: The Zoo.* Edina, MN: Abdo & Daughters.

Knowles, Sheena. (1998). *Edward the Emu.* (Rev. ed.). Illustrated by Rod Clement. New York: HarperTrophy.

Innovative Kids. (1999). *Soft Shapes: Animals.* Illustrated by Bob Fillipowich. Norwalk, CT: Author.

Martin, Bill Jr. (1997). *Polar Bear, Polar Bear, What Do You Hear?* (Board Book). Illustrated by Eric Carle. New York: Henry Holt.

Martin, Bill Jr. (1983). *Brown Bear, Brown Bear, What Do You See?* Illustrated by Eric Carle. New York: Henry Holt.

Noble, Kate. (1994). *The Blue Elephant* (Zoo stories). Illustrated by Rachel Bass. New York: Silver Seahorse.

Ormerod, Jan. (1991). *When We Went to the Zoo.* New York: Lothrop, Lee & Shepard.

Oxenbury, Helen. (1991). *Monkey See, Monkey Do.* (Board Book). New York: Dial.

Paxton, Tom. (1996). *Going to the Zoo.* Illustrated by Karen Schmidt. New York: William Morrow.

Prelutsky, Jack, and Paul O. Zelinsky. (1983). *Zoo Doings: Animal Poems.* New York: William Morrow.

Rathman, Peggy. (1996). *Good Night, Gorilla.* New York: Putnam.

Rosen, Michael. (1989). *We're Going on a Bear Hunt.* New York: Macmillan.

Smith, Dale. (1997). *Nighttime at the Zoo.* New York: Golden Anchor.

Smith, Roland. (1993). *Inside the Zoo Nursery.* Photographs by William Munoz. New York: Cobblehill/Dutton.

Stamper, Judith. (1989). *Zoo Worker.* Illustrated by Kathleen Garry-McCord. Mahwah, NJ: Troll.

Tucker, Siam. (1995). *Animal Splash.* New York: Little Simon.

Van Fleet, Matthew. (2003). *Tails.* San Diego: Harcourt.

Waber, Bernard, and Barbara Waber. (1996). *A Lion Named Shirley Williamson.* New York: Houghton Mifflin.

Waddell, Martin. (1993). *Let's Go Home, Little Bear.* Illustrated by Barbara Firth. Cambridge, MA: Candlewick Press.

Family Letter (Preschool)

Dear Family,

Here we go with another new theme, "Zoo," for the children to explore. We are studying the zoo and zoo animals. We will provide opportunities for the children to learn the following:

- A zoo is a place where people can safely see wild animals.
- Zoo animals from all over the world are kept in cages, houses, and fenced areas similar to their natural habitats.
- Giraffes, bears, elephants, lions, tigers, zebras, monkeys, gorillas, hippopotamuses, and rhinoceroses are zoo animals.
- Baby animals usually are kept with their mothers. Sometimes they are placed in a zoo nursery for extra care.
- Zookeepers and veterinarians take care of all of the animals and keep them safe, fed, watered, exercised, and healthy.

We will be talking about the following:

- types of wild animals
- the names of the mothers and babies
- the animals' natural habitats
- how zookeepers and veterinarians care for the animals
- activities at the zoo

Some things to do at home with your child to support our classroom learning include:

- Look at pictures of the zoo and zoo animals in magazines and books.
- Talk to your child about your visits to the zoo when you were young.
- Go on a family trip to a zoo or a petting zoo. Take photographs for your child to keep and share with classmates.

Opportunities for you to participate at school include:

- Go with us on our field trip to the zoo.
  Date _____ Time _____
- Come visit our classroom to see the bulletin board and block zoo the children have created.
  Date _____ Time _____
- Please tell us if you know of a veterinarian who takes care of baby animals and would bring one to show the children.

Our wish list for this theme includes:

pictures of wild animals

empty, clean baby bottles

Styrofoam™ cups

wallpaper and fabric scraps, preferably striped, patterned, and spotted

Thanks!

**DOMESTICATED (FARM)
TYPES OF ANIMALS**

Chicken and chick	Sheep and lamb
Turkey and chick	Goat and kid
Cow and calf	Duck and duckling
Pig (sow) and piglet	Goose and gosling
Horse and foal	
Donkey (mule) and foal	

SHELTERS
Coop — nesting
and roosting
Pen
Barn
Stable
Stall
Shed

**THEME 21
Farm**

**ACTIVITIES ON
THE FARM**
Milk cows
Collect eggs
Shear sheep
PLANT AND HARVEST

Corn	Wheat
Oats	Cotton
Hay	

CARE OF ANIMALS
Farmer
Veterinarian
Food and water
Grazing pasture
Fenced fields
Clean shelters

THEME GOALS

To provide opportunities for children to learn the following:

▶ A farm is located outside of a city.

▶ A farm is land on which crops and animals are raised.

▶ A farmer is the person who owns the farm and, along with family members and employees, works long hours to care for the animals and crops.

▶ Chickens, turkeys, cows, pigs, horses, donkeys, sheep, goats, ducks, and geese are some of the farm animals.

▶ Farm animals are sheltered in coops, pens, barns, stables, stalls, and sheds.

▶ Much of the food we eat and the clothing we wear comes from the animals and crops raised on farms.

Children-Created Bulletin Board

This bulletin board focuses on the farm. It should express what the children know and want to find out about life on the farm. The bulletin board should change in appearance as the theme progresses.

▶ Cover the bulletin board with a light background.

▶ Ask the children to help you make a sun and some cotton-ball clouds.

▶ Provide many pictures so the children can see actual farm life.

▶ Encourage some of the children to make a barn. Others can make a scarecrow standing in the cornfield.

▶ Have available mother farm animals with babies for the children to match in appropriate pairs and put on the bulletin board.

▶ Activities throughout this theme will provide additional content to make the board interactive.

VOCABULARY STARTERS

Let the children add words.

barn — a farm building where animals are protected and crops are stored.

crop — any type of food grown on a farm.

farm — a piece of land, usually with a house and barn, on which crops and animals are raised.

harvest — collecting crops when they are ripe.

pasture — a field where farm animals can eat grass and other plants.

plant — to put seeds into the ground.

veterinarian — a doctor for animals.

LANGUAGE EXPERIENCES

NURSERY RHYMES

"Little Bo-Peep"

Little Bo-Peep has lost her sheep,
And can't tell where to find them;
Leave them alone, and they'll come home,
Wagging their tails behind them.

"Sing a Song of Sixpence"

Sing a song of sixpence,
A pocket full of rye;
Four and twenty blackbirds
Baked in a pie.
  When the pie was opened,
  The birds began to sing;
  Was not that a dainty dish,
  To set before the king?
The king was in his counting-house
Counting out his money;
The queen was in the parlor
Eating bread and honey.
  The maid was in the garden
  Hanging out the clothes,
  There came a little blackbird,
  That sat on her nose.

"Hey! Diddle, Diddle"

Hey! Diddle, diddle!
The cat and the fiddle.
The cow jumped over the moon;
The little dog laughed to see such sport,
And the dish ran away with the spoon.

"Little Boy Blue"

Little boy blue, come blow your horn,
The sheep's in the meadow,
The cow's in the corn.
Where's the boy that looks after the sheep?
He's under the haystack, fast asleep.
Will you wake him? No, not I;
For if I do, he'll be sure to cry.

"This Little Pig Went to Market"

This little pig went to market;
This little pig stayed at home;
This little pig ate roast beef;
This little pig had none;
This little pig said, "Wah, wah,
I can't find my way home."

"There Were Two Blackbirds"

There were two blackbirds sitting on a hill,
The one named Jack, the other named Jill.
Fly away Jack!
Fly away Jill!
Come again Jack!
Come again Jill!

WHAT WOULD I BE?

This activity encourages dictating and writing skills and creativity.

▶ Ask the children to write about the following idea: "If I could be a farm animal, which one would I be?"

- Have the children write about what they would look like, what they would do all day, who their friends would be, and anything else they want to say.

- The children also may illustrate their words.

- Younger children can dictate their ideas for you to write down.

BOW-WOW! BOW-BOW! VOW-VOW! HUF-HUF!

Introduce this activity by asking the children to think about the sounds animals make.

- Ask the children to talk about the animals they have actually seen and heard. Ask: "How do they sound?" "Do they all sound alike?"

- Read DeZutter's *Who Says a Dog Goes Bow-Wow?*, listed in the Children's Books section of this theme. This book offers an imaginative way to present different languages to children. As the author says, "Where people live and what language *they're* using determine what animals say to us humans."

- Have the children experiment with making the international sounds introduced in the book, such as how the rooster crows: cock-a-doodle-doo (English), kee-kee-ree-kee (Spanish, Italian), ku-ku-ru-ku (Turkish), and coco-rico (French).

- Ask the children to locate, on a globe or map, the countries where the languages are spoken.

- Set up art easels and put out markers, crayons, all kinds of paper, scissors, and glue on the art table for children who want to create their own animals or books.

DRAMATIC PLAY

ON THE FARM

- Involve the class in a project to turn the dramatic play area into a farm.

- Read books, share pictures, watch videos, and talk about life on a farm.

- What would the children like to do if they lived on a farm? How many of them have been on a farm? Do any of their family members live on a farm?

- Write down all of the children's comments, suggestions, and ideas.

- Decide on props to complete the farm area. Some examples are a saddle for make-believe horse riding; a scarecrow for the corn- or wheatfield the children make; and a "cow to milk," based on the next Dramatic Play activity.

- The indoor dramatic play area can become the farmhouse and the barn.

- The outdoor playground area can become the pasture or planting fields.

- Once the children become involved in the process, this project could last many days. Be flexible!

MILKING A PRETEND COW

Read Aliki's *Milk: From Cow to Carton,* listed in the Children's Books section of this theme. This book takes the children on a guided tour through the milking process and a trip to the dairy and ends with the different foods made from milk. The story also connects with the Creative Food Experiences section of this theme.

- To help the children understand more about cows, have them "milk a glove."

- Make a pinhole in each fingertip of a pair of latex gloves.

- Outside, hang a clothesline about three feet above the ground and away from the main "traffic areas" of the playground.

- Attach to the clothesline the prepared gloves about three feet apart with a spring-type clothespin.

- Place a pail below each glove and a low stool or chair beside each one.

- Fill the prepared gloves with water.

- Let the children take turns squeezing the fingertips of the glove as if milking, so that the water goes into the bucket.

- Be prepared to answer the children's questions. Otherwise, step back and become an observer.

PUPPET PLAY

FARM PUPPETS

▶ Make a horse puppet by using a child-size sock.

▶ Add yarn pieces to represent a mane.

▶ Add facial features. Refer to the Sock Puppet activity in theme 2 for additional suggestions.

▶ Make a scarecrow hand puppet, based on the Scarecrow Puppet in theme 12.

OLD MacDONALD FINGER PUPPETS

▶ Create, with the children, some rooster, horse, duck, cow, and pig finger puppets to act out "Old MacDonald Had a Farm."

▶ For this activity, you will need one or more child-size and adult-size cloth gloves (such as garden gloves), scraps of colored felt, some Velcro™ (both hooked and soft sides), and some Velcro™ glue.

▶ To construct the finger puppets, glue a small square piece of soft-sided Velcro™ to each glove finger, and let dry thoroughly.

▶ Cut out each animal head (as suggested in the illustration) from a felt scrap, keeping in the one-inch to two-inch size range. Make as many sets of animals as there are gloves.

▶ Using felt-tipped markers, draw animal features on each felt cutout, and then glue a small square of hook-sided Velcro™ to the back.

▶ When ready to sing the song, the children can press into place each animal head on the glove fingers as the song names it.

▶ Store each glove and set of animals in a small plastic bag to protect them, and place in the dramatic play area to be used by the children whenever they wish.

MUSIC

SONG: "My Kitty Just Says 'Meow'" by Jo Eklof

The bird in the tree says, "cheep cheep cheep. The dog says, "bow wow wow." The duck in the pond says, "quack quack quack." my kit-ty just says, "meow."

Additional verses:

"Cocka doodle doo," says the rooster. "Oink oink," says the sow.
"He haw he haw," hear the donkey say. My kitty just says, "meow."

"Baa," says the fluffy lamb. "Moo," says the cow.
"Buzz buzz buzz," says the honey bee. My kitty just says, "meow."

(See page 307 for enlargement.)

MOVEMENT

SIMON SAYS "GO TO THE FARM"

"Simon Says" is a familiar game played by many young children. Change it so it is appropriate for your group of children.

▶ For toddlers, the pace should be slow, with every action a "Simon Says" one. If the "Simon Says" concept seems too difficult, then substitute a name with which the children are comfortable.

▶ It is helpful to model the actions along with the toddlers.

▶ For preschoolers and kindergartners, pick up the pace of the game.

▶ For all ages, use the farm animals to help "Simon." For example:
- Trot like a horse.
- Strut like a rooster.
- Run like a goat.
- Walk like a piglet.
- Chew like a cow.
- Scratch like a hen.
- Waddle like a duck.
- Hop like a rabbit.
- Fly like a goose.
- Kick like a donkey.

TOPPLE THE MILK CARTONS

▶ Collect at least 10 quart-size, empty, and clean milk cartons.

▶ Collect several soft medium-size balls.

▶ Put a masking-tape line on the floor or a wide chalk line on the sidewalk.

▶ Place the line farther away from the cartons for the older children.

▶ Set up the milk cartons.

▶ Standing at the line, each child can try to knock down the cartons with a ball.

▶ The older children can play while standing with their backs to the cartons and throwing the ball between their legs, or throwing the ball with an overhand pitch.

▶ Let the children make up the rules. It is their game.

SENSORY ART

MUD PLAY

Children like to play in the mud, and many do not have the opportunity to do so.

▶ Put some dirt and water in plastic tubs, along with plastic farm animals, including a lot of pigs.

▶ Let interested children mix the mud and play with it.

FARM FUN

▶ Put farm animal cookie cutters in the art center. The cookie cutters are available at many craft and discount stores.

▶ Add different-colored tempera paint and paper.

▶ The children can discover that dipping the cookie cutters into the paint and pressing them onto the paper make interesting animal designs.

▶ Place some horseshoes and brushes on the art table with the tempera paint and paper.

▶ The children can explore painting the horseshoes and then pressing paper on top of them to make other types of interesting prints.

▶ Add oatmeal to the tempera paint for another sensory art experience.

IT'S CORN

▶ Put out corn kernels, bowls, and tweezers on a table.

▶ Encourage the children to move the corn from one bowl to another with the tweezers.

▶ This is an activity that you can put out and leave, so the children can play with it whenever they want.

▶ This activity promotes small muscle development and eye-hand coordination.

▶ To make this into a one-on-one activity with you and the child, ask her to count the number of pieces of corn she moves from one bowl to the next.

RECYCLABLES

▶ Have the children create farm animals from assorted recyclable materials.

▶ Furnish materials, such as feathers, Styrofoam™, plastic lids, buttons, ribbons, paper, yarn, fabric scraps, paper towel rolls, odds and ends of wrapping paper, and small plastic containers.

▶ After the children have made their "farm animals," ask them to label each one and place them on a display table that you have covered with recyclable burlap or gunnysacks.

CREATIVE FOOD EXPERIENCES

ANIMAL CINNAMON TOAST

You will need:

> bread (two slices per child)
> margarine
> 3 tablespoons sugar
> 1 teaspoon cinnamon

1. Wash hands.
2. Children spread softened margarine onto bread with plastic knives.
3. Mix cinnamon and sugar. Sprinkle on bread.
4. Use animal cookie cutters to cut bread.
5. Put in toaster oven until margarine melts, approximately one minute. Enjoy!

ANIMAL CINNAMON TOAST

Wash hands.

Spread softened margarine on 2 slices of bread.

Mix 3 tablespoons sugar with 1 teaspoon cinnamon.

Sprinkle mixture on bread.

Use animal cookie cutters to cut bread.

Put in toaster oven until margarine melts. ENJOY!

COOKING EGGS

▶ Talk about how chickens lay eggs for us to eat.
▶ Give each child an uncooked egg to hold and gently explore.

▶ If an egg is dropped, simply let the child clean it up with a paper towel. This is part of the learning experience.
▶ Next, hard-boil an egg for each child. See the Creative Food Experiences section of theme 10 for a scrambled eggs activity.
▶ Give a whole cooked egg to each child.
▶ Ask the children to try cutting the egg in half with a plastic knife. This is a fun thing to do.
▶ If the children succeed, then they can try to cut it into fourths.
▶ Some of the eggs will be eaten before the activity reaches this point. That is okay. It is the process that is important!

HAYSTACKS AND MOO STACKS

(See Creative Food Experiences for theme 15.)

Important: Before preparing this snack, ensure that no children are allergic to milk products. If so, use another food as the basis of this snack, such as popcorn (from corn grown on a farm) or wheat crackers (from wheat grown on a farm).

You will need the following:

> cow milk
> goat milk
> cottage cheese
> Swiss cheese
> chocolate milk
> buttermilk
> cheddar cheese
> Colby cheese

1. Wash hands.
2. Give each child a sample of the milk products.
3. Talk about each of the products. Did the children know that all of these come from cows?

MATH

BARN AND ANIMAL PLAY

▶ Make a flannelboard barn with a door that opens and closes and animal characters to use on the flannelboard.

▶ Make the animals in family sets, such as a rooster, hen, and chicks.

▶ Working with small groups, ask the children to place the animals "in or out" of the barn, put a cow "on top" of the barn, "by the side," "on the left side," "far away," and so on.

▶ To extend this activity, read Rounds's *Three Billy Goats Gruff*, listed in the Children's Books section of this theme.

▶ Make flannelboard characters to correspond to the story.

▶ Ask the children to help you tell the story with the flannelboard pieces.

▶ Emphasize math concepts in the story, such as how many goats, the number of legs each goat has, the total number of legs of all of the goats, various sizes (small, medium, large), their order in crossing the bridge, and other concepts.

ADDING AND SUBTRACTING EGGS

▶ Collect empty egg cartons and plastic eggs.

▶ Have each child start with a full carton of eggs.

▶ Take away some of the eggs, and ask the child to tell you how many are left. Observe how the children determine their answers.

▶ Continue adding and subtracting the eggs in the carton.

▶ With older children, ask them to write down a number sentence on a sentence strip to show what you did when you took out two eggs.

▶ Continue giving the children examples of addition and subtraction for them to write down in number sentences. Observe how they determine their answers.

SCIENCE

WHERE'S MY MAMA?

▶ Read Gibbons's *Farming* and Chang's *Are You My Baby?*

▶ Talk about the hard work the farmer does to provide food for people to buy at the grocery store.

▶ In the spring, one of the tasks of the farmer is to care for the baby animals.

▶ Guide the children in learning the following names of the baby animals and their parents:

Family	Father	Mother	Baby
chicken	rooster	hen	chick
cattle	bull	cow	calf
pigs (hogs)	boar	sow	piglet
horse	stallion	mare	foal
sheep	ram	ewe	lamb
goat	billy	nanny	kid
duck	drake	duck	duckling

▶ Have available puzzles, pictures, and books to demonstrate visually what you are talking about.

▶ Put plastic animal families in the manipulative and block centers for the children.

SOCIAL STUDIES

IT'S FARM DAY!

To bring closure to the "Farm" theme, have a "Farm Day." If possible, take the activities outdoors.

▶ Invite a veterinarian to bring to class a baby farm animal to share with the children.

▶ Have the children dress like farmers, with overalls, boots, hats, and jeans.

▶ Some of the activities might include: find the milk caps in the hay, shuck corn to be cooked and eaten later, bean bag toss at milk cartons, milk the cow, described in the Dramatic Play section of this theme, sit in the saddle to ride the "pretend horse" of choice, and dance to recorded country music.

▶ Invite family members to stay for a picnic supper when they pick up their children.

▶ Infants and young toddlers can participate, when appropriate, or observe what the older children are doing.

CHILDREN'S BOOKS

Aliki. (1992). *Milk: From Cow to Carton (Let's-Read-and-Find-Out Book).* (Rev. ed.). New York: HarperCollins.

Ancona, George. (1997). *The American Family Farm: A Photo Essay.* (Rev. ed.). Photographs by Joan Anderson. San Diego: Harcourt.

Asch, Frank. (1998). *Barnyard Lullaby.* New York: Simon & Schuster.

Boynton, Sandra. (1993). *Barnyard Dance!* (Board Book). New York: Workman.

Brown, Margaret Wise, and Aida E. Marcuse. (1996). *Big Red Barn/El Gran Granero Rojo.* (Rev. ed.). Illustrated by Felicia Bond. New York: HarperCollins.

Burton, Jane. (1992). *Chick, Chick.* New York: Lodestar Books Dutton.

Carle, Eric. (1992). *Rooster's Off to See the World.* New York: Simon & Schuster.

Carter, David A. (2001). *Old MacDonald Had a Farm.* New York: Scholastic.

Chang, Cindy. (1996). *Are You My Baby?* (Board Book). Illustrated by Willabel L. Tong and Jill Dubin. New York: Random House.

Clayton, Gordon. (1993). *Calf (See How They Grow).* Photographs by Mary and Bill Ling. New York: DK Publishing.

Crews, Donald. (1998). *Bigmama's.* (Rev. ed.). New York: Mulberry.

Demi. (1993). *Little Baby Lamb.* New York: Grossett & Dunlap.

DeZutter, Hank. (1993). *Who Says a Dog Goes Bow-Wow?* Illustrated by Suse MacDonald. New York: Bantam Doubleday.

Ehlert, Lois, (1997). *Color Farm.* (Board ed.). New York: HarperCollins.

Fleming, Denise. (1994). *Barnyard Banter.* New York: Henry Holt.

Galdone, Paul, and Maria A. Fiol. (1996). *Three Billy Goats Gruff/Los Tres Chivitos Gruff.* New York: Lectorum.

Gibbons, Gail. (2003). *Horses!* New York: Holiday House.

Gibbons, Gail. (1990). *Farming.* New York: Holiday House.

Horenstein, Henry. (1994). *My Mom's a Vet.* Cambridge, MA: Candlewick Press.

Jones, Carol. (1998). *Old MacDonald Had a Farm.* Boston: Houghton Mifflin.

Jordan, Sandra. (1996). *Down on Casey's Farm.* New York: Orchard Books.

London, Jonathan. (1995). *Like Butter on Pancakes.* Illustrated by G. Brian Karas. New York: Viking.

Martin, Bill Jr. (1988). *Barn Dance.* New York: Henry Holt.

McDonnell, Flora. (1994). *I Love Animals.* Cambridge, MA: Candlewick Press.

Nicholson, Sue. (1999). *A Day at Greenhill Farm.* New York: DK Publishing.

Peters, Lisa W. (1995). *The Hayloft.* New York: Dial.

Rounds, Glen. (1994). *Three Billy Goats Gruff.* New York: Holiday House.

Sovak, Jan. (2001). *Learning about Animals.* New York: Dover.

Tafuri, Nancy. (1995). *The Barn Party.* New York: Greenwillow.

Tresselt, Alvin, and Carolyn Ewing. (1991). *Wake Up, Farm.* New York: Lothrop, Lee & Shepard.

Wallner, Alexandra. (1998). *The Farmer in the Dell.* New York: Holiday House.

Wildsmith, Brian. (1999). *The Bremen Town Band.* New York: Oxford University Press.

Wormell, Mary. (1995). *Hilda Hen's Happy Birthday.* San Diego: Harcourt.

Family Letter (Toddler)

Dear Family,

We are now learning about animals and life on the "Farm," as we begin our new theme. The children will learn the following:

- *A farm is a piece of land located outside of a city where crops and animals are raised.*
- *Many animals live on farms, such as chickens, turkeys, cows, pigs, horses, donkeys, sheep, goats, ducks, and geese.*
- *Farm animals are sheltered in coops, pens, barns, stables, stalls, and sheds.*
- *A farmer is the person who owns the farm and, along with family members and employees, works long hours to care for the animals and crops.*
- *Much of the food we eat and the clothing we wear comes from the animals and crops raised on farms.*

We will be talking about the following:

- *farm animals and their babies*
- *milking cows*
- *types of animal homes*
- *collecting eggs*
- *how farm animals are cared for*
- *sounds of animals*
- *activities on the farm*
- *foods from the farm*

Try some of the following at home with your child:

- *Go for a ride in the country. Talk about the farms and animals that you see.*
- *Read books about the farm.*
- *Play music, and sing songs about farm animals.*

Family participation opportunities at school will include:

- *Come and join us for our tasting and cooking activities.*
  Date _____ Time _____
- *Come have fun with us on "Farm Day."*
  Date _____ Time _____

Our wish list for this theme includes:

animal cookie cutters

old, clean, child-size socks

paper towel rolls

empty, washed, quart-size milk cartons

plastic lids

egg cartons

Thanks!

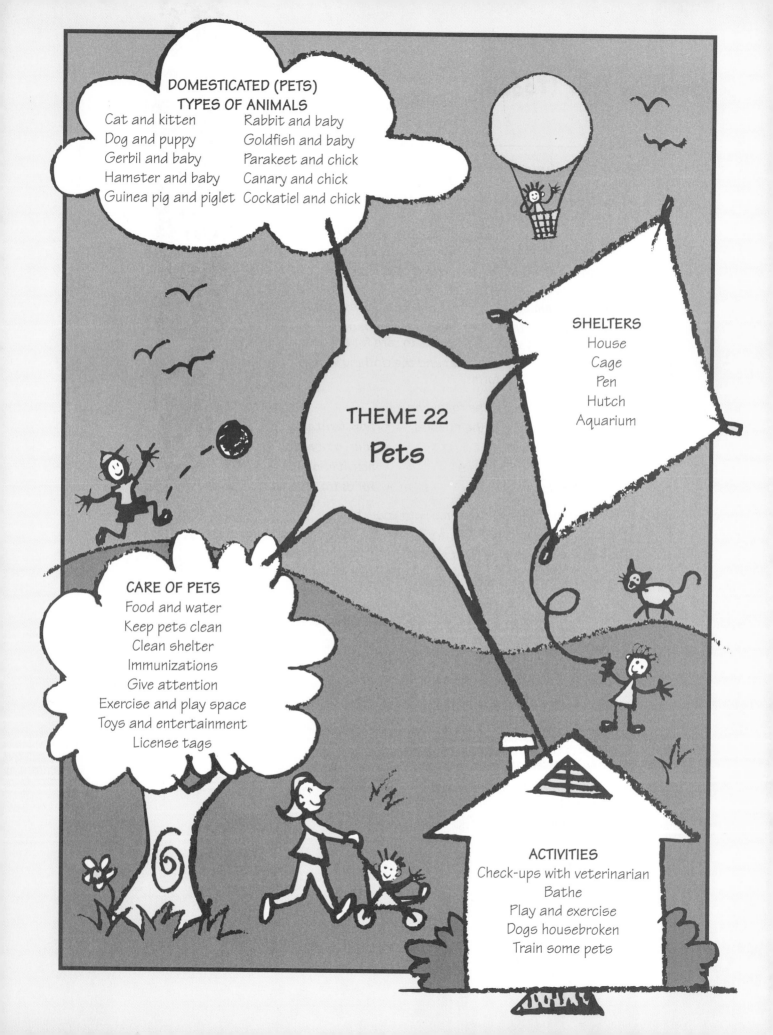

**DOMESTICATED (PETS)
TYPES OF ANIMALS**

Cat and kitten   Rabbit and baby
Dog and puppy   Goldfish and baby
Gerbil and baby   Parakeet and chick
Hamster and baby   Canary and chick
Guinea pig and piglet   Cockatiel and chick

**THEME 22
Pets**

SHELTERS
House
Cage
Pen
Hutch
Aquarium

CARE OF PETS
Food and water
Keep pets clean
Clean shelter
Immunizations
Give attention
Exercise and play space
Toys and entertainment
License tags

ACTIVITIES
Check-ups with veterinarian
Bathe
Play and exercise
Dogs housebroken
Train some pets

THEME GOALS

To provide opportunities for children to learn the following:

▶ A pet is a tame animal that is taken care of and kept as a special friend.

▶ Pets need food, water, shelter, and plenty of attention and love.

▶ Pets need to be handled carefully and gently.

▶ Pets also need exercise, a clean and safe home, and visits to the veterinarian.

▶ Some common house pets are cats, dogs, gerbils, hamsters, guinea pigs, cockatiels, parakeets, and goldfish.

▶ Families need to learn how to take care of a pet before getting one.

Children-Created Bulletin Boards

This bulletin board gives the children an opportunity to share their pets with their classmates. Children who do not have a pet can choose an animal they would like to have as a pet.

▶ Title the bulletin board "Our Pets."

▶ Ask the children to bring a photo of the family pet to put on the board.

▶ Ask children who do not have a pet to cut out a picture of the animal they would like to have as a pet. Supply magazines for the children.

▶ The children also can draw a picture of a pet to put on the board.

▶ The bulletin board should reflect the children's interests and change throughout the theme.

▶ Put modeling clay in the art center, and leave it out for the children to make clay pets whenever they would like.

▶ On a small table in front of the bulletin board, place the clay animals the children have made.

VOCABULARY STARTERS

Let the children add words.

domesticated — animals that are not wild and are used to living around people.

feathers — the covering of birds.

fur — soft, thick hair that covers some animals.

scales — hard covering of fish and reptiles.

veterinarian — a doctor of animals.

LANGUAGE EXPERIENCES

FINGERPLAY:
"I Have a Pet"

I have a pet mouse
And her name is Rose.
She runs up my arm
And sits on my nose.
   (the fingers run up an arm and onto the nose)
I have a pet turtle
And his name is Bill.
He crawls a little bit
Then he just stands still.
   (the fingers on one hand "crawl" and stand still)
I have a pet canary
Her name is Miss Peep.
She flies around my head
And goes "cheep, cheep, cheep."
   (the fingers fly around the head)
I have a pet goldfish
His name is Joe.
He can't say a word
Just
   (make lips round and form three "O's" in time with the verse).

Philip Jackman

POEM:

"Pet Guessing Game"

My name is Lulu,
And I'm black and white.
I wander around the house at night.
I like to play with a piece of string.
My paws are soft, but my claws can sting.
What am I? *(Cat)*

My name is Petey and my coat is brown,
I love to run and jump up and down.
I like to chew on a big old bone,
And I bark at the sound of a telephone.
What am I? *(Dog)*
My name is Poky and I'm hard on top.
My legs are so short I can't run or hop.
When I get scared and want to hide,
I can pull my head and my legs inside.
What am I? *(Turtle)*
My name is Cookie, I'm yellow and white.
I sing and sit on my perch all night.
I like to eat seeds with my little sharp beak,
If you cover my cage, you won't hear a squeak.
What am I? *(Cockatiel)*

Philip Jackman

DRAMATIC PLAY

THREE LITTLE KITTENS

Young children enjoy the story told in the familiar poem "Three Little Kittens." They also like to act out being the kittens in the retelling of the story.

▶ Have mittens for the children to put on and take off as they act out the story. See Puppet Play in this theme for easy mittens to make.

▶ With toddlers, use fewer verses to tell the story.

▶ Ask preschoolers what the three little kittens could have done to keep their mittens clean.

▶ Give the children opportunities to retell the story in a different way.

▶ Brett's *The Mitten: A Ukrainian Folktale* and Tressellet's *The Mitten* (see the Children's Books section in this theme) tell another story about a mitten.

"Three Little Kittens"

Three little kittens
  Lost their mittens
And they began to cry,
  "Oh mother dear,
Come here, come here,
  Our mittens we have lost."
"Lost your mittens!
  My little kittens!
Then you shall have no pie."
  "Mee-ow, mee-ow

Now we shall have no pie.
   Mee-ow, mee-ow, mee-ow."
The three little kittens
   Found their mittens
And they began to cry,
   "Oh mother dear,
See here, see here,
   Our mittens we have found."
"Put on your mittens,
   My little kittens,
Now you shall have some pie."
   "Purr-r, purr-r, purr-r."
The three little kittens
   Put on their mittens
And soon ate up the pie.
   "Oh, mother dear,
Look here, look here,
   Our mittens we have soiled."
"Soiled your mittens!
   My little kittens!"
Then they began to cry,
   "Mee-ow, mee-ow,"
Then they began to cry,
   "Mee-ow, mee-ow, mee-ow."
The three little kittens
   Washed their mittens
And hung them out to dry.
   "Oh, mother dear,
See here, see here,
   Our mittens we have washed."
"Washed your mittens?
   My little kittens,
Now off you go to bed."
   "Purr-r, purr-r, purr-r."

PUPPET PLAY

PUPPETS FOR INFANTS

- Make this puppet for the older infants to enjoy.
- Use nontoxic, permanent markers to draw animal faces of pets on felt fabric.
- Cut out the faces.
- Measure the elastic around an infant's hand, then cut it, allowing an extra half inch at each end.
- Sew the strip together at the ends with a quarter-inch seam.
- Sew a face on the elastic covering the seam. Be sure the felt is securely sewn onto the elastic.

- Measure and sew other elastic strips for the other pet faces.
- Place a puppet on the infant's hand, and show him how to make the puppet move and talk.

MITTENS FOR KITTENS

This activity can be related to the Dramatic Play activity in this theme.

- Put out colored construction paper, various colors of yarn, pencils, crayons, markers, rulers, scissors, paper clips, and a paper punch on a table near the dramatic play center. Felt can be used as well.
- In small groups, invite children to make a puppet at the table.
- Guide the children to draw around their hands on construction paper. Younger children may need some guidance from you to help them make their mitten puppets.
- Measuring with a ruler, help the children enlarge their hand drawings one to two inches (see illustration).
- Place this sheet over another, and fasten them together with a paper clip.
- Cut out the mittens, both sheets at once. For younger children, cutting one sheet at a time works better.
- Punch holes around the edges of each of the mittens, *not* the bottom. Weave a piece of yarn through the holes, and tie off the ends so that the two halves of the mittens are fastened together, as shown in the illustration.

▶ The children can draw faces on their mittens if they would like. This adds to the personality of the mitten puppet.

▶ The children put on their mitten puppets by inserting their hands into the open end.

MUSIC

SONG: "How I Wish I Had a Little Dog" by Jo Eklof

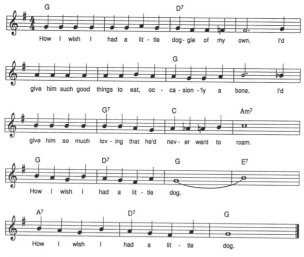

Second verse:

How I wish I had a little doggie brown and white.
We'd romp around the yard all day. He's sleep near me at night.
We'd do many things together, life would seem just right.
How I wish I had a little dog. How I wish I had a little dog.

© 1980 by Jo Eklof. All rights reserved. Used with permission.

(See page 308 for enlargement.)

MOVEMENT

LET'S HAVE A PET PARTY

▶ Read Carle's *Have You Seen My Cat?*, Morley and Orbell's *Me and My Pet Fish,* and Flanagan's *Buying a Pet from Ms. Chavez,* listed in the Children's Books section of this theme.

▶ Talk about the pets the children have, or the pets they would like to have.

▶ Tell the children that they are going to have a "pet party"! Half of the group will get to act out being favorite pets, and the other half will be the pet owners.

▶ Suggest activities, such as: the owner can have the pet do tricks, take the pet for a walk, pretend to feed the pet, and put the pet to "bed."

▶ After the children have played for several minutes, suggest that the owners and pets switch roles.

▶ While the children are playing, encourage the positive aspects of pet care they demonstrate, such as: "Carmen, I like the way you are so gentle with your kitty"; "Jared, you are very patient teaching your puppy to do that trick"; "Chris, when you pat your bunny like that, she knows you love her, doesn't she?"

SENSORY ART

PETS OF CLAY

Introduce the children to making creative pets out of clay (ceramic clay, play dough, and Plasticine®). They can pull, tear, roll, cut, and create with clay. Clay offers a unique tactile and sensorimotor experience for the children.

▶ Purchase clay from a teacher resource store, *and* make some play dough in the class with the children.

▶ Have the children make their pets out of clay. They can make and remake the animals as often as they wish.

▶ Place the finished animals on a table near the bulletin board.

▶ Play dough recipes are given in the Sensory Art sections in themes 6 and 10.

CREATIVE FOOD EXPERIENCES

ROLL-AND-PAT "MOUSE" COOKIES

Read Numeroff's *If You Give a Mouse a Cookie* to the children. Everyone can then bake cookies.
You will need the following:

> 1 cup Bisquick
> 1 package instant pudding
> 1/4 cup oil
> 1 egg
> raisins, chocolate chips, or shredded coconut (optional)

You may need to double the recipe for more than 10 children.

1. Wash hands.
2. Mix ingredients.
3. Give each child a ball of dough on a piece of waxed paper.
4. Use a hand to press the dough flat.
5. Decorate with raisins, chocolate chips, or coconut.
6. Bake 8 minutes at 350 degrees.
7. Yum!

ROLL-AND-PAT "MOUSE" COOKIES

Wash hands.

Mix together 1 cup Bisquick, 1 package instant pudding,

1/4 cup oil, and 1 egg.

On wax paper, use your hand to flatten a ball of dough.

Decorate with raisins, chocolate chips, or coconut.

Bake 8 minutes at 350 degrees. YUM!

MATH

FEED THE DOG MATCH

▶ Take an ordinary file folder, open it, and draw 10 doghouses inside of the folder. (See the illustration.)
▶ Put a number on each doghouse, not sequentially.
▶ Write "Feed the Dog" on the cover of the folder.
▶ Laminate the file folder.
▶ Draw 10 small dog bones on a piece of tagboard.
▶ Put dots on each bone, from 1 to 10, to correspond to the doghouse numbers.
▶ For younger children, you can put the numeral on the opposite side of the bone to make the activity self-correcting. (See the illustration.)
▶ Laminate the "bones," then cut them out.
▶ Put these pieces into a resealable plastic bag, and staple or glue to the back of the folder.
▶ Put the matching folder game in the math or manipulative center for the children to discover.

FIND THE GERBIL FOOD FOLDER GAME

▶ Draw a circular maze inside of a file folder. (See the illustration.)
▶ Place "Start" at the beginning of the maze.
▶ At the "Stop" point, have an illustration of a gerbil's food box.

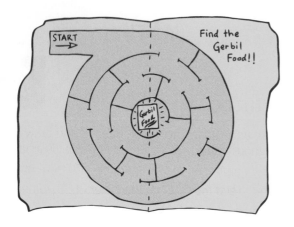

- On the cover of the file folder, write "Find the Gerbil Food."
- Laminate the file folder.
- Provide a rub-off crayon or washable marker and a roll of paper towels for corrections and wipe off when the folder is ready to be returned to the math center.
- The child playing the game begins at "Start," and he then marks a path to the gerbil food box.

SCIENCE

LET'S GET A PET

- Read Ziefert's *Let's Get a Pet*, listed in the Children's Books section of this theme.
- Later, put this in the book center for the children to have as a reference.
- With the children's help, make a list of the animals that make the best pets. Put this list on the bulletin board.
- Talk about what you should do *before* getting a pet.
- Make a list of these things to think about, such as:
  - Read about different kinds of pets.
  - Decide which kind of animal you want.
  - Decide how much money you have to spend to buy a pet.
  - Remember that some animals, such as dogs, can get big.
  - You have to clean up after pets.
  - Some animals shed.
  - Some friends or family members might be allergic to pets.
  - Are you kind? Are you gentle?
  - Will you take the responsibility to take care of your pet?

- Will you feed your pet and give it water?
- Will you play with your pet?
- Put this list on the bulletin board.
- If possible, set up a pet center in the classroom. Check with your state's licensing department to learn which pets are acceptable in an early childhood classroom.
- Let the children take turns sharing responsibility for the class pet(s).

LET'S OBSERVE

- Observe a classroom pet. If you do not have a pet, perhaps you could borrow one for the day or bring a pet from home.
- In small groups, suggest to the children that they sit quietly and watch the animal.
- Younger children can tell you what they saw the animal doing. Write down what they describe.
- Children can also draw pictures to show what they saw.
- Older children can keep a chart of the animal's activities and movements during the day. At the end of the observation time, they can report what they observed.
- Discuss what the children learned about the classroom pet. What new questions do they have?

SOCIAL STUDIES

A VISIT TO A PET STORE

- Make arrangements to visit a pet store in your community.
- Go there first by yourself to arrange a special time for the field trip and to be sure the store is appropriate for young children to visit.
- It is important for someone to be available to show the children all of the pets and to answer questions the children may have.
- Perhaps there will be one animal that the children can pet very gently.
- Follow up by sending thank-you notes from the class.
- Encourage the children to talk about the experience and to draw pictures and dictate stories about it.

CHILDREN'S BOOKS

Angelou, Maya. (1994). *My Painted House, My Friendly Chicken.* Photographed by Margaret Courtney-Clark. New York: Clarkson N. Potter.

Bauer, Marion Dane. (1997). *If You Were Born a Kitten.* Illustrated by Joellen M. Stammen. New York: Simon & Schuster.

Beaton, Clare. (1997). *Los Animales/Animals.* New York: Barron's Juveniles.

Brett, Jan. (1996). *The Mitten: A Ukrainian Folktale.* New York: Putnam.

Buck, Nola. (1998). *Oh, Cats! (My First I Can Read Book).* Illustrated by Nadine B. Westcott. New York: HarperTrophy.

Cabrera, Jane. (1997). *Cats' Colors.* New York: Dial.

Carle, Eric. (1996). *Have You Seen My Cat?* New York: Little Simon.

Cole, Joanna. (1995). *My New Kitten.* Photographed by Margaret Miller. New York: William Morrow.

Dodd, Emma. (2001). *Dog's Colorful Day — A Messy Story about Colors and Counting.* New York: Dutton.

Duke, Kate. (1998). *One Guinea Pig Is Not Enough.* New York: Dutton.

Eastman. P.D. (2003). *Big Dog . . . Little Dog.* New York: Random House.

Flanagan, Alice K. (1998). *Buying a Pet from Ms. Chavez.* Chicago: Children's Press.

Gibbons, Gail. (1998). *Cats.* New York: Holiday House.

Gibbons, Gail. (1996). *Dogs.* New York: Holiday House.

Hathon, Elizabeth. (1993). *Soft As a Kitten.* (Board Book). New York: Grosset & Dunlap.

Keats, Ezra Jack. (1988). *Hi, Cat.* New York: Aladdin.

King-Smith, Dick. (1997). *Puppy Love.* Illustrated by Anita Jeram. Cambridge, MA: Candlewick Press.

Kunhardt, Edith, and Dorothy Kunhardt. (1994). *Pat the Bunny and Friends.* (Board Book). New York: Golden Press.

Landau, Elaine. (1998). *Your Pet Gerbil (True Books — Animals).* Chicago: Children's Press.

McBratney, San. (1995). *Guess How Much I Love You.* Illustrated by Anita Jeram. Cambridge, MA: Candlewick Press.

McCully, Emily. (2001). *Four Hungry Kittens.* New York: Dial.

Morley, Christine, and Carole Orbell. (1997). *Me and My Pet Fish (Me and My Pet Series).* Illustrated by Brita Granstrom. New York: World Book.

Numeroff, Laura Joffe. (1997). *If You Give a Mouse a Cookie.* Illustrated by Felicia Bond. New York: HarperTrophy.

Roth, Susan L. (1998). *Cinnamon's Day Out: A Gerbil Adventure.* New York: Dial.

Sun, Chyng-Feng. (1996). *Cat and Cat-Face.* Illustrated by Lesley Liu. Boston: Houghton Mifflin.

Tan, Amy. (2001). *SAGWA, the Chinese Siamese Cat.* Illustrated by Gretchen Shields. New York: Aladdin.

Tressellet, Alvin. (1964). *The Mitten.* Illustrated by Yaroslava. New York: William Morrow.

Voake, Charlotte. (1997). *Ginger.* Cambridge, MA: Candlewick Press.

Wolf, Jake. (1998). *Daddy, Could I Have an Elephant?* Illustrated by Marylin Hafner. New York: Puffin.

Ziefert, Harriet. (1993). *Let's Get a Pet.* Illustrated by Mavis Smith. New York: Viking.

Family Letter (Preschool)

Dear Family,

Our new theme is "Pets." We will provide opportunities for the children to learn the following:

- A pet is a tame animal that is taken care of and kept as a special friend.
- Pets need food, water, shelter, and plenty of attention and love.
- Pets need to be handled carefully and gently.
- Pets also need exercise, a clean and safe home, and visits to the veterinarian.
- Some common house pets are cats, dogs, gerbils, hamsters, guinea pigs, cockatiels, parakeets, and goldfish.
- Families need to learn how to take care of a pet before getting one.

We will be talking about the following:

- domesticated types of animals, birds, and fish
- shelters for pets
- care of pets
- activities of pets

Things to do at home with your child to support and reinforce our classroom activities include the following:

- If you are thinking about getting a pet, read and talk about which kind of animal the family wants, how much will it cost, who will be responsible for taking care of the pet, and other considerations.
- If you already have a pet, watch and talk about all of the different things your pet does.
- Visit a pet store to see different kinds of pets.
- Check out books about pets from the library to read together at home.

Family participation opportunities at school include:

- Come with us on our visit to the pet store.
  Date _____ Time _____
- Visit our class to see what is going on.
  Date _____ Time _____

Our wish list for this theme includes:
  magazines with pictures of animals
  file folders
  wide elastic strips
  yarn

Thanks!

TYPES AND CHARACTERISTICS OF INSECTS

Three body parts
Four wings (some)
Six legs (three pairs)
Two sensors (antennae)
Egg, caterpillar (larva), cocoon, chrysalis, pupa, butterfly or moth

Ladybugs
Cockroaches
Mosquitoes
Crickets
Grasshoppers

Bees
Flies
Wasps
Beetles

THEME 23
Insects and Spiders

HABITATS OF INSECTS

Ants — colony
Bees — hive
Wasps — nests
Other insects
water   trees
grass   ground
pollinating plants

TYPES AND CHARACTERISTICS OF SPIDERS

Two body parts
Eight legs (four pairs)
No antennae or wings
Spin webs to catch insects
Tarantula
Daddy longlegs
Others

ACTIVITIES OF INSECTS

Ants — break down dead plant material and add to soil
Butterflies — pollinate flowers
Bees — make honey
All insects — help us by feeding on plant and animal waste and are part of the food chain for spiders, birds, frogs, and bats

THEME GOALS

To provide opportunities for children to learn the following:

▶ There are many kinds of insects, and they are found all over the world.

▶ Insects come in many sizes, shapes, and colors.

▶ Insects have three body parts: head, thorax (middle section), and abdomen (usually the largest of the sections).

▶ Insects wear their skeleton outside as a hard outer skin called the "exoskeleton."

▶ Insects have six legs (three pairs), two antennae, and, if winged, four wings.

▶ Insects help us by making honey and pollinating flowers and fruits.

▶ Spiders are not insects.

▶ Insects and spiders come from eggs.

▶ Spiders have eight legs (four pairs), two body parts, two feelers, and no wings or antennae.

▶ A spider spins silk to get its food, build its shelter, protect its eggs, and to travel safely.

▶ Spiders help us by eating insects.

Children-Created Bulletin Board

With the children's help, create this bulletin board from the point of view of an insect and a spider. As always, this board should be interactive, reflecting the children's input throughout the theme.

▶ Title this board "Look Everywhere for Insects and Spiders."

▶ On one side, create a spider's web using white thread or thin yarn. Children can make and add spiders to the web whenever they want to do so.

▶ Place grass at the bottom with insects that the children have made "hiding" throughout.

▶ Make flowers out of wallpaper or gift wrap to brighten the bulletin board. Put bees on and around the flowers.

▶ Place rocks made with burlap-covered cardboard or crumpled brown paper around the board. Attach some of them at one end so they may be lifted to reveal insects underneath.

▶ Label the items as they are placed on the board.

▶ Continue to add the children's creations as they work on this theme.

VOCABULARY STARTERS

Let the children add words. Include pictures, where appropriate.

antennae — two sensors on an insect that stick out from the head.

arachnids — class of eight-legged creatures (*not* insects) that includes spiders.

chrysalis — hard covering that protects the pupa inside of the cocoon.

cocoon — silky covering around the caterpillar as it sleeps and slowly changes.

head, thorax, and **abdomen** — the three body parts of an insect.

larva — caterpillar stage of a butterfly's or moth's life.

metamorphosis — life cycle of an insect from one stage to another, such as caterpillar to butterfly.

pupa — stage of life of a butterfly, a moth, or an ant before it becomes an adult.

web — net that spiders weave from a spun thread.

LANGUAGE EXPERIENCES

"I CAN'T" SAID THE ANT

▶ Read Cameron's *"I Can't" Said the Ant,* listed in the Children's Books section of this theme.

▶ This book is a favorite of young children. It offers opportunities for exploring letter-sound associations, rhyming words, and dramatizing the story.

▶ Some children will ask you to read the book again and again. Use flannelboard characters that the children can manipulate.

▶ Older children can read the book themselves and then write their own story.

▶ Children can work together or individually to create a classroom Big Book of their story.

▶ Encourage the children to think of other ways to retell the story, such as drawing or painting the story sequentially, discussing what clues they used to predict what would come next, and recalling their favorite rhyming lines.

▶ An example of the delightful language includes:
  — "What's all the clatter?" asked the platter.
  — "Teapot fell," said the dinner bell.
  — "Teapot broke," said the artichoke.
  — "She went kerplop!" said the mop.

▶ *"I Can't" Said the Ant* also promotes working cooperatively. Have the children talk about how the ants and other characters worked together to solve the problem.

LET'S CREATE A SPIDER'S WEB

▶ To introduce chapter books to the children, read White's *Charlotte's Web,* listed in the Children's Books section of this theme. A video also is available.

▶ As Charlotte starts to build her web, have the children start to build a web in one corner of the classroom using white yarn or twine.

▶ The class web can continue to grow along with Charlotte's.

▶ Guide the children into making spiders and putting them on the web with two-sided sticky tape.

▶ The children will think of additional insects to "get caught" in the web, as well as writing words in the web, just as Charlotte did.

DRAMATIC PLAY

ANTS AT A PICNIC

▶ Put several large picnic baskets in the dramatic play area. Add play food.

▶ Make a box tunnel by taking the ends out of boxes. Line the boxes up, and tape them together to form a tunnel.

▶ Use a cloth tunnel, if you already have one, to have more than one tunnel for the ants.

▶ The children can pretend to be ants taking the "food" from the picnic basket to their home through the tunnels.

▶ Continue to add items that the children want to use.

INSECTS HAVE SIX LEGS

▶ Brainstorm with the children to think of what they could make to add extra legs onto themselves. This helps them focus on the fact that insects have six legs.

- Walking on hands and knees is an easy way to create four legs.

- What can be done to make two more? One idea is to make long tube shapes from black material. Stuff the tubes with newspaper, and sew them onto a band for tying around the child's waist.

- Add antennae by using a headband and attaching pipe cleaners to it.

- Ask a child to select an insect. Then, act out how she thinks the insect moves.

PUPPET PLAY

PAPER BAG BEES

- Put out pictures and books showing real bees around the area for the children to look at.

- For children who want to make puppets, have them color or paint paper lunch sacks yellow and black.

- When the paint has dried, have the children stuff newspaper into the sacks.

- Tape on yellow construction paper for wings, but let the children use any color construction paper if they do not want to make the wings yellow.

- The children can "fly" the bees all over inside and outside as they play with their puppets.

- Later, if the children agree, take the puppets, attach string, and hang them around the bulletin board.

OTHER PAPER BAG PUPPETS

- Put out paper sacks, construction paper, pipe cleaners, scissors, glue, crayons, and markers on a table.

- Put out pictures of insects, including caterpillars, around the area.

- For toddlers, precut small, medium, and large circles for them to glue as body parts onto the paper sacks. Accept whatever they do with the circles.

- Model how you put your hand inside of the sack to make the puppet move and "talk."

MUSIC

SONG: "I Like to Look at Bugs" by Jo Eklof

When the sun comes out and the winter goes away, I like to go out on a nice warm day. I like to run and I like to play and I like to look at bugs. (Do they jiggle and jump? Yes, they jiggle and jump. Do they wiggle and bump? Yes, they wiggle and bump.) I like to look at bugs.

Additional verses:
Do they crawl and creep? Do they like to leap?

(See page 309 for enlargement.)

SONG:
"Shoo Fly"

This traditional song, "Shoo Fly," easily combines music and movement. It promotes coordination of action and words and gives practice in following directions. Ask the children to form a circle and join hands. Then do the following:

Sing: *Shoo fly, don't bother me.*
  Walk: four steps to the center.
Sing: *Shoo fly, don't bother me.*
  Walk: four steps back.
Sing: *Shoo fly, don't bother me.*
  Walk: four steps to the center.
Sing: *I belong to somebody.*
  Walk: four steps back.
Sing: *I feel, I feel, I feel like a morning star.*
  Walk: with joined hands, in a circle to the right.
Sing: *I feel, I feel, I feel like a morning star.*
  Walk: drop hands, in a circle to the left.

Repeat from the beginning up to:

Sing: *I feel, I feel, I feel like a morning star.*
  Walk: two children form an arch with their hands.
Sing: *I feel, I feel, I feel like a morning star.*
  Walk: one child leads the other children through the arch and begins another circle.
Sing: *Shoo fly, don't bother me. Shoo fly, don't bother me. I belong to somebody.*
Say: *"Shoo Fly!"* Use hand motions to get rid of the flies.

MOVEMENT

THE VERY HUNGRY CATERPILLAR

▶ Read Carle's *The Very Hungry Caterpillar* to the children.

▶ Ask the children to get their naptime blanket out of their cubbies. Or, ask families to send an extra small blanket to school.

▶ Have the children wrap up inside of their blankets.

▶ After a short time, the children unwrap from their "cocoons" and become beautiful butterflies, using their blankets for wings.

▶ Put some music on so the "butterflies" can dance and move to the music.

LET'S MOVE LIKE INSECTS

▶ Play a cassette or CD of Rimski-Korsakov's *Flight of the Bumblebee.*

▶ Play a portion first, so the children can hear the music.

▶ Have the children "fly like the bees" in rhythm to the music.

▶ Then change the music to a song the children like.

▶ Ask the children to jump like grasshoppers to the lively music.

▶ Ask the children to crawl like a bug: slowly, like a caterpillar, fast, like a flea, and so on.

SENSORY ART

A GROUP CATERPILLAR

The children can do this activity over a period of time.

▶ Each day, place a long piece of butcher paper on the art table with pie tins containing various colors of paint.

▶ Whenever a child wants to do so, she puts a hand, with fingers extended, into one of the paints and makes a handprint on the butcher paper. Ask the child to put her handprint next to another handprint with thumbs touching (see illustration).

▶ Some children may put fingers only on the caterpillar. Fingerpainting is fun. Whatever they do adds their special touch.

▶ After eight or so children have made handprints, ask one of the children to draw a face on the caterpillar.

▶ Display the caterpillar mural.

3-D INSECTS

▶ Collect large bottle caps, small container tops, thread spools, cardboard, construction paper, foil, felt and fabric scraps, pipe cleaners, yarn, string, Styrofoam™ spheres and squiggles, buttons, play dough, modeling clay, cotton balls, paper fasteners, garbage bag ties, twigs, and toothpicks.

▶ Put these items, along with glue, crayons, markers, tempera paints, small brushes, scissors, single-hole paper punches, and staplers, on a long table.

▶ Leave the materials out during the theme. This way the children can create unique "insects" as they explore the theme further.

▶ Take photos of the children making their bugs, and add these to the bulletin board.

CREATIVE FOOD EXPERIENCES

CRUNCHY STRAWBERRIES

This cooking experience goes well with the story of *The Very Hungry Caterpillar.*

You will need the following:

  2 tablespoons strawberry yogurt per child
  2 whole strawberries per child
  1 teaspoon granola per child (optional)
  1 small plastic bowl per child

1. Wash hands.
2. Have each child cut up the strawberries with a plastic knife and place them in her bowl.
3. Spoon the yogurt on top.
4. Cover with granola, if desired.

SURPRISE MUFFINS

You will need the following:

  English muffins
  cream cheese
  red food coloring
  raisins
  lettuce leaves

1. Wash hands.
2. Give each child a lettuce leaf on a paper plate.
3. Place half of an English muffin on the lettuce.
4. Give each child a small amount of cream cheese.
5. Add a few drops of red food coloring to the cream cheese.
6. Each child spreads the red cheese on her English muffin with a plastic knife.
7. Add raisins (dots) on top of the cream cheese.
8. Surprise! It is a ladybug muffin!

SURPRISE MUFFINS

Wash hands.

Place 1/2 of an English muffin on a leaf of lettuce.

Mix a few drops of red food coloring into a small amount of

cream cheese. Spread the red cheese on the English muffin.

Add raisins on top of the cream cheese.

Surprise! It's a ladybug muffin!

LET'S MAKE "DIRT CAKE"

You will need the following:

  1 20-ounce package of chocolate sandwich cookies
  1 8-ounce package of cream cheese
  1/2 stick of margarine
  1 cup powered sugar
  3 1/2 cups milk
  2 packages of instant chocolate pudding
  1 12-ounce tub of whipped topping
  1/4 cup mini-marshmallows
  gummy worms

1. Wash hands.
2. Put the chocolate cookies in a resealable plastic bag.
3. Have one or two of the children crush the chocolate cookies with a rolling pin.
4. Have one or two other children cream the margarine, sugar, and cream cheese in a bowl.
5. Another child can mix the milk and pudding. Let this sit until thick.
6. Stir the whipped topping into the cream cheese mixture, and add this to the milk and pudding mixture. Combine well.
7. Put one-third of the cookie crumbs into the bottom of a nine-by-nine-inch glass pan.
8. Add one-half of the cream cheese mixture.
9. Repeat cookie crumbs and cream cheese mixture, adding some gummy worms and the mini-marshmallows.
10. Add extra crumbs on top to look like dirt. Refrigerate overnight.
11. Serve the next day as a special treat.

▶ Punch holes on one side of each page. Later, the children can tie the pages together with yarn or staple the pages.

▶ Put out books and pictures the children can use for reference in the math area.

▶ Ask the children to write on the cover what they want to name their book, for example, "My Insect Book," "Ricardo's Insect Book," or "Insects."

▶ Ask the children to draw the three body parts of an insect on the second page (head, thorax/middle section, abdomen/large third section).

▶ On the third page, children draw the body parts again and add the six legs of the insect.

▶ On the fourth page, children draw the three body parts and six legs and add the two antennae.

▶ On the fifth page, children draw the three body parts, six legs, two antennae, and four wings (some insects have wings).

▶ On the sixth page, ask the children to write what they know about insects. The younger ones can dictate to you what they want to say.

MATH

GEOMETRIC DESIGNS

▶ Read McDermott's *Anansi the Spider,* listed in the Children's Books section of this theme.

▶ The bold, vivid colors and the geometric style of the illustrations can suggest to children a new way to look at math.

▶ Talk about all of the shapes, sizes, and configurations of lines the children discover.

▶ Put out all kinds of paper, crayons, markers, and paints in the math center.

▶ Encourage the children to experiment with their own designs and create new ways to draw the insects they are studying.

MATH BOOK OF INSECTS

▶ Working with a small group of children at a time, encourage them to make a six-page booklet, including the cover.

SCIENCE

SEE WHAT WE CAN FIND

▶ In a corner of the playground or in a special place that you have prepared, let the children dig up several cupfuls of dirt.

▶ Dump the dirt onto a newspaper that has been spread out on the sidewalk or floor.

▶ Ask the children to examine the dirt to see what they can find.

▶ Small sifters and magnifying glasses are useful tools to help search through a pile of dirt.

BUGS!

Make a bug jar! Spring is a wonderful time for the children to find and observe bugs. Provide magnifying glasses.

▶ In a plastic jar or bottle with a wide neck, put grass, twigs, leaves, and a wet cotton ball.

▶ Put all of the bugs the children find in the bug jar.

▶ Attach some lightweight netting (found in fabric stores) to the top of the jar with a rubber band.

▶ Encourage the children to release the insects outside after they have completed their observations.

SOCIAL STUDIES

MIGRATING MONARCH BUTTERFLIES

▶ Read Heiligmam's *From Caterpillar to Butterfly,* Gibbons's *Monarch Butterfly,* or Feltwell's *Butterflies and Moths,* listed in the Children's Books section of this theme.

▶ Discuss with children the fact that some butterflies travel or migrate every year to escape cold weather.

▶ In the fall, many thousands of monarch butterflies fly from the northern United States and Canada south to Southern California and Mexico, where they spend the winter. The monarchs can cover whole trees.

▶ Have the children find these places on a globe or map.

▶ Ask the children where they would like to go if they could "migrate" for the winter.

▶ Point out the locations on the globe or map.

▶ Next, talk about how in late winter or early spring, adult monarchs mate, lay eggs, and begin the journey north.

▶ The new eggs hatch, go through the metamorphosis cycle, and the butterflies fly north as well.

▶ With the children, create a chart showing the life cycle of the monarch butterfly.

▶ With the older children, extend the activity. Ask them how they think monarch butterflies can travel so far. Does the wind help them fly?

▶ Demonstrate by having an electric fan blow pieces of paper.

▶ You also can blow up some medium-size balloons and hold the opening closed with your fingers.

▶ Everyone counts to three, and the balloons are released. Discovery: when air is trapped, as with currents, it can become a power source and push objects.

▶ Wind currents help the monarchs by letting them glide and by pushing them on.

CHILDREN'S BOOKS

Cameron, Polly. (1961). *"I Can't" Said the Ant.* New York: Scholastic.

Carle, Eric. (1997). *The Very Quiet Cricket.* (Board Book). New York: Putnam.

Carle, Eric. (1996). *The Grouchy Ladybug.* New York: HarperCollins.

Carle, Eric. (1995). *The Very Busy Spider.* New York: Philomel.

Carle, Eric. (1994). *The Very Hungry Caterpillar.* (Board Book). New York: Philomel.

Cassie, Brian, and Jerry Pallotta. (1995). *The Butterfly Alphabet Book.* Illustrated by Mark Astrella. Watertown, MA: Charlesbridge.

Climo, Shirley. (1995). *The Little Red Ant and the Great Big Crumb: A Mexican Fable.* Illustrated by Francisco X. Mora. New York: Clarion.

Cole, Joanna, and Stephanie Calmenson. (1996). *Bug in a Rug: Reading Fun for Just-Beginners.* Illustrated by Alan Tiegreen. New York: William Morrow.

Cutts, David, and Diane Cutts. (1998). *I Can Read about Bees and Wasps.* Illustrated by Janice Kinnealy. New York: Troll.

Feltwell, John. (1997). *Butterflies and Moths (Eyewitness Explorers).* New York: DK Publishers.

Fleming, Denise. (1995). *In the Tall, Tall Grass.* New York: Henry Holt.

Fowler, Allan. (1998). *Inside an Ant Colony.* Chicago: Children's Press.

Fowler, Allan, Robert Hillerich, and Fay Robinson. (1996). *Busy, Buzzy Bees.* Chicago: Children's Press.

Gibbons, Gail. (1991). *Monarch Butterfly.* New York: Holiday House.

Grifalconi, Ann. (1987). *Darkness and the Butterfly.* Boston: Little, Brown.

Hartley, Karen, and Chris Marco. (2001). *Ant.* Des Plaines, IL: Heinemann.

Heiligmam, Deborah. (1996). *From Caterpillar to Butterfly.* Illustrated by Bari Weisman. New York: HarperTrophy.

Johnson, Sylvia A., and Isao Kishida. (1989). *Silkworms.* New York: First Avenue Editions.

Lambert, Jonathan. (1994). *Dottie the Ladybug Plays Hide and Seek.* (Baby Bug Books). New York: Random House.

McDermott, Gerald. (1986). *Anansi the Spider.* New York: Henry Holt.

Mudd, Maria M. (1991). *The Butterfly.* Illustrated by Wendy Smith-Griswold. New York: Stewart, Tabori & Chang, Inc./Workman.

Polacco, Patricia. (1993). *The Bee Tree.* New York: Philomel.

Rockwell, Anne. (2001). *Bugs Are Insects.* Illustrated by Steve Jenkins. New York: HarperCollins.

Trapani, Iza. (1993). *The Itsy Bitsy Spider.* New York: Whispering Coyote Press.

Wallace, Karen. (2000). *Born to Be a Butterfly.* New York: DK Publishing.

Wallace, Karen. (1999). *Busy, Buzzy Bee.* New York: DK Publishing.

White, E. B. (1974). *Charlotte's Web.* New York: Harper.

Family Letter (Primary grade)

Dear Family,

We are now beginning our new theme, "Insects and Spiders." We will provide opportunities for the children to learn the following:

- There are many kinds of insects, and they are found all over the world.
- Insects come in many sizes, shapes, and colors.
- Insects have three body parts: head, thorax (middle section), and abdomen (usually the largest of the sections).
- Insects have six legs (three pairs), two antennae, and, if winged, four wings.
- Insects help us by making honey and pollinating flowers and fruits.
- Spiders are not insects.
- Insects and spiders come from eggs.
- Spiders have eight legs (four pairs), two body parts, two feelers, and no wings or antennae.
- A spider spins silk to get its food, build its shelter, protect its eggs, and to travel safely.
- Spiders help us by eating insect pests.

We will be talking about the following:

- types and characteristics of insects
- habitats of insects
- activities of insects
- types and characteristics of spiders

Try one or more of the following at home with your child:

- Take a walk around your yard and neighborhood. Look for insects, spiders, and spider webs. Talk about what you find.
- Let your child tell you what he or she has learned about spiders and insects.
- Visit the public library, and check out books that will help your child further his or her interest in nature.

Join us for the following family participation opportunities at school:

- Visit our classroom to see the spider web that we have "spun" and all of the activities that are taking place.
  Date _____ Time _____
- Come help us make and eat our "dirt cake."
  Date _____ Time _____

Our wish list for this theme includes:

pipe cleaners	white twine and yarn
lunch-size paper bags	old newspapers

Thanks!

TYPES AND CHARACTERISTICS OF FISH

Gills — to breathe
Fins — to move and swim
Oxygen — to live
Sensitive detectors
Camouflage
Rays

Most lay eggs;
  some do not
Bony fish —
  skeletons and scales
Sharks
Jawless fish

HABITATS
Oceans
Rivers
Lakes
Ponds
Fish farms
Aquariums

THEME 24
Fish

ACTIVITIES

FISH		PEOPLE
Breathe	Eat	Fishing
See	Swim	Aquariums — visiting
Hear	Jump	and having a small
Smell	Chase	one at home
Taste	Hide	
School of fish		

FISH

FRESHWATER	SALTWATER
Goldfish	Salmon
Carp	Sea horse
Sunfish	Flying fish
Bass	Shark
Perch	Swordfish
Trout	Tuna
Catfish	Flounder
Minnow	Herring

THEME GOALS

To provide opportunities for children to learn the following:

▶ Fish come in a large variety of shapes, sizes, patterns, and colors.

▶ All fish have certain things in common that make them different from other creatures living in the oceans, lakes, rivers, and ponds of the world.

▶ All fish live in the water, have gills for breathing oxygen in the water, fins for swimming, and scales for protection.

▶ Fish rise or sink in the water by inflating or deflating a swim bladder, like a small balloon in their abdomens.

▶ Fish depend on insects, other water-living animals, and plants for their food.

▶ Fish provide food, entertainment, and sport for people.

Children-Created Bulletin Board

This bulletin board should invite the children to create an underwater wonderland filled with all kinds of fish drawings, creations, and stories. The board changes often as the children make it an important part of their thematic environment.

▶ Cover the bulletin board with a blue background.

▶ Title it "Our Aquarium."

▶ Have the children glue bright aquarium gravel along the bottom of the board.

▶ Ask the children to make a colorful school of fish to go all around the border of the board.

▶ Extend the bulletin board out to the side by placing colored fish netting (available at craft stores) around the board.

▶ Put clothespins on the netting for the children to add their stories, drawings, and anything else they choose.

▶ Put a big fish in the middle of the board labeled with the parts of the fish body: gills, fins, scales, mouth, and eyes.

VOCABULARY STARTERS

Let the children add words. Include pictures, where appropriate.

aquarium — a building, tank, or other container where live fish and water plants are kept.

bony fish — the biggest group, have skeletons made of bone and thin scales covering their bodies. Oysters, starfish, and jellyfish are not fish, because they do not have a backbone.

camouflage — colors or patterns on something (a fish, for example) that help it blend into its surroundings, making it difficult to see.

fins — parts of the fish that help it move and balance in the water.

gills — parts of a fish's body used for breathing.

school — a large group of fish swimming together, sometimes for protection.

LANGUAGE EXPERIENCES

POEM:

"Do You Know?"

▶ With infants, move their hands and arms in rhythm to the words.

▶ Let the older children enjoy moving along with the motion of the words.

Do you know how the fish
Swim up and down the ocean?
If they don't have arms or legs
How do they make their motion?
  I'll tell you a secret
  If you promise not to tell.
  It is really very easy.
  You can do it very well.
Put your hands on your hips,
Put your elbows out wide,
And you wiggle and you waggle
From side-to-side.
  To do it like a fish
  You have to do it faster.
  So you wiggle waggle wiggle
  Waggle wiggle waggle faster.
You wiggle waggle wiggle
Waggle wiggle waggle faster.
You wiggle waggle wiggle
Waggle wiggle waggle faster.

Philip Jackman

THAT'S MY NAME

▶ To practice name recognition, you and the children make a fish for each child.

▶ Have each child write his name on it.

▶ Laminate the fish.

▶ Place a fish bowl on the floor or a table and put all of the fish into the bowl.

▶ Have each of the children, one at a time, take a fish out of the bowl and hold it up.

▶ When each child recognizes his name, he gets the fish.

▶ At the end of the activity, put all of the fish back into the fish bowl.

▶ This can be repeated many times and used as a transition activity as well.

DRAMATIC PLAY

AQUARIUM FUN

▶ Turn the dramatic play area into an aquarium.

▶ Set up a small table at the entrance to the area with a toy cash register, play money, or money and tickets the children make.

▶ With the children, make some tagboard fish to hang from the ceiling and a special tank filled with colorful foam board fish. (See the Sensory Art section of this theme.)

▶ Put the water table or plastic tubs of water with "fish" and small aquarium nets in the area also.

▶ Place many kinds and sizes of seashells, starfish, pictures, and books of fish all around.

▶ Add items that the children suggest.

▶ If possible, visit an actual aquarium during the study of this theme.

PUPPET PLAY

FISH PUPPETS

▶ Have the children bring some of their old socks from home.

- Guide the children into making a "fish" sock puppet.
- Put out yarn, thread, felt scraps, buttons, sequins, glue, and markers at the art table.
- Older children can sew on buttons using large, dull needles and thick thread.
- Have available pictures of fish for reference, especially those that show the varied colors and patterns of fish scales.
- Ready-made household hot mitts designed as fish also can be used to create another variety of hand puppets.

MUSIC

"THIS IS THE WAY THE GOLDFISH SWIM"

The traditional tune to this activity is "This is the Way We Wash Our Clothes," or sometimes called "Lazy Mary Will You Wake Up?" The children enjoy "swimming" along, "nibbling" with their fingers, and "gill breathing" with their elbows.

This is the way the goldfish swim —
  Back and forth, back and forth.
This is the way the goldfish swim —
  Back and forth in the water.
This is the way they move their gills —
  In and out, in and out.

This is the way they move their gills —
  When the goldfish are breathing.
This is the way they nibble their food,
  Nibble their food, nibble their food.
This is the way they nibble their food —
  When the goldfish are hungry.
This is the way the goldfish jump,
  Goldfish jump, goldfish jump.
This is the way the goldfish jump —
When the goldfish are playing.

Philip Jackman

MOVEMENT

SWIM LIKE A FISH

This movement activity is best to do after the children have had a chance to observe live fish in an aquarium and to study how they move.

- Place six to eight chairs in any arrangement you choose in the middle of a cleared area, indoors or outdoors.
- Have each child decide which kind of fish he would like to be and then practice "swimming" about.
- Explain to the children that they are going to go exploring around the chairs, the way fish explore around rocks under water.
- Have each child take a turn. Make appropriate comments, such as: "Evan's fish is swimming around all the rocks," "Look, Keesha's fish is zigzagging around the rocks," and, "See how Juan's goes fast, then slow."
- After each child has taken a turn, have all of the children swim in and around each other and the chairs.
- You also might suggest changes in movement by asking the children to explore way down low and way up high, and to hover motionless, as fish often do.
- To help create a "swimming mood," play an excerpt from appropriate music, such as Debussy's *La Mer (The Sea)*. Encourage the children to swim as the music makes them feel.

SENSORY ART

CATCH THE FISH AND PUT IT BACK

▶ Take different colored pieces of foam board (available at craft stores), and cut dozens of little fish in all colors and shapes.

▶ Put these in the water table or a plastic tub with a small amount of water.

▶ The fish float, and the children enjoy catching the fish with small aquarium fish nets.

MAKE A FISH

▶ On a table, put out a variety of sizes and colors of construction paper, tagboard, pencils, crayons, markers, and scissors.

▶ Leave these out for the children to draw, cut out, and color fish of their choosing. They can make them in all shapes, patterns, and sizes — the bigger, the better. These fish will later be hung around the dramatic play area, which will become a giant aquarium.

▶ For older children, suggest that they experiment with folding and cutting the paper to form fish. The illustration is just an example of one way to do this.

▶ Variety and creativity are important in this activity. Let the children experiment with the materials and apply their imaginations!

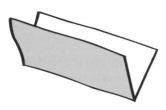

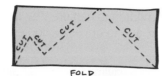

FOLD

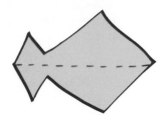

FELT FISH AQUARIUM

▶ Use a small aquarium without a top.

▶ Tie thread across the top from corner to corner, and from side to side across the middle. The fish will hang from these.

▶ Put out various colors of construction paper, felt, sequins, foil, beads, glue, yarn, thread, pipe cleaners, wire, and markers on the art table.

▶ Throughout the theme, the children can make small fish to put into the aquarium.

▶ For younger children, provide a few fish templates for them to trace around.

▶ Punch holes in the top of each fish, put thread through the holes, and attach to the thread across the top of the aquarium.

▶ Put this in the dramatic play area.

CREATIVE FOOD EXPERIENCES

FISH IN THE CUP

You will need the following:

    packages of green or blue gelatin
    gummy fish

1. Wash hands.
2. With the children's help, make green or blue gelatin according to the directions on the box.
3. Put equal portions, enough for the class, into clear plastic cups.
4. After the gelatin has cooled in the refrigerator and is partially set, add some gummy fish to each cup.
5. Refrigerate until the treat is completely set.
6. Eat!

MAKE A FISH

You will need the following:

    wheat bread (2 slices per child)
    cheese
    raisins
    mini-marshmallows

1. Wash hands.
2. The children cut the bread slices with fish-shaped cookie cutters.
3. Grate some cheese, or use prepackaged shredded cheese, and spread around bread for "fish scales."
4. Use raisins for eyes. Make a marshmallow mouth.
5. Put bread pieces on a cookie sheet, and bake in oven or toaster oven until cheese melts.

See Theme 18, "Oceans and Lakes," for additional cooking recipes that work well with this theme.

MAKE A FISH

Wash hands.

Cut 2 slices of bread with fish shape cookie cutters.

Spread shredded cheese around bread for "fish scales".

Use raisins for eyes and a mini-marshmallow for a mouth.

Put bread pieces on a cookie sheet.

Bake in toaster oven until cheese melts.

EAT!

MATH

FIND THE FISH SCHOOL OF FRIENDS

This is a board game in which one to four children move "fish" around the board until they reach their "school of friends."

▶ To construct the game, you will need a large piece of poster board or heavy cardboard, markers to draw the game (see the illustration), and scraps of cardboard on which to draw and then cut out the game pieces.

▶ In addition, you need one die for play with younger children, or a pair of dice for older children.

▶ Besides stimulating the children's interest in fish, this game emphasizes math skills.

▶ Keep the game pieces in a resealable plastic bag clipped to the game board.

▶ Place the game in the math or manipulative center so the children can play with it when they wish.

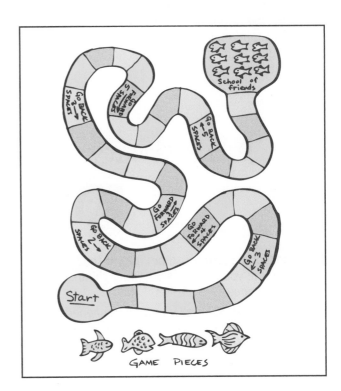

SCIENCE

SETTING UP AN AQUARIUM

▶ Setting up an aquarium in the classroom is a fascinating learning experience for the children. It integrates all content areas of the curriculum.

▶ Set up a budget and involve the children in how the money should be spent.

▶ To begin, provide the children with pictures and books on how an aquarium works, including the importance of keeping it clean, filtering and aerating the water, checking water temperature, and carefully feeding fish on a schedule.

▶ Decide on the size, and make a list of what should be purchased and how much everything will cost.

▶ Next, visit a pet store and consult with the personnel about purchasing the aquarium tank, pump and aerator, supplies and accessories, and fish.

▶ Back in the classroom, the children, with your supervision, can fill the aquarium, add the parts, and place the fish in their new home.

▶ Once the aquarium is in operation, the children can make a schedule of what their responsibilities will be.

▶ The children can observe the fish and write their daily observations about each fish and its behavior in an aquarium journal or book. The journal can include the children's drawings of the aquarium and its fish.

SOCIAL STUDIES

THE WORLD OF FISH

▶ Read Lionni's *Fish Is Fish* or Pfister's *The Rainbow Fish* to the younger children. Older children can read the books themselves.

▶ Ask the children to tell you what happened in the book. "How do you think the fish felt?" "What made the fish happy?" "Would you tell me what happened in the book?"

▶ As you continue to discuss the stories with the children, guide them toward thinking about the concepts that are discussed in each of the books: sharing, feelings, giving, receiving, and helping others.

▶ Talk about how the children fulfill these actions every day in the world of the classroom and in their family world at home.

▶ Have the children write a story about a fish. Suggest that they work together in a small group or with a partner.

CHILDREN'S BOOKS

Ancona, George. (1991). *The Aquarium Book.* New York: Clarion.

Andres, Katherine. (1993). *Fish Story.* New York: Simon & Schuster.

Angelfish, Christopher. (1997). *The Fish Book.* Illustrated by Joseph Veno. New York: Golden Books.

Arnosky, Jim. (1993). *Crinkleroot's 25 Fish Every Child Should Know.* New York: Bradbury.

Coffelt, Nancy. (1994). *Tom's Fish.* New York: Gulliver Books.

Cohen, Caron Lee, and S. D. Schindler. (1998). *How Many Fish? (I Can Read Book).* Illustrated by Lillian Hoban. New York: HarperCollins.

Cole, Joanna. (1997). *Magic School Bus Goes Upstream: A Book about Salmon Migration.* Illustrated by Bruce Degen. New York: Scholastic.

Ehlert, Lois. (1992). *Fish Eyes: A Book You Can Count On.* San Diego: Harcourt.

Frieden, Sarajo. (1996). *The Care and Feeding of Fish: A Story with Pictures.* Boston: Houghton Mifflin.

Krawczyk, Sabine. (Ed.). (1998). *Fish (First Discovery Book).* New York: Scholastic.

Lionni, Leo. (1987). *Fish Is Fish.* (Rev. ed.). New York: Knopf.

MacLeod, Heather. (1995). *The Fish.* Illustrated by Janice Skivington. Chicago: Children's Press.

McKissack, Pat, and Dena Schutzer. (1996). *A Million Fish . . . More or Less.* New York: Dragonfly.

Morley, Christine, and Carole Orbell. (1997). *Me and My Pet Fish.* Illustrated by Brita Granstrom. New York: World Book.

Pallotta, Jerry. (1991). *The Underwater Alphabet Book.* Illustrated by Edgar Stuart. Watertown, MA: Charlesbridge.

Palmer, Helen. (1989). *A Fish Out of Water.* New York: Random House.

Pfeffer, Wendy, and Holly Keller. (1996). *What's It Like to Be a Fish? (Let's-Read-and-Find-Out Science).* Illustrated by Wendy Keller. New York: HarperTrophy.

Pfister, Marcus. (1995). *Rainbow Fish to the Rescue.* New York: North-South Books.

Pfister, Marcus. (1992) *The Rainbow Fish.* New York: North-South Books.

Ryder, Joanne, and Carol Schwartz. (1993). *One Small Fish.* New York: Morrow Junior Books.

Snedden, Robert. (1993). *What Is a Fish?* Photographed by Oxford Scientific Films. Illustrated by Adrian Lascomb. San Francisco: Sierra Club Books.

Toft, Kim Michelle. (1998). *One Less Fish.* Illustrated by Allan Sheather. Watertown, MA: Charlesbridge.

Wallwork, Amanda. (1998). *Find the Fish: That Looks Like This.* (Rev. ed.). New York: Puffin.

Wildsmith, Brian. (1987). *Fishes.* New York: Oxford University Press.

Wu, Norbert. (1997). *Fish Faces.* (Rev. ed.). New York: Owlet.

Wylie, JoAnne, and David Wylie. (1983). *A Fishy Color Story.* Chicago: Children's Press.

Family Letter (Preschool)

Dear Family,

The wonderful world of "Fish" is our new theme. The children will learn the following:

- Fish come in a large variety of shapes, sizes, patterns, and colors.
- All fish have certain things in common that make them different from other creatures living in the oceans, lakes, rivers, and ponds of the world.
- All fish live in the water, have gills for breathing oxygen in the water, fins for swimming, and scales for protection.
- Fish rise or sink in the water by inflating or deflating a swim bladder, like a small balloon in their abdomens.
- Fish depend on insects, other water-living animals, and plants for their food.
- Fish provide food, entertainment, and sport for people.

We will be talking about the following:

- types and characteristics of fish
- habitats of fish
- freshwater and saltwater fish
- activities of fish

Some things to do at home with your child include:

- Visit a pet store or an aquarium with your child. Talk about and observe the fish.
- Read books about fish to your child.
- Talk about what people can do to stop polluting the oceans, rivers, lakes, and ponds.

Come in and participate at school in the following activities:

- Go with us to visit the aquarium.
  Date _____ Time _____
- Come have lunch with us one day.
  Date _____ Time _____

Our wish list items for this theme include:

> clean, old socks
> beads and sequins
> pictures of and magazines about fish
> yarn
> fish food

Thanks!

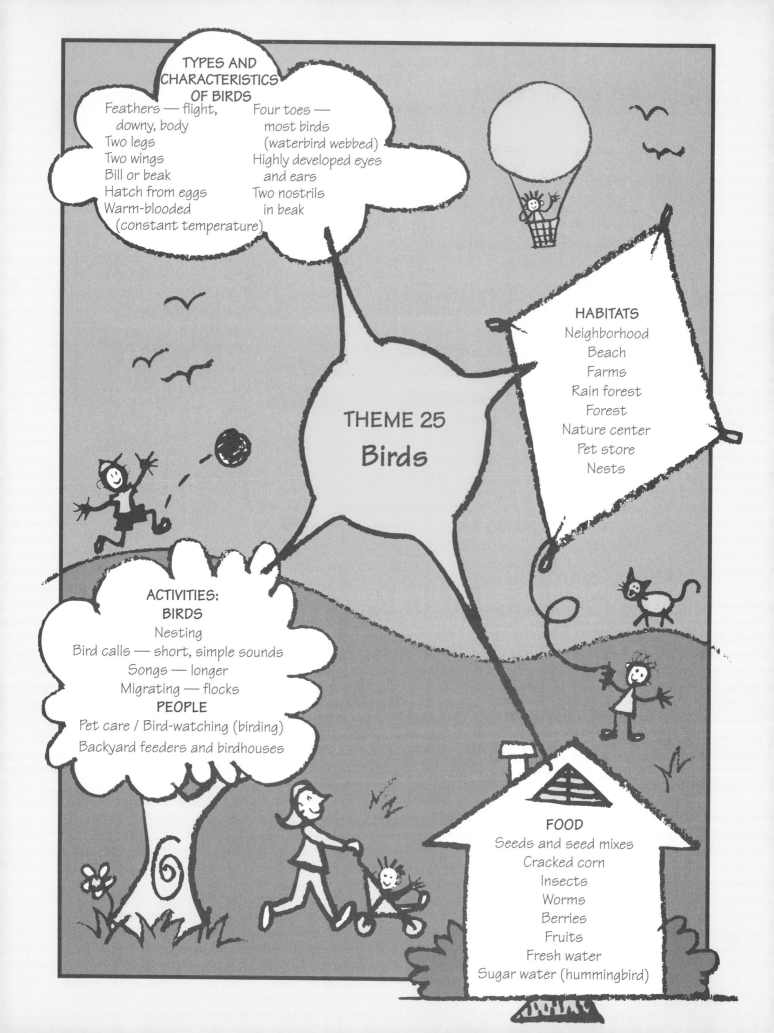

TYPES AND CHARACTERISTICS OF BIRDS

Feathers — flight, downy, body
Two legs
Two wings
Bill or beak
Hatch from eggs
Warm-blooded (constant temperature)

Four toes — most birds (waterbird webbed)
Highly developed eyes and ears
Two nostrils in beak

THEME 25
Birds

HABITATS
Neighborhood
Beach
Farms
Rain forest
Forest
Nature center
Pet store
Nests

ACTIVITIES:
BIRDS
Nesting
Bird calls — short, simple sounds
Songs — longer
Migrating — flocks
PEOPLE
Pet care / Bird-watching (birding)
Backyard feeders and birdhouses

FOOD
Seeds and seed mixes
Cracked corn
Insects
Worms
Berries
Fruits
Fresh water
Sugar water (hummingbird)

THEME GOALS

To provide opportunities for children to learn the following:

▶ Birds are found everywhere in the world, from the city to the rain forest.

▶ All birds have feathers: flight feathers, downy feathers, and body feathers.

▶ All birds have wings, but not all of them can fly.

▶ All birds hatch from eggs in nests.

▶ Birds come in many sizes, shapes, and colors. They all have feet and either a beak or bill.

Children-Created Bulletin Board

Each time the bulletin board is blank and ready to welcome a new theme, the children become interested. Keep their attention and curiosity alive by having them help you create the new bulletin board.

▶ Cover your board with all of the pictures of birds you can find.

▶ With the children, divide the birds into categories, such as neighborhood birds, pet birds, beach and waterbirds, birds that do not fly, farm birds, and endangered birds.

▶ Label the largest bird (ostrich) and the smallest bird (hummingbird).

▶ Add to the board as the children draw pictures and write about the different kinds of birds.

▶ Glue on bird food and feathers for a textured effect.

▶ It is fun to see the birds "flying" all around the bulletin board.

VOCABULARY STARTERS

Let the children add words. Include pictures, where appropriate.

aviary — a place or large building where birds are kept.

colony — a group of birds nesting near one another.

flock — a group of birds.

migration — the movement of creatures, such as birds, fish, and butterflies, from one place to another.

molting — shedding feathers and growing others to replace them.

ornithology — the study of birds.

perch — a place where a bird sits.

preening — birds cleaning and oiling their feathers.

roost — a place where birds rest.

seabirds — birds that cannot fly but can swim as well as fish, such as penguins.

LANGUAGE EXPERIENCES

FINGERPLAY: "What Do Birds Do?"

The tiny sparrow says chirp-chirp-chirp.
   (make a sparrow beak with thumb and fingers; point beak up, open and close for each "chirp")
And eats some seeds with a peck-peck-peck.
   (point beak down and peck seeds on the other hand)
Then flies away with a flap, flap, flap.
   (cross hands in front, flap fingers on both hands)
The big blackbird says caw, caw, caw.
   (make a blackbird beak with both hands and fingers cupped together; point beak up, open and close on each "caw")
And eats some berries with a chomp-chomp-chomp.
   (point beak toward front, and chomp three berries in a row)
Then flies away with a whoosh-whoosh-whoosh.
   (flap arms and hands like large wings)

Philip Jackman

POEM: "Look! I See Birds!"

High, high, high in the sky,
See the eagle circle and fly.
Down, down, down on the ground,
See the pigeon walking around.
Glide, glide, glide on the pool,
See the swan quiet and cool.
Up, up, up in the tree,
See the owl staring at me.
Far, far, far and alone,
See the geese flying back home.

Philip Jackman

POEM: "On Yonder Hill There Stands a Tree"

This is a traditional poem, author unknown, that the children enjoy learning and repeating.

▶ Start slowly. As they learn it, the children like to say it faster and faster.

▶ Ask the children to add lines.

On yonder hill there stands a tree:
   Tree on the hill, and the hill stood still.
And on the tree there was a branch:
   Branch on the tree, tree on the hill, and the hill stood still.
And on the branch there was a nest:
   Nest on the branch, branch on the tree, tree on the hill, and the hill stood still.
And in the nest there was an egg:
   Egg in the nest, nest on the branch, branch on the tree, tree on the hill, and the hill stood still.
And in the egg there was a bird:
   Bird in the egg, egg in the nest, nest on the branch, branch on the tree, tree on the hill, and the hill stood still.
And on the bird there was a feather:
   Feather on the bird, bird in the egg, egg in the nest, nest on the branch, branch on the tree, tree on the hill, and the hill stood still.

DRAMATIC PLAY

LET'S BUILD A NEST

This activity fits in nicely after the children have been learning about the characteristics of various types of birds, including the varied ways they build their nests.

▶ Turn the dramatic play area or a corner of the playground into a nest-building site.

▶ Collect a variety of materials, such as strips of assorted types of paper (butcher paper, newspaper, toilet paper, paper towels), cardboard, paper towel tubes, cloth scraps, string, yarn, small tree branches, twigs, craft sticks, glue, clay, and anything else that might be useful and safe for building a nest.

▶ By working cooperatively and creatively, the children can problem solve, divide up tasks, and figure out how to build the nest.

PUPPET PLAY

IT'S A PUPPET BIRD!

▶ This is fun and easy for the older children to make at any time. It also is a great way to recycle old file folders.

▶ Supply file folders, pencils, markers, crayons, scissors, glue, feathers (available at teacher supply stores), and construction paper.

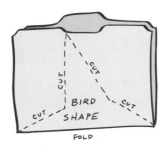

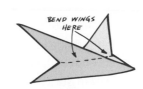

▶ Draw a simple bird outline on one side of a folder, with the fold at the bottom.

▶ Cut out the bird shape, cutting both halves of the folder at the same time.

▶ The wings can be bent out to either side.

▶ The children can complete their bird any way they wish.

▶ The birds are now ready to "fly," by simply holding the bottom of the puppets and moving them up and down quickly until the wings move.

▶ A lot of dramatic play can emerge from these puppets.

MUSIC

SONG: "Birds on the Rooftop"

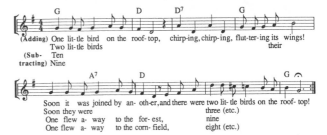

*Reproduced by permission of B. Wolf - 1995
Copyright B. Wolf - 1993*

(See page 310 for enlargement.)

LET'S LISTEN

▶ Introduce the children to the portion of Saint-Saëns *Carnival of the Animals* that relates to the theme of birds. Be familiar with the piece prior to sharing it with the students.

▶ Listen to the instruments that make these sounds:
  – "hens and roosters" (string section)
  – "cuckoo" (clarinet)
  – "birds" (flutes and violins)

▶ After the children have listened to the music once, ask them to imitate the birds through movement and in response to the music the next time you play it.

▶ Offer several follow-up activities, such as playing the rhythm instruments along with the recording, drawing special pictures while the music is playing, and playing the entire recording of *Carnival of the Animals* as background music throughout the following days.

MOVEMENT

SOAR LIKE A BIRD

▶ After spending some time observing birds outdoors and looking at pictures and books of different types of birds, talk about the various birds the children have seen.

▶ Find out which is each child's favorite bird. What does she like most about it? Why?

▶ Ask the children to pantomime their favorite birds in flight. Ask them to show how their wings move, how their heads move, and how fast or slow they fly.

▶ Add music to the children's "flying." A good selection could be the "Sunrise" part of Grofé's *Grand Canyon Suite,* because it builds, flows, and soars. Skip the opening, because it is very slow in building.

▶ You might give the children word pictures to help them get started. For example, ask them to imagine their bird waking up in a nest, stretching, looking around, and then taking off. What does flying feel like? What do they see down below?

▶ Encourage students to use the whole space to "fly," but to be careful to avoid other birds, just as real birds avoid touching each other.

▶ After a time, you might fade the music out slowly, suggesting that birds get tired and have to rest now and then.

▶ Have the children imagine where they come to rest. Is it a nest, tree, housetop, or mountaintop?

▶ Let each child conclude the activity at her own pace.

SENSORY ART

FINGER AND HAND PAINTING

▶ Show the children pictures of red, blue, and multicolored birds.

▶ Talk to the children about the colors of the birds and show them the paint colors (they should be the same as the colors of the birds) you have put out.

▶ With smocks on and sleeves rolled up, older infants and toddlers can really get into finger and hand painting. Sometimes the children use their whole bodies.

▶ Children can paint on trays, tables, and paper.

▶ To make prints from the tray and table designs, slowly press white paper on top, and gently pull it up.

FEATHER PAINTING

▶ Set up the easels and the art table.

▶ Make available several colors and thicknesses of tempera paint in flat shallow pans or trays, along with all kinds and shapes of paper, feathers, and feather dusters for the children.

▶ Let the children explore painting with these new kinds of "brushes."

WHY DO DUCKS STAY DRY?

This activity can be done by one to three children at a time.

▶ Have the children draw two pictures of a duck.

▶ Cut the ducks out of paper bags.

▶ Ask the children to leave one duck plain and to rub vegetable oil on the other.

▶ Have the children sprinkle or spray water on both ducks to observe what happens.

▶ How does the oil that ducks rub on their feathers while they are preening help them stay dry?

▶ This activity can lead to many more discoveries about ducks and how they survive in their environment.

CREATIVE FOOD EXPERIENCES

NIBBLE A "NEST"

You will need the following:

> 2 large shredded wheat biscuits
> 1/4 cup coconut
> 1 tablespoon brown sugar
> 1/4 cup liquid margarine
> strawberry yogurt
> fruity jelly beans

Ingredients are for six servings. Double or triple the recipe as needed for your class.

1. Wash hands.
2. With the children's help, use fingers to crumble shredded wheat biscuits in a bowl.
3. Stir in coconut, brown sugar, and margarine.
4. Line six muffin tins with foil.
5. Press the shredded wheat mixture into the bottoms and up the sides of the foil-lined cups.
6. Bake in a 350-degree oven for about 10 minutes, or until crisp. Let cool.

7. Remove the "nests" from the cups by lifting up on the foil. Carefully peel off the foil.
8. Fill the "nest" with a spoonful of yogurt, and place jelly bean "eggs" on top.
9. Enjoy the treat!

MATH

IT'S FOR THE BIRDS

▶ Fill the sand/water table or plastic tubs with wild birdseed.

▶ Provide the children with measuring cups, measuring spoons, sifters, funnels, and many sizes of bowls.

▶ Add materials that the children ask for to help them count, measure, pour, and stir.

- -

BIRD PUZZLES

▶ Make some large cardboard or tagboard cards.

▶ Write a numeral on the bottom.

▶ At the top of the card, place the corresponding number of bird stickers. For younger children, make all of the birds the same.

▶ Cut the cards in two. Use different types or configurations of cuts, such as zigzag, diamond, straight, curved, and diagonal.

▶ This will help the children put the puzzle card sets together correctly.

▶ As a follow-up activity for older children, let them make another set of card puzzles.

▶ Supply the materials. Let the students decide what the bird puzzles will look like and how they will make them.

NIBBLE A "NEST"

 Wash hands.

 Crumble 2 large shredded wheat biscuits into a mixing bowl.

    Stir in 1/4 cup coconut, 1 tablespoon brown sugar,

   and 1/4 cup liquid margarine. Line 6 muffin tins with foil.

Press the shredded wheat mixture onto the bottoms and up the sides of the foil-lined cups. Bake in 350 degree oven for 10 minutes or until crisp. Let cool.

Remove the "nests" from the cups. Carefully peel off foil.

Fill the "nest" with a spoonful of yogurt and place

 jelly bean "eggs" on top. Enjoy the treat!

SCIENCE

LOOK AT THE PICTURES

▶ Put pictures of birds in the sides of a photo cube. These can be photos you take or pictures from magazines.

▶ Point to each picture, and say the name of the bird to the children.

▶ Make several picture cubes, and leave them around the room for the children to play with.

▶ Take the children outside, and point out the birds you see.

▶ Repeat this activity to help the children learn about birds. Repetition is important for very young children.

WHAT'S IN A NEST?

▶ To tie in with the nest building in the dramatic play area, put items that birds might like to use for a nest outside of the windows. Put these in a box so items will not blow away.

▶ Let the suggestions come from the children. For example, yarn and ribbon pieces, scraps of paper, small twigs, dryer lint, grass, wads of wet tissue, mud, and broken craft sticks are some things birds use in their nests.

▶ Include all of the items. It is important to have some things that the birds will not take.

▶ Watch the objects each day, and write down which things the birds like best.

BUILD A BIRD FEEDER TOGETHER

Make feeders at home and at school. This is a project that the children, their family members, and you can do together.

▶ A suggestion for a feeder is to make one from an empty, clean, one-half gallon milk carton. Simply cut away two adjoining sides of a carton, leaving two inches at the top and bottom.

▶ Punch two holes in the top of the carton. Thread some strong string through the holes and tie it, making a loop for hanging.

▶ Put wild bird feed, sunflowers seeds, or bread crumbs in the feeder.

▶ Hang it from a tree branch outside.

▶ This will attract birds to the yard or playground. It probably will attract squirrels too, giving the children more to watch.

▶ Get several pairs of inexpensive binoculars, and keep them out at all times.

▶ Have a disposable camera for the children to take their own pictures.

▶ Invite someone from the local Audubon Society or a bird rehabilitator to talk to the families and the children at an early evening get-together.

▶ He or she can bring a bird, talk about local birds and their habits, and discuss rain forests, migrating birds, and endangered species.

▶ Everyone can share their experiences with bird-watching.

▶ An activity like this that connects home and school can make everyone excited about learning.

SOCIAL STUDIES

A DUCKY FIELD TRIP

▶ Plan a field trip to a local pond, lake, or park that is a duck habitat.

▶ This will give the children a chance to observe ducks in their natural environment. They can see other birds too.

- Bring binoculars, cameras, paper and pencils, a tape recorder and blank tapes, and a bird field guide or other reference book.

- Remind the children that this is an *observation* field trip. Nothing should be done to disturb the waterfowl or nesting wildlife.

- Observe the different behaviors of ducks. Try to identify preening, waddling, swimming, flying, diving, and dabbling (head down and tail up in shallow water to feed).

- Are there any ducklings to observe? What type of behaviors do they exhibit?

- Having children draw and write about their experience would be a good follow-up activity to this interesting field trip.

CHILDREN'S BOOKS

Appelt, Kathia, and Jane Dyer. (2000). *Oh My Baby, Little One.* San Diego: Harcourt.

Arnosky, Jim. (1993). *Crinkleroot's 25 Birds Every Child Should Know.* New York: Bradbury.

Cannon, Janell. (1993). *Stellaluna.* San Diego: Harcourt.

Cherry, Lynne. (1997). *Flute's Journey: The Life of a Wood Thrush.* New York: Gulliver Books.

Eastman, P. D. (1988). *Are You My Mother?* New York: Random House.

Ehlert, Lois. (2001). *Waiting for Wings.* San Diego: Harcourt.

Ehlert, Lois. (1993). *Feathers for Lunch.* San Diego: Harcourt.

Ehlert, Lois, and Gloria Dee Aragon Andujar. (1997). *Cuckoo = Cucu: A Mexican Folktale = UN Cuento.* San Diego: Harcourt.

Gibbons, Gail. (1998). *Soaring with the Wind: The Bald Eagle.* New York: William Morrow.

Green, Jen. (1998). *Birds: Explore the Amazing World of Birds.* New York: Smithmark.

Hutchins, Pat. (1990). *Good-Night Owl!* (Rev. ed.). New York: Aladdin.

Inches, Alison, and Cheryl Medenhal. (2001). *Dizzy's Bird Watch.* New York: Simon Spotlight.

Landau, Elaine. (1992). *State Birds.* New York: Franklin Watts.

Lerner, Carol. (1996). *Backyard Birds of Summer.* New York: William Morrow.

Massie, Diane R., and Steven Kellogg. (2000). *The Baby Bee Bird.* Illustrated by Steven Kellogg. New York: Harper-Collins.

McCloskey, Robert. (1976). *Make Way for Ducklings.* New York: Viking.

Muntean, Michaela. (1998). *Big Bird's Baby Book.* New York: Golden Books/Sesame Workshop.

National Wildlife Federation. (1997). *Birds, Birds, Birds! (Ranger Rick's Naturescope Guides).* (Rev. ed.). New York: McGraw Hill.

Neitzel, Shirley. (1997). *The House I'll Build for the Wrens.* Illustrated by Nancy Winslow Parker. New York: Greenwillow.

Parsons, Alexandra. (1990). *Amazing Birds.* Photographed by Jerry Young. New York: Knopf.

Rider, Joanne. (2003). *Wild Birds.* Illustrated by Susan E. Kwas. New York: HarperCollins.

Rockwell, Anne F. (1992). *Our Yard Is Full of Birds.* New York: HarperCollins.

Rockwell, Anne F., and Harlow Rockwell. (1996). *My Spring Robin.* Illustrated by Lizzie Rockwell. New York: Demco Media.

Sill, John, and Cathryn P. Sill. (1997). *About Birds: A Guide for Children.* New York: Peachtree Publishers.

Waddell, Martin. (1996). *Owl Babies.* Illustrated by Patrick Benson. Cambridge, MA: Candlewick Press.

Wildsmith, Brian. (1992). *The Owl and the Woodpecker.* New York: Oxford University Press/Franklin Watts.

Ziefert, Harriet. (2001). *Birdhouse for Rent.* Boston: Houghton Mifflin.

Family Letter (Primary grade)

Dear Family,

Please join us as we begin our new theme, "Birds." We will provide opportunities for the children to learn the following:

- Birds are found everywhere in the world, from the city to the rain forest.
- All birds have feathers: flight feathers, downy feathers, and body feathers.
- All birds have wings, but not all of them can fly.
- All birds hatch from eggs in nests.
- Birds come in many sizes, shapes, and colors, have feet, and have either a beak or bill.

We will be talking about the following:

- types and characteristics of birds
- habitats of birds
- food that birds eat
- activities of birds
- activities of people (bird-watching or birding)

Some things to do at home with your child include:

- Build a backyard bird feeder.
- Watch birds around your house and in the neighborhood.
- Read books and magazines about birds.
- Learn about birds that are endangered species.

Opportunities for you to participate at school include:

- Join us for the family meeting, share the bird feeder you and your child made, and hear our guest speaker from the Audubon Society.
  Date _____ Time _____
- Go with us on our field trip to a duck habitat.
  Date _____ Time _____

Our wish list for this theme includes:

newspapers	string
paper towel tubes	cardboard scraps
foil	sifters
funnels	ribbon scraps
empty, clean, half-gallon milk cartons	

Thanks!

PEOPLE
Ringmaster
Clowns
Musicians
Trapeze artists
Acrobats
High-wire (tightrope) walkers
Animal trainers
Jugglers
Grounds crew

THEME 26
Circus

ANIMALS
Lions
Tigers
Elephants
Horses
Seals
Bears
Dogs

ACTIVITIES
Parade
Music — band
Putting up and taking down tents
Taking care of animals
Circus trains and trucks
Performing circus arts

PERFORMANCE AREAS
Tents
Arenas
Fairgrounds
(state and county)
Circus rings

THEME GOALS

To provide opportunities for children to learn the following:

▶ The circus is family entertainment that takes place in big tents or arenas.

▶ Many thrilling performers can be seen at the circus, such as trapeze artists and high-wire walkers.

▶ Clowns are an important part of the circus, because they make us laugh and keep the action moving.

▶ Circus animals do special tricks.

▶ The animal trainer teaches the animals how to do tricks and takes care of them.

▶ Circus musicians play lively music from the beginning of the show to the end.

▶ The ringmaster announces all of the circus acts.

Children-Created Bulletin Board

This bulletin board should reflect the children's enthusiasm about going to the circus. It should be bright, colorful, and ever-changing.

▶ With the children's help, glue sawdust or confetti on a butcher paper background.

▶ Place balloons or streamers all around the board.

▶ Divide the board into three or four rings.

▶ Within the rings, place items the children suggest or create.

▶ Attach a strip of burlap along the bottom of the board as an extension on which to place the children's writing and drawings.

▶ Title the bulletin board "It Is Circus Time!"

VOCABULARY STARTERS

Let the children add words. Include pictures, where appropriate.

acrobat — a person who performs tumbling and balancing acts.

circus — traveling show of animals, clowns, acrobats, and others.

circus backyard — small village of trucks and trailers surrounding the tent or arena. This is where the circus family lives.

juggler — a person who is able to keep many objects in the air at the same time.

ringmaster — person in charge of the circus performance.

trapeze — a high swing used for aerial circus acts.

LANGUAGE EXPERIENCES

MAKE A CIRCUS BOOK

▶ Make a circus book for younger children. Mount pictures of animals, clowns, and circus performers on poster board squares, and put them in resealable plastic bags.

▶ Stack the bags on top of each other with the resealable section at the top.

▶ Punch holes along one side of the plastic bags, and tie them together with yarn. This makes flipping through the book easy for children. It also is easy for you to change the pictures as you find others.

▶ Talk about the pictures with the children.

▶ Leave the circus book out for the older infants and toddlers to play with and "read."

POEM: "Toodles the Clown"

With a drum-drum-drum and rooty-toot-toot
The circus has come to town.
Say, who's that man in that funny suit?
I think it's Toodles the Clown.
　He's got a green hat and a big red nose
　And a polka-dot bow tie.
　His shoes have holes — I can see his toes —
　And he's carrying a pie.
Look out! Look out! And don't fall down,
Or you'll surely drop your pie!
Oh, my! Oh, my! He fell on the ground
And his pie got pushed in his eye!
　"Help, help!" He says, "Come help me please.
　I can't see with pie on my face."
　Now he's up on his elbow, he's up on his knees
　Now he wobbles all over the place.
He staggers and stumbles and finally stands,
But he's OK, I think,
'Cause he sneaks us a smile as he licks his hands,
Then gives us a great big wink.
　Be sure you remember the next time you hear
　That the circus is coming to town
　To look for the clown with the big red nose.
　He's Toodles — Toodles the Clown!

Philip Jackman

DRAMATIC PLAY

CIRCUS PLAY

It is fun time in the dramatic play area when you bring in the circus prop box!

▶ Have clown costumes, ballet shoes, ballet costumes, wigs, hats, small umbrellas, and stuffed animals. The children can bring their stuffed animals too.

▶ Place hula hoops on the floor to create the rings at the circus. These mark a well-defined space that can be put anywhere.

▶ Put masking tape in a straight line on the floor to be used as a tightrope.

▶ Place a few sturdy boxes around for the ringmaster and performing acts.

▶ Mix face cream with a small amount of powdered tempera or food coloring for clown makeup.

▶ You also can add some soap to liquid tempera paint and use a small brush to put on the makeup. Remember to include mirrors!

▶ Put mats on the floor for the tumbling acts.

▶ Outside, have a circus parade. Decorate the tricycles and wagons with crepe paper.

▶ Here comes the band! Play recorded, lively marching music while the children play their rhythm instruments.

PUPPET PLAY

MARIONETTES

Marionettes, controlled by strings, require muscle control and coordination that usually are developed in older preschoolers, kindergartners, and primary-grade children.

▶ A fun way for the children to begin is to tightly tie yarn or strings to the head and arms of stuffed animals. (Moving the legs in addition is more complicated.)

▶ Attach the other ends of the yarn or string to a dowel rod, ruler, stick, or paper towel tube.

▶ The children can pull the strings and start talking to each other.

▶ If the older children want to try another type of marionette, the first question should be, "What do you want it to do?"

▶ It is important to think through and plan each step in the creation of a marionette. The "airplane control" is the easiest design to manipulate (see illustration).

▶ Start with one string to the head and a string to each hand. Strings to the legs can be added later.

▶ The children need time to experiment with their marionettes and to work through the frustration of the puppet not working the first time. It is the process that is important for young children.

▶ The children should hang up the marionettes when they are done playing. This eliminates tangled strings.

MUSIC

"THIS IS THE WAY THE CIRCUS GOES"

▶ This a rhythmical beat poem that can be said or sung. The tune is a traditional song, "This Is the Way We Wash Our Clothes." The dashes in the song indicate pauses allowing for the up-and-down movement.

▶ Add rhythm instruments and body movements to vary the activity.

This is the way the trapeze man
Swings up — and down — up — and down.
This is the way the trapeze woman
Swings up — and down — at the circus.
  This is the way the acrobat
  Jumps up — and down — up — and down.
  This is the way the acrobat
  Jumps up — and down — at the circus.
This is the way the horses gallop
Round and round, round and round.
This is the way the horses gallop
Round and round at the circus.
  This is the way the clowns go round
  Clowns go round — and fall on the ground.
  This is the way the clowns go round
  And fall on the ground at the circus.

Philip Jackman

MOVEMENT

BE A CLOWN

▶ It is fun for the children to act silly! Ask them if they have ever seen a clown. Where? When?

▶ Talk about clowns and what they do.

- Let the children decide if they want to pretend to be clowns one at a time, with a partner, or everyone together.

- Ask the children to do the following, first in pantomime, then with words:
  — Walk in a silly way.
  — Do silly tricks.
  — Make silly faces.
  — Sing a silly song.
  — Do a silly dance.

- Ask the children to show you what else they can do to act like a clown.

- By pretending to be a clown, a child can play away many fears he may have from previous experiences with clowns.

SENSORY ART

WASH THE ANIMALS

- Young children enjoy water play. For older infants and toddlers, fill a plastic tub or the sand/water table with soap and water.

- Put some small plastic animals into the water.

- Let the children wash the animals.

- Have plenty of paper towels for the drying area.

- This activity works best if two to four children play together.

DRAW A CLOWN

- The "draw a clown" activity, based on the "draw a child" activity, is a favorite of young children.

- For toddlers, draw around each child lying on a large piece of paper.

- Older children can choose a partner and draw around each other.

- Have available plenty of fabric scraps, yarn, ribbon, construction paper, markers, crayons, paints, glue, and scissors for the children.

- Each child can color and draw a clown face, add hair, and decorate the rest of the clown.

CIRCUS PUTTY

- Make an entertaining, stretchy, puttylike material. Children enjoy pulling and making shapes with the putty and creating animal shapes by using animal cookie cutters.

- Use equal amounts of white school glue and liquid laundry starch, approximately $\frac{1}{4}$ cup of each per child.

- Pour glue and starch into a small bowl for each child.

- Let the children mix with their fingers. Closely supervise the young toddlers.

- The putty will be very sticky until *well* mixed.

- If it is too sticky, add more starch in very small amounts, and mix until you get a smooth, rubbery consistency.

- Store the mixture in an airtight container or a plastic bag. The putty does not need to be refrigerated.

CIRCUS CRAYON ETCHING

The children can do this creative activity after they have talked about the circus, looked at pictures and books, and investigated the many features of the circus. Younger children will enjoy exploring this activity, while older ones should be encouraged to investigate detailed images and patterns.

- Put out paper, crayons, craft sticks, paper clips, and waxed paper on a table.

- Guide the children in using their crayons to cover the paper with many bright colors in assorted shapes. They need to press down hard to leave a thick layer of colors.

- After filling the paper, have the children color heavily over the whole paper using black crayons.

- Ask the children to think about a circus design that they would like to draw.

- Using the craft stick or paper clip, scrape or scratch through the layer of black crayon in whatever circus designs the children choose.

- The light colors will show through when the black is scraped away.

▶ Polish the picture using waxed paper to give it a shine.

▶ Leave the materials out for the children to use again whenever they wish.

CREATIVE FOOD EXPERIENCES

BIG TOP SNACK

You will need the following:

> 6 cups popped popcorn
> 1 cup candy-coated milk chocolate pieces
> 1 cup raisins
> 1 cup peanuts (optional)
> 1 to 2 cups animal crackers

1. Wash hands.
2. Place all ingredients into a big paper bag, a one-gallon, resealable plastic bag, or a container.
3. Shake everything up!
4. Pour into individual bowls, and enjoy!

- -

CIRCUS TRAINS

You will need the following:

> celery sticks
> peanut butter or pimento cheese (*Note*: if any child is allergic to peanut butter substitute pimento cheese.)
> carrots
> animal crackers

1. Wash hands.
2. Cut the carrots into circles.
3. Use toothpicks to stick the carrot "rounds" onto a piece of celery. These are the "wheels."
4. Spread the peanut butter on the inside of the celery.
5. Stand the animal crackers in the peanut butter.
6. This is the animal car on the circus train.
7. Look at the train, then eat! . . . but be careful of the toothpicks!

CIRCUS TRAINS

Wash hands.

Cut a carrot into circles.

Use toothpicks to stick the carrot "wheels" onto

a piece of celery. Spread some peanut butter inside the celery.

Stand some animal crackers in the peanut butter.

Look at your Circus Train Animal Car, then eat!

MATH

LET'S BUILD A CIRCUS

▶ Expand the block center so the children can build a circus and circus grounds.

▶ In addition to the blocks, provide the children with craft sticks, toothpicks, dowel rods, wooden clothespins, clay, fabric, string, yarn, plastic animals and people, cardboard boxes, and small, interlocking block pieces.

▶ Ask the children for ideas about what else they will need to set up the circus.

▶ Leave the area open for expansion for the duration of this theme.

▶ The block center offers many opportunities for children to apply math concepts.

SCIENCE

BALANCING ACTS

Most circus performers — and that includes animals as well as people — have developed a sharp sense of balance. If they did not have it, they could not walk on a tightrope, fly on a trapeze, perform acrobatics, juggle, or balance large objects. This balancing activity explores some of the principles of balance that circus performers understand.

▶ On a floor (not on carpet), put down a six-to-eight-foot-long piece of masking tape.

▶ Ask the children, one at a time, to try to "tightrope walk" its length with their arms at their sides and to observe how easy or hard it is to do.

▶ Next, have children walk the tape, but this time with their arms held out to either side, observing how easy or hard it is.

▶ Ask the children to compare the two methods and tell you which one makes balancing easier.

▶ Talk about children's answers. (Balancing is easier with the arms extended. Why is this?)

▶ Have children walk the tape with only *one* arm extended. What happens? (They have to lean to the opposite side. Why? To balance the weight of the extended arm.)

▶ This experiment demonstrates that the more a person distributes his body weight outward from the center of balance, the *longer* it takes him to fall sideways. This gives him more time to shift weight and regain balance, which is why high-wire artists at the circus walk with long poles.

▶ To make this experience a little more challenging for the older children, place a six-foot length of one-inch by three-inch lumber on its wide side on the floor.

▶ When children balance on this, it is more like being on a tightrope.

SOCIAL STUDIES

TUMBLING TIME

Since most circus acts involve various forms of tumbling and gymnastics, you could introduce the children to these skills by inviting a qualified gymnastics or physical education instructor to visit the class.

▶ In making arrangements for a class visitor, be sure to explain to the person that the children are studying the circus so that he or she can tie in the presentation to this theme.

▶ Ask the visiting instructor to demonstrate some simple tumbling and gymnastics exercises.

▶ Be sure that safe procedures are used, and that you know exactly what the children will be asked to do.

▶ Place some mats on the floor so the children can practice some easy rolls and cartwheels, if *they* want to do so.

▶ Give the children plenty of time to ask questions.

CHILDREN'S BOOKS

Bauer, Marion. (2001). *If You Had a Nose Like an Elephant's Trunk.* New York: Holiday House.

Bourguignon, Laurence. (1996). *A Friend for Tiger.* New York: Bridgewater Books.

Brett, Jan. (1996). *Berlioz the Bear.* New York: Paper Star.

Bulloch, Ivan, and Diane James. (1997). *A Clown (I Want to Be Series).* New York: World Book.

Chwast, Seymour. (1996). *The Twelve Circus Rings.* San Diego: Harcourt.

Dr. Seuss (pseud. for Theodor Geisel). (1994). *If I Ran the Circus.* (Rev. issue). New York: Random Library.

Dr. Seuss. (1966). *Horton Hatches the Egg.* New York: Random House.

Ehlert, Lois. (1992). *Circus.* New York: HarperCollins.

Flaconer, Ian. (2001). *Olivia Saves the Circus.* New York: Atheneum.

Hill, Eric. (1994). *Spot Goes to the Circus.* (Rev. ed.). New York: Puffin.

Hopp, Lisa. (1997). *Circus of Colors (Poke and Look).* Illustrated by Chiara Bordoni. New York: Grosset & Dunlap.

Johnson, Crockett. (1981). *Harold's Circus.* New York: HarperCollins.

Johnson, Neil. (1995). *Big-Top Circus.* New York: Dial.

Kastner, Jill, and Virginia Duncan. (1997). *Barnyard Big Top.* New York: Simon & Schuster.

Millman, Isaac. (2003). *Moses Goes to the Circus.* New York: Frances Foster.

Murphy, Stuart J. (1998). *Circus Shapes.* Illustrated by Edward Miller. New York: HarperCollins.

Paxton, Tom. (1997). *Engelbert Joins the Circus.* Illustrated by Roberta Wilson. New York: William Morrow and Company.

Prelutsky, Jack. (1989). *Circus.* Illustrated by Arnold Lobel. New York: Aladdin.

Sampson, Michael. (1997). *Star of the Circus.* Illustrated by Mary Beth Sampson and Jose Aruego. New York: Henry Holt.

Schumaker, Ward. (1997). *Sing a Song of Circus.* San Diego: Harcourt.

Xiong, Blia, and Cathy Spagnoli. (1989). *Nine-in-One GRR! GRR!: A Folktale from the Hmong People of Laos.* Illustrated by Nancy Hom. San Francisco: Children's Book Press.

Family Letter (Toddler)

Dear Family,

We are beginning our new theme, the "Circus." We will provide opportunities for the children to learn the following:

- *The circus is family entertainment that takes place in big tents or arenas.*
- *Many thrilling performers can be seen at the circus, such as trapeze artists and high-wire walkers.*
- *Clowns are an important part of the circus, because they make us laugh and keep the action moving.*
- *Circus animals do special tricks.*
- *The animal trainer teaches the animals how to do tricks and takes care of them.*
- *Circus musicians play lively music from the beginning of the show to the end.*
- *The ringmaster announces all of the circus acts.*

We will be talking about the following:

- *people in the circus*
- *animals in the circus*
- *performance areas of the circus*
- *activities and performance acts at the circus*

Some things to do at home with your child include:

- *Read books about the circus and circus life.*
- *Read books about clowns, and talk about what you see.*
- *Visit the zoo to see elephants, lions, and tigers.*
- *Enjoy eating popcorn and cotton candy together.*
- *Take your child to the circus when it comes to town.*

Family participation opportunities at school will include:

- *Come visit us, and see what "circus activities" we are doing.*
  Date _____ Time _____
- *Come read a book to my friends and me.*
  Date _____ Time _____
- *Come have lunch with my friends and me.*
  Date _____ Time _____

Our wish list items for this theme include:

pictures of circus animals
pictures of clowns
paper towel tubes
string

Thanks!

CHARACTERISTICS
Hatched from eggs
Meat eating
Plant eating
Varied sizes, weights, and shapes
Four legs; some walked on two
Many with heavy body shells,
horns, and spikes for protection

THEME 27
Dinosaurs

**WHERE TO LOOK
FOR INFORMATION**
Museums
Books
Videos
Internet
Dinosaur parks
and digs

FAMILIAR TYPES
Ankylosaurus
Brachiosaurus
Brontosaurus (Apatosaurus)
Compsognathus
Parasaurolophus
Spinosaurus
Stegosaurus
Triceratops
Tyrannosaurus Rex
Velociraptor

SCIENTIFIC FINDINGS
Paleontologists
Dinosaur digs
Fossils
Footprints
Bones
Teeth
Nest with eggs

THEME GOALS

To provide opportunities for children to learn the following:

▶ Dinosaurs lived long ago, before there were any people.

▶ Some dinosaurs were big and some were small, with varying body shapes.

▶ Some dinosaurs ate plants, some ate meat, and some ate both.

▶ Dinosaurs hatched from eggs.

▶ No one really knows why they died out (became extinct).

▶ Scientists who study dinosaurs look for fossils of dinosaur footprints, bones, teeth, and eggs.

Children-Created Bulletin Board

Young children are fascinated by dinosaurs. This bulletin board, as with all boards in an early childhood classroom, should reflect the interests and participation of the children.

▶ Start with a completely blank bulletin board.

▶ Let the children suggest the color of the background and what should be added first.

▶ "Where are the dinosaurs?" is usually the first question asked. This presents an opportunity for the children to draw and place their images of the dinosaurs on the bulletin board.

▶ Throughout the theme, children's conceptions will change, and new artwork can be placed on the board as well.

▶ At some point, resource pictures of dinosaurs also should be added.

▶ Trees, plants, sun, rocks, and mountains can be created for a three-dimensional effect.

▶ To make the mountains, the children dampen brown paper bags, crush them, and then paint them. The children can add the "mountains" to the bulletin board after they are dry.

▶ Tree trunks can be made from corrugated paper.

▶ Glue on dry leaves and dry grass.

▶ Foil makes a great lake.

▶ As the theme progresses, the bulletin board should change.

VOCABULARY STARTERS

Let the children add words.

dinosaur — "terrible lizard," a prehistoric reptile with upright legs.

extinct — a type of animal or plant that has disappeared and no longer exists.

fossil — rocklike remains of prehistoric animals and plants.

paleontologist — a scientist who digs up dinosaur fossils and brings them to museums.

LANGUAGE EXPERIENCES

FINGERPLAY: Five Big Dinosaurs

Five BIG dinosaurs practicing a roar,
   (hold up five fingers)
One went away and then there were four.
   (hold up four fingers)
Four BIG dinosaurs munching on a tree,
One went away and then there were three.
   (hold up three fingers)
Three BIG dinosaurs didn't know what to do,
One went away and then there were two.
   (hold up two fingers)
Two BIG dinosaurs enjoying the sun,
One went away and then there was one.
   (hold up one finger)
One BIG dinosaur as lonesome as could be,
It went away and none were left to see.
   (hold up no fingers)

Author Unknown

WHAT IF . . . ?

▶ Ask questions that will lead the children to imaginative thinking, abstract imagery, and language development. The answers also can give you insight into how much the children know about dinosaurs. Ask: "What can you tell me about dinosaurs?" "What would the world be like if dinosaurs were still alive?" "Would we keep dinosaurs as pets?" "What would you teach your 'pet'?"

▶ Write down what the children say, and put their comments into a Big Book.

▶ Have the children illustrate their words.

▶ As an extension of this activity, ask the older children to write a letter to their families and neighbors, convincing them that it would be beneficial for the students if they could keep a dinosaur as a pet.

▶ The children can share their letters with each other if they wish.

DINOSAUR RIDDLES

Children enjoy making up riddles and jokes. Their sense of humor is delightful.

▶ Write down riddles the children dictate on sentence strips, and post them around the room. Older children can write their own.

▶ Have available blank sentence strips in the language center.

▶ A few examples of children's humor follow:

What do you call Tyrannosaurus rex when it wears a cowboy hat and boots? — Tyrannosaurus tex!

What kind of dinosaur can you ride in a rodeo? — A bronco-saurus!

Which dinosaurs were the best police officers? — Tricera-cops!

What did dinosaurs have that no other animals had? — Baby dinosaurs!

What should you do if you find a dinosaur in your bed? — Find somewhere else to sleep!

DRAMATIC PLAY

PREHISTORIC TIMES

▶ In the dramatic play area and book center, have plenty of books, pictures, and items for the children. Also provide plastic dinosaur figures, clay, dinosaur model sets, and other related objects.

▶ Read Pfister's *Dazzle the Dinosaur* (see the Children's Books section in this theme).

▶ Provide an extra-large cardboard shape of "Dazzle" (stegosaurus).

▶ Have the children glue on wads of newspaper to fill out the body, and then completely cover the shape with sheets of newspaper to create a paintable surface.

▶ Lay "Dazzle" flat, and paint. Then sprinkle sand all over to add texture.

▶ It is fun to cover the plates on the dinosaur's back with glitter or foil.

▶ When the dinosaur stands up, the children enjoy measuring themselves against "Dazzle." This offers a concrete way for them to visualize the size of the dinosaurs. The Sensory Art section of this theme offers more ideas for creating dinosaurs, and the Science section has more information about them.

PUPPET PLAY

DINOSAUR SHADOW PUPPETS

▶ Provide the children with tagboard, poster board, transparent or masking tape, and craft sticks.

▶ Children can use books and other materials containing pictures of dinosaurs, particularly side views, for reference.

▶ The children draw their own creative outlines of several dinosaurs on tagboard and cut them out.

▶ Tape a craft stick so that it projects down from the bottom of each dinosaur. This serves as a handle for the puppeteer.

▶ For a quick, easy screen, tape a white sheet over an open doorway, and place a light behind it.

▶ For a more durable shadow puppet screen, construct one from a large piece of poster board or cardboard. Cut a large rectangular hole in the middle, then fasten a piece of white fabric, such as a sheet, to the back side of it. Cut the fabric slightly larger than the hole.

▶ Bend back two "wings" on either side of the screen to serve as supports, as shown in the illustration.

▶ Put the screen on a table, and set up a bright light behind it.

▶ Some of the children can have fun throwing shadows of dinosaurs on the screen, making them move however they wish, while others can watch from the front.

▶ Create opportunities for the children to make up plays, enjoy the puppets, watch others with their puppets, and experiment with different kinds of puppets in shadow play.

MUSIC

SONG: "I Wish That I Could See a Dinosaur" by Jo Eklof

I wish that I could see a din-o-saur.

I'd like to see him move and hear him ro-ar.

I'd like to count each scale, look him o-ver head to tail.

I wish that I could see a din-o-saur, but

but I wish that I could see a din-o-saur.

Second verse:

But I will never see a dinosaur, for dinosaurs aren't living any more.
So I'll have to read and look at their pictures in a book,
For I will never see a dinosaur, but I wish that I could see a dinosaur.

(See page 311 for enlargement.)

MOVEMENT

DINOSAUR STOMP

This activity combines music and movement.

▶ Have available paper sacks for the children to tie onto their feet and stomp around like the dinosaurs to music.

▶ Add rhythmic beats, first as clapping, then as stomping steps.

▶ Young children really enjoy saying dinosaur names. They like the sound and rhythm of them.

▶ Repeat the names with the children several times.

▶ Clap the syllables as you say the names.

▶ Stomp the syllables as you say the names.

▶ Use rhythm instruments to emphasize the syllables as you say the names.

▶ Here are some of the most familiar dinosaur names:

Ankylosaurus — áng-ka-low-śawr-us

Brachiosaurus — brak-e-o-śawr-us

Brontosaurus — bron-to-śawr-us (also called Apatosaurus — a-pat-o-śawr-us)

Compsognathus — comp-śog-na-thus

Parasaurolophus — pear-a-śawr-o-lofus

Spinosaurus — spy-no-śawr-us

Stegosaurus — śteg-o-śawr-us

Triceratops — try-śer-a-tops

Tyrannosaurus rex — tie-ran-o-śawr-us

Velociraptor — ve-lah-si-rap-tor

SENSORY ART

DINOSAUR LACING CARDS

Older toddlers and young preschoolers enjoy this activity. It promotes hand-eye coordination and small muscle development.

▶ Draw several different dinosaur shapes on cardboard or poster board.

▶ Punch large holes just inside the edges of each dinosaur.

▶ You will need 10- to 15-inch-long cotton shoelaces.

▶ Tie one end of the lace to the dinosaur.

▶ Modeling how to push the string through the holes can be helpful if the children have not done this kind of activity before.

LOOK FOR THE FOSSILS

▶ Collect a variety of bones, such as chicken or turkey bones. Have enough for each child to have more than one to use in the sensory activities.

▶ *Boil and clean* the bones thoroughly, *or soak them overnight* in a household bleach solution (3/4 cup of bleach to 1 gallon of water).

▶ The children can enjoy several activities. One is to cook up a batch of play dough (see theme 6 and theme 11 for recipes).

▶ The children take a bone, place it inside of a lump of dough, and cover it completely.

▶ Put the dough-wrapped bones on a cookie sheet, and slowly bake the dough in the oven until it is "rock" hard.

▶ Now it is time for the children to become paleontologists. How can they break the "rocks" without destroying the bones and the imprints inside?

▶ Let the children experiment with a variety of instruments and brushes. Give them plenty of time to complete this process. The activity works best in small groups. If a lot of children want to participate at the same time, spread out onto two or three tables.

▶ For younger children, hide the bones in the sand table or outside in the sandbox.

▶ The children can be paleontologists and find miniature "dinosaur" bones.

CREATIVE FOOD EXPERIENCES

UNUSUAL BISCUITS

▶ Read Hoff's *Danny and the Dinosaur* to the children, listed in the Children's Books section of this theme.

▶ Talk about dinosaurs, explaining that they are animals that lived a long time ago.

▶ Put out dinosaur cookie cutters (available at kitchenware stores and some teacher's resource stores) along with canned biscuit dough.

▶ Let the children make dinosaur biscuits. Some may not want to use the cookie cutters. That is okay. It is fun to shape the dough with your hands.

▶ Bake the biscuits. Be sure to mark the placement of each child's biscuit on a chart, so she gets to eat her own biscuit.

▶ Enjoy biscuits at snack time.

DINOSAUR NESTS

You will need the following:

chocolate chips
jelly beans
chow mein noodles

1. Wash hands.

2. Melt the chocolate chips. (Teacher melts the chips, while the children watch the process. Cook in small groups.)

DINOSAUR NESTS

Wash hands.

Melt some chocolate chips. Pour spoonfuls of melted chocolate

onto 1/4 to 1/2 cup of chow mein noodles.

As the chocolate is cooling, place jelly bean "eggs" into the

dinosaur "nest" with a spoon.

Let the chocolate cool until it hardens. Eat and enjoy!

---

3. Let the children serve themselves 1/4 to 1/2 cup of chow mein noodles on a paper plate labeled with each child's name.

4. Pour spoonfuls of chocolate onto the noodles until they are covered.

5. As the chocolate cools, the children place jelly bean "eggs" into the nest with a spoon.

6. Let the chocolate cool until it hardens.

7. Eat and enjoy.

COOKIE FIND

This activity is not only fun, it also helps develop small muscle skills and hand-eye coordination.

▶ Give the children several chocolate chip cookies and toothpicks.

▶ Ask the children if they would like to carefully dig out each chocolate chip while trying not to damage it.

▶ After all of the chips are removed (or before, for some children), children eat the cookies and chips!

MATH

HOW LONG WAS A DINOSAUR?

▶ With the children's help, cut pieces of yarn into one-foot lengths.

▶ Have the children line up the pieces of yarn along the floor to measure the length of a dinosaur; for example, 12 pieces of yarn for a 12-foot dinosaur.

▶ How many dinosaurs would fit into the classroom? How many could play on the playground?

▶ Perhaps the children could continue measuring when they go home. Ask: "How many dinosaurs would fit in your room at home?" "In your backyard?"

▶ What about dinosaur tracks? How many of the children's footprints would fit inside of a dinosaur track?

▶ Consult reference books and dinosaur resources on the Internet for information.

TOOTHPICK SKELETON

This activity can be done in small groups or individually. It encourages sharing ideas and working together to solve a problem.

▶ Ask the children to estimate how many toothpicks (representing bones) it will take to create a dinosaur skeleton on a 9-by-12-inch piece of construction paper.

▶ Give each child the number of toothpicks she estimated.

▶ After the toothpicks are glued into place to form the skeleton, ask the children to figure out the number of toothpicks they overestimated. Did they underestimate? How many more do they need to complete the dinosaur skeleton?

SCIENCE

LET'S MAKE A "BOXOSAURUS"

This is a problem-solving, creative thinking, and scientific investigating type of activity. Allow plenty of time over many days for this project, until the children say that it is completed. This process is fascinating to observe.

▶ Collect many sizes of cardboard boxes, paper plates, paint, fabric scraps, yarn, glue, scissors, and anything else the children might need.

▶ After the children have seen books, pictures, and reference materials, encourage them, as a class, to make a dinosaur out of boxes.

▶ *Children* need to decide how tall and how long the "boxosaurus" should be. Does it have a long tail? Short or long front legs? Is it a plant eater or meat eater? What color is it?

WHICH DINOSAUR IS WHICH?

▶ To help the children see the differences in the dinosaurs, place many pictures of both plant- and meat-eating dinosaurs around the classroom and in activity centers.

▶ Some additional information follows that might be helpful:

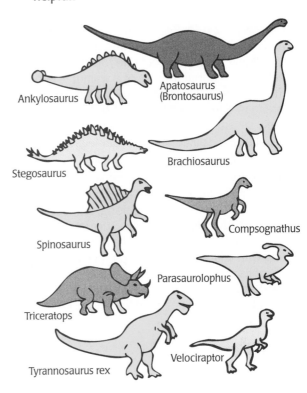

Plant Eaters

Ankylosaurus (áng-ka-low-śawr-us) — A huge, armored dinosaur, twenty-five to thirty feet long, six feet wide, four feet tall, and weighing five tons. It had four short legs, a short neck, and a wide skull with a tiny brain.

Brachiosaurus (brak-e-o-śawr-us) — One of the tallest and largest dinosaurs found, eighty-five feet long, forty to fifty feet tall, weighing fifty to eighty tons. It had a long neck, a small head, a thick tail, front legs longer than its hind legs, and nostrils on top of its head. It was probably one of the slowest of the dinosaurs.

Brontosaurus (bron-to-śawr-us)/**Apatosaurus** (a-pat-o-sawr-us) — In some reference materials, both names are used. This was one of the largest land animals that ever existed at seventy to ninety-five feet long, fifteen feet tall, and weighing thirty-five to fifty tons. It had a long neck, a long, whiplike tail, a very tiny brain, hind legs larger than the front legs, and nostrils on top of its head.

Parasaurolophus (pear-a-śawr-o-lofus) — A long-crested (six feet), duck-billed dinosaur, thirty-three feet long, sixteen feet tall, and weighing about three to four tons. Its nostrils, located at the end of its snout, went up through the crest and back down. It had a notch in its back, right where the crest would touch the back when its head leaned backward.

Stegosaurus (steg-o-sawr-us) — This dinosaur was twenty-five to thirty feet long, and nine to eleven feet tall and weighed about one ton. It had a very small brain — about the size of a walnut — and it carried its head close to the ground, probably no more than three feet high. It also had approximately seventeen bony plates embedded in its back, a heavy, spiked tail, and rear legs longer and straighter than its front legs.

Triceratops (try-ser-a-tops) — This dinosaur looked somewhat like the rhinoceros does today, but much bigger. It was about thirty feet long, ten feet tall, and weighed six to twelve tons. Triceratops walked on four sturdy legs and had three horns on its face, along with a large, bony plate projecting from the back of its skull. This dinosaur had one of the largest skulls of any land animal ever discovered; its head was nearly one-third as long as its body.

Meat Eaters

Compsognathus (comp-sog-na-thus) — This was a birdlike dinosaur that walked on two long, thin legs. It was from twenty-eight inches to four feet long, weighed about six and one-half pounds, and was about the size of a chicken. It was a very fast, agile dinosaur with a small pointed head, short arms, with two clawed fingers on each hand, and three-toed feet.

Spinosaurus (spy-no-sawr-us) — Called a "spiny lizard" because it had a series of large spines up to six feet long coming out if its back, this dinosaur was about forty to fifty feet long and weighed four tons or more. It walked on two legs and had arms smaller than its legs.

Tyrannosaurus rex (tie-ran-o-sawr-us) — This dinosaur was huge, about forty feet long, and fifteen to twenty feet tall and weighed five to seven tons. It could not run very fast. It walked on two powerful legs with claws, had tiny, two-fingered arms, and had a slim, pointed tail for balance and quick turning while running.

Velociraptor (ve-lah-so-rap-tor) — This was a fierce, fast dinosaur about six feet long and three feet tall that walked on two legs. It had about thirty very sharp, curved teeth, long, thin arms with three-fingered clawed hands, and four-toed, clawed feet. It was very intelligent and may have hunted in packs.

▶ Many Internet sites offer a wealth of information on dinosaurs. You may want to investigate some of them.

SOCIAL STUDIES

MEET A SCIENTIST

▶ Plan a field trip to a museum. Arrange beforehand for someone familiar with dinosaurs and fossils, and how fossils are found and collected, to talk to the children.

▶ Ask the museum staff to show the children around the museum and, if possible, to show actual dinosaur bones or fossils.

▶ You may want to discuss with the children what a museum is and what to expect when they get there. Share McGowan's book *Discover Dinosaurs: A Royal Ontario Museum Book, is* listed in the Children's Books section of this theme.

▶ If you cannot visit a museum, invite a college or high school science instructor to talk to the children about dinosaurs to tell them how scientists use fossils to learn more about dinosaurs.

▶ Ask the visitor to bring some fossils to show the children. If possible, have him or her help you set up a "dig" on a part of the playground.

▶ Follow up by asking the children to draw pictures or write stories about what they learned.

▶ Children can also write thank-you notes to the individual who helped them at the museum or visited the class.

CHILDREN'S BOOKS

Aliki. (1988). *Digging Up Dinosaurs.* New York: Ty Crowell.

Aliki. (1985). *Dinosaurs Are Different.* New York: Ty Crowell.

Barner, Bob. (2001). *Dinosaur Bones.* New York: Chronicle.

Barton, Byron. (1994). *Dinosaurs, Dinosaurs.* New York: HarperTrophy.

Barton, Byron. (1990). *Bones, Bones, Dinosaur Bones.* New York: Ty Crowell.

Berenstain, Michael. (1997). *Baby Dinosaurs.* New York: Good Times.

Dodson, Peter, and Wayne D. Barlowe. (1995). *An Alphabet of Dinosaurs.* New York: Scholastic.

Grambling, Lois G. (2000). *Can I Have a Tyrannosaurus Rex, Dad? Please!* Illustrated by Penny L. C. Houffe. Mahwah, NJ: Troll.

Hennessy, B.G. (1991). *The Dinosaur Who Lived in My Backyard.* (Rev. ed.). Illustrated by Susan Davis. New York: Puffin.

Hoff, Syd. (1998). *Danny and the Dinosaur Go to Camp.* (Rev. ed.). New York: HarperTrophy.

Hoff, Syd. (1993). *Danny and the Dinosaur.* (Rev. ed.). New York: HarperTrophy.

Joyce, William. (1998). *Dinosaur Bob.* New York: Harper-Collins.

McGowan, Chris. (1992). *Discover Dinosaurs: A Royal Ontario Museum Book.* New York: Addison-Wesley.

McLaughlin, Annmarie. (2001). *Soft Shapes: Dinosaurs.* Illustrated by Bob Filipowich. Norwalk, CT: Innovative Kids.

Pallotta, Jerry. (1990). *The Dinosaur Alphabet Book.* Illustrated by Ralph Masiello. Watertown, MA: Charlesbridge.

Petty, Kate. (1997). *Dinosaurs Laid Eggs (I Didn't Know That).* Illustrated by James Field, Mike Lacy, and Jo Moore. New York: Millbrook Press.

Pfister, Marcus. (1994). *Dazzle the Dinosaur.* New York: North-South Books.

Prelutsky, Jack. (1992). *Tyrannosaurus Was a Beast: Dinosaur Poems.* Illustrated by Arnold Lobel. New York: Mulberry.

Pringle, Laurence. (1995). *Dinosaur!: Strange and Wonderful.* Illustrated by Carol Heyer. New York: Boyds Mills Press.

Sattler, Helen Roney. (1984). *Baby Dinosaurs.* New York: Lothrop, Lee & Shepard.

Stevenson, James. (2000). *The Most Amazing Dinosaur.* New York: Greenwillow.

Thomson, Ruth. (2000). *Dinosaur's Day.* New York: DK Publishing.

Yolen, Jane. (2000). *How Do Dinosaurs Say Goodnight?* Illustrated by Mark Teague. New York: Blue Sky Press.

Family Letter (Preschool)

Dear Family,

We are very excited about beginning our new theme, "Dinosaurs." We will provide opportunities for the children to learn the following:

- Dinosaurs lived long ago, before there were any people.
- Some dinosaurs were big and some were small, with varying body shapes.
- Some dinosaurs ate plants, some ate meat, and some ate both.
- Dinosaurs hatched from eggs.
- No one really knows why they died out (became extinct).
- Scientists who study dinosaurs look for fossils of dinosaur footprints, bones, teeth, and eggs.

We will be talking about the following:

- characteristics of dinosaurs
- ten of the most familiar types of dinosaurs
- scientific findings of the paleontologists
- where to find information about dinosaurs

Try doing some of the following at home with your child:

- Read books and talk about dinosaurs.
- Take your child to a museum.
- Visit a store that has all kinds of rocks to observe.
- Try to answer your child's dinosaur riddles.

Family participation opportunities at school will include:

- Come visit us and see what we have added to our room.
  Date _____ Time _____
- Go with us on our field trip to the museum.
  Date _____ Time _____

Our wish list for this theme includes:

foil

toothpicks

large pieces of white fabric or a sheet

cardboard boxes (various sizes)

Thanks!

Transportation

Early childhood curriculum builds upon what children already know and are able to do. It is important to strengthen their knowledge and encourage learning new concepts and skills.

With this in mind, the activities in this theme suggest ways to continue expanding the experiences of children. The content also takes into consideration the children's ages, stages of development, and individual differences in prior experiences and community involvement. Mix and match the activities to meet the needs of the children in your classroom.

The following themes are included in Section VI, "Transportation":

Theme 28 — Cars, Trucks, and Buses

Theme 29 — Airplanes

Theme 30 — Trains and Tracks

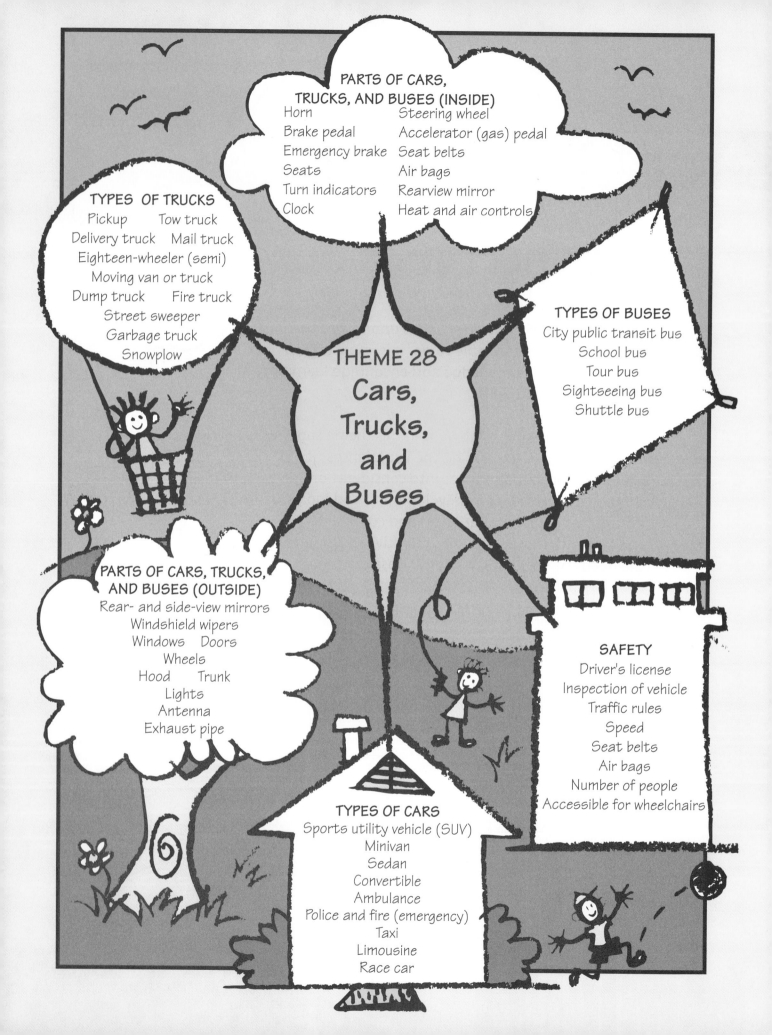

PARTS OF CARS, TRUCKS, AND BUSES (INSIDE)

Horn — Steering wheel
Brake pedal — Accelerator (gas) pedal
Emergency brake — Seat belts
Seats — Air bags
Turn indicators — Rearview mirror
Clock — Heat and air controls

TYPES OF TRUCKS

Pickup — Tow truck
Delivery truck — Mail truck
Eighteen-wheeler (semi)
Moving van or truck
Dump truck — Fire truck
Street sweeper
Garbage truck
Snowplow

TYPES OF BUSES

City public transit bus
School bus
Tour bus
Sightseeing bus
Shuttle bus

**THEME 28
Cars,
Trucks,
and
Buses**

PARTS OF CARS, TRUCKS, AND BUSES (OUTSIDE)

Rear- and side-view mirrors
Windshield wipers
Windows — Doors
Wheels
Hood — Trunk
Lights
Antenna
Exhaust pipe

SAFETY

Driver's license
Inspection of vehicle
Traffic rules
Speed
Seat belts
Air bags
Number of people
Accessible for wheelchairs

TYPES OF CARS

Sports utility vehicle (SUV)
Minivan
Sedan
Convertible
Ambulance
Police and fire (emergency)
Taxi
Limousine
Race car

THEME GOALS

To provide opportunities for children to learn the following:

▶ Cars, trucks, and buses are forms of transportation that move people and things from place to place.

▶ There are many kinds, colors, and sizes of cars, trucks, and buses.

▶ A driver's license is required to operate these vehicles.

▶ All vehicles need to be inspected, repaired, and kept clean.

▶ Many occupations involve car, truck, and bus transportation.

Children-Created Bulletin Board

This bulletin board gives the children an opportunity to share what they know and what they want to know about cars, trucks, and buses. Throughout the theme, the board changes as children become more aware of and learn new information about these methods of transportation.

▶ Let the children create a border for the bulletin board by "tire track painting" with toy cars and trucks dipped into paint and rolled onto strips of paper.

▶ Title the board, "Transportation: Cars, Trucks, Buses, and Wheels."

▶ At the beginning of this theme, have the children draw or cut out pictures of land transportation vehicles and put them on the bulletin board to make a collage.

▶ Provide pictures of tricycles, bicycles, and wagons, wheeled vehicles with which children are familiar.

▶ Throughout the theme, more of the children's ideas, safety rules, drawings, and stories will be added to the collage background.

VOCABULARY STARTERS

Let the children add words.

cab — the driver's area of a truck.

driver — a person who operates a vehicle.

eighteen-wheeler — a large truck with eight wheels on the trailer and 10 on the tractor, or cab, unit.

fuel — material, such as gasoline or diesel fuel, used to produce power to move a vehicle.

mechanic — a person who repairs (fixes) a vehicle.

LANGUAGE EXPERIENCES

SAFETY RULES

To introduce this theme, it is helpful to talk about safety rules. Write down each rule that the children suggest.

▶ Older children can write their own rules on sentence strips.

▶ Make one safety list for riding in a car and another for riding in a bus.

▶ Examples from children for riding safely in the car include:

Buckle up your seat belt.

Young children should ride in the backseat.

Do not bother the driver.

Red means **stop**; yellow means **slow down** and **be ready to stop**; green means **go**.

▶ Safety suggestions from children for riding the bus include:

Use the handrail when getting on and off the bus.

No dogs on the bus.

Be quiet on the bus so the driver can pay attention to driving.

Be nice.

Do not stand on your seat.

▶ Encourage each child to draw a picture that illustrates his safety rule.

▶ Put the lists and pictures on the bulletin board.

DRAMATIC PLAY

BUS RIDE

▶ Collect items for a prop box, such as a bus driver's cap, coins, tickets, a steering wheel made from cardboard or a Styrofoam™ plate, a bicycle horn, and a cassette tape of traffic sounds. Tape the sounds yourself, including sirens and honking horns.

▶ Arrange chairs to form a line for seats on a bus.

▶ Tie one end of heavy ribbon pieces onto the chairs for seat belts.

▶ Put Velcro™ on the other ends of the ribbons so the seat belts will fasten.

▶ Encourage the children to take turns being the bus driver and the passengers.

▶ Model safe ways to get on and off the bus.

PLAYGROUND GAS STATION AND CAR WASH

▶ Ask the children to tell you about when they went with a family member to a service station or car wash.

▶ Let the children help you set up a gas station and car wash on the playground.

▶ Attach an old hose to a post or tree to use as a gas hose. Use other hoses for air and water. Label each.

▶ Place a "toolbox" in the area. This can be a prop box filled with an air pump, safety glasses, all kinds of tools, flashlights, car diagnostic papers and service diagrams collected from car dealers and service stations, receipt books, car magazines, tool catalogs, and car advertisements from the newspaper.

▶ The children can drive their trikes, wagons, or cardboard-box cars to the station to get fuel or to be repaired or washed.

▶ Set up the car wash with a couple of buckets of soapy water, smocks, sponges, spray bottles, some rags or old towels for drying, and a cash register for the attendant.

▶ Add toy trucks and cars, Big Wheels™, and trikes.

▶ Allow plenty of time for the children to explore and enjoy this outdoor dramatic play area.

LET'S MAKE A CAR! LET'S MAKE A BUS!

▶ Cardboard boxes can provide hours of fun and learning experiences for young children. Provide a collection of large, medium, and small boxes, cutting tools, construction paper, paint, crayons, brushes, tape, glue, brads, yarn, ribbon, and plenty of space for creating.

▶ Large boxes are available from furniture and appliance stores. Medium boxes are found in grocery stores, offices, and homes. Ask families to save small, sturdy boxes such as those that come with shoes, stationery, and bank checks.

▶ Offer suggestions and encouragement, but avoid giving patterns or models to copy as the children design and make cars, trucks, or buses.

▶ Let the children "drive" their cars, trucks, or buses. (See the Sensory Art section of this theme for ways to make a driver's license.)

▶ Expand the dramatic play area by opening up a "fast food drive-through window." The children can build a "drive-through" window in the block center for small vehicles.

PUPPET PLAY

COMMUNITY TRUCK AND DRIVER PUPPETS

▶ Have available pictures and books of trucks for the children.

▶ Read Behrens's *I Can Be a Truck Driver,* Barton's *Trucks,* and Becker's *You Can Name 100 Trucks!* (See the Children's Books section of this theme.) Make the books available for the children.

▶ Talk about all of the different kinds of trucks.

▶ Discuss how both women and men drive trucks.

▶ Do any of the children's family members drive trucks?

▶ Guide the older children into making truck and driver puppets. Examples are tow truck, tractor-trailer truck, dump truck, and trash truck. See illustrations.

▶ Use cardboard or tagboard for the base, and provide craft sticks, dowel rods, straws, crayons, markers, paint, felt and fabric scraps, scissors, glue, and yarn.

▶ Younger children can create stick puppets using a truck picture or stencil to draw a truck on a piece of paper and attach it to a straw.

▶ Older children can make a set of truck and driver puppets if they wish.

MUSIC

"DO YOU WANT TO TAKE A TRIP?"

This song, sung to the traditional tune "She'll Be Comin' Round the Mountain," talks about the major types of land transportation in a way that emphasizes *response singing* and has fun with sound effects. Use the rhythm instruments to accompany the song, and add a "bicycle horn" and a "train whistle."

Do you want to take a trip?
  Response: *Yes we do! Uh-huh!*
Do you want to take a trip?
  Response: *Yes we do! Uh-huh!*
Do you want to take a trip,
A zippety-dippity-trip?
Do you want to take a trip?
  Response: *Yes we do! Uh-huh!*
Do you want to drive a car?
  Response: *Yes we do! Beep-beep!*
Do you want to drive a car?
  Response: *Yes we do! Beep-beep!*
If you want to drive a car
You can drive it pretty far.
Do you want to drive a car?
  Response: *Yes we do! Beep-beep!*
Do you want to ride a bus?
  Response: *Yes we do! Honk, honk!*
Do you want to ride a bus?
  Response: *Yes we do! Honk, honk!*
If you want to ride a bus
I don't want to hear you fuss.

Do you want to ride a bus?
   Response: *Yes we do! Honk, honk!*
Do you want to take a truck?
   Response: *Yes we do! Zoom-zoom!*
Do you want to take a truck?
   Response: *Yes we do! Zoom-zoom!*
If you want to take a truck
Just be careful – don't get stuck!
Do you want to take a truck?
   Response: *Yes we do! Zoom-zoom!*
Do you want to take a train?
   Response: *Yes we do! Toot-toot!*
Do you want to take a train?
   Response:*Yes we do! Toot-toot!*
Do you want to take a train
And go see your Auntie Jane?
Do you want to take a train?
   Response: *Yes we do! Toot-toot!*

Philip Jackman

MOVEMENT

LET'S PLAY RED LIGHT– GREEN LIGHT

This is a traditional game that continues to be played by young children.

▶ One person is the traffic light with a green circle and a red circle. It is easy to add a yellow circle for "slow down."

▶ All children who want to play start out in a line facing the traffic light player.

▶ When the green light is shown, everyone moves forward.

▶ When the yellow light is shown, everyone slows down.

▶ When the red light is shown, everyone stops!

▶ If a child moves instead of stopping, he goes back to the starting line and begins again.

▶ Continue until the whole group reaches the traffic light, or the children decide to stop.

▶ For a change, use "Walk" and "Do Not Walk" symbols instead of red, yellow, and green lights.

START YOUR ENGINES

▶ Have the children sit in a circle and number off one through four.

▶ Let the children in each number group decide on the name of their car (Jaguar, Chevrolet, Porsche, etc.).

▶ The game leader, chosen by the entire group, calls a car name, and those cars get up and run around the outside of the circle.

▶ The first person back to his spot wins that round.

▶ *But,* there is a *surprise* to this game: the cars can have something wrong with them. (The leader decides.) For example, "flat tire" (hop around the circle on one foot); "run out of gas" (crab walk around the circle); or "no muffler" (make noises while slowly running around the circle).

▶ The children can think up things that could go wrong before the game starts.

SENSORY ART

SAND AND WATER TABLE PLAY

▶ Children enjoy playing with small cars and trucks. To make the activity multisensory, put sand, salt, cornmeal, or gravel in the sand table or in large plastic tubs. Add fresh salt and cornmeal often if these materials are chosen.

▶ Add the cars and trucks.

▶ Continue to add objects, such as paper towel rolls (tunnels), blocks (ramps), and small traffic safety signs, such as "Stop" and "Yield."

Another entertaining sensory activity using the sand and water table or plastic tubs follows:

▶ Clean out the table or tubs. Put in a small amount of water.

▶ Add bubble wrap and plastic toy cars to the sensory table.

▶ The children drive their cars over the bubble wrap to make popping noises. The water provides extra-sensory fun.

LICENSE PLATE RUBBINGS

▶ Collect expired license plates. Put tape around the edges for safety. If possible, have some plates from other states to show the children.

▶ Talk to the children about the purpose of license plates.

▶ Explain to the children that each state has a different design, and that each plate within that state is different.

▶ Put the old license plates, paper, and crayons in the art center so the children can make rubbings.

▶ Ask the older children to look for license plates when they are riding in their family's vehicle or on the bus and to keep a list to share with their classmates.

PERSONAL DRIVER'S LICENSE

▶ Put tagboard, crayons, markers, pencils, a small bathroom scale, a tape measure, and a yardstick in the art center.

▶ Show the children your driver's license, and ask families to do the same.

▶ The children can make their driver's licenses based on real ones, or they can design new ones.

▶ Take a picture of each child to be used on the license. Children can also draw pictures of themselves.

▶ Have the children figure out how much they weigh and how tall they are. Add this information to the driver's license.

▶ Put the licenses on the bulletin board if the children wish to do so.

CREATIVE FOOD EXPERIENCES

STOPLIGHT COOKIES

You will need the following:

packaged sugar cookie dough in a roll (enough for each child to have three cookies)

white icing

red, yellow, and green food coloring

1. Wash hands.
2. Bake sugar cookies according to instructions on package.
3. Divide white icing into three equal portions.
4. Add red food coloring to one bowl of icing, yellow food coloring to another bowl of icing, and green food coloring to the third bowl of icing.
5. Each child spreads icing on his cookies with a plastic knife to make Stoplight Cookies. Yum!

TRUCK STOP PANCAKES

You will need the following:

2 eggs

4 tablespoons sugar

2 cups all-purpose flour

2 teaspoons baking powder

1 teaspoon salt

2 cups milk

4 tablespoons oil

1 teaspoon vanilla **or** cinnamon for added flavor

1. Wash hands.
2. Start with 2 cups of milk, and mix with other ingredients.

TRUCK STOP PANCAKES

Wash hands.

Mix 2 cups milk, 2 eggs, 4 tablespoons sugar.

2 cups all-purpose flour, 2 teaspoons baking powder.

1 teaspoon salt, 4 tablespoons oil, and

1 teaspoon vanilla or cinnamon.

Spray skillet with fat free cooking spray. Cook pancakes on

medium heat. Turn when bubbles have formed and edges are

cooked enough. Turn only once.   ENJOY!

3. For thicker pancakes, use less milk; for thinner ones, add more milk.

4. Spray skillet with fat-free cooking spray.

5. Cook pancakes on medium heat, not high, or the sugar will scorch your pancakes.

6. Turn when bubbles have formed and edges are cooked enough. Turn only once.

7. Recipe serves 4 to 6. Enjoy!

MATH

RACE CAR TRACK

This game is best when played by small groups of children. Use an old sheet to make this math game.

▶ With the children's help, draw a large, oval shape on the sheet.

▶ Draw four lines inside and parallel to the oval shape to form lanes. Mark these lanes into small spaces, similar to the way lanes are drawn in board games.

▶ In the open area inside the lanes, draw a large rectangular grid to create small squares. Randomly number each square with a number from 1 to 10.

▶ Each child chooses a small car and puts it in a lane space marked "Start." Then, in turn, each child stands outside the sheet and tosses a large washer or other round disk onto the numbered squares.

▶ The child advances his car the number of spaces indicated. If the washer does not land on a numbered square, he loses a turn.

▶ Continue playing until all cars have reached the finish line or the children choose to stop the game.

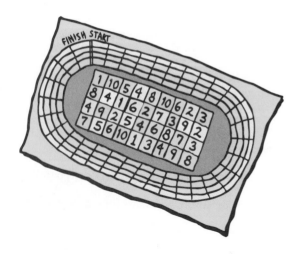

SCIENCE

WHEELS

▶ Have available pictures and books for the children.

▶ Have toy cars, trucks, and buses, along with trikes, wagons, and tires, for the children to inspect.

▶ Use these to help the children visualize different kinds of wheels.

▶ Explain to the children that there would be no wagons, trikes, bicycles, skates, or cars if we did not have wheels.

▶ Discuss with the children the many different materials used in making wheels.

▶ Go for a walk around the neighborhood with the children, and look for wheels.

▶ Show the children pictures and talk about the different "wheels at work." Ask them to name some of these in their community, such as ambulances, fire trucks, garbage trucks, mail trucks, pickup trucks, cement mixers, dump trucks, and eighteen-wheelers.

▶ Add different kinds of wheels to the block center.

DRIVING IN TRAFFIC

Go for a drive without ever leaving the classroom. With the children's help, lay out some short streets by placing masking tape on the floor in a zigzag pattern, as described.

▶ With the tape, mark a starting place with an "X."

▶ Then, start *forward* with the masking tape for four feet. Each street segment is four feet long.

▶ Turn 90 degrees *left* for four feet, then *right*, then *right* again, then *left*, then *left* again, then *right*, then *right* again, then *left* for the final four feet, ending with "Stop," marked on the floor.

▶ The children who want to play sit in a circle around the "streets," with two children at a time acting as "driver" and "police officer."

- The driver follows the tape from "X" to each turn, at which point he must signal with the appropriate hand before turning, say either "left" or "right," and then make the turn.

- The police officer follows behind the driver. If the driver does not make the correct signal and say left or right before turning, then the officer issues a warning ticket. Let the children design this ticket.

- The driver continues to the "Stop" sign, and his turn is over.

- Let the children take turns being driver and officer until all who wish to do so have participated.

- For younger children, let them "drive" along the streets, one child at a time. If they can identify left from right, let them do so. Otherwise, it is fun for them to just drive.

- Ask questions to the group about the activity. "Why do drivers need to signal in traffic?" "Do real drivers put their hand out before turning?" (Yes, if they are on a bicycle, or if their turn indicator signal is not working.) "How do real drivers signal a turn?" "Why do we need to have police officers watching drivers?" "Do you know what happens if a driver is given a real ticket for a violation, like not signaling or wearing a seat belt?"

- Make this activity available as long as the children are "driving."

SOCIAL STUDIES

WHAT DOES A MECHANIC DO?

- To introduce this activity, read Flanagan's *Mr. Yee Fixes Cars,* Delafosse's *Cars and Trucks and Other Vehicles,* Leslie's *Let's Look Inside the Red Car: A Lift-the-Flap-Book* or Radford's *Harry at the Garage,* listed in the Children's Books section of this theme.

- Invite a car, truck, or bus mechanic to visit the class, or take a field trip to a garage and visit with a mechanic there.

- Ask the mechanic to show and talk about the tools he or she uses to repair vehicles, and to demonstrate how the tools are used and what they do.

- The children always enjoy seeing the mechanic take a ride on the "creeper," a piece of equipment used to slide under vehicles.

- Perhaps the mechanic can show the children what an engine looks like or what the car or truck looks like when raised on "the rack."

- After the visit, the children can write thank-you notes and draw or write about what they learned.

CHILDREN'S BOOKS

Barton, Byron. (2001). *My Car.* New York: Greenwillow.

Barton, Byron. (1998). *Trucks.* New York: HarperCollins.

Becker, Jim. (1994). *You Can Name 100 Trucks!* Illustrated by Randy Cherning. New York: Cartwheel Books.

Behrens, June. (1985). *I Can Be a Truck Driver.* Chicago: Children's Press.

Bingham, Caroline, and Deni Brown. (1995). *Fire Truck: And Other Emergency Machines.* New York: DK Publishers.

Bloom, Suzanne. (2001). *The Bus for Us.* Honesdale, PA: Boyds Mills Press.

Crews, Donald. (1997). *Truck.* Tupelo, MS: Tupelo Books.

Crews, Donald. (1993). *School Bus: For the Buses, the Riders, and the Watchers.* New York: Mulberry Books.

Deesing, Jim. (Ed.). (1997). *Busy Trucks: A Pop-Up Book.* Illustrated by Richard Stergulz. New York: Random House.

Delafosse, Claude. (Ed.). (1996). *Cars and Trucks and Other Vehicles.* New York: Cartwheel Books.

Dingus, Bill N. (1998). *Jeffery the Jeep.* Illustrated by Carol B. Murray. New York: Overmountain Press.

Eick, Jean. (1998). *Bulldozers.* New York: Raintree/Steck-Vaughn.

Flanagan, Romie. (1998). *Mr. Yee Fixes Cars.* Chicago: Children's Press.

Hoban, Tana. (1997). *Construction Zone.* New York: Greenwillow.

Kirk, Daniel. (1997). *Trash Trucks.* New York: Putnam.

Leslie, Amanda. (1997a). *Let's Look Inside the Red Car: A Lift-the-Flap Book.* (Rev. ed.). Cambridge, MA: Candlewick Press.

Leslie, Amanda. (1997b). *Let's Look Inside the Yellow Truck: A Lift-the-Flap Book.* (Rev. ed.). Cambridge, MA: Candlewick Press.

Osinski, Christine. (1998). *Riding the School Bus with Mrs. Kramer.* Illustrated by Alice K. Flanagan. Chicago: Children's Press.

Oxlade, Chris. (1997). *Car (Take It Apart).* Illustrated by Mike Grey. New York: Silver Burdett.

Pienkowski, Jan. (1997). *Trucks and Other Working Wheels.* Illustrated by Renee Jablow and Helen Balmer. New York: Dutton.

Piers, Helen. (1996). *Is There Room on the Bus?: An Around-the-World Counting Story.* Illustrated by Hannah Giffard. New York: Simon & Schuster.

Pomerantz, Charlotte. (1997). *How Many Trucks Can a Tow Truck Tow?* Illustrated by R. W. Alley. New York: Random House.

Pritchard, Louise. (1998). *Cars, Trucks, and Buses.* New York: DK Publishers.

Radford, Derek. (1997). *Harry at the Garage.* Cambridge, MA: Candlewick Press.

Raffi. (1998). *The Wheels on the Bus (Songs to Read).* Illustrated by Sylvie K. Wickstrom. New York: Crown.

Rockwell, Anne F. (1992). *Cars.* New York: Dutton.

Royston, Angela. (1999). *Truck Trouble.* New York: DK Publishing.

Royston, Angela. (1991). *Diggers and Dump Trucks.* New York: Little Simon.

Scarry, Richard. (1997). *Cars and Trucks and Things That Go.* New York: Golden Press.

Siebert, Diane. (1987). *Truck Song.* Illustrated by Byron Barton. New York: HarperTrophy.

Wilson-Max, Ken. (1997a). *Big Red Fire Truck.* New York: Cartwheel Books.

Wilson-Max, Ken. (1997b). *Little Green Tow Truck.* New York: Cartwheel Books.

Wilson-Max, Ken. (1996). *Big Yellow Taxi.* New York: Scholastic.

Ziefert, Harriet, and Andrea Baruffi. (1992). *Where Is Mommy's Truck?* New York: HarperCollins.

Family Letter (Toddler)

Dear Family,

We are starting to study transportation, and our theme is "Cars, Trucks, and Buses."
We will provide opportunities for the children to learn the following:

- Cars, trucks, and buses are forms of transportation that move people and things from place to place.
- There are many kinds, colors, and sizes of cars, trucks, and buses.
- A driver's license is required to operate these vehicles.
- All vehicles need to be inspected, repaired, and kept clean.
- Many occupations involve car, truck, and bus transportation.

We will be talking about the following:

- types of cars
- types of trucks
- types of buses
- parts of cars, trucks, and buses (inside)
- parts of cars, trucks, and buses (outside)
- safety

Try some of the following things at home with your child:

- Take your child with you when you go to the service station, go through the car wash, or have your car repaired.
- Talk to your child about the family car. For example, the type of car, the parts of the car, how you take care of the car, and the importance of wearing seat belts.
- When you and your child are in the car, look for stop signs, yield signs, traffic lights, and different types of cars, trucks, and buses.

Some opportunities for you to participate at school will include:

- Come join us when we cook truck stop pancakes, and stay to help us eat them.
  Date _____ Time _____
- Go with us on our field trip to the mechanic's garage.
  Date _____ Time _____

Our wish list for this theme includes:

    all sizes of cardboard boxes
    out-of-date (expired) license plates
    paper towel tubes
    car, truck, and bus magazines

Thanks!

TYPES OF AIRCRAFT

Commercial airplane   Private small craft
Helicopter   Glider
Blimp   Cargo plane
Mail plane   Small jet
Seaplane   Rescue care flight
Military aircraft

**THEME 29
Airplanes**

OCCUPATIONS
Pilots
Copilots
Flight engineers
Flight attendants
Air traffic controllers
Airline mechanics
Radio operators
Ticket agents
Baggage handlers
Ground crews

SAFETY
Traffic control tower
Runway lights
Wind socks
Radar
Safety checks
Safety standards of
Federal Aviation Administration (FAA)
Pilot's license
Seat belts

AIRPORT
Terminal
Moving Sidewalk
Tram
Concourse
TV screens with flight numbers
Runways
Baggage claim area
Security checkpoint
Ticket counters

THEME GOALS

To provide opportunities for children to learn the following:

▶ Airplanes are a form of transportation with wings. Airplanes move people and things from place to place.

▶ There are many kinds and sizes of airplanes.

▶ A pilot's license is required to operate an airplane.

▶ All airplanes have to be carefully inspected and repaired to keep them operating safely.

▶ Many occupations involve airplane transportation.

Children-Created Bulletin Board

This bulletin board is an interactive discovery area that will keep changing during the airplane theme. Encourage the children to think of things to put on the bulletin board, and to discover what you have added.

▶ Cover the board with a light-blue background.

▶ Title the board, "Transportation: Going on an Airplane."

▶ The top part of the board could represent the sky with cotton ball clouds, sun, or raindrops. Change the weather as the actual weather changes.

▶ The bottom half of the board can be the airport.

▶ Encourage the children to place planes all over the board. The planes can be ones that they draw, cut out, or make from craft sticks.

▶ As the theme progresses, the children can add the control tower, people, and anything else they want to contribute.

▶ Cut a large front and back cover for a suitcase-shaped book with a handle out of poster board.

▶ Attach this book below the bulletin board. Ask the children to paint or color the front and back covers.

▶ Using the cover for a pattern, cut pages for the book. Staple the pages together.

▶ Cover the staples by binding the book along the edge with clear mailing tape or duct tape.

▶ Let the children fill the pages with pictures, drawings, or written stories that fit inside of the "suitcase."

▶ Ask the children to number the pages.

VOCABULARY STARTERS

Let the children add words.

airline — a company that owns and operates airplanes.

airplane or **aircraft** — a vehicle that travels in the air.

airport — the place at which airplanes take off and land.

FAA — Federal Aviation Administration, which sets safety standards for airlines.

terminal — the building at the airport where people buy tickets and wait for airplanes.

wind sock — a sleevelike tube that indicates wind direction for the pilot.

LANGUAGE EXPERIENCES

**FINGERPLAY:
My Little Airplane**

This fingerplay may be recited as a poem or sung to the traditional tune of "I'm a Little Teapot."

▶ With infants and young toddlers, demonstrate the hand motions. They do not yet have the muscle control needed, but they do enjoy watching the motions and will try to do them with you.

My little airplane sits on the ground.
   (put one hand flat on floor or table)
I turn the propeller round and round.
   (with other hand, turn the propeller at tips of fingers)
I go down the runway, then up in the sky
   (move hand forward, then hand zooms straight up)
And loop-the-loop — just look at me fly!
   (hand does one or more loops over the head)
In a big circle I go round and round,
   (make a circle over the head)
Then tip the plane over and dive to the ground.
   (fingers point down, then hand zooms down)
I circle near the ground and get ready to land,
   (circle hand near floor or table)
Then come to a stop as nice as I can.
   (hand moves forward, then comes to a stop)

Philip Jackman

- -

**POEM:
"That's My Air-r-r-r-r-plane"**

This poem has a strong jazz beat and calls for lots of body movement and hand clapping. Each line has two strong beats. However, on the last line of each verse, "Air-r-r-r-r-plane" is dragged out for four beats.

Let me tell you 'bout an airplane,
   It's silver and blue.
It flies up high
   And down low too.
It has a smart pilot
   and a wonderful crew.
That's my air-r-r-r-r-plane.
We're going down to Houston,
   Then, what do you say,
We'll fly to Seattle,
   Then on to L.A.
We're having lots of fun
   Just flyin' around
In our air-r-r-r-r-plane.
Do you want to fly too?
   Well, hop right on.
We're headin' on up
   To Saskatchewan.
We'll visit cousin Bob
   Then we'll jump back on
Our big air-r-r-r-r-plane.
Look down there!
   We're comin' back home.
Man, I love to ramble
   And I love to roam,
But I've run out of tickets
   And I've run out of poem
'Bout my air-r-r-r-r-plane.

Philip Jackman

DRAMATIC PLAY

AIRPLANE TRIP

This activity encourages planning together as a family, sequencing, problem solving, sharing, taking turns, and creativity.

▶ Expand the home living/dramatic play center to three times its usual size. You can close another center to make room for this.

▶ Make one portion of the expanded area for the "planning stage" of the trip. The children can make lists of what to take and what they are going to do.

▶ Place maps or road atlases, travel brochures, and travel posters here.

▶ Take another part of the area and make it the "getting ready to go on a trip" space.

▶ In this section, place suitcases, clothes to pack, shoes, toy or discarded cameras, sunglasses, hats, scarves, backpacks, envelopes, picture postcards, and airplane tickets and passports the children have made.

- For younger children's luggage, use small suitcases, camera cases, briefcases, or backpacks.

- In another area, arrange chairs in rows with two or three chairs side by side to form seats in an airplane. To make seat belts, tie one end of the ribbons to the chairs, and put Velcro™ on the other ends to connect.

- The children take their seats, fasten their seat belts, put their luggage under their seats, and prepare for takeoff.

PUPPET PLAY

PILOT, COPILOT, AND FLIGHT ATTENDANT PUPPETS

- With the children's help, cut out cardboard circles 8 to 10 inches in diameter, or use large paper plates.

- For infants and young toddlers, draw large, simple facial features on the cardboard circles.

- Attach a stick, such as a paint stirring stick or tongue depressor, to make a puppet.

- Play peekaboo by placing the face in front of an adult's or a baby's face.

- Older children can create a set of pilot, copilot, and flight attendant stick puppet faces themselves.

- Have available construction paper, crayons, markers, scissors, and glue for the children to add hats and uniforms to their puppets.

- The children can play with their puppets in the dramatic play area or in other learning centers.

MUSIC

SONG: "I Love to Go Up in an Airplane"

Flying in an airliner is a great adventure for a small child and may be quite frightening at first. These original lyrics, sung to the folk tune "My Bonnie Lies Over the Ocean," try to create a friendly, reassuring feeling for young children.

I love to go up in an airplane,
I love to go up in the sky.
I love to go up in an airplane,
I feel like a bird when I fly.
Up, up, up, up, up in an airplane I'll fly, I'll fly,
Up, up, up, up, up in an airplane I'll fly.
  The airplane has powerful engines,
  They all make a great roaring sound.
  The wings lift us up like a feather,
  Oh, look, we are up off the ground!
  Up, up, up, up, up in our airplane we fly, we fly,
  Up, up, up, up, up in our airplane we fly.
The pilot's in charge of the airplane,
And knows how to make it fly high.
For helpers we have flight attendants,
They'll take care of us as we fly.
Up, up, up, up, up like a bird in the sky, the sky,
Up, up, up, up, up like a bird in the sky.

Philip Jackman

MOVEMENT

LANDING AT THE AIRPORT GAME

This simple game can be adapted to different age levels. It is based on the idea that to land an airplane safely, the pilot must put it down on the center of the runway and follow it straight to the terminal. The game is best when played with small groups of children.

- Clear an area on the floor on which you can, using masking tape, lay out a "runway" that is 2 feet wide and 6 to 12 feet long.

- To get the children used to the concept of flying and landing, ask them to hold out their arms and pretend to be planes flying, circling in, and landing on the masking tape runway.

- Children have to watch out for the other planes and line up to land one at a time.

- Then, show the children a ball, approximately two to five inches in diameter, that represents an "airplane."

- To help the child aim the airplane (ball), put down another piece of tape on the center of the runway.

- At the end of the runway, place a small open box, which represents the terminal, on its side, with the open side facing the pilot (child) trying to land.

- Each pilot rolls the airplane down the runway and tries to reach the terminal.

- If the ball fails to go into the box, the pilot must go to the end of the line while other pilots try to land.

- Play continues until all airplanes have arrived safely to the terminal, or until the children choose to stop playing.

- Tape or clip one piece of construction paper over each picture so the one-inch opening shows only a portion of the picture.

- Discuss with the children what it could be. Let them guess.

- Then lift the construction paper to show the children the picture.

- Show the children another covered picture, and play again.

- Have the children make some surprise pictures. They can play the guessing game with each other.

SENSORY ART

AIRPLANE EASEL PAINTING

This type of sensory art develops eye-hand coordination and provides a creative and an imaginative self-expression activity.

- An airplane is a big transportation vehicle.

- Painting airplanes on a large piece of newsprint or newspaper attached to an easel can help young children learn to express the concepts of form, shape, and size.

- Put two easels close together so children can socialize and share their ideas about their paintings.

LOOK AND SEE

- Collect several pictures from magazines, travel brochures, and newspapers that show airplanes and other types of transportation.

- Cut a one-inch hole shaped like a circle or square in several pieces of construction paper.

CREATIVE FOOD EXPERIENCES

AIRPLANE PRETZEL COOKIES

You will need the following:

1 1/2 sticks butter or margarine

1/2 cup sugar

1 teaspoon vanilla

1 3/4 cup enriched all-purpose flour

2 tablespoons milk

1 egg

1. Wash hands.

2. Combine butter or margarine, sugar, and vanilla. Beat until blended.

3. Add flour and milk. Chill dough.

4. Divide dough into four parts.

5. Divide each part into eight pieces, and place each piece on individual waxed paper pieces. Each child gets two pieces.

6. Roll each piece into a long strand about the width of a pencil.

7. Twist dough into an airplane-shaped pretzel.

8. Beat egg slightly, brush tops of pretzels, and sprinkle with sugar.

9. Bake 8 to 10 minutes at 350 degrees on a greased cookie sheet. Eat!

See theme 17 for a different pretzel recipe.

AIRPLANE PRETZEL COOKIES

Wash hands.

Combine 1 1/2 sticks butter, 1/2 cup sugar,

and 1 teaspoon vanilla. Beat until blended.

Add 1 3/4 cup flour and 2 tablespoons milk. Chill dough.

Divide dough into 4 parts. Then divide each part into

8 pieces. Roll each piece into a long strand and twist dough

into an airplane shaped pretzel. Beat 1 egg slightly, brush

tops of pretzels and sprinkle with sugar. Bake 8 to 10 minutes

at 350 degrees on a greased cookie sheet. EAT!

▶ Cut out three squares from each color of construction paper, with each square the same size as the blank grid squares. Draw each type of airplane on each color.

▶ Laminate the folder and all game pieces. Be sure to laminate the pocket *before* attaching it to the folder.

SCIENCE

MATH

AIRPLANE COLOR MATCHING GAME

PRESCHOOL-K

The object of this game is to match each of four types of airplane to each of three colors.

▶ You will need a standard file folder, a piece of tagboard for a "pocket," three sheets of construction paper, and sturdy game pieces made of cardboard or tagboard.

▶ On the right side of the open folder, draw a grid (see illustration).

▶ At the top, glue three squares of three different colors.

▶ Down the left side, draw four different types of airplanes. The illustration shows two types of propeller-driven airplanes and two types of jets with varying numbers of engines.

▶ In the middle of the left half of the folder, glue or tape a pocket made from a piece of tagboard.

MAKE A PARACHUTE

PRIMARY-GRADE

You may use a parachute for outdoor fun. The children may have seen parachutes at air shows or on television. In this activity, each child makes her own parachute, only with the "jumper" attached.

▶ Provide plenty of tissue paper squares, about the size of a paper napkin, string, ruler, scissors, wooden clothespins, crayons, and markers for the children.

▶ After the children draw designs on their tissue paper, they measure and cut four pieces of string 12 inches long.

▶ Next, tie a piece of string to each of the four corners of the tissue paper. Tie the loose ends together.

▶ The children may want to decorate the clothespin "jumper" before clipping it to the knotted strings.

▶ Then, it is time to "launch" the parachutes! Give the parachute, with "jumper" attached, a toss into the air. The parachute should billow open and float the "jumper" to the floor or ground. It may take a few tries for the children to accomplish this.

▶ As the children try out their parachutes, ask them questions about what is happening, such as: "Why

doesn't the parachute jumper come down faster?"
"If she didn't have a parachute, would she come
down faster?"

▶ Questions such as these deal with the interplay
between gravity and the wind resistance of falling
objects, important issues in aviation.

SOCIAL STUDIES

AIRPORTS AND AIRPLANES

▶ Arrange a field trip to an airport. Most airports and
airlines welcome children and teachers and have
orientations and tours to accommodate all ages.
(Large airports may have changed the rules and do
not offer field trips.)

▶ If the children do not get a chance to go to the airport, invite a pilot, copilot, or flight attendant to
visit the class. This will allow time for questions to
be answered and personal stories to be shared.

▶ Talk about going through a security checkpoint
with the older children.

▶ As a follow-up to the visits, talk about safety rules.
You and the children develop a list of safety rules
for airplane travel. Many airlines offer educational
packets for teachers.

▶ Suggestions to get the children started include:

Put everything you will need in carry-on luggage.

Bring safe, soft toys to play with.

Electronic games may interfere with an aircraft's
navigational system.

Stay in your seat. Wear your seat belt.

Pay attention to what the pilot and flight attendant
say. They are there to help us.

▶ Put the list and pictures that the children have
drawn on the bulletin board.

▶ With the children, build an airport with runways,
wind socks, a terminal, and streets. Place small airplanes and cars in their proper places at the gates
and parking lots. Add people.

▶ This type of activity will let you know what the
children have learned and whatever else they
want to know.

CHILDREN'S BOOKS

Barton, Byron. (1998). *Planes.* New York: HarperCollins.

Bellville, Cheryl. (1992). *The Airplane Book.* Minneapolis, MN: Carolrhoda Books.

Benjamin, Cynthia. (1997). *Working Hard with the Rescue Helicopter.* Illustrated by Steven J. Petruccio. New York: Cartwheel Books.

Benjamin, Cynthia. (1994). *I Am a Pilot.* Illustrated by Miriam Sagastis. New York: Barron's.

Berger, Melvin. (1996). *How Do Airplanes Fly?* Illustrated by Paul Babb. New York: Hambleton-Hill.

Bingham, Caroline. (Ed.). (2001). *Big Book of Airplanes.* New York: DK Publishing.

Blackburn, Ken, and Jeff Lammers. (1996). *Kids' Paper Airplane Book.* New York: Workman.

Bursik, Rose. (1994). *Amelia's Fantastic Flight.* New York: Henry Holt.

Cooper, Jason. (1992). *Airports: Great Places to Visit.* Vero Beach, FL: Rourke Books.

Evans, Frank. (1994). *All Aboard Airplanes.* Illustrated by George Guzzi. New York: Price Stern Sloan.

Felix, Monique. (1995a). *The Plane.* New York: Creative Education.

Felix, Monique. (1995b). *The Wind.* New York: Creative Education.

Kalman, Bobbie. (1995). *Wings, Wheels, and Sails.* New York: Crabtree.

Maynard, Christopher, and Deni Brown. (1995). *Airplane and Other Airport Machines.* New York: DK Publishers.

Pallotta, Jerry, and Fred Stillwell. (1997). *The Airplane Alphabet Book.* Illustrated by Rob Bolster. Watertown, MA: Charlesbridge.

Petty, Kate. (1998). *Some Planes Hover (I Didn't Know That).* Illustrated by Ross Walton and Jo Moore. New York: Copper Beech Books.

Robison, Fay. (1997). *Pilots Fly Planes.* New York: The Child's World.

Rockwell, Anne F. (1998). *I Fly.* Illustrated by Annette Cable. New York: Dragonfly.

Scarry, Huck. (2001). *Richard Scarry's A Day at the Airport.* New York: Random House.

Siebert, Diane. (1995). *Plane Song.* Illustrated by Vincent Nasta. New York: HarperTrophy.

Stott, Dorothy. (1995). *Up, Up in a Plane!* New York: Grosset & Dunlap.

Tucker, Sian. (1993). *The Little Plane.* (Board Book). New York: Little Simon.

Wilson-Max, Ken. (1995). *Little Red Plane.* New York: Cartwheel Books.

Family Letter (Primary Grade)

Dear Family,

We are studying transportation, and we are beginning our theme "Airplanes." The children will learn the following:

- *Airplanes are a form of transportation with wings. Airplanes move people and things from place to place.*
- *There are many kinds and sizes of airplanes.*
- *A pilot's license is required to operate an airplane. All airplanes have to be carefully inspected and repaired to keep them operating safely.*
- *Many occupations involve airplane transportation.*

We will be talking about the following:

- *types of aircraft*
- *occupations*
- *airports and airport regulations*
- *safety*

Some things to do at home with your child include:

- *Point things out to your child, and talk about them when you take someone to or pick someone up from the airport.*
- *Read books about aviation, aircraft, and careers in airplane transportation.*
- *Talk to your child about all of the planning it takes to prepare for a trip on an airplane.*

Some opportunities for you to participate in at school include:

- *Go with us on our field trip to the airport.*
  Date _____ Time _____
- *Let us know if any family member or friend is a pilot, copilot, or flight attendant, or if he or she works in any capacity for an airline or airport. We would like to invite this person to visit the classroom and talk to the children.*

Our wish list items for this theme include:

maps
used/cancelled airplane tickets
small suitcases
file folders
clothespins

Thanks!

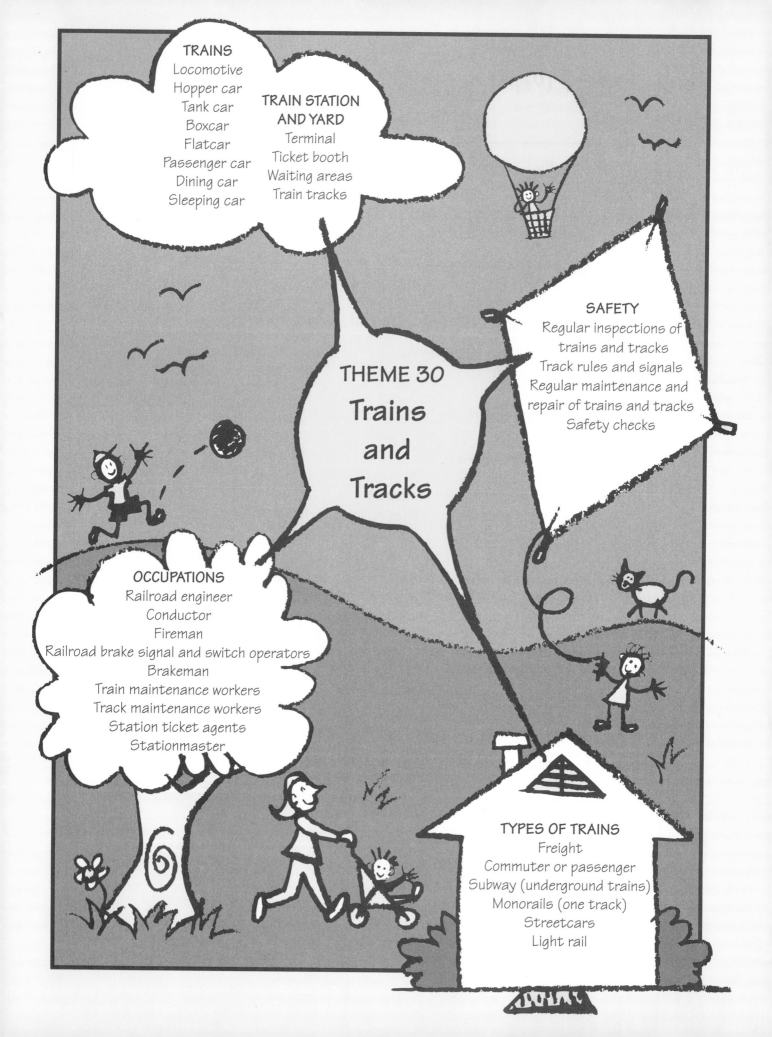

THEME GOALS

To provide opportunities for children to learn the following:

▶ A train is a form of transportation that moves people and things from place to place on tracks.

▶ There are different kinds of trains.

▶ Some trains run on tracks above ground, and some run on tracks below ground.

▶ All trains have to be inspected and repaired to operate safely.

▶ Many occupations involve train transportation.

Children-Created Bulletin Board

This bulletin board offers you and the children an opportunity to explore the world of trains, through our theme "Trains and Tracks." This should be a cooperative project in which each child is involved in adding to and changing the bulletin board throughout the theme.

▶ You and the children make a train with one car for each child and you, plus a locomotive (engine).

▶ Extend the train and tracks, made from craft sticks, outside the border of the bulletin board.

▶ Have the train move from left to right, consistent with how we read.

▶ Encourage the children to cut out, draw, or paint a picture, or to write something to put in their train car.

▶ The bulletin board should keep changing throughout the theme. The children will come up with additions as they continue to explore and discover trains and tracks.

VOCABULARY STARTERS

Let the children add words.

brakeman — a person who operates and repairs the brake systems of trains.

conductor — a person responsible for the general safety of passengers, crew, and freight aboard the train.

fireman — a person who assists in the safe operation of the train and is the assistant engineer.

throttle — the lever that controls the speed of the train.

train engineer — a person responsible for safely driving the train.

train or rail yard — an area where trains are put together, safety checked, fueled, and switched to the right track.

Zooming by the crossroads,
   (one hand "zooms" across chest)
Wheels go "clackety clack."
   (hands roll over one another)
Soon it's at the station,
   (pull back the "brake" motion)
Loading up the cars,
   (bend down and pick up "crates")
Some have bikes or roller skates,
Some hold candy bars.
When the cars are hitched on,
   (each child gets in train formation by putting his
   hands on the waist of the child in front of him)
The brakeman says okay,
The engineer blows "toot-toot"
And we're on our way!

Author unknown

LANGUAGE EXPERIENCES

ACTION POEM: "Choo-Choo Train"

When sharing this poem with infants, it is helpful for you to move the babies' arms and hands as you sing.

Here's the choo-choo train.
   (bend arms at elbows)
Puffing down the track.
   (rotate forearms in rhythm)
Now it's going forward,
Now it's going back.
Now the bell is ringing.
   (pull bell with closed fist)
Ding, ding, ding.
Now the whistle blows.
   (hold hands around the mouth)
Wooo-wooo-wooo!
It makes a lot of noise
Everywhere it goes!
   (cover ears with hands)

Author unknown

ACTION POEM: "Here Comes the Freight Train"

Here comes the freight train
   (move arms back and forth)
Chugging down the track,
   (make "chugging" sounds)

CLOTHESLINE STORY

This activity helps develop communication and sequencing skills and left-to-right progression.

▶ Read to the children Piper's *The Little Engine That Could,* listed in the Children's Books section of this theme.

▶ With toddlers, retell the story with flannelboard characters. They love interacting with the engine that keeps saying "I think I can — I think I can."

▶ With older children, retell the story using the characters the children have drawn and cut out. Laminate these figures.

▶ When everyone is ready to tell the story, ask two children to hold a nylon cord, approximately 36 inches long, to form a clothesline.

▶ As the story is being told, other children pin the characters on the clothesline with the clothespins, beginning on the left and proceeding to the right.

▶ Make the materials available to the children so that they can read the story and put the characters on the clothesline whenever they choose.

DRAMATIC PLAY

RIDE THE RAILS

▶ Visit an appliance or an electronic equipment store, or check with families to see if they have a large packing carton to make into a train car.

▶ Put the box in the dramatic play area.

▶ With the children's help, tape a second, smaller box to the front of the big box to represent the engine.

▶ Some of the children can paint and decorate the train car and engine.

▶ Other children can color paper plates to tape along the sides of the box to make the wheels. Older ones can punch small holes in the box, insert large brads, and attach the paper plates to keep them firmly on the box.

▶ A paper towel tube can be taped inside the front of the large box for the throttle.

▶ If the children want to add boxes to make the train longer, collect other boxes and tape them to the big box. The children will decide what else is needed.

▶ To keep the train from interfering with other classroom activities, outline train tracks on the floor with masking tape. The train should stay on the tracks.

▶ Put travel posters all around the room.

▶ Add a train whistle recording or a bell to create a more realistic train effect.

▶ The children can take along a snack to eat as they travel down the tracks (see the Creative Food Experiences section of this theme).

▶ Enjoy riding the rails!

PUPPET PLAY

PUPPET TRAVEL

▶ Select one of your favorite puppet characters. It can be made out of a sock, sack, paper plates, kitchen gadgets, or other objects. Refer to Puppet Play sections in other themes for suggestions.

▶ Introduce the puppet as a character who is going on a trip and needs the children's help.

▶ In a large bag, put in small toy vehicles, such as train cars, airplanes, helicopters, cars, trucks, boats, and buses.

▶ The puppet tells the children that he is going to visit his grandmother (let the children help you decide where), and that he does not have a way to get there.

▶ Ask a child to reach into the bag to select a vehicle that will help the puppet get to his destination. The children keep selecting objects from the bag until it is empty.

▶ In order for the puppet to make a decision, the toy vehicles have to be sorted according to which ones are suitable for travel by air, land, or water. The children sort them.

▶ Finally, the puppet makes a decision. He will go by train, because that is what the children are studying.

▶ Make the puppet and all of the toys available for the children to play with again.

MUSIC

WE'RE GOING TO TAKE A TRAIN RIDE

▶ Let's take a train ride! The song starts very slowly, just the way a train starts, then it gets faster and faster, finally slowing down until it stops.

▶ The lyrics are original, and the tune is the traditional song "Skip to My Lou," which is rhythmic and easily remembered.

▶ The song also suggests trainlike movements, with the children starting slowly, speeding up, and finally slowing to a stop.

Get on the train, hear the whistle blow.
Get on the train, hear the whistle blow.
Get on the train, hear the whistle blow.
We're going to take a train ride.
   The train starts to move, it's going kind of slow.
   The train starts to move, it's going kind of slow.
   The train starts to move, it's going kind of slow.
   We're starting to take a train ride.
The wheels are turning, we're picking up speed.
The wheels are turning, we're picking up speed.
The wheels are turning, we're picking up speed.
We're moving along on our train ride.
   Look at us go, we're going pretty fast.
   Look at us go, we're going pretty fast.
   Look at us go, we're going pretty fast.
   We have lots of fun on our train ride.

The wheels are slowing, we'll be there soon.
The wheels are slowing, we'll be there soon.
The wheels are slowing, we'll be there soon.
We'll soon be finished with our train ride.
  Here comes the station, the whistle goes "toot."
  Here comes the station, the whistle goes "toot."
  Here comes the station, the whistle goes "toot."
  We're almost finished with our train ride.
The train is stopping, we're almost there.
The train is stopping, we're almost there.
The train is stopping, we're almost there.
We've come to the end of our train ride.

Philip Jackman

MOVEMENT

LOOSE CABOOSE

This is a fun game to play outside.

▶ One of the children is the "loose caboose."

▶ The rest of the children divide into trains with three cars each.

▶ The first player in the train is the engine.

▶ The other players can choose what they want to be, such as a hopper car, flatcar, boxcar, or tank car.

▶ The object is for the loose caboose to try to attach to a train at the end.

▶ When all the children are aboard, the "trains" chug around the train yard making sounds.

▶ The trains dodge and turn to keep away from the caboose.

▶ When the caboose attaches to a train, the engine of that train becomes the new loose caboose.

Note: Modern freight trains no longer have a caboose (last car on a train), but this is still a fun game to play.

SENSORY ART

SHOE BOX TRAINS

▶ Have younger children color shoe boxes.

▶ Add two wheels on each side of the shoe box. Make the wheels with corrugated cardboard circles or small paper plates, and attach them with brads.

▶ String the boxes together.

▶ Add a string with a large bead tied securely onto the end so the children can pull their train.

▶ Older children can make a flatcar by using the bottom of the shoe box and attaching wheels to it.

▶ Children can put small cars, blocks, or anything they choose to fill up the flatcar.

I SPY A TRAIN

▶ Read and look closely at Micklethwait's *I Spy a Freight Train: Transportation in Art,* listed in the Children's Books section of this theme.

▶ As the author says, "You don't need to have any knowledge of art to introduce a child to a painting. . . . All that is important is there in front of you in the picture, waiting to be discovered."

▶ Gather books of paintings from the library and postcards of paintings from a local art store or museum.

▶ Make these into a display that invites the children to look for details in each painting.

▶ For this theme, include many paintings representing transportation, especially trains. For example, Mary Cassatt's *In the Omnibus (The Tramway),* Vincent Van Gogh's *The Langlois Drawbridge,* Ernst Thoms's *Train,* and Claude Monet's *Gare Saint-Lazare, Arrival of a Train.*

▶ If possible, follow up this activity with a visit to the art museum or gallery with the children.

CREATIVE FOOD EXPERIENCES

NUTRITIOUS SNACK FOR BABY

Before you prepare this snack, check with the family to be sure the baby is not allergic to any of the ingredients. This can be used by families when traveling with their infant.

You will need the following:

  2 teaspoons low-fat plain yogurt
  3 teaspoons any fruit baby food
  2 teaspoons rice cereal (you can substitute barley or oatmeal cereal)

Mix well and serve!

TRAIN TAKE-ALONG SNACK MIX

You will need the following:

> 1 1/2 tablespoons of butter or margarine
> 2 1/2 tablespoons of honey
> 1 cup of Cheerios
> 1 cup of Crispix cereal
> 1/2 cup of peanuts (optional)
> 1/2 cup of thin stick pretzels, broken in half
> 1/2 cup of raisins
> 1 cup of chocolate mini-baking bits

1. Wash hands.
2. Let the children measure and put ingredients in individual bowls, ready for you to pour into a hot skillet.
3. In large skillet, over low heat, melt butter.
4. Add honey until blended. Add cereal, nuts, pretzels, and raisins, stirring until all pieces are evenly coated.
5. Continue cooking over low heat about 10 minutes, stirring often.

6. Remove from heat, and immediately place on waxed paper or a cookie sheet to cool.
7. Add chocolate mini-baking bits.
8. Store in a tightly covered container.

MATH

WHICH FREIGHT TRAIN CAR IS MISSING?

This is an activity to do with small groups of children or one-on-one with the teacher.

▶ Make individual *freight train* car drawings on index cards, and laminate the cards. For examples of these cars, see the illustration.

▶ You also can play the same game by using small toy train cars.

▶ Put out some of the cards or toy trains on a tray.

▶ For younger children, use fewer items.

▶ Ask the children playing the game to look at each item and name it.

▶ Have the children close their eyes while you take an object away.

▶ Ask the children to guess which item is missing.

▶ Continue, and take several of the train cars away.

▶ Make the game available for the children in the math center.

LOCOMOTIVE: The engine that pulls the train. The engineer, who drives the train, rides near the front.

HOPPER CAR: It carries the type of freight that has to be poured into it, such as coal, sand, or wheat. It is open on top.

FLATCAR: It carries very large or long things, such as logs, steel beams, or machinery. Loads have to be tied down.

BOXCAR: It carries all kinds of smaller things, such as washing machines, television sets, toys, paper products, and food.

TANK CAR: It carries liquid freight, such as oil, gasoline, and chemicals.

CABOOSE: It is the last car on a Freight Train. Inside it are offices and beds for the train crew.

TRAIN TAKE-ALONG SNACK MIX

Wash hands.

Melt 1 1/2 tablespoons butter -- add 2 1/2 tablespoons honey

until blended. Add 1 cup Cheerios, 1 cup Crispix cereal,

1/2 cup peanuts (optional), 1/2 cup broken stick pretzels, and

1/2 cup raisins stirring until all pieces are evenly coated.

Continue cooking over low heat about 10 minutes, stirring

often. Remove from heat and immediately place on wax paper

or cookie sheet to cool. Add 1 cup chocolate covered mini

baking bits. YUMMY!

SCIENCE

MAKE A MINIATURE RAILROAD

All you need to make a classroom railroad is a smooth, flat, rigid surface, some regular craft sticks, a marble, and a bottle of rubber cement. This kind of activity helps children develop skills relating to cause and effect and work together to solve a problem.

▶ At one end of your flat surface, which can be cardboard, plywood, or foam core, the children start "laying tracks." It is helpful for you to guide the younger ones. They run two parallel lines of craft sticks end to end, separated by 1/2 inch.

▶ Put rubber cement at each end of each stick to hold it in place.

▶ As the children lay the track, they should gently curve it first in one direction, then in another, in an "S" pattern until they reach the far edge of the cardboard, plywood, or foam board.

▶ When the track is done, slightly elevate the edge where the children began.

▶ Put the marble between the two tracks, and start it rolling downhill.

▶ If the surface is not tilted enough, the marble may stop rolling. Tilt it too much, and the "train" jumps the track.

▶ Children need to experiment to get just the right tilt.

▶ If the sticks are angled too sharply on the curves, the train may keep stopping. Children may need to redesign the curve to make it less angular.

▶ Talk to the children about how this experiment in making a railroad presents the same problems that real railroads have: Trains must be careful not to go too fast on curves, or they will jump the tracks; the people who lay the tracks must not make curves so sharp that trains have difficulty going around them.

SOCIAL STUDIES

TRAINS IN OUR COMMUNITY

▶ Call the local train information center in your community to check on the times that trains arrive at your train station.

▶ Take the children on a field trip to see the trains.

▶ Many train stations have a tour and an orientation session for children. If you live in a city with light rail transportation or subways, the children probably already are familiar with trains and tracks.

▶ Discuss the safety equipment located at train crossings within a city and its outlying areas. **Signal arms** are found at train crossings on very busy roads. These are lowered to block the road so cars cannot cross the tracks when a train passes by. **Blinking lights** are seen where train crossings and crowded roads intersect. The lights blink on and off to warn cars that a train is coming. **Warning signs** are placed at train crossings on roads that are not heavily traveled. The signs tell drivers to stop and look both ways to see if a train is coming before crossing the tracks.

▶ You also can invite a community or family member who is a train enthusiast to show the children some of his or her electric trains. These miniature train cars help children identify the individual cars and learn even more about trains.

CHILDREN'S BOOKS

Awdry, W. (1994). *New Tracks for Thomas.* Illustrated by Owain Bell. New York: Random House.

Aylesworth, Jim. (1995). *Country Crossing.* Illustrated by Ted Rand. New York: Aladdin.

Barton, Byron. (1998). *Trains.* New York: HarperCollins.

Brown, Margaret Wise. (2001). *Two Little Trains.* Illustrated by Leo and Dianne Dillon. New York: HarperCollins.

Burton, Virginia Lee. (1997). *Maybelle the Cable Car.* Boston: Houghton Mifflin.

Chall, Marsha Wilson. (2003). *Prairie Train.* Illustrated by John Thompson. New York: HarperCollins.

Crampton, Gertrude. (1997). *Tootle.* Illustrated by Tibor Gergely. New York: Golden Books.

Crebbin, June. (1996). *The Train Ride.* Illustrated by Stephen Lambert. Cambridge, MA: Candlewick Press.

Crews, Donald. (2001). *Inside Freight Trains.* New York: William Morrow.

Crews, Donald. (1992). *Freight Train.* New York: Mulberry.

Demarest, Chris L. (1997). *All Aboard!* San Diego: Harcourt.

Galef, David. (1996). *Tracks.* Illustrated by Tedd Arnold. New York: Morrow.

Gerver, Jane E. (2001). *A Crack in the Track.* New York: Random House.

Gibbons, Gail. (1988). *Trains.* New York: Holiday House.

Jeunesse, Gallimard. (1998). *Trains (First Discovery Book).* Illustrated by James Prunier and Wendy Barish. New York: Scholastic.

Johnston, Tony. (1996). *How Many Miles to Jacksonville?* Illustrated by Bart Forbes. New York: Putnam.

Magee, Doug. (1994). *All Aboard ABC.* New York: Puffin.

McMillan, Bruce. (1995). *Grandfather's Trolley.* Cambridge, MA: Candlewick Press.

Merriam, Eve. (1994). *Train Leaves the Station.* Illustrated by Dale Gottlieb. New York: Henry Holt.

Micklethwait, Lucy. (1996). *I Spy a Freight Train: Transportation in Art.* New York: Greenwillow.

Mills, Claudia. (1998). *Gus and Grandpa Ride the Train.* Illustrated by Catherine Stock. New York: Farrar, Straus & Giroux.

Petty, Kate. (1997). *Some Trains Run on Water: And Other Amazing Facts about Rail Transport (I Didn't Know That).* Illustrated by Ross Walton and Jo Moore. New York: Millbrook Press.

Pinkney, Gloria Jean. (1994). *The Sunday Outing.* New York: Dial.

Piper, Watty. (1978). *The Little Engine That Could.* Illustrated by George and Doris Hauman. New York: Grosset & Dunlap.

Quattlebaum, Mary. (1997). *Underground Train.* Illustrated by Cat Bowman Smith. New York: Bantam.

Royston, Angela. (1992). *Eye Openers — Trains.* New York: Little Simon.

Scarry, Richard. (1995). *Richard Scarry's Longest Book Ever/8 Feet of Lift-the-Flap Fun!* New York: Little Simon.

Sturges, Phileman. (2001). *I Love Trains!* Illustrated by Shari Halpern. New York: HarperCollins.

Suen, Anastasia. (1998). *Window Music.* Illustrated by Wade Zahares. New York: Viking.

Torres, Leyla. (1997). *Gorrion Del Metro/Subway Sparrow.* New York: Farrar, Straus & Giroux.

Voake, Charlotte. (1998). *Here Comes the Train.* Cambridge, MA: Candlewick Press.

Welply, Michael, and Dawn Bentley. (1998). *Choo-Choo Charlie: The Littletown Train.* New York: Piggy Toes Press.

Williams, Sam. (2001). *Long Train: 101 Cars on the Track.* Illustrated by Ken Wilson-Max. New York: Cartwheel Books.

Wilson-Max, Ken. (1996). *Big Blue Engine.* New York: Cartwheel Books.

Family Letter (Preschool)

Dear Family,

We will be starting our new theme, "Trains and Tracks," this week. We will provide opportunities for the children to learn the following:

- A train is a form of transportation that moves people and things from place to place on tracks.
- There are different kinds of trains.
- Some trains run on tracks above ground, and some run on tracks below ground.
- All trains have to be inspected and repaired to operate safely.
- Many occupations involve train transportation.

We will be talking about the following:

- types of trains
- occupations
- train station and yard
- safety

Some things to do at home with your child include:

- Talk about the train tracks and trains you see around your community. Ask your child what she or he sees, which type of train is her or his favorite, and why.
- Talk about the blinking lights, warning signs, and signal arms at each train crossing in the community. This is a perfect time to talk about car safety too.
- Visit the library, and check out books to read to your child about trains and tracks.

Family participation opportunities at school will include:

- Let us know of a family member or friend who is an electric train enthusiast. We would like to invite this person to visit the class, show some of the trains, and talk to the children.
- Come visit our classroom to see all of the activities we are doing as we learn about trains and tracks.
    Date _____ Time _____

Our wish list for this theme includes:
    clothespins
    shoe boxes
    cardboard boxes
    marbles
    paper towel tubes

Thanks!

Appendix A: Music (Full Size)

"Name Song"

Bea Wolf

_____ , that's my name; that's what peo- ple call me.
(your)   (you).

_____ , _____ ! That's a ver- y fine name, in- deed!

"It's So Good to Be with Friends"

Jo Eklof

It's so good to be with friends in

an - y kind of wea - ther. We could go for a walk or

sit and talk. We love to be to - geth - er.

Additional verses:

It's fun in the snow with friends in cold and snowy weather.
We could shiver and play all through the day. We love to be together.

It's fun to swim with friends in warm and sunny weather.
We could splash and play all through the day. We love to be together.

www.missjo.com

"I Am a Member of My Family"

Jo Eklof

I am a mem-ber of my fam - i - ly. We live to - geth - er

peace - ful - ly. We help each oth - er yes - sir - ree!

I am a mem ber of my fam - i - ly.

Additional verses:
We love each other . . .
We're kind to each other . . .
We laugh with each other . . .
We take care of each other . . .
We play with each other . . .
We smile at each other . . .
We hug each other . . .
We cheer up each other . . .

"I Have Two Ears"

Jo Eklof

"Brr, It's Cold Today!"

Jo Eklof

"When I Wear Red"

Jo Eklof

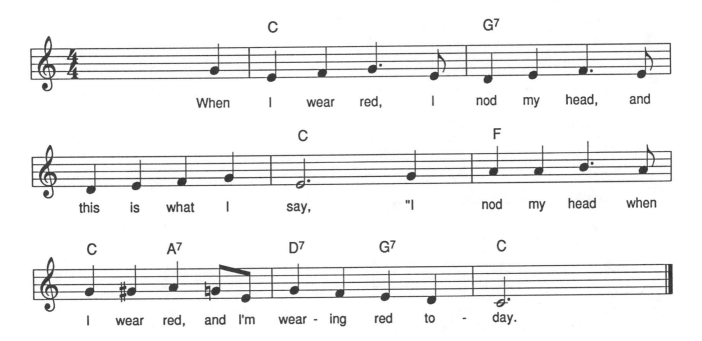

When I wear red, I nod my head, and this is what I say, "I nod my head when I wear red, and I'm wear-ing red to - day.

Additional verses:

Have children make up what action to do with other colors, for instance, "When I wear green, I always lean.

"The Frog Song"

Jo Eklof

Late last night while you and I were in our beds a - sleep, the

frogs came out and sang this song, "rib - bit   rib - bit

rib - bit   rib - bit   rib - bit ba - reep!"

"My Kitty Just Says 'Meow'"

Jo Eklof

The bird in the tree says, "cheep cheep cheep. The dog says, "bow wow wow." The duck in the pond says, "quack quack quack." my kit-ty just says, "meow."

Additional verses:

"Cocka doodle doo," says the rooster. "Oink oink," says the sow.
"He haw he haw," hear the donkey say. My kitty just says, "meow."

"Baa," says the fluffy lamb. "Moo," says the cow.
"Buzz buzz buzz," says the honey bee. My kitty just says, "meow."

"How I Wish I Had a Little Dog"

Jo Eklof

Second verse:
How I wish I had a little doggie brown and white.
We'd romp around the yard all day. He'd sleep near me at night.
We'd do many things together, life would seem just right.
How I wish I had a little dog. How I wish I had a little dog.

"I Like to Look at Bugs"

Jo Eklof

When the sun comes out and the win-ter goes a-way, I

like to go out on a nice warm day. I like to run and I

like to play and I like to look at bugs. (Do they

jig-gle and jump? Yes, they jig-gle and jump. Do they wig-gle and bump? Yes, they

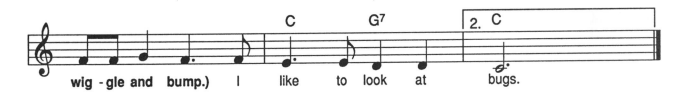

wig-gle and bump.) I like to look at bugs.

Additional verses:

Do they crawl and creep? Do they like to leap?

Do they hop and fly? Way up in the sky?

"Birds on the Rooftop"

Bea Wolf

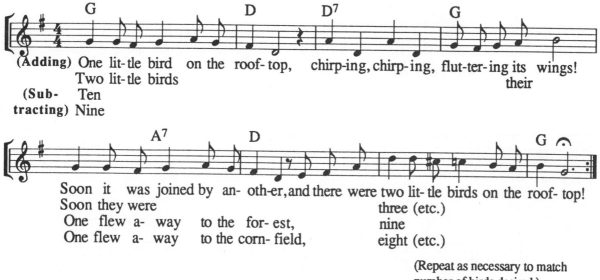

(Adding) One lit-tle bird on the roof-top, chirp-ing, chirp-ing, flut-ter-ing its wings!
Two lit-tle birds   their
(Sub- Ten
tracting) Nine

Soon it was joined by an-oth-er, and there were two lit-tle birds on the roof-top!
Soon they were   three (etc.)
One flew a-way   to the for-est,   nine
One flew a-way   to the corn-field,   eight (etc.)

(Repeat as necessary to match
number of birds desired.)

"I Wish That I Could See a Dinosaur"

Jo Eklof

Second verse:

But I will never see a dinosaur, for dinosaurs aren't living any more.
So I'll have to read and look at their pictures in a book,
For I will never see a dinosaur, but I wish that I could see a dinosaur.

www.missjo.com

Appendix B: Developmentally Appropriate Materials and Supplies for Curriculum Areas

Additional materials and supplies are listed in many of the *Theme Activities* throughout this book. You will add other items as well. Some of the items listed are not appropriate for infants and toddlers; be cautious in what you select.

LITERACY AND LANGUAGE ARTS

The following materials and supplies offer children a print-rich environment that includes things to write with, write on, and write in:

▶ all types of books that are displayed attractively and within easy access of the children

▶ books made and written by individual children

▶ calendars

▶ carbon paper

▶ cardboard and poster board

▶ child dictation, writing, and drawings displayed

▶ children's names displayed

▶ crayons of various sizes, colors, and thicknesses

▶ date stamp and pad

▶ envelopes

▶ folders and notebooks

▶ graph paper

▶ index cards

▶ labels on materials, supplies, and equipment, and in learning centers throughout the classroom and outdoors

▶ large and individual chalkboards, dry-erase boards, and magic slates

▶ magnetic letters and numbers

▶ maps and globes

▶ markers of various colors, fine tipped, thick tipped, washable, permanent, and scented

▶ message boards

▶ paper of various sizes, colors, and textures; lined and unlined paper, drawing paper; construction paper; scraps

▶ paper clips, hole punch, and stickers

▶ pencil sharpener

▶ pencils, pens, and chalk of various sizes and colors

▶ Post-its™

▶ rebus, symbol, and alphabet charts

▶ rulers, tape, glue, scissors, stapler, and stickers

▶ stationery and note pads

▶ typewriters and computers

DRAMATIC PLAY AND PUPPETS

Play is the natural language of children, and having available the following materials and supplies will enable young children to create many learning experiences as they play:

▶ artificial fruit and vegetables, grocery boxes, telephones, coupons, and shopping lists

▶ children's books

▶ boxes, buttons, wiggly eyes, and clothespins

▶ cloth scraps of felt, lace, and cotton; towels and washcloths

▶ cotton balls, steel wool, pipe cleaners, corks, and hair curlers

▶ craft sticks, tongue depressors, dowel rods, paper towel rolls, ice cream sticks, and straws

▶ crayons, markers, pencils, pens, and paints

▶ doll buggies, wagons, wheelbarrows, and trucks

▶ dolls and doll-size furniture

▶ dress-up clothes with shoes, gloves, purses, and community helpers clothing items

▶ empty food boxes, shopping bags, and lunch boxes

▶ flannelboard with flannelboard pieces

- gloves, mittens, and hot pad mitts
- paper plates, paper sacks, and paper cups
- pots, pans, lids, boxes, plastic cups, bowls, and baskets
- multicultural puppets and small dolls to dress
- scissors, glue, gummed labels and stickers, staples, stapler, and rulers
- socks — especially those that will fit a child's hand, plus soccer socks for adult-size puppets
- sturdy boxes with lids for prop boxes
- Styrofoam™ balls and scraps
- toy cash register, calculator, play money, price tags, and sales slip pads
- yarn, string, ribbons, and shoelaces

MUSIC AND MOVEMENT

Using the body and the voice along with the following materials and supplies can easily offer many opportunities for creative movement and music activities:

- balls and beanbags
- books to look at or read while listening to tapes and CDs
- boxes, especially large appliance boxes
- coffee can- and oatmeal-box drums, paper bags, pan lids, aluminum pie pans, and sandpaper-covered wooden blocks
- headphones and a jack box designed for several children to listen at one time
- hoops
- parachute or old sheets and lightweight blankets
- scarves, streamers, and ribbons
- stuffed animals or rag dolls as dance partners
- tambourines, wooden maracas, wood blocks, xylophone, rhythm sticks, drums, finger cymbals, bells, ankle bells, triangles, and rain sticks
- tape player, CD player, and a wide variety of tapes and CDs, including story tapes
- tape recorder with microphone to record children singing, individually or in a group
- tumbling mats and lightweight vinyl shapes
- tunnels
- wind chimes, gongs, and music boxes

SENSORY ART

Young children learn through their five senses, and the following materials and supplies will give them multiple opportunities to do this:

- aprons, smocks, sponges, and paper towels
- blocks and boxes
- brushes of all sizes
- construction paper, tissue paper, corrugated paper, white butcher paper, brown wrapping paper, foil, gift wrapping paper, fabric scraps, old greeting cards, wallpaper samples, newspapers, and catalogs
- cooking utensils, bowls, measuring cups and spoons, mixing spoons, graters, peelers, wire whisks, eggbeaters, funnel, tongs, colander, sifter, cookie cutters, muffin tins, waxed paper, foil, and plastic wrap
- easels
- fingerpaints, tempera, chalk, crayons, markers, pencils, pens, and watercolors
- gadget or object painting with corks, combs, string, and cookie cutters
- new and unused Styrofoam™ trays
- play dough and clay
- sand and water table, outdoor sandbox
- scissors, paper clips, brads, rubber bands, staples, stapler, and rulers
- texture board with matching pieces
- various sizes of paper plates, paper cups, index cards, and box lids
- wading pool, dishpan, and infant tub
- washed gravel, seashells, Styrofoam™ pieces, and birdseed
- water, sand, and mud
- white glue, flour and water paste, glue sticks, masking tape, and clear tape
- woodworking bench, hammers, nails, soft wood, sandpaper, glue, clamps, and braces and bits

COOKING AND CREATIVE FOOD EXPERIENCES

Plan to cook on days when another adult can help you. Supervision is critical to ensure the children's safety. Creative food experiences involve young children in the cooking process from planning to cleanup and provide an opportunity for the children to use real kitchen utensils and equipment. A list of suggested supplies follows:

▶ airtight containers with lids
▶ bread loaf pans, cake pans, and muffin tins
▶ can opener
▶ colander and funnel
▶ cookie cutters and cookie sheets
▶ electric blender and/or mixer
▶ electric wok
▶ hand eggbeater
▶ hand-squeezing orange juicer
▶ hot pads and mitts or holders
▶ hot plate or electric skillet
▶ individual bowls for children
▶ measuring cups and spoons
▶ paper towels and paper napkins
▶ pastry brushes
▶ plastic cutting boards or trays
▶ plastic grater
▶ plastic, serrated knives (for younger children)
▶ potato masher
▶ rolling pins
▶ rubber spatula
▶ serrated steel knives and kitchen shears (for older children)
▶ sifter
▶ slotted spoons and tongs
▶ smocks or aprons (not the ones used in the art center)
▶ sponges used just for cooking activities
▶ timer
▶ toaster oven
▶ unbreakable nesting bowls for mixing
▶ unbreakable pitchers
▶ vegetable peelers
▶ waxed paper, foil, plastic wrap, and plastic bags
▶ wire whisks
▶ wooden stirring spoons

Basic ingredients to keep on hand include:

▶ baking soda and baking powder
▶ cornmeal and cornstarch
▶ flour
▶ honey
▶ milk
▶ oil
▶ salt
▶ sugar
▶ vinegar

MATH

The following materials offer children many ways to develop their understanding of math concepts, such as classification, seriation, patterning, measurement, and numbers:

▶ bingo cards, lotto cards, board games, and checkers
▶ calendar
▶ cans or egg cartons with numbers on them; a matching number of objects can be put into them
▶ children's socks, shoes, mittens, and gloves to match in pairs
▶ clocks with numerals (*not* digital)
▶ geometric boards (geoboards) to manipulate rubber bands or elastic loopers to form shapes or designs
▶ magnetic board with plastic numerals
▶ manipulatives, such as puzzles, sewing cards with yarn, pegs, and pegboards
▶ measuring cups, spoons, and pitchers
▶ milk cartons to demonstrate liquid measures and relationships between half-pints, pints, quarts, and gallons
▶ number strips and counting boards
▶ objects to count, sort, and classify, such as buttons, paper clips, pennies, colored cubes, bottle caps, aluminum washers, colored plastic clothespins, empty spools, shells, Popsicle™ or craft sticks, keys, nuts, and bolts
▶ rulers, yardsticks, and measuring tapes
▶ sandpaper numerals
▶ scales
▶ shape puzzles and flannelboard characters, such as a circle, a square, an oval, and so on
▶ table games, such as parquetry blocks and pattern blocks

- telephones, both dial and touch-tone
- timer
- unit, hollow, shape, and table blocks
- wooden pegboard and pegs

SCIENCE

Many of the following materials and supplies can be donated and many can be recycled. Others can be purchased inexpensively. All offer children opportunities to actively observe, predict, experiment, and analyze:

- aluminum foil pans
- aquariums with contents and supplies
- binoculars
- birdhouse and bird feeders
- compass
- corks, plugs, and stoppers
- dried plants, such as flowers and grasses
- eggbeaters and wire whisks
- eyedroppers
- feathers
- flashlights
- food coloring
- fossils
- garden hose
- instant print camera
- kitchen timer
- magnets, such as bar and horseshoe types
- magnifying glasses and tripod magnifier stand
- pinecones
- pipe cleaners
- plants
- plastic bottles, jars, and trays
- prisms
- rain gauges
- rock and seashell collections
- rulers, tape measures, and yardsticks
- scales
- seeds and seed catalogs
- sieves, sifters, funnels, and shallow pans

- skeleton
- soil samples, such as clay and sand
- stethoscope
- sundial
- telescope
- terrarium
- thermometers, both indoor and outdoor
- tongs and tweezers
- watering cans
- X-rays (discarded ones from family members who are doctors or veterinarians)

SOCIAL STUDIES

Like other curriculum areas, social studies needs to be experienced firsthand by children. This can be achieved by using the following materials and supplies:

- artifacts from many cultures
- boxes and blocks of different sizes and textures with people and animal figures; cars, trucks, and other items representing the community; pieces of fabric, scrap wood, boxes, and other materials for building homes from other parts of the world; a set of wooden international signs
- books, videos, computer software, and photographs representing cultures from around the world
- calendar of events in the community and other places
- CD or tape player with music from other places
- clothing, props, and puppets for children to use in role-playing experiences
- eating and cooking utensils, such as chopsticks, *matate* (Mexican mortar and pestle for grinding corn), and various types of cooking pots
- folk art, such as rain sticks, pottery, weaving, quilts, jewelry, wood carving, stories, music, and songs
- maps, map puzzles, globes, and atlases
- pictures and posters of different places in the community and the world
- stamps and coins from the United States and different parts of the world

Dear Family,

You will receive a daily report about your infant that informs you about her or his eating, sleeping, and elimination habits, along with requests for diapers, clothing, and supplies. This will give us a daily communication with you.

You also will receive this weekly family letter to give you a weekly update on your infant's

Health —

Sleeping —

Eating —

Elimination pattern —

Special activities —

Accomplishments —

Each week, we will suggest books and toys that will be available for you to borrow from the center.

Our theme this week is _____

Books to borrow —

Toys to borrow —

From time to time we will ask for some items that we need for our classroom activities. This week we need the following:

Thanks!

INFANT LESSON PLAN

TEACHER(S):   DATES: THEME:

CENTER / ACTIVITY	MONDAY	TUESDAY	WEDNESDAY	THURSDAY	FRIDAY
SENSORY: ART, MUSIC, TACTILE ACTIVITIES					
COGNITIVE & LANGUAGE ACTIVITIES					
SMALL MUSCLE & LARGE MUSCLE ACTIVITIES					
SELF-AWARENESS, SELF-ESTEEM, SELF-HELP ACTIVITIES					
SPECIAL ACTIVITIES					
BOOKS OF THE WEEK					
SPECIAL NOTES					

TODDLER LESSON PLAN

TEACHER(S):

CONCEPTS:

DATES:

THEME:

SKILLS:

DAY	LARGE GROUP ACTIVITIES	SMALL GROUP ACTIVITIES
MONDAY		
TUESDAY		
WEDNESDAY		
THURSDAY		
FRIDAY		

SENSORY ACTIVITIES	DRAMATIC PLAY / HOME LIVING & PUPPETS	MOVEMENT / OUTDOOR ACTIVITIES
MUSIC ACTIVITIES	SELF-AWARENESS, SELF-ESTEEM, SELF-HELP ACTIVITIES	SMALL MUSCLE / MANIPULATIVE ACTIVITIES
ART ACTIVITIES	LANGUAGE ACTIVITIES	TRANSITIONS
ACTIVITIES / NOTES	BOOKS OF THE WEEK	

PRESCHOOL LESSON PLAN

TEACHER(S):

CONCEPTS:

DATES:

SKILLS:

THEME:

CENTERS & ACTIVITIES	MONDAY	TUESDAY	WEDNESDAY	THURSDAY	FRIDAY
MORNING GROUP ACTIVITY					
AFTERNOON GROUP ACTIVITY					
LANGUAGE & LITERACY					
ART					
MUSIC & MOVEMENT					
DRAMATIC PLAY					
HOME LIVING					
MATH					
MANIPULATIVE					
SCIENCE & DISCOVERY					
BLOCKS		OUTDOOR / LARGE MUSCLE		TRANSITIONS	
SENSORY CENTERS		SOCIAL STUDIES		BOOKS OF THE WEEK	

SPECIAL ACTIVITIES & NOTES

K–3 LESSON PLAN

TEACHER(S)

DATES:

ACTIVITIES	MONDAY	TUESDAY	WEDNESDAY	THURSDAY	FRIDAY
LARGE/SMALL GROUP ACTIVITY					
LANGUAGE & LITERACY					
MATH & MANIPULATIVE					
SCIENCE & DISCOVERY					
SOCIAL STUDIES & COMMUNITY INVOLVMENT					
MUSIC, ART, & CREATIVE DRAMATICS					
HEALTH & PHYSICAL EDUCATION					

SPECIAL ACTIVITIES & NOTES: WHILE USING *SING ME A STORY! TELL ME A SONG!* AS A RESOURCE, ALWAYS CONSULT STATE AND DISTRICT REQUIRED CURRICULA.